More praise for
Guns, Germs, and Steel

"No scientist brings more experience from the laboratory and field, none thinks more deeply about social issues or addresses them with greater clarity, than Jared Diamond as illustrated by *Guns, Germs, and Steel*. In this remarkably readable book he shows how history and biology can enrich one another to produce a deeper understanding of the human condition."
—Edward O. Wilson, Pellegrino University Professor, Harvard University

"Serious, groundbreaking biological studies of human history only seem to come along once every generation or so. . . . Now Jared Diamond must be added to their select number. . . . Diamond meshes technological mastery with historical sweep, anecdotal delight with broad conceptual vision, and command of sources with creative leaps. No finer work of its kind has been published this year, or for many past."
—Martin Sieff, *Washington Times*

"[Diamond's] masterful synthesis is a refreshingly unconventional history informed by anthropology, behavioral ecology, linguistics, epidemiology, archeology, and technological development."
—*Publishers Weekly* (starred review)

"[Jared Diamond] is broadly erudite, writes in a style that pleasantly expresses scientific concepts in vernacular American English, and deals almost exclusively in questions that should interest everyone concerned about how humanity has developed. . . . [He] has done us all a great favor by supplying a rock-solid alternative to the racist answer. . . . A wonderfully interesting book."   —Alfred W. Crosby, *Los Angeles Times*

"Fascinating and extremely important. . . . [A] synopsis doesn't do credit to the immense subtlety of this book."
—David Brown, *Washington Post Book World*

"Deserves the attention of anyone concerned with the history of mankind at its most fundamental level. It is an epochal work. Diamond has written a summary of human history that can be accounted, for the time being, as Darwinian in its authority." —Thomas M. Disch, *New Leader*

"A wonderfully engrossing book. . . . Jared Diamond takes us on an exhilarating world tour of history that makes us rethink all our ideas about ourselves and other peoples and our places in the overall scheme of things." —Christopher Ehret, Professor of African History, UCLA

"Jared Diamond masterfully draws together recent discoveries in fields of inquiry as diverse as archaeology and epidemiology, as he illuminates how and why the human societies of different continents followed widely divergent pathways of development over the past 13,000 years."
—Bruce D. Smith, Director, Archaeobiology Program, Smithsonian Institution

"The question, 'Why did human societies have such diverse fates?' has usually received racist answers. Mastering information from many different fields, Jared Diamond convincingly demonstrates that head starts and local conditions can explain much of the course of human history. His impressive account will appeal to a vast readership."
—Luca Cavalli-Sforza, Professor of Genetics, Stanford University

To Andy, This is a book that appeals to the geographer in all of us. I hope you enjoy it, and that you will remember with fondness your trip to Peru whenever you see it on your bookshelf.

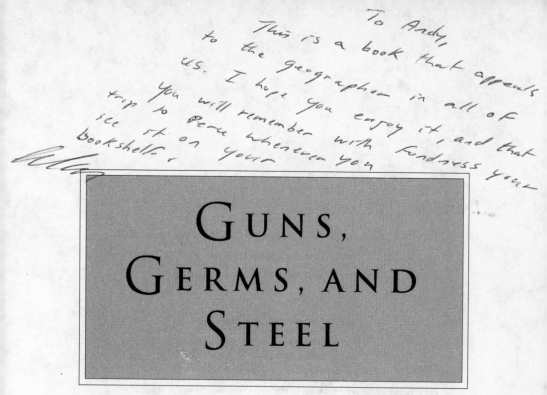

GUNS, GERMS, AND STEEL

THE FATES OF HUMAN SOCIETIES

Jared Diamond

W. W. Norton & Company
New York London

To Esa, Kariniga, Omwai, Paran, Sauakari, Wiwor,
and all my other New Guinea friends and teachers—
masters of a difficult environment

Copyright © 1999, 1997 by Jared Diamond

All rights reserved
Printed in the United States of America
First published as a Norton paperback 1999

For information about permission to reproduce selections from this book,
write to Permissions, W. W. Norton & Company, Inc., 500 Fifth Avenue, New
York, NY 10110.

The text of this book is composed in Sabon
with the display set in Trajan Bold
Composition and manufacturing by the Maple-Vail Book
Manufacturing Group
Book design by Chris Welch

Library of Congress Cataloging-in-Publication Data
Diamond, Jared M.
Guns, germs, and steel : the fates of human societies / Jared Diamond.
p.   cm.
Includes bibliographical references and index.
ISBN 0-393-31755-2
1. Social evolution.   2. Civilization—History.   3. Ethnology.   4. Human
beings—Effect of environment on.   5. Culture diffusion.   I. Title.
HM206.D48   1997
303.4—dc21   96-37068
                                                                CIP

W. W. Norton & Company, Inc., 500 Fifth Avenue, New York, N.Y. 10110
http://www.wwnorton.com

W. W. Norton & Company Ltd., 10 Coptic Street, London WC1A 1PU

4 5 6 7 8 9 0

CONTENTS

Preface to the Paperback Edition   9

PROLOGUE   YALI'S QUESTION

    The regionally differing courses of history   I 3

PART ONE   FROM EDEN TO CAJAMARCA   3 3

    CHAPTER 1   UP TO THE STARTING LINE
    What happened on all the continents before 11,000 B.C.?   3 5

    CHAPTER 2   A NATURAL EXPERIMENT
    OF HISTORY
    How geography molded societies on Polynesian islands   5 3

    CHAPTER 3   COLLISION AT CAJAMARCA
    Why the Inca emperor Atahuallpa did not capture
    King Charles I of Spain   6 7

PART TWO   THE RISE AND SPREAD OF FOOD
PRODUCTION   8 3

    CHAPTER 4   FARMER POWER
    The roots of guns, germs, and steel   8 5

CHAPTER 5 HISTORY'S HAVES AND
HAVE-NOTS
Geographic differences in the onset of food production   9 3

CHAPTER 6 TO FARM OR NOT TO FARM
Causes of the spread of food production   1 0 4

CHAPTER 7 HOW TO MAKE AN ALMOND
The unconscious development of ancient crops   1 1 4

CHAPTER 8 APPLES OR INDIANS
*Why did peoples of some regions fail to domesticate
plants?*   1 3 1

CHAPTER 9 ZEBRAS, UNHAPPY MARRIAGES, AND
THE *ANNA KARENINA* PRINCIPLE
*Why were most big wild mammal species never
domesticated?*   1 5 7

CHAPTER 10 SPACIOUS SKIES AND
TILTED AXES
*Why did food production spread at different rates on
different continents?*   1 7 6

PART THREE FROM FOOD TO GUNS,
GERMS, AND STEEL   1 9 3

CHAPTER 11 LETHAL GIFT OF LIVESTOCK
The evolution of germs   1 9 5

CHAPTER 12 BLUEPRINTS AND BORROWED
LETTERS
The evolution of writing   2 1 5

CHAPTER 13 NECESSITY'S MOTHER
The evolution of technology   2 3 9

CHAPTER 14 FROM EGALITARIANISM TO
KLEPTOCRACY
The evolution of government and religion   2 6 5

PART FOUR AROUND THE WORLD
IN FIVE CHAPTERS   2 9 3

CHAPTER 15 YALI'S PEOPLE
The histories of Australia and New Guinea   2 9 5

CHAPTER 16 HOW CHINA BECAME CHINESE
The history of East Asia   322

CHAPTER 17 SPEEDBOAT TO POLYNESIA
The history of the Austronesian expansion   334

CHAPTER 18 HEMISPHERES COLLIDING
The histories of Eurasia and the Americas compared   354

CHAPTER 19 HOW AFRICA BECAME BLACK
The history of Africa   376

EPILOGUE THE FUTURE OF HUMAN
HISTORY AS A SCIENCE   403

Acknowledgments   427
Further Readings   429
Credits   459
Index   461

WHY IS WORLD HISTORY
LIKE AN ONION?

T HIS BOOK ATTEMPTS TO PROVIDE A SHORT HISTORY OF everybody for the last 13,000 years. The question motivating the book is: Why did history unfold differently on different continents? In case this question immediately makes you shudder at the thought that you are about to read a racist treatise, you aren't: as you will see, the answers to the question don't involve human racial differences at all. The book's emphasis is on the search for ultimate explanations, and on pushing back the chain of historical causation as far as possible.

Most books that set out to recount world history concentrate on histories of literate Eurasian and North African societies. Native societies of other parts of the world—sub-Saharan Africa, the Americas, Island Southeast Asia, Australia, New Guinea, the Pacific Islands—receive only brief treatment, mainly as concerns what happened to them very late in their history, after they were discovered and subjugated by western Europeans. Even within Eurasia, much more space gets devoted to the history of western Eurasia than of China, India, Japan, tropical Southeast Asia, and other eastern Eurasian societies. History before the emergence of writing around 3,000 B.C. also receives brief treatment, although it constitutes 99.9% of the five-million-year history of the human species.

Such narrowly focused accounts of world history suffer from three disadvantages. First, increasing numbers of people today are, quite understandably, interested in other societies besides those of western Eurasia. After all, those "other" societies encompass most of the world's population and the vast majority of the world's ethnic, cultural, and linguistic groups. Some of them already are, and others are becoming, among the world's most powerful economies and political forces.

Second, even for people specifically interested in the shaping of the modern world, a history limited to developments since the emergence of writing cannot provide deep understanding. It is not the case that societies on the different continents were comparable to each other until 3,000 B.C., whereupon western Eurasian societies suddenly developed writing and began for the first time to pull ahead in other respects as well. Instead, already by 3,000 B.C., there were Eurasian and North African societies not only with incipient writing but also with centralized state governments, cities, widespread use of metal tools and weapons, use of domesticated animals for transport and traction and mechanical power, and reliance on agriculture and domestic animals for food. Throughout most or all parts of other continents, none of those things existed at that time; some but not all of them emerged later in parts of the Native Americas and sub-Saharan Africa, but only over the course of the next five millennia; and none of them emerged in Aboriginal Australia. That should already warn us that the roots of western Eurasian dominance in the modern world lie in the preliterate past before 3,000 B.C. (By western Eurasian dominance, I mean the dominance of western Eurasian societies themselves and of the societies that they spawned on other continents.)

Third, a history focused on western Eurasian societies completely bypasses the obvious big question. Why were those societies the ones that became disproportionately powerful and innovative? The usual answers to that question invoke proximate forces, such as the rise of capitalism, mercantilism, scientific inquiry, technology, and nasty germs that killed peoples of other continents when they came into contact with western Eurasians. But why did all those ingredients of conquest arise in western Eurasia, and arise elsewhere only to a lesser degree or not at all?

All those ingredients are just proximate factors, not ultimate explanations. Why didn't capitalism flourish in Native Mexico, mercantilism in sub-Saharan Africa, scientific inquiry in China, advanced technology in Native North America, and nasty germs in Aboriginal Australia? If one responds by invoking idiosyncratic cultural factors—e.g., scientific inquiry supposedly stifled in China by Confucianism but stimulated in western Eurasia by Greek or Judaeo-Christian traditions—then one is continuing to ignore the need for ultimate explanations: why didn't traditions like Confucianism and the Judaeo-Christian ethic instead develop in western

Eurasia and China, respectively? In addition, one is ignoring the fact that Confucian China was technologically more advanced than western Eurasia until about A.D. 1400.

It is impossible to understand even just western Eurasian societies themselves, if one focuses on them. The interesting questions concern the distinctions between them and other societies. Answering those questions requires us to understand all those other societies as well, so that western Eurasian societies can be fitted into the broader context.

Some readers may feel that I am going to the opposite extreme from conventional histories, by devoting too little space to western Eurasia at the expense of other parts of the world. I would answer that some other parts of the world are very instructive, because they encompass so many societies and such diverse societies within a small geographical area. Other readers may find themselves agreeing with one reviewer of this book. With mildly critical tongue in cheek, the reviewer wrote that I seem to view world history as an onion, of which the modern world constitutes only the surface, and whose layers are to be peeled back in the search for historical understanding. Yes, world history is indeed such an onion! But that peeling back of the onion's layers is fascinating, challenging—and of overwhelming importance to us today, as we seek to grasp our past's lessons for our future.

J. D.

YALI'S QUESTION

W E ALL KNOW THAT HISTORY HAS PROCEEDED VERY DIF-
ferently for peoples from different parts of the globe. In the
13,000 years since the end of the last Ice Age, some parts of the world
developed literate industrial societies with metal tools, other parts developed only nonliterate farming societies, and still others retained societies
of hunter-gatherers with stone tools. Those historical inequalities have cast
long shadows on the modern world, because the literate societies with
metal tools have conquered or exterminated the other societies. While
those differences constitute the most basic fact of world history, the reasons for them remain uncertain and controversial. This puzzling question
of their origins was posed to me 25 years ago in a simple, personal form.

In July 1972 I was walking along a beach on the tropical island of New
Guinea, where as a biologist I study bird evolution. I had already heard
about a remarkable local politician named Yali, who was touring the district then. By chance, Yali and I were walking in the same direction on that
day, and he overtook me. We walked together for an hour, talking during
the whole time.

Yali radiated charisma and energy. His eyes flashed in a mesmerizing
way. He talked confidently about himself, but he also asked lots of probing
questions and listened intently. Our conversation began with a subject then

on every New Guinean's mind—the rapid pace of political developments. Papua New Guinea, as Yali's nation is now called, was at that time still administered by Australia as a mandate of the United Nations, but independence was in the air. Yali explained to me his role in getting local people to prepare for self-government.

After a while, Yali turned the conversation and began to quiz me. He had never been outside New Guinea and had not been educated beyond high school, but his curiosity was insatiable. First, he wanted to know about my work on New Guinea birds (including how much I got paid for it). I explained to him how different groups of birds had colonized New Guinea over the course of millions of years. He then asked how the ancestors of his own people had reached New Guinea over the last tens of thousands of years, and how white Europeans had colonized New Guinea within the last 200 years.

The conversation remained friendly, even though the tension between the two societies that Yali and I represented was familiar to both of us. Two centuries ago, all New Guineans were still "living in the Stone Age." That is, they still used stone tools similar to those superseded in Europe by metal tools thousands of years ago, and they dwelt in villages not organized under any centralized political authority. Whites had arrived, imposed centralized government, and brought material goods whose value New Guineans instantly recognized, ranging from steel axes, matches, and medicines to clothing, soft drinks, and umbrellas. In New Guinea all these goods were referred to collectively as "cargo."

Many of the white colonialists openly despised New Guineans as "primitive." Even the least able of New Guinea's white "masters," as they were still called in 1972, enjoyed a far higher standard of living than New Guineans, higher even than charismatic politicians like Yali. Yet Yali had quizzed lots of whites as he was then quizzing me, and I had quizzed lots of New Guineans. He and I both knew perfectly well that New Guineans are on the average at least as smart as Europeans. All those things must have been on Yali's mind when, with yet another penetrating glance of his flashing eyes, he asked me, "Why is it that you white people developed so much cargo and brought it to New Guinea, but we black people had little cargo of our own?"

It was a simple question that went to the heart of life as Yali experienced it. Yes, there still is a huge difference between the lifestyle of the average

New Guinean and that of the average European or American. Comparable differences separate the lifestyles of other peoples of the world as well. Those huge disparities must have potent causes that one might think would be obvious.

Yet Yali's apparently simple question is a difficult one to answer. I didn't have an answer then. Professional historians still disagree about the solution; most are no longer even asking the question. In the years since Yali and I had that conversation, I have studied and written about other aspects of human evolution, history, and language. This book, written twenty-five years later, attempts to answer Yali.

ALTHOUGH YALI'S QUESTION concerned only the contrasting life-styles of New Guineans and of European whites, it can be extended to a larger set of contrasts within the modern world. Peoples of Eurasian origin, especially those still living in Europe and eastern Asia, plus those transplanted to North America, dominate the modern world in wealth and power. Other peoples, including most Africans, have thrown off European colonial domination but remain far behind in wealth and power. Still other peoples, such as the aboriginal inhabitants of Australia, the Americas, and southernmost Africa, are no longer even masters of their own lands but have been decimated, subjugated, and in some cases even exterminated by European colonialists.

Thus, questions about inequality in the modern world can be reformulated as follows. Why did wealth and power become distributed as they now are, rather than in some other way? For instance, why weren't Native Americans, Africans, and Aboriginal Australians the ones who decimated, subjugated, or exterminated Europeans and Asians?

We can easily push this question back one step. As of the year A.D. 1500, when Europe's worldwide colonial expansion was just beginning, peoples on different continents already differed greatly in technology and political organization. Much of Europe, Asia, and North Africa was the site of metal-equipped states or empires, some of them on the threshold of industrialization. Two Native American peoples, the Aztecs and the Incas, ruled over empires with stone tools. Parts of sub-Saharan Africa were divided among small states or chiefdoms with iron tools. Most other peoples—including all those of Australia and New Guinea, many Pacific islands, much of the Americas, and small parts of sub-Saharan Africa—lived as farming tribes or even still as hunter-gatherer bands using stone tools.

Of course, those technological and political differences as of A.D. 1500 were the immediate cause of the modern world's inequalities. Empires with steel weapons were able to conquer or exterminate tribes with weapons of stone and wood. How, though, did the world get to be the way it was in A.D. 1500?

Once again, we can easily push this question back one step further, by drawing on written histories and archaeological discoveries. Until the end of the last Ice Age, around 11,000 B.C., all peoples on all continents were still hunter-gatherers. Different rates of development on different continents, from 11,000 B.C. to A.D. 1500, were what led to the technological and political inequalities of A.D. 1500. While Aboriginal Australians and many Native Americans remained hunter-gatherers, most of Eurasia and much of the Americas and sub-Saharan Africa gradually developed agriculture, herding, metallurgy, and complex political organization. Parts of Eurasia, and one area of the Americas, independently developed writing as well. However, each of these new developments appeared earlier in Eurasia than elsewhere. For instance, the mass production of bronze tools, which was just beginning in the South American Andes in the centuries before A.D. 1500, was already established in parts of Eurasia over 4,000 years earlier. The stone technology of the Tasmanians, when first encountered by European explorers in A.D. 1642, was simpler than that prevalent in parts of Upper Paleolithic Europe tens of thousands of years earlier.

Thus, we can finally rephrase the question about the modern world's inequalities as follows: why did human development proceed at such different rates on different continents? Those disparate rates constitute history's broadest pattern and my book's subject.

While this book is thus ultimately about history and prehistory, its subject is not of just academic interest but also of overwhelming practical and political importance. The history of interactions among disparate peoples is what shaped the modern world through conquest, epidemics, and genocide. Those collisions created reverberations that have still not died down after many centuries, and that are actively continuing in some of the world's most troubled areas today.

For example, much of Africa is still struggling with its legacies from recent colonialism. In other regions—including much of Central America,

Mexico, Peru, New Caledonia, the former Soviet Union, and parts of Indonesia—civil unrest or guerrilla warfare pits still-numerous indigenous populations against governments dominated by descendants of invading conquerors. Many other indigenous populations—such as native Hawaiians, Aboriginal Australians, native Siberians, and Indians in the United States, Canada, Brazil, Argentina, and Chile—became so reduced in numbers by genocide and disease that they are now greatly outnumbered by the descendants of invaders. Although thus incapable of mounting a civil war, they are nevertheless increasingly asserting their rights.

In addition to these current political and economic reverberations of past collisions among peoples, there are current linguistic reverberations—especially the impending disappearance of most of the modern world's 6,000 surviving languages, becoming replaced by English, Chinese, Russian, and a few other languages whose numbers of speakers have increased enormously in recent centuries. All these problems of the modern world result from the different historical trajectories implicit in Yali's question.

BEFORE SEEKING ANSWERS to Yali's question, we should pause to consider some objections to discussing it at all. Some people take offense at the mere posing of the question, for several reasons.

One objection goes as follows. If we succeed in explaining how some people came to dominate other people, may this not seem to justify the domination? Doesn't it seem to say that the outcome was inevitable, and that it would therefore be futile to try to change the outcome today? This objection rests on a common tendency to confuse an explanation of causes with a justification or acceptance of results. What use one makes of a historical explanation is a question separate from the explanation itself. Understanding is more often used to try to alter an outcome than to repeat or perpetuate it. That's why psychologists try to understand the minds of murderers and rapists, why social historians try to understand genocide, and why physicians try to understand the causes of human disease. Those investigators do not seek to justify murder, rape, genocide, and illness. Instead, they seek to use their understanding of a chain of causes to interrupt the chain.

Second, doesn't addressing Yali's question automatically involve a Eurocentric approach to history, a glorification of western Europeans, and an obsession with the prominence of western Europe and Europeanized

America in the modern world? Isn't that prominence just an ephemeral phenomenon of the last few centuries, now fading behind the prominence of Japan and Southeast Asia? In fact, most of this book will deal with peoples other than Europeans. Rather than focus solely on interactions between Europeans and non-Europeans, we shall also examine interactions between different non-European peoples—especially those that took place within sub-Saharan Africa, Southeast Asia, Indonesia, and New Guinea, among peoples native to those areas. Far from glorifying peoples of western European origin, we shall see that most basic elements of their civilization were developed by other peoples living elsewhere and were then imported to western Europe.

Third, don't words such as "civilization," and phrases such as "rise of civilization," convey the false impression that civilization is good, tribal hunter-gatherers are miserable, and history for the past 13,000 years has involved progress toward greater human happiness? In fact, I do not assume that industrialized states are "better" than hunter-gatherer tribes, or that the abandonment of the hunter-gatherer lifestyle for iron-based statehood represents "progress," or that it has led to an increase in human happiness. My own impression, from having divided my life between United States cities and New Guinea villages, is that the so-called blessings of civilization are mixed. For example, compared with hunter-gatherers, citizens of modern industrialized states enjoy better medical care, lower risk of death by homicide, and a longer life span, but receive much less social support from friendships and extended families. My motive for investigating these geographic differences in human societies is not to celebrate one type of society over another but simply to understand what happened in history.

DOES YALI'S QUESTION really need another book to answer it? Don't we already know the answer? If so, what is it?

Probably the commonest explanation involves implicitly or explicitly assuming biological differences among peoples. In the centuries after A.D. 1500, as European explorers became aware of the wide differences among the world's peoples in technology and political organization, they assumed that those differences arose from differences in innate ability. With the rise of Darwinian theory, explanations were recast in terms of natural selection and of evolutionary descent. Technologically primitive peoples were considered evolutionary vestiges of human descent from apelike ancestors. The displacement of such peoples by colonists from industrialized societies exemplified the survival of the fittest. With the later rise of genetics, the explanations were recast once again, in genetic terms. Europeans became considered genetically more intelligent than Africans, and especially more so than Aboriginal Australians.

Today, segments of Western society publicly repudiate racism. Yet many (perhaps most!) Westerners continue to accept racist explanations privately or subconsciously. In Japan and many other countries, such explanations are still advanced publicly and without apology. Even educated white Americans, Europeans, and Australians, when the subject of Australian Aborigines comes up, assume that there is something primitive about the Aborigines themselves. They certainly look different from whites. Many of the living descendants of those Aborigines who survived the era of European colonization are now finding it difficult to succeed economically in white Australian society.

A seemingly compelling argument goes as follows. White immigrants to Australia built a literate, industrialized, politically centralized, democratic state based on metal tools and on food production, all within a century of colonizing a continent where the Aborigines had been living as tribal hunter-gatherers without metal for at least 40,000 years. Here were two successive experiments in human development, in which the environment was identical and the sole variable was the people occupying that environment. What further proof could be wanted to establish that the differences between Aboriginal Australian and European societies arose from differences between the peoples themselves?

The objection to such racist explanations is not just that they are loathsome, but also that they are wrong. Sound evidence for the existence of human differences in intelligence that parallel human differences in technology is lacking. In fact, as I shall explain in a moment, modern "Stone Age" peoples are on the average probably more intelligent, not less intelligent, than industrialized peoples. Paradoxical as it may sound, we shall see in Chapter 15 that white immigrants to Australia do not deserve the credit usually accorded to them for building a literate industrialized society with the other virtues mentioned above. In addition, peoples who until recently were technologically primitive—such as Aboriginal Australians and New Guineans—routinely master industrial technologies when given opportunities to do so.

An enormous effort by cognitive psychologists has gone into the search for differences in IQ between peoples of different geographic origins now living in the same country. In particular, numerous white American psychologists have been trying for decades to demonstrate that black Americans of African origins are innately less intelligent than white Americans of European origins. However, as is well known, the peoples compared differ greatly in their social environment and educational opportunities. This fact creates double difficulties for efforts to test the hypothesis that intellectual differences underlie technological differences. First, even our cognitive abilities as adults are heavily influenced by the social environment that we experienced during childhood, making it hard to discern any influence of preexisting genetic differences. Second, tests of cognitive ability (like IQ tests) tend to measure cultural learning and not pure innate intelligence, whatever that is. Because of those undoubted effects of childhood environment and learned knowledge on IQ test results, the psychologists' efforts to date have not succeeded in convincingly establishing the postulated genetic deficiency in IQs of nonwhite peoples.

My perspective on this controversy comes from 33 years of working with New Guineans in their own intact societies. From the very beginning of my work with New Guineans, they impressed me as being on the average more intelligent, more alert, more expressive, and more interested in things and people around them than the average European or American is. At some tasks that one might reasonably suppose to reflect aspects of brain function, such as the ability to form a mental map of unfamiliar surroundings, they appear considerably more adept than Westerners. Of course, New Guineans tend to perform poorly at tasks that Westerners have been trained to perform since childhood and that New Guineans have not. Hence when unschooled New Guineans from remote villages visit towns, they look stupid to Westerners. Conversely, I am constantly aware of how stupid I look to New Guineans when I'm with them in the jungle, displaying my incompetence at simple tasks (such as following a jungle trail or erecting a shelter) at which New Guineans have been trained since childhood and I have not.

It's easy to recognize two reasons why my impression that New Guineans are smarter than Westerners may be correct. First, Europeans have for thousands of years been living in densely populated societies with central governments, police, and judiciaries. In those societies, infectious epidemic diseases of dense populations (such as smallpox) were historically the major cause of death, while murders were relatively uncommon and a state of war was the exception rather than the rule. Most Europeans who escaped fatal infections also escaped other potential causes of death and proceeded to pass on their genes. Today, most live-born Western infants survive fatal infections as well and reproduce themselves, regardless of their intelligence and the genes they bear. In contrast, New Guineans have been living in societies where human numbers were too low for epidemic diseases of dense populations to evolve. Instead, traditional New Guineans suffered high mortality from murder, chronic tribal warfare, accidents, and problems in procuring food.

Intelligent people are likelier than less intelligent ones to escape those causes of high mortality in traditional New Guinea societies. However, the differential mortality from epidemic diseases in traditional European societies had little to do with intelligence, and instead involved genetic resistance dependent on details of body chemistry. For example, people with blood group B or O have a greater resistance to smallpox than do people with blood group A. That is, natural selection promoting genes for intelligence has probably been far more ruthless in New Guinea than in more densely populated, politically complex societies, where natural selection for body chemistry was instead more potent.

Besides this genetic reason, there is also a second reason why New Guineans may have come to be smarter than Westerners. Modern European and American children spend much of their time being passively entertained by television, radio, and movies. In the average American household, the TV set is on for seven hours per day. In contrast, traditional New Guinea children have virtually no such opportunities for passive entertainment and instead spend almost all of their waking hours actively doing something, such as talking or playing with other children or adults. Almost all studies of child development emphasize the role of childhood stimulation and activity in promoting mental development, and stress the irreversible mental stunting associated with reduced childhood stimulation. This effect surely contributes a non-genetic component to the superior average mental function displayed by New Guineans.

That is, in mental ability New Guineans are probably genetically superior to Westerners, and they surely are superior in escaping the devastating developmental disadvantages under which most children in industrialized societies now grow up. Certainly, there is no hint at all of any intellectual *dis*advantage of New Guineans that could serve to answer Yali's question.

The same two genetic and childhood developmental factors are likely to distinguish not only New Guineans from Westerners, but also hunter-gatherers and other members of technologically primitive societies from members of technologically advanced societies in general. Thus, the usual racist assumption has to be turned on its head. Why is it that Europeans, despite their likely genetic disadvantage and (in modern times) their undoubted developmental disadvantage, ended up with much more of the cargo? Why did New Guineans wind up technologically primitive, despite what I believe to be their superior intelligence?

A GENETIC EXPLANATION isn't the only possible answer to Yali's question. Another one, popular with inhabitants of northern Europe, invokes the supposed stimulatory effects of their homeland's cold climate and the inhibitory effects of hot, humid, tropical climates on human creativity and energy. Perhaps the seasonally variable climate at high latitudes poses more diverse challenges than does a seasonally constant tropical climate. Perhaps cold climates require one to be more technologically inventive to survive, because one must build a warm home and make warm clothing, whereas one can survive in the tropics with simpler housing and no clothing. Or the argument can be reversed to reach the same conclusion: the long winters at high latitudes leave people with much time in which to sit indoors and invent.

Although formerly popular, this type of explanation, too, fails to survive scrutiny. As we shall see, the peoples of northern Europe contributed nothing of fundamental importance to Eurasian civilization until the last thousand years; they simply had the good luck to live at a geographic location where they were likely to receive advances (such as agriculture, wheels, writing, and metallurgy) developed in warmer parts of Eurasia. In the New World the cold regions at high latitude were even more of a human backwater. The sole Native American societies to develop writing arose in Mexico south of the Tropic of Cancer; the oldest New World pottery comes from near the equator in tropical South America; and the New World society generally considered the most advanced in art, astronomy, and other respects was the Classic Maya society of the tropical Yucatán and Guatemala in the first millennium A.D.

Still a third type of answer to Yali invokes the supposed importance of lowland river valleys in dry climates, where highly productive agriculture depended on large-scale irrigation systems that in turn required centralized bureaucracies. This explanation was suggested by the undoubted fact that the earliest known empires and writing systems arose in the Tigris and Euphrates Valleys of the Fertile Crescent and in the Nile Valley of Egypt. Water control systems also appear to have been associated with centralized political organization in some other areas of the world, including the Indus Valley of the Indian subcontinent, the Yellow and Yangtze Valleys of China, the Maya lowlands of Mesoamerica, and the coastal desert of Peru.

However, detailed archaeological studies have shown that complex irrigation systems did not *accompany* the rise of centralized bureaucracies but *followed* after a considerable lag. That is, political centralization arose for some other reason and then permitted construction of complex irrigation systems. None of the crucial developments preceding political centralization in those same parts of the world were associated with river valleys or with complex irrigation systems. For example, in the Fertile Crescent food production and village life originated in hills and mountains, not in lowland river valleys. The Nile Valley remained a cultural backwater for about 3,000 years after village food production began to flourish in the hills of the Fertile Crescent. River valleys of the southwestern United States eventually came to support irrigation agriculture and complex societies, but only after many of the developments on which those societies rested had been imported from Mexico. The river valleys of southeastern Australia remained occupied by tribal societies without agriculture.

Yet another type of explanation lists the immediate factors that enabled Europeans to kill or conquer other peoples—especially European guns, infectious diseases, steel tools, and manufactured products. Such an explanation is on the right track, as those factors demonstrably *were* directly responsible for European conquests. However, this hypothesis is incomplete, because it still offers only a proximate (first-stage) explanation identifying immediate causes. It invites a search for ultimate causes: why were Europeans, rather than Africans or Native Americans, the ones to end up with guns, the nastiest germs, and steel?

While some progress has been made in identifying those ultimate causes in the case of Europe's conquest of the New World, Africa remains a big puzzle. Africa is the continent where protohumans evolved for the longest time, where anatomically modern humans may also have arisen, and where native diseases like malaria and yellow fever killed European explorers. If a long head start counts for anything, why didn't guns and steel arise first in Africa, permitting Africans and their germs to conquer Europe? And what accounts for the failure of Aboriginal Australians to pass beyond the stage of hunter-gatherers with stone tools?

Questions that emerge from worldwide comparisons of human societies formerly attracted much attention from historians and geographers. The best-known modern example of such an effort was Arnold Toynbee's 12-volume *Study of History*. Toynbee was especially interested in the internal dynamics of 23 advanced civilizations, of which 22 were literate and 19 were Eurasian. He was less interested in prehistory and in simpler, nonliterate societies. Yet the roots of inequality in the modern world lie far back in prehistory. Hence Toynbee did not pose Yali's question, nor did he come to grips with what I see as history's broadest pattern. Other available books on world history similarly tend to focus on advanced literate Eurasian civilizations of the last 5,000 years; they have a very brief treatment of pre-Columbian Native American civilizations, and an even briefer discussion of the rest of the world except for its recent interactions with Eurasian civilizations. Since Toynbee's attempt, worldwide syntheses of historical causation have fallen into disfavor among most historians, as posing an apparently intractable problem.

Specialists from several disciplines have provided global syntheses of their subjects. Especially useful contributions have been made by ecological geographers, cultural anthropologists, biologists studying plant and animal domestication, and scholars concerned with the impact of infectious diseases on history. These studies have called attention to parts of the puzzle, but they provide only pieces of the needed broad synthesis that has been missing.

Thus, there is no generally accepted answer to Yali's question. On the one hand, the proximate explanations are clear: some peoples developed guns, germs, steel, and other factors conferring political and economic power before others did; and some peoples never developed these power factors at all. On the other hand, the ultimate explanations—for example, why bronze tools appeared early in parts of Eurasia, late and only locally in the New World, and never in Aboriginal Australia—remain unclear.

Our present lack of such ultimate explanations leaves a big intellectual gap, since the broadest pattern of history thus remains unexplained. Much more serious, though, is the moral gap left unfilled. It is perfectly obvious to everyone, whether an overt racist or not, that different peoples have fared differently in history. The modern United States is a European-molded society, occupying lands conquered from Native Americans and incorporating the descendants of millions of sub-Saharan black Africans brought to America as slaves. Modern Europe is not a society molded by sub-Saharan black Africans who brought millions of Native Americans as slaves.

These results are completely lopsided: it was not the case that 51 percent of the Americas, Australia, and Africa was conquered by Europeans, while 49 percent of Europe was conquered by Native Americans, Aboriginal Australians, or Africans. The whole modern world has been shaped by lopsided outcomes. Hence they must have inexorable explanations, ones more basic than mere details concerning who happened to win some battle or develop some invention on one occasion a few thousand years ago.

It *seems* logical to suppose that history's pattern reflects innate differences among people themselves. Of course, we're taught that it's not polite to say so in public. We read of technical studies claiming to demonstrate inborn differences, and we also read rebuttals claiming that those studies suffer from technical flaws. We see in our daily lives that some of the conquered peoples continue to form an underclass, centuries after the conquests or slave imports took place. We're told that this too is to be attributed not to any biological shortcomings but to social disadvantages and limited opportunities.

Nevertheless, we have to wonder. We keep seeing all those glaring, persistent differences in peoples' status. We're assured that the seemingly transparent biological explanation for the world's inequalities as of A.D. 1500 is wrong, but we're not told what the correct explanation is. Until we have some convincing, detailed, agreed-upon explanation for the broad pattern of history, most people will continue to suspect that the racist biological explanation is correct after all. That seems to me the strongest argument for writing this book.

AUTHORS ARE REGULARLY asked by journalists to summarize a long book in one sentence. For this book, here is such a sentence: "History followed different courses for different peoples because of differences among peoples' environments, not because of biological differences among peoples themselves."

Naturally, the notion that environmental geography and biogeography influenced societal development is an old idea. Nowadays, though, the view is not held in esteem by historians; it is considered wrong or simplistic, or it is caricatured as environmental determinism and dismissed, or else the whole subject of trying to understand worldwide differences is shelved as too difficult. Yet geography obviously has *some* effect on history; the open question concerns how much effect, and whether geography can account for history's broad pattern.

The time is now ripe for a fresh look at these questions, because of new information from scientific disciplines seemingly remote from human history. Those disciplines include, above all, genetics, molecular biology, and biogeography as applied to crops and their wild ancestors; the same disciplines plus behavioral ecology, as applied to domestic animals and their wild ancestors; molecular biology of human germs and related germs of animals; epidemiology of human diseases; human genetics; linguistics; archaeological studies on all continents and major islands; and studies of the histories of technology, writing, and political organization.

This diversity of disciplines poses problems for would-be authors of a book aimed at answering Yali's question. The author must possess a range of expertise spanning the above disciplines, so that relevant advances can be synthesized. The history and prehistory of each continent must be similarly synthesized. The book's subject matter is history, but the approach is that of science—in particular, that of historical sciences such as evolutionary biology and geology. The author must understand from firsthand experience a range of human societies, from hunter-gatherer societies to modern space-age civilizations.

These requirements seem at first to demand a multi-author work. Yet that approach would be doomed from the outset, because the essence of the problem is to develop a unified synthesis. That consideration dictates single authorship, despite all the difficulties that it poses. Inevitably, that single author will have to sweat copiously in order to assimilate material from many disciplines, and will require guidance from many colleagues.

My background had led me to several of these disciplines even before Yali put his question to me in 1972. My mother is a teacher and linguist; my father, a physician specializing in the genetics of childhood diseases. Because of my father's example, I went through school expecting to become a physician. I had also become a fanatical bird-watcher by the age of seven. It was thus an easy step, in my last undergraduate year at university, to shift from my initial goal of medicine to the goal of biological research. However, throughout my school and undergraduate years, my training was mainly in languages, history, and writing. Even after deciding to obtain a Ph.D. in physiology, I nearly dropped out of science during my first year of graduate school to become a linguist.

Since completing my Ph.D. in 1961, I have divided my scientific research efforts between two fields: molecular physiology on the one hand, evolutionary biology and biogeography on the other hand. As an unforeseen bonus for the purposes of this book, evolutionary biology is a historical science forced to use methods different from those of the laboratory sciences. That experience has made the difficulties in devising a scientific approach to human history familiar to me. Living in Europe from 1958 to 1962, among European friends whose lives had been brutally traumatized by 20th-century European history, made me start to think more seriously about how chains of causes operate in history's unfolding.

For the last 33 years my fieldwork as an evolutionary biologist has brought me into close contact with a wide range of human societies. My specialty is bird evolution, which I have studied in South America, southern Africa, Indonesia, Australia, and especially New Guinea. Through living with native peoples of these areas, I have become familiar with many technologically primitive human societies, from those of hunter-gatherers to those of tribal farmers and fishing peoples who depended until recently on stone tools. Thus, what most literate people would consider strange lifestyles of remote prehistory are for me the most vivid part of my life. New Guinea, though it accounts for only a small fraction of the world's land area, encompasses a disproportionate fraction of its human diversity. Of the modern world's 6,000 languages, 1,000 are confined to New Guinea. In the course of my work on New Guinea birds, my interests in language were rekindled, by the need to elicit lists of local names of bird species in nearly 100 of those New Guinea languages.

Out of all those interests grew my most recent book, a nontechnical account of human evolution entitled The Third Chimpanzee. Its Chapter 14, called "Accidental Conquerors," sought to understand the outcome of the encounter between Europeans and Native Americans. After I had completed that book, I realized that other modern, as well as prehistoric, encounters between peoples raised similar questions. I saw that the question with which I had wrestled in that Chapter 14 was in essence the question Yali had asked me in 1972, merely transferred to a different part of the world. And so at last, with the help of many friends, I shall attempt to satisfy Yali's curiosity—and my own.

THIS BOOK'S CHAPTERS are divided into four parts. Part 1, entitled "From Eden to Cajamarca," consists of three chapters. Chapter 1 provides a whirlwind tour of human evolution and history, extending from our divergence from apes, around 7 million years ago, until the end of the last Ice Age, around 13,000 years ago. We shall trace the spread of ancestral humans, from our origins in Africa to the other continents, in order to understand the state of the world just before the events often lumped into the term "rise of civilization" began. It turns out that human development on some continents got a head start in time over developments on others.

Chapter 2 prepares us for exploring effects of continental environments on history over the past 13,000 years, by briefly examining effects of island environments on history over smaller time scales and areas. When ancestral Polynesians spread into the Pacific around 3,200 years ago, they encountered islands differing greatly in their environments. Within a few millennia that single ancestral Polynesian society had spawned on those diverse islands a range of diverse daughter societies, from hunter-gatherer tribes to proto-empires. That radiation can serve as a model for the longer, larger-scale, and less understood radiation of societies on different continents since the end of the last Ice Age, to become variously hunter-gatherer tribes and empires.

The third chapter introduces us to collisions between peoples from different continents, by retelling through contemporary eyewitness accounts the most dramatic such encounter in history: the capture of the last independent Inca emperor, Atahuallpa, in the presence of his whole army, by Francisco Pizarro and his tiny band of conquistadores, at the Peruvian city of Cajamarca. We can identify the chain of proximate factors that enabled Pizarro to capture Atahuallpa, and that operated in European conquests of other Native American societies as well. Those factors included Spanish germs, horses, literacy, political organization, and technology (especially ships and weapons). That analysis of proximate causes is the easy part of this book; the hard part is to identify the ultimate causes leading to them and to the actual outcome, rather than to the opposite possible outcome of Atahuallpa's coming to Madrid and capturing King Charles I of Spain.

Part 2, entitled "The Rise and Spread of Food Production" and consisting of Chapters 4–10, is devoted to what I believe to be the most important constellation of ultimate causes. Chapter 4 sketches how food production—that is, the growing of food by agriculture or herding, instead of the hunting and gathering of wild foods—ultimately led to the immediate factors permitting Pizarro's triumph. But the rise of food production varied around the globe. As we shall see in Chapter 5, peoples in some parts of the world developed food production by themselves; some other peoples acquired it in prehistoric times from those independent centers; and still others neither developed nor acquired food production prehistorically but remained hunter-gatherers until modern times. Chapter 6 explores the numerous factors driving the shift from the hunter-gatherer lifestyle toward food production, in some areas but not in others.

Chapters 7, 8, and 9 then show how crops and livestock came in prehistoric times to be domesticated from ancestral wild plants and animals, by incipient farmers and herders who could have had no vision of the outcome. Geographic differences in the local suites of wild plants and animals available for domestication go a long way toward explaining why only a few areas became independent centers of food production, and why it arose earlier in some of those areas than in others. From those few centers of origin, food production spread much more rapidly to some areas than to others. A major factor contributing to those differing rates of spread turns out to have been the orientation of the continents' axes: predominantly west–east for Eurasia, predominantly north–south for the Americas and Africa (Chapter 10).

Thus, Chapter 3 sketched the immediate factors behind Europe's conquest of Native Americans, and Chapter 4 the development of those factors from the ultimate cause of food production. In Part 3 ("From Food to Guns, Germs, and Steel," Chapters 11–14), the connections from ultimate to proximate causes are traced in detail, beginning with the evolution of germs characteristic of dense human populations (Chapter 11). Far more Native Americans and other non-Eurasian peoples were killed by Eurasian germs than by Eurasian guns or steel weapons. Conversely, few or no distinctive lethal germs awaited would-be European conquerors in the New World. Why was the germ exchange so unequal? Here, the results of recent molecular biological studies are illuminating in linking germs to the rise of food production, in Eurasia much more than in the Americas.

Another chain of causation led from food production to writing, possibly the most important single invention of the last few thousand years

(Chapter 12). Writing has evolved de novo only a few times in human history, in areas that had been the earliest sites of the rise of food production in their respective regions. All other societies that have become literate did so by the diffusion of writing systems or of the idea of writing from one of those few primary centers. Hence, for the student of world history, the phenomenon of writing is particularly useful for exploring another important constellation of causes: geography's effect on the ease with which ideas and inventions spread.

What holds for writing also holds for technology (Chapter 13). A crucial question is whether technological innovation is so dependent on rare inventor-geniuses, and on many idiosyncratic cultural factors, as to defy an understanding of world patterns. In fact, we shall see that, paradoxically, this large number of cultural factors makes it easier, not harder, to understand world patterns of technology. By enabling farmers to generate food surpluses, food production permitted farming societies to support full-time craft specialists who did not grow their own food and who developed technologies.

Besides sustaining scribes and inventors, food production also enabled farmers to support politicians (Chapter 14). Mobile bands of hunter-gatherers are relatively egalitarian, and their political sphere is confined to the band's own territory and to shifting alliances with neighboring bands. With the rise of dense, sedentary, food-producing populations came the rise of chiefs, kings, and bureaucrats. Such bureaucracies were essential not only to governing large and populous domains but also to maintaining standing armies, sending out fleets of exploration, and organizing wars of conquest.

Part 4 ("Around the World in Five Chapters," Chapters 15–19) applies the lessons of Parts 2 and 3 to each of the continents and some important islands. Chapter 15 examines the history of Australia itself, and of the large island of New Guinea, formerly joined to Australia in a single continent. The case of Australia, home to the recent human societies with the simplest technologies, and the sole continent where food production did not develop indigenously, poses a critical test of theories about intercontinental differences in human societies. We shall see why Aboriginal Australians remained hunter-gatherers, even while most peoples of neighboring New Guinea became food producers.

Chapters 16 and 17 integrate developments in Australia and New Guinea into the perspective of the whole region encompassing the East

Asian mainland and Pacific islands. The rise of food production in China spawned several great prehistoric movements of human populations, or of cultural traits, or of both. One of those movements, within China itself, created the political and cultural phenomenon of China as we know it today. Another resulted in a replacement, throughout almost the whole of tropical Southeast Asia, of indigenous hunter-gatherers by farmers of ultimately South Chinese origin. Still another, the Austronesian expansion, similarly replaced the indigenous hunter-gatherers of the Philippines and Indonesia and spread out to the most remote islands of Polynesia, but was unable to colonize Australia and most of New Guinea. To the student of world history, all those collisions among East Asian and Pacific peoples are doubly important: they formed the countries where one-third of the modern world's population lives, and in which economic power is increasingly becoming concentrated; and they furnish especially clear models for understanding the histories of peoples elsewhere in the world.

Chapter 18 returns to the problem introduced in Chapter 3, the collision between European and Native American peoples. A summary of the last 13,000 years of New World and western Eurasian history makes clear how Europe's conquest of the Americas was merely the culmination of two long and mostly separate historical trajectories. The differences between those trajectories were stamped by continental differences in domesticable plants and animals, germs, times of settlement, orientation of continental axes, and ecological barriers.

Finally, the history of sub-Saharan Africa (Chapter 19) offers striking similarities as well as contrasts with New World history. The same factors that molded Europeans' encounters with Africans molded their encounters with Native Americans as well. But Africa also differed from the Americas in all these factors. As a result, European conquest did not create widespread or lasting European settlement of sub-Saharan Africa, except in the far south. Of more lasting significance was a large-scale population shift within Africa itself, the Bantu expansion. It proves to have been triggered by many of the same causes that played themselves out at Cajamarca, in East Asia, on Pacific islands, and in Australia and New Guinea.

I harbor no illusions that these chapters have succeeded in explaining the histories of all the continents for the past 13,000 years. Obviously, that would be impossible to accomplish in a single book even if we did understand all the answers, which we don't. At best, this book identifies several constellations of environmental factors that I believe provide a large part of the answer to Yali's question. Recognition of those factors emphasizes the unexplained residue, whose understanding will be a task for the future.

The Epilogue, entitled "The Future of Human History as a Science," lays out some pieces of the residue, including the problem of the differences between different parts of Eurasia, the role of cultural factors unrelated to environment, and the role of individuals. Perhaps the biggest of these unsolved problems is to establish human history as a historical science, on a par with recognized historical sciences such as evolutionary biology, geology, and climatology. The study of human history does pose real difficulties, but those recognized historical sciences encounter some of the same challenges. Hence the methods developed in some of these other fields may also prove useful in the field of human history.

Already, though, I hope to have convinced you, the reader, that history is not "just one damn fact after another," as a cynic put it. There really are broad patterns to history, and the search for their explanation is as productive as it is fascinating.

PART ONE

FROM EDEN TO CAJAMARCA

CHAPTER 1

UP TO THE STARTING
LINE

A SUITABLE STARTING POINT FROM WHICH TO COMPARE
historical developments on the different continents is around
11,000 B.C.* This date corresponds approximately to the beginnings of
village life in a few parts of the world, the first undisputed peopling of the
Americas, the end of the Pleistocene Era and last Ice Age, and the start of
what geologists term the Recent Era. Plant and animal domestication
began in at least one part of the world within a few thousand years of that
date. As of then, did the people of some continents already have a head
start or a clear advantage over peoples of other continents?

If so, perhaps that head start, amplified over the last 13,000 years, pro-

*Throughout this book, dates for about the last 15,000 years will be quoted as so-
called calibrated radiocarbon dates, rather than as conventional, uncalibrated radiocarbon dates. The difference between the two types of dates will be explained in Chapter
5. Calibrated dates are the ones believed to correspond more closely to actual calendar
dates. Readers accustomed to uncalibrated dates will need to bear this distinction in
mind whenever they find me quoting apparently erroneous dates that are older than the
ones with which they are familiar. For example, the date of the Clovis archaeological
horizon in North America is usually quoted as around 9000 B.C. (11,000 years ago),
but I quote it instead as around 11,000 B.C. (13,000 years ago), because the date usually
quoted is uncalibrated.

vides the answer to Yali's question. Hence this chapter will offer a whirlwind tour of human history on all the continents, for millions of years, from our origins as a species until 13,000 years ago. All that will now be summarized in less than 20 pages. Naturally, I shall gloss over details and mention only what seem to me the trends most relevant to this book.

Our closest living relatives are three surviving species of great ape: the gorilla, the common chimpanzee, and the pygmy chimpanzee (also known as bonobo). Their confinement to Africa, along with abundant fossil evidence, indicates that the earliest stages of human evolution were also played out in Africa. Human history, as something separate from the history of animals, began there about 7 million years ago (estimates range from 5 to 9 million years ago). Around that time, a population of African apes broke up into several populations, of which one proceeded to evolve into modern gorillas, a second into the two modern chimps, and the third into humans. The gorilla line apparently split off slightly before the split between the chimp and the human lines.

Fossils indicate that the evolutionary line leading to us had achieved a substantially upright posture by around 4 million years ago, then began to increase in body size and in relative brain size around 2.5 million years ago. Those protohumans are generally known as *Australopithecus africanus, Homo habilis,* and *Homo erectus,* which apparently evolved into each other in that sequence. Although *Homo erectus,* the stage reached around 1.7 million years ago, was close to us modern humans in body size, its brain size was still barely half of ours. Stone tools became common around 2.5 million years ago, but they were merely the crudest of flaked or battered stones. In zoological significance and distinctiveness, *Homo erectus* was more than an ape, but still much less than a modern human.

All of that human history, for the first 5 or 6 million years after our origins about 7 million years ago, remained confined to Africa. The first human ancestor to spread beyond Africa was *Homo erectus,* as is attested by fossils discovered on the Southeast Asian island of Java and conventionally known as Java man (see Figure 1.1). The oldest Java "man" fossils— of course, they may actually have belonged to a Java woman—have usually been assumed to date from about a million years ago. However, it has recently been argued that they actually date from 1.8 million years ago. (Strictly speaking, the name *Homo erectus* belongs to these Javan fossils, and the African fossils classified as *Homo erectus* may warrant a different name.) At present, the earliest unquestioned evidence for humans in

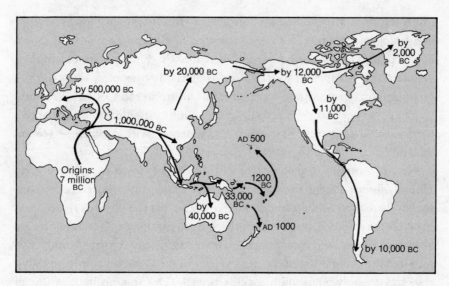

Figure 1.1. The spread of humans around the world.

Europe stems from around half a million years ago, but there are claims of an earlier presence. One would certainly assume that the colonization of Asia also permitted the simultaneous colonization of Europe, since Eurasia is a single landmass not bisected by major barriers.

That illustrates an issue that will recur throughout this book. Whenever some scientist claims to have discovered "the earliest X"—whether X is the earliest human fossil in Europe, the earliest evidence of domesticated corn in Mexico, or the earliest anything anywhere—that announcement challenges other scientists to beat the claim by finding something still earlier. In reality, there must be some truly "earliest X," with all claims of earlier X's being false. However, as we shall see, for virtually any X, every year brings forth new discoveries and claims of a purported still earlier X, along with refutations of some or all of previous years' claims of earlier X. It often takes decades of searching before archaeologists reach a consensus on such questions.

By about half a million years ago, human fossils had diverged from older *Homo erectus* skeletons in their enlarged, rounder, and less angular skulls. African and European skulls of half a million years ago were sufficiently similar to skulls of us moderns that they are classified in our species, *Homo sapiens,* instead of in *Homo erectus.* This distinction is arbitrary, since *Homo erectus* evolved into *Homo sapiens*. However, these early *Homo sapiens* still differed from us in skeletal details, had brains significantly smaller than ours, and were grossly different from us in their artifacts and behavior. Modern stone-tool-making peoples, such as Yali's great-grandparents, would have scorned the stone tools of half a million years ago as very crude. The only other significant addition to our ancestors' cultural repertoire that can be documented with confidence around that time was the use of fire.

No art, bone tool, or anything else has come down to us from early *Homo sapiens* except for their skeletal remains, plus those crude stone tools. There were still no humans in Australia, for the obvious reason that it would have taken boats to get there from Southeast Asia. There were also no humans anywhere in the Americas, because that would have required the occupation of the nearest part of the Eurasian continent (Siberia), and possibly boat-building skills as well. (The present, shallow Bering Strait, separating Siberia from Alaska, alternated between a strait and a broad intercontinental bridge of dry land, as sea level repeatedly rose and fell during the Ice Ages.) However, boat building and survival in cold Siberia were both still far beyond the capabilities of early *Homo sapiens*.

After half a million years ago, the human populations of Africa and western Eurasia proceeded to diverge from each other and from East Asian populations in skeletal details. The population of Europe and western Asia between 130,000 and 40,000 years ago is represented by especially many skeletons, known as Neanderthals and sometimes classified as a separate species, *Homo neanderthalensis*. Despite being depicted in innumerable cartoons as apelike brutes living in caves, Neanderthals had brains slightly larger than our own. They were also the first humans to leave behind strong evidence of burying their dead and caring for their sick. Yet their stone tools were still crude by comparison with modern New Guineans' polished stone axes and were usually not yet made in standardized diverse shapes, each with a clearly recognizable function.

The few preserved African skeletal fragments contemporary with the Neanderthals are more similar to our modern skeletons than to Neanderthal skeletons. Even fewer preserved East Asian skeletal fragments are known, but they appear different again from both Africans and Neanderthals. As for the lifestyle at that time, the best-preserved evidence comes from stone artifacts and prey bones accumulated at southern African sites. Although those Africans of 100,000 years ago had more modern skeletons than did their Neanderthal contemporaries, they made essentially the same crude stone tools as Neanderthals, still lacking standardized shapes. They had no preserved art. To judge from the bone evidence of the animal species on which they preyed, their hunting skills were unimpressive and mainly directed at easy-to-kill, not-at-all-dangerous animals. They were not yet in the business of slaughtering buffalo, pigs, and other dangerous prey. They couldn't even catch fish: their sites immediately on the seacoast lack fish bones and fishhooks. They and their Neanderthal contemporaries still rank as less than fully human.

Human history at last took off around 50,000 years ago, at the time of what I have termed our Great Leap Forward. The earliest definite signs of that leap come from East African sites with standardized stone tools and the first preserved jewelry (ostrich-shell beads). Similar developments soon appear in the Near East and in southeastern Europe, then (some 40,000 years ago) in southwestern Europe, where abundant artifacts are associated with fully modern skeletons of people termed Cro-Magnons. Thereafter, the garbage preserved at archaeological sites rapidly becomes more and more interesting and leaves no doubt that we are dealing with biologically and behaviorally modern humans.

Cro-Magnon garbage heaps yield not only stone tools but also tools of bone, whose suitability for shaping (for instance, into fishhooks) had apparently gone unrecognized by previous humans. Tools were produced in diverse and distinctive shapes so modern that their functions as needles, awls, engraving tools, and so on are obvious to us. Instead of only single-piece tools such as hand-held scrapers, multipiece tools made their appearance. Recognizable multipiece weapons at Cro-Magnon sites include harpoons, spear-throwers, and eventually bows and arrows, the precursors of rifles and other multipiece modern weapons. Those efficient means of killing at a safe distance permitted the hunting of such dangerous prey as rhinos and elephants, while the invention of rope for nets, lines, and snares allowed the addition of fish and birds to our diet. Remains of houses and sewn clothing testify to a greatly improved ability to survive in cold climates, and remains of jewelry and carefully buried skeletons indicate revolutionary aesthetic and spiritual developments.

Of the Cro-Magnons' products that have been preserved, the best known are their artworks: their magnificent cave paintings, statues, and musical instruments, which we still appreciate as art today. Anyone who has experienced firsthand the overwhelming power of the life-sized painted

bulls and horses in the Lascaux Cave of southwestern France will understand at once that their creators must have been as modern in their minds
as they were in their skeletons.

Obviously, some momentous change took place in our ancestors' capabilities between about 100,000 and 50,000 years ago. That Great Leap
Forward poses two major unresolved questions, regarding its triggering
cause and its geographic location. As for its cause, I argued in my book
The Third Chimpanzee for the perfection of the voice box and hence for
the anatomical basis of modern language, on which the exercise of human
creativity is so dependent. Others have suggested instead that a change in
brain organization around that time, without a change in brain size, made
modern language possible.

As for the site of the Great Leap Forward, did it take place primarily in
one geographic area, in one group of humans, who were thereby enabled
to expand and replace the former human populations of other parts of the
world? Or did it occur in parallel in different regions, in each of which
the human populations living there today would be descendants of the
populations living there before the leap? The rather modern-looking
human skulls from Africa around 100,000 years ago have been taken to
support the former view, with the leap occurring specifically in Africa.
Molecular studies (of so-called mitochondrial DNA) were initially also
interpreted in terms of an African origin of modern humans, though the
meaning of those molecular findings is currently in doubt. On the other
hand, skulls of humans living in China and Indonesia hundreds of thousands of years ago are considered by some physical anthropologists to
exhibit features still found in modern Chinese and in Aboriginal Australians, respectively. If true, that finding would suggest parallel evolution
and multiregional origins of modern humans, rather than origins in a single Garden of Eden. The issue remains unresolved.

The evidence for a localized origin of modern humans, followed by their
spread and then their replacement of other types of humans elsewhere,
seems strongest for Europe. Some 40,000 years ago, into Europe came the
Cro-Magnons, with their modern skeletons, superior weapons, and other
advanced cultural traits. Within a few thousand years there were no more
Neanderthals, who had been evolving as the sole occupants of Europe for
hundreds of thousands of years. That sequence strongly suggests that the
modern Cro-Magnons somehow used their far superior technology, and
their language skills or brains, to infect, kill, or displace the Neanderthals,

leaving behind little or no evidence of hybridization between Neanderthals and Cro-Magnons.

THE GREAT LEAP Forward coincides with the first proven major extension of human geographic range since our ancestors' colonization of Eurasia. That extension consisted of the occupation of Australia and New Guinea, joined at that time into a single continent. Many radiocarbon-dated sites attest to human presence in Australia / New Guinea between 40,000 and 30,000 years ago (plus the inevitable somewhat older claims of contested validity). Within a short time of that initial peopling, humans had expanded over the whole continent and adapted to its diverse habitats, from the tropical rain forests and high mountains of New Guinea to the dry interior and wet southeastern corner of Australia.

During the Ice Ages, so much of the oceans' water was locked up in glaciers that worldwide sea levels dropped hundreds of feet below their present stand. As a result, what are now the shallow seas between Asia and the Indonesian islands of Sumatra, Borneo, Java, and Bali became dry land. (So did other shallow straits, such as the Bering Strait and the English Channel.) The edge of the Southeast Asian mainland then lay 700 miles east of its present location. Nevertheless, central Indonesian islands between Bali and Australia remained surrounded and separated by deep-water channels. To reach Australia / New Guinea from the Asian mainland at that time still required crossing a minimum of eight channels, the broadest of which was at least 50 miles wide. Most of those channels divided islands visible from each other, but Australia itself was always invisible from even the nearest Indonesian islands, Timor and Tanimbar. Thus, the occupation of Australia / New Guinea is momentous in that it demanded watercraft and provides by far the earliest evidence of their use in history. Not until about 30,000 years later (13,000 years ago) is there strong evidence of watercraft anywhere else in the world, from the Mediterranean.

Initially, archaeologists considered the possibility that the colonization of Australia / New Guinea was achieved accidentally by just a few people swept to sea while fishing on a raft near an Indonesian island. In an extreme scenario the first settlers are pictured as having consisted of a single pregnant young woman carrying a male fetus. But believers in the fluke-colonization theory have been surprised by recent discoveries that still other islands, lying to the east of New Guinea, were colonized soon after New Guinea itself, by around 35,000 years ago. Those islands were New Britain and New Ireland, in the Bismarck Archipelago, and Buka, in the Solomon Archipelago. Buka lies out of sight of the closest island to the west and could have been reached only by crossing a water gap of about 100 miles. Thus, early Australians and New Guineans were probably capable of intentionally traveling over water to visible islands, and were using watercraft sufficiently often that the colonization of even invisible distant islands was repeatedly achieved unintentionally.

The settlement of Australia / New Guinea was perhaps associated with still another big first, besides humans' first use of watercraft and first range extension since reaching Eurasia: the first mass extermination of large animal species by humans. Today, we regard Africa as *the* continent of big mammals. Modern Eurasia also has many species of big mammals (though not in the manifest abundance of Africa's Serengeti Plains), such as Asia's rhinos and elephants and tigers, and Europe's moose and bears and (until classical times) lions. Australia / New Guinea today has no equally large mammals, in fact no mammal larger than 100-pound kangaroos. But Australia / New Guinea formerly had its own suite of diverse big mammals, including giant kangaroos, rhinolike marsupials called diprotodonts and reaching the size of a cow, and a marsupial "leopard." It also formerly had a 400-pound ostrichlike flightless bird, plus some impressively big reptiles, including a one-ton lizard, a giant python, and land-dwelling crocodiles.

All of those Australian / New Guinean giants (the so-called megafauna) disappeared after the arrival of humans. While there has been controversy about the exact timing of their demise, several Australian archaeological sites, with dates extending over tens of thousands of years, and with prodigiously abundant deposits of animal bones, have been carefully excavated and found to contain not a trace of the now extinct giants over the last 35,000 years. Hence the megafauna probably became extinct soon after humans reached Australia.

The near-simultaneous disappearance of so many large species raises an obvious question: what caused it? An obvious possible answer is that they were killed off or else eliminated indirectly by the first arriving humans. Recall that Australian / New Guinean animals had evolved for millions of years in the absence of human hunters. We know that Galápagos and Antarctic birds and mammals, which similarly evolved in the absence of humans and did not see humans until modern times, are still incurably tame today. They would have been exterminated if conservationists had not imposed protective measures quickly. On other recently discovered islands where protective measures did not go into effect quickly, exterminations did indeed result: one such victim, the dodo of Mauritius, has become virtually a symbol for extinction. We also know now that, on every one of the well-studied oceanic islands colonized in the prehistoric era, human colonization led to an extinction spasm whose victims included the moas of New Zealand, the giant lemurs of Madagascar, and the big flightless geese of Hawaii. Just as modern humans walked up to unafraid dodos and island seals and killed them, prehistoric humans presumably walked up to unafraid moas and giant lemurs and killed them too.

Hence one hypothesis for the demise of Australia's and New Guinea's giants is that they met the same fate around 40,000 years ago. In contrast, most big mammals of Africa and Eurasia survived into modern times, because they had coevolved with protohumans for hundreds of thousands or millions of years. They thereby enjoyed ample time to evolve a fear of humans, as our ancestors' initially poor hunting skills slowly improved. The dodo, moas, and perhaps the giants of Australia / New Guinea had the misfortune suddenly to be confronted, without any evolutionary preparation, by invading modern humans possessing fully developed hunting skills.

However, the overkill hypothesis, as it is termed, has not gone unchallenged for Australia / New Guinea. Critics emphasize that, as yet, no one has documented the bones of an extinct Australian / New Guinean giant with compelling evidence of its having been killed by humans, or even of its having lived in association with humans. Defenders of the overkill hypothesis reply: you would hardly expect to find kill sites if the extermination was completed very quickly and long ago, such as within a few millennia some 40,000 years ago. The critics respond with a countertheory: perhaps the giants succumbed instead to a change in climate, such as a severe drought on the already chronically dry Australian continent. The debate goes on.

Personally, I can't fathom why Australia's giants should have survived innumerable droughts in their tens of millions of years of Australian history, and then have chosen to drop dead almost simultaneously (at least on a time scale of millions of years) precisely and just coincidentally when the first humans arrived. The giants became extinct not only in dry central Australia but also in drenching wet New Guinea and southeastern Australia. They became extinct in every habitat without exception, from deserts to cold rain forest and tropical rain forest. Hence it seems to me most likely that the giants were indeed exterminated by humans, both directly (by being killed for food) and indirectly (as the result of fires and habitat modification caused by humans). But regardless of whether the overkill hypothesis or the climate hypothesis proves correct, the disappearance of all of the big animals of Australia / New Guinea had, as we shall see, heavy consequences for subsequent human history. Those extinctions eliminated all the large wild animals that might otherwise have been candidates for domestication, and left native Australians and New Guineans with not a single native domestic animal.

THUS, THE COLONIZATION of Australia / New Guinea was not achieved until around the time of the Great Leap Forward. Another extension of human range that soon followed was the one into the coldest parts of Eurasia. While Neanderthals lived in glacial times and were adapted to the cold, they penetrated no farther north than northern Germany and Kiev. That's not surprising, since Neanderthals apparently lacked needles, sewn clothing, warm houses, and other technology essential to survival in the coldest climates. Anatomically modern peoples who did possess such technology had expanded into Siberia by around 20,000 years ago (there are the usual much older disputed claims). That expansion may have been responsible for the extinction of Eurasia's woolly mammoth and woolly rhinoceros.

With the settlement of Australia / New Guinea, humans now occupied three of the five habitable continents. (Throughout this book, I count Eurasia as a single continent, and I omit Antarctica because it was not reached by humans until the 19th century and has never had any self-supporting human population.) That left only two continents, North America and South America. They were surely the last ones settled, for the obvious reason that reaching the Americas from the Old World required either boats (for which there is no evidence even in Indonesia until 40,000 years ago and none in Europe until much later) in order to cross by sea, or else it required the occupation of Siberia (unoccupied until about 20,000 years ago) in order to cross the Bering land bridge.

However, it is uncertain when, between about 14,000 and 35,000 years ago, the Americas were first colonized. The oldest unquestioned human remains in the Americas are at sites in Alaska dated around 12,000 B.C., followed by a profusion of sites in the United States south of the Canadian border and in Mexico in the centuries just before 11,000 B.C. The latter sites are called Clovis sites, named after the type site near the town of Clovis, New Mexico, where their characteristic large stone spearpoints were first recognized. Hundreds of Clovis sites are now known, blanketing all 48 of the lower U.S. states south into Mexico. Unquestioned evidence of human presence appears soon thereafter in Amazonia and in Patagonia. These facts suggest the interpretation that Clovis sites document the Americas' first colonization by people, who quickly multiplied, expanded, and filled the two continents.

One might at first be surprised that Clovis descendants could reach Patagonia, lying 8,000 miles south of the U.S.-Canada border, in less than a thousand years. However, that translates into an average expansion of only 8 miles per year, a trivial feat for a hunter-gatherer likely to cover that distance even within a single day's normal foraging.

One might also at first be surprised that the Americas evidently filled up with humans so quickly that people were motivated to keep spreading south toward Patagonia. That population growth also proves unsurprising when one stops to consider the actual numbers. If the Americas eventually came to hold hunter-gatherers at an average population density of somewhat under one person per square mile (a high value for modern hunter-gatherers), then the whole area of the Americas would eventually have held about 10 million hunter-gatherers. But even if the initial colonists had consisted of only 100 people and their numbers had increased at a rate of only 1.1 percent per year, the colonists' descendants would have reached that population ceiling of 10 million people within a thousand years. A population growth rate of 1.1 percent per year is again trivial: rates as high as 3.4 percent per year have been observed in modern times when people colonized virgin lands, such as when the HMS *Bounty* mutineers and their Tahitian wives colonized Pitcairn Island.

The profusion of Clovis hunters' sites within the first few centuries after their arrival resembles the site profusion documented archaeologically for the more recent discovery of New Zealand by ancestral Maori. A profusion of early sites is also documented for the much older colonization of Europe by anatomically modern humans, and for the occupation of Australia / New Guinea. That is, everything about the Clovis phenomenon and its spread through the Americas corresponds to findings for other, unquestioned virgin-land colonizations in history.

What might be the significance of Clovis sites' bursting forth in the centuries just before 11,000 B.C., rather than in those before 16,000 or 21,000 B.C.? Recall that Siberia has always been cold, and that a continuous ice sheet stretched as an impassable barrier across the whole width of Canada during much of the Pleistocene Ice Ages. We have already seen that the technology required for coping with extreme cold did not emerge until after anatomically modern humans invaded Europe around 40,000 years ago, and that people did not colonize Siberia until 20,000 years later. Eventually, those early Siberians crossed to Alaska, either by sea across the Bering Strait (only 50 miles wide even today) or else on foot at glacial times when Bering Strait was dry land. The Bering land bridge, during its millennia of intermittent existence, would have been up to a thousand miles wide, covered by open tundra, and easily traversable by people adapted to cold conditions. The land bridge was flooded and became a strait again most recently when sea level rose after around 14,000 B.C. Whether those early Siberians walked or paddled to Alaska, the earliest secure evidence of human presence in Alaska dates from around 12,000 B.C.

Soon thereafter, a north–south ice-free corridor opened in the Canadian ice sheet, permitting the first Alaskans to pass through and come out into the Great Plains around the site of the modern Canadian city of Edmonton. That removed the last serious barrier between Alaska and Patagonia for modern humans. The Edmonton pioneers would have found the Great Plains teeming with game. They would have thrived, increased in numbers, and gradually spread south to occupy the whole hemisphere.

One other feature of the Clovis phenomenon fits our expectations for the first human presence south of the Canadian ice sheet. Like Australia / New Guinea, the Americas had originally been full of big mammals. About 15,000 years ago, the American West looked much as Africa's Serengeti Plains do today, with herds of elephants and horses pursued by lions and cheetahs, and joined by members of such exotic species as camels and giant ground sloths. Just as in Australia / New Guinea, in the Americas most of those large mammals became extinct. Whereas the extinctions took place probably before 30,000 years ago in Australia, they occurred around 17,000 to 12,000 years ago in the Americas. For those extinct American mammals whose bones are available in greatest abundance and have been dated especially accurately, one can pinpoint the extinctions as having occurred around 11,000 B.C. Perhaps the two most accurately dated extinctions are those of the Shasta ground sloth and Harrington's mountain goat in the Grand Canyon area; both of those populations disappeared within a century or two of 11,100 B.C. Whether coincidentally or not, that date is identical, within experimental error, to the date of Clovis hunters' arrival in the Grand Canyon area.

The discovery of numerous skeletons of mammoths with Clovis spearpoints between their ribs suggests that this agreement of dates is not a coincidence. Hunters expanding southward through the Americas, encountering big animals that had never seen humans before, may have found those American animals easy to kill and may have exterminated them. A countertheory is that America's big mammals instead became extinct because of climate changes at the end of the last Ice Age, which (to confuse the interpretation for modern paleontologists) also happened around 11,000 B.C.

Personally, I have the same problem with a climatic theory of megafaunal extinction in the Americas as with such a theory in Australia / New Guinea. The Americas' big animals had already survived the ends of 22 previous Ice Ages. Why did most of them pick the 23rd to expire in concert, in the presence of all those supposedly harmless humans? Why did they disappear in all habitats, not only in habitats that contracted but also in ones that greatly expanded at the end of the last Ice Age? Hence I suspect that Clovis hunters did it, but the debate remains unresolved. Whichever theory proves correct, most large wild mammal species that might otherwise have later been domesticated by Native Americans were thereby removed.

Also unresolved is the question whether Clovis hunters really were the first Americans. As always happens whenever anyone claims the first anything, claims of discoveries of pre-Clovis human sites in the Americas are constantly being advanced. Every year, a few of those new claims really do appear convincing and exciting when initially announced. Then the inevitable problems of interpretation arise. Were the reported tools at the site really tools made by humans, or just natural rock shapes? Are the reported radiocarbon dates really correct, and not invalidated by any of the numerous difficulties that can plague radiocarbon dating? If the dates are correct, are they really associated with human products, rather than just being a 15,000-year-old lump of charcoal lying next to a stone tool actually made 9,000 years ago?

To illustrate these problems, consider the following typical example of an often quoted pre-Clovis claim. At a Brazilian rock shelter named Pedro Furada, archaeologists found cave paintings undoubtedly made by humans. They also discovered, among the piles of stones at the base of a cliff, some stones whose shapes suggested the possibility of their being crude tools. In addition, they came upon supposed hearths, whose burnt charcoal yielded radiocarbon dates of around 35,000 years ago. Articles on Pedro Furada were accepted for publication in the prestigious and highly selective international scientific journal *Nature*.

But none of those rocks at the base of the cliff is an obviously human-made tool, as are Clovis points and Cro-Magnon tools. If hundreds of thousands of rocks fall from a high cliff over the course of tens of thousands of years, many of them will become chipped and broken when they hit the rocks below, and some will come to resemble crude tools chipped and broken by humans. In western Europe and elsewhere in Amazonia, archaeologists have radiocarbon-dated the actual pigments used in cave paintings, but that was not done at Pedro Furada. Forest fires occur frequently in the vicinity and produce charcoal that is regularly swept into caves by wind and streams. No evidence links the 35,000-year-old charcoal to the undoubted cave paintings at Pedro Furada. Although the original excavators remain convinced, a team of archaeologists who were not involved in the excavation but receptive to pre-Clovis claims recently visited the site and came away unconvinced.

The North American site that currently enjoys the strongest credentials as a possible pre-Clovis site is Meadowcroft rock shelter, in Pennsylvania, yielding reported human-associated radiocarbon dates of about 16,000 years ago. At Meadowcroft no archaeologist denies that many human artifacts do occur in many carefully excavated layers. But the oldest radiocarbon dates don't make sense, because the plant and animal species associated with them are species living in Pennsylvania in recent times of mild climates, rather than species expected for the glacial times of 16,000 years ago. Hence one has to suspect that the charcoal samples dated from the oldest human occupation levels consist of post-Clovis charcoal infiltrated with older carbon. The strongest pre-Clovis candidate in South America is the Monte Verde site, in southern Chile, dated to at least

15,000 years ago. It too now seems convincing to many archaeologists, but caution is warranted in view of all the previous disillusionments.

If there really were pre-Clovis people in the Americas, why is it still so hard to prove that they existed? Archaeologists have excavated hundreds of American sites unequivocally dating to between 2000 and 11,000 B.C., including dozens of Clovis sites in the North American West, rock shelters in the Appalachians, and sites in coastal California. Below all the archaeological layers with undoubted human presence, at many of those same sites, deeper older layers have been excavated and still yield undoubted remains of animals—but with no further evidence of humans. The weaknesses in pre-Clovis evidence in the Americas contrast with the strength of the evidence in Europe, where hundreds of sites attest to the presence of modern humans long before Clovis hunters appeared in the Americas around 11,000 B.C. Even more striking is the evidence from Australia / New Guinea, where there are barely one-tenth as many archaeologists as in the United States alone, but where those few archaeologists have nevertheless discovered over a hundred unequivocal pre-Clovis sites scattered over the whole continent.

Early humans certainly didn't fly by helicopter from Alaska to Meadowcroft and Monte Verde, skipping all the landscape in between. Advocates of pre-Clovis settlement suggest that, for thousands or even tens of thousands of years, pre-Clovis humans remained at low population densities or poorly visible archaeologically, for unknown reasons unprecedented elsewhere in the world. I find that suggestion infinitely more implausible than the suggestion that Monte Verde and Meadowcroft will eventually be reinterpreted, as have other claimed pre-Clovis sites. My feeling is that, if there really had been pre-Clovis settlement in the Americas, it would have become obvious at many locations by now, and we would not still be arguing. However, archaeologists remain divided on these questions.

The consequences for our understanding of later American prehistory remain the same, whichever interpretation proves correct. Either: the Americas were first settled around 11,000 B.C. and quickly filled up with people. Or else: the first settlement occurred somewhat earlier (most advocates of pre-Clovis settlement would suggest by 15,000 or 20,000 years ago, possibly 30,000 years ago, and few would seriously claim earlier); but those pre-Clovis settlers remained few in numbers, or inconspicuous, or had little impact, until around 11,000 B.C. In either case, of the five habitable continents, North America and South America are the ones with the shortest human prehistories.

WITH THE OCCUPATION of the Americas, most habitable areas of the continents and continental islands, plus oceanic islands from Indonesia to east of New Guinea, supported humans. The settlement of the world's remaining islands was not completed until modern times: Mediterranean islands such as Crete, Cyprus, Corsica, and Sardinia between about 8500 and 4000 B.C.; Caribbean islands beginning around 4000 B.C.; Polynesian and Micronesian islands between 1200 B.C. and A.D. 1000; Madagascar sometime between A.D. 300 and 800; and Iceland in the ninth century A.D. Native Americans, possibly ancestral to the modern Inuit, spread throughout the High Arctic around 2000 B.C. That left, as the sole uninhabited areas awaiting European explorers over the last 700 years, only the most remote islands of the Atlantic and Indian Oceans (such as the Azores and Seychelles), plus Antarctica.

What significance, if any, do the continents' differing dates of settlement have for subsequent history? Suppose that a time machine could have transported an archaeologist back in time, for a world tour at around 11,000 B.C. Given the state of the world then, could the archaeologist have predicted the sequence in which human societies on the various continents would develop guns, germs, and steel, and thus predicted the state of the world today?

Our archaeologist might have considered the possible advantages of a head start. If that counted for anything, then Africa enjoyed an enormous advantage: at least 5 million more years of separate protohuman existence than on any other continent. In addition, if it is true that modern humans arose in Africa around 100,000 years ago and spread to other continents, that would have wiped out any advantages accumulated elsewhere in the meantime and given Africans a new head start. Furthermore, human genetic diversity is highest in Africa; perhaps more-diverse humans would collectively produce more-diverse inventions.

But our archaeologist might then reflect: what, really, does a "head start" mean for the purposes of this book? We cannot take the metaphor of a footrace literally. If by head start you mean the time required to populate a continent after the arrival of the first few pioneering colonists, that time is relatively brief: for example, less than 1,000 years to fill up even the whole New World. If by head start you instead mean the time required to adapt to local conditions, I grant that some extreme environments did take time: for instance, 9,000 years to occupy the High Arctic after the occupation of the rest of North America. But people would have explored and adapted to most other areas quickly, once modern human inventiveness had developed. For example, after the ancestors of the Maori reached New Zealand, it apparently took them barely a century to discover all worthwhile stone sources; only a few more centuries to kill every last moa in some of the world's most rugged terrain; and only a few centuries to differentiate into a range of diverse societies, from that of coastal hunter-gatherers to that of farmers practicing new types of food storage.

Our archaeologist might therefore look at the Americas and conclude that Africans, despite their apparently enormous head start, would have been overtaken by the earliest Americans within at most a millennium. Thereafter, the Americas' greater area (50 percent greater than Africa's) and much greater environmental diversity would have given the advantage to Native Americans over Africans.

The archaeologist might then turn to Eurasia and reason as follows. Eurasia is the world's largest continent. It has been occupied for longer than any other continent except Africa. Africa's long occupation before the colonization of Eurasia a million years ago might have counted for nothing anyway, because protohumans were at such a primitive stage then. Our archaeologist might look at the Upper Paleolithic flowering of south-western Europe between 20,000 and 12,000 years ago, with all those famous artworks and complex tools, and wonder whether Eurasia was already getting a head start then, at least locally.

Finally, the archaeologist would turn to Australia / New Guinea, noting first its small area (it's the smallest continent), the large fraction of it covered by desert capable of supporting few humans, the continent's isolation, and its later occupation than that of Africa and Eurasia. All that might lead the archaeologist to predict slow development in Australia / New Guinea.

But remember that Australians and New Guineans had by far the earliest watercraft in the world. They were creating cave paintings apparently at least as early as the Cro-Magnons in Europe. Jonathan Kingdon and Tim Flannery have noted that the colonization of Australia / New Guinea from the islands of the Asian continental shelf required humans to learn to deal with the new environments they encountered on the islands of central

Indonesia—a maze of coastlines offering the richest marine resources, coral reefs, and mangroves in the world. As the colonists crossed the straits separating each Indonesian island from the next one to the east, they adapted anew, filled up that next island, and went on to colonize the next island again. It was a hitherto unprecedented golden age of successive human population explosions. Perhaps those cycles of colonization, adaptation, and population explosion were what selected for the Great Leap Forward, which then diffused back westward to Eurasia and Africa. If this scenario is correct, then Australia / New Guinea gained a massive head start that might have continued to propel human development there long after the Great Leap Forward.

Thus, an observer transported back in time to 11,000 B.C. could not have predicted on which continent human societies would develop most quickly, but could have made a strong case for any of the continents. With hindsight, of course, we know that Eurasia was the one. But it turns out that the actual reasons behind the more rapid development of Eurasian societies were not at all the straightforward ones that our imaginary archaeologist of 11,000 B.C. guessed. The remainder of this book consists of a quest to discover those real reasons.

CHAPTER 2

A NATURAL EXPERIMENT
OF HISTORY

O N THE CHATHAM ISLANDS, 500 MILES EAST OF NEW
Zealand, centuries of independence came to a brutal end for the
Moriori people in December 1835. On November 19 of that year, a ship
carrying 500 Maori armed with guns, clubs, and axes arrived, followed on
December 5 by a shipload of 400 more Maori. Groups of Maori began to
walk through Moriori settlements, announcing that the Moriori were now
their slaves, and killing those who objected. An organized resistance by
the Moriori could still then have defeated the Maori, who were outnumbered two to one. However, the Moriori had a tradition of resolving disputes peacefully. They decided in a council meeting not to fight back but
to offer peace, friendship, and a division of resources.

Before the Moriori could deliver that offer, the Maori attacked en
masse. Over the course of the next few days, they killed hundreds of Moriori, cooked and ate many of the bodies, and enslaved all the others, killing
most of them too over the next few years as it suited their whim. A Moriori
survivor recalled, "[The Maori] commenced to kill us like sheep. . . . [We]
were terrified, fled to the bush, concealed ourselves in holes underground,
and in any place to escape our enemies. It was of no avail; we were discovered and killed—men, women, and children indiscriminately." A Maori
conqueror explained, "We took possession. . . in accordance with our cus-

toms and we caught all the people. Not one escaped. Some ran away from us, these we killed, and others we killed—but what of that? It was in accordance with our custom."

The brutal outcome of this collision between the Moriori and the Maori could have been easily predicted. The Moriori were a small, isolated population of hunter-gatherers, equipped with only the simplest technology and weapons, entirely inexperienced at war, and lacking strong leadership or organization. The Maori invaders (from New Zealand's North Island) came from a dense population of farmers chronically engaged in ferocious wars, equipped with more-advanced technology and weapons, and operating under strong leadership. Of course, when the two groups finally came into contact, it was the Maori who slaughtered the Moriori, not vice versa.

The tragedy of the Moriori resembles many other such tragedies in both the modern and the ancient world, pitting numerous well-equipped people against few ill-equipped opponents. What makes the Maori-Moriori collision grimly illuminating is that both groups had diverged from a common origin less than a millennium earlier. Both were Polynesian peoples. The modern Maori are descendants of Polynesian farmers who colonized New Zealand around A.D. 1000. Soon thereafter, a group of those Maori in turn colonized the Chatham Islands and became the Moriori. In the centuries after the two groups separated, they evolved in opposite directions, the North Island Maori developing more-complex and the Moriori less-complex technology and political organization. The Moriori reverted to being hunter-gatherers, while the North Island Maori turned to more intensive farming.

Those opposite evolutionary courses sealed the outcome of their eventual collision. If we could understand the reasons for the disparate development of those two island societies, we might have a model for understanding the broader question of differing developments on the continents.

MORIORI AND MAORI history constitutes a brief, small-scale natural experiment that tests how environments affect human societies. Before you read a whole book examining environmental effects on a very large scale— effects on human societies around the world for the last 13,000 years— you might reasonably want assurance, from smaller tests, that such effects really are significant. If you were a laboratory scientist studying rats, you might perform such a test by taking one rat colony, distributing groups of those ancestral rats among many cages with differing environments, and coming back many rat generations later to see what had happened. Of course, such purposeful experiments cannot be carried out on human societies. Instead, scientists must look for "natural experiments," in which something similar befell humans in the past.

Such an experiment unfolded during the settlement of Polynesia. Scattered over the Pacific Ocean beyond New Guinea and Melanesia are thousands of islands differing greatly in area, isolation, elevation, climate, productivity, and geological and biological resources (Figure 2.1). For most of human history those islands lay far beyond the reach of watercraft. Around 1200 B.C. a group of farming, fishing, seafaring people from the Bismarck Archipelago north of New Guinea finally succeeded in reaching some of those islands. Over the following centuries their descendants colonized virtually every habitable scrap of land in the Pacific. The process was mostly complete by A.D. 500, with the last few islands settled around or soon after A.D. 1000.

Thus, within a modest time span, enormously diverse island environments were settled by colonists all of whom stemmed from the same founding population. The ultimate ancestors of all modern Polynesian populations shared essentially the same culture, language, technology, and set of domesticated plants and animals. Hence Polynesian history constitutes a natural experiment allowing us to study human adaptation, devoid of the usual complications of multiple waves of disparate colonists that often frustrate our attempts to understand adaptation elsewhere in the world.

Within that medium-sized test, the fate of the Moriori forms a smaller test. It is easy to trace how the differing environments of the Chatham Islands and of New Zealand molded the Moriori and the Maori differently. While those ancestral Maori who first colonized the Chathams may have been farmers, Maori tropical crops could not grow in the Chathams' cold climate, and the colonists had no alternative except to revert to being hunter-gatherers. Since as hunter-gatherers they did not produce crop surpluses available for redistribution or storage, they could not support and feed nonhunting craft specialists, armies, bureaucrats, and chiefs. Their prey were seals, shellfish, nesting seabirds, and fish that could be captured by hand or with clubs and required no more elaborate technology. In addi-

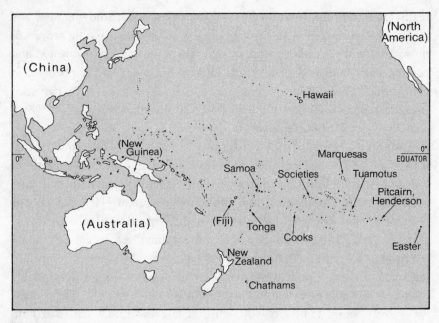

Figure 2.1. Polynesian islands. (Parentheses denote some non-Polynesian lands.)

tion, the Chathams are relatively small and remote islands, capable of supporting a total population of only about 2,000 hunter-gatherers. With no other accessible islands to colonize, the Moriori had to remain in the Chathams, and to learn how to get along with each other. They did so by renouncing war, and they reduced potential conflicts from overpopulation by castrating some male infants. The result was a small, unwarlike population with simple technology and weapons, and without strong leadership or organization.

In contrast, the northern (warmer) part of New Zealand, by far the largest island group in Polynesia, was suitable for Polynesian agriculture. Those Maori who remained in New Zealand increased in numbers until there were more than 100,000 of them. They developed locally dense populations chronically engaged in ferocious wars with neighboring populations. With the crop surpluses that they could grow and store, they fed craft specialists, chiefs, and part-time soldiers. They needed and developed varied tools for growing their crops, fighting, and making art. They erected elaborate ceremonial buildings and prodigious numbers of forts.

Thus, Moriori and Maori societies developed from the same ancestral society, but along very different lines. The resulting two societies lost awareness even of each other's existence and did not come into contact again for many centuries, perhaps for as long as 500 years. Finally, an Australian seal-hunting ship visiting the Chathams en route to New Zealand brought the news to New Zealand of islands where "there is an abundance of sea and shellfish; the lakes swarm with eels; and it is a land of the karaka berry. . . . The inhabitants are very numerous, but they do not understand how to fight, and have no weapons." That news was enough to induce 900 Maori to sail to the Chathams. The outcome clearly illustrates how environments can affect economy, technology, political organization, and fighting skills within a short time.

As I already mentioned, the Maori-Moriori collision represents a small test within a medium-sized test. What can we learn from all of Polynesia about environmental influences on human societies? What differences among societies on different Polynesian islands need to be explained?

Polynesia as a whole presented a much wider range of environmental conditions than did just New Zealand and the Chathams, although the latter define one extreme (the simple end) of Polynesian organization. In their subsistence modes, Polynesians ranged from the hunter-gatherers of the Chathams, through slash-and-burn farmers, to practitioners of intensive food production living at some of the highest population densities of any human societies. Polynesian food producers variously intensified production of pigs, dogs, and chickens. They organized work forces to construct large irrigation systems for agriculture and to enclose large ponds for fish production. The economic basis of Polynesian societies consisted of more or less self-sufficient households, but some islands also supported guilds of hereditary part-time craft specialists. In social organization, Polynesian societies ran the gamut from fairly egalitarian village societies to some of the most stratified societies in the world, with many hierarchically ranked lineages and with chief and commoner classes whose members married within their own class. In political organization, Polynesian islands ranged from landscapes divided into independent tribal or village units, up to multi-island proto-empires that devoted standing military establishments to invasions of other islands and wars of conquest.

Finally, Polynesian material culture varied from the production of no more than personal utensils to the construction of monumental stone architecture. How can all that variation be explained?

Contributing to these differences among Polynesian societies were at least six sets of environmental variables among Polynesian islands: island climate, geological type, marine resources, area, terrain fragmentation, and isolation. Let's examine the ranges of these factors, before considering their specific consequences for Polynesian societies.

The climate in Polynesia varies from warm tropical or subtropical on most islands, which lie near the equator, to temperate on most of New Zealand, and cold subantarctic on the Chathams and the southern part of New Zealand's South Island. Hawaii's Big Island, though lying well within the Tropic of Cancer, has mountains high enough to support alpine habitats and receive occasional snowfalls. Rainfall varies from the highest recorded on Earth (in New Zealand's Fjordland and Hawaii's Alakai Swamp on Kauai) to only one-tenth as much on islands so dry that they are marginal for agriculture.

Island geological types include coral atolls, raised limestone, volcanic islands, pieces of continents, and mixtures of those types. At one extreme, innumerable islets, such as those of the Tuamotu Archipelago, are flat, low atolls barely rising above sea level. Other former atolls, such as Henderson and Rennell, have been lifted far above sea level to constitute raised limestone islands. Both of those atoll types present problems to human settlers, because they consist entirely of limestone without other stones, have only very thin soil, and lack permanent fresh water. At the opposite extreme, the largest Polynesian island, New Zealand, is an old, geologically diverse, continental fragment of Gondwanaland, offering a range of mineral resources, including commercially exploitable iron, coal, gold, and jade. Most other large Polynesian islands are volcanoes that rose from the sea, have never formed parts of a continent, and may or may not include areas of raised limestone. While lacking New Zealand's geological richness, the oceanic volcanic islands at least are an improvement over atolls (from the Polynesians' perspective) in that they offer diverse types of volcanic stones, some of which are highly suitable for making stone tools.

The volcanic islands differ among themselves. The elevations of the higher ones generate rain in the mountains, so the islands are heavily weathered and have deep soils and permanent streams. That is true, for instance, of the Societies, Samoa, the Marquesas, and especially Hawaii, the Polynesian archipelago with the highest mountains. Among the lower islands, Tonga and (to a lesser extent) Easter also have rich soil because of volcanic ashfalls, but they lack Hawaii's large streams.

As for marine resources, most Polynesian islands are surrounded by shallow water and reefs, and many also encompass lagoons. Those environments teem with fish and shellfish. However, the rocky coasts of Easter, Pitcairn, and the Marquesas, and the steeply dropping ocean bottom and absence of coral reefs around those islands, are much less productive of seafood.

Area is another obvious variable, ranging from the 100 acres of Anuta, the smallest permanently inhabited isolated Polynesian island, up to the 103,000 square miles of the minicontinent of New Zealand. The habitable terrain of some islands, notably the Marquesas, is fragmented into steep-walled valleys by ridges, while other islands, such as Tonga and Easter, consist of gently rolling terrain presenting no obstacles to travel and communication.

The last environmental variable to consider is isolation. Easter Island and the Chathams are small and so remote from other islands that, once they were initially colonized, the societies thus founded developed in total isolation from the rest of the world. New Zealand, Hawaii, and the Marquesas are also very remote, but at least the latter two apparently did have some further contact with other archipelagoes after the first colonization, and all three consist of many islands close enough to each other for regular contact between islands of the same archipelago. Most other Polynesian islands were in more or less regular contact with other islands. In particular, the Tongan Archipelago lies close enough to the Fijian, Samoan, and Wallis Archipelagoes to have permitted regular voyaging between archipelagoes, and eventually to permit Tongans to undertake the conquest of Fiji.

AFTER THAT BRIEF look at Polynesia's varying environments, let's now see how that variation influenced Polynesian societies. Subsistence is a convenient facet of society with which to start, since it in turn affected other facets.

Polynesian subsistence depended on varying mixes of fishing, gathering wild plants and marine shellfish and crustacea, hunting terrestrial birds and breeding seabirds, and food production. Most Polynesian islands originally supported big flightless birds that had evolved in the absence of predators, New Zealand's moas and Hawaii's flightless geese being the best-known examples. While those birds were important food sources for the initial colonists, especially on New Zealand's South Island, most of them were soon exterminated on all islands, because they were easy to hunt down. Breeding seabirds were also quickly reduced in number but continued to be important food sources on some islands. Marine resources were significant on most islands but least so on Easter, Pitcairn, and the Marquesas, where people as a result were especially dependent on food that they themselves produced.

Ancestral Polynesians brought with them three domesticated animals (the pig, chicken, and dog) and domesticated no other animals within Polynesia. Many islands retained all three of those species, but the more isolated Polynesian islands lacked one or more of them, either because livestock brought in canoes failed to survive the colonists' long overwater journey or because livestock that died out could not be readily obtained again from the outside. For instance, isolated New Zealand ended up with only dogs; Easter and Tikopia, with only chickens. Without access to coral reefs or productive shallow waters, and with their terrestrial birds quickly exterminated, Easter Islanders turned to constructing chicken houses for intensive poultry farming.

At best, however, these three domesticated animal species provided only occasional meals. Polynesian food production depended mainly on agriculture, which was impossible at subantarctic latitudes because all Polynesian crops were tropical ones initially domesticated outside Polynesia and brought in by colonists. The settlers of the Chathams and the cold southern part of New Zealand's South Island were thus forced to abandon the farming legacy developed by their ancestors over the previous thousands of years, and to become hunter-gatherers again.

People on the remaining Polynesian islands did practice agriculture based on dryland crops (especially taro, yams, and sweet potatoes), irrigated crops (mainly taro), and tree crops (such as breadfruit, bananas, and coconuts). The productivity and relative importance of those crop types varied considerably on different islands, depending on their environments. Human population densities were lowest on Henderson, Rennell, and the atolls because of their poor soil and limited fresh water. Densities were also low on temperate New Zealand, which was too cool for some Polynesian crops. Polynesians on these and some other islands practiced a nonintensive type of shifting, slash-and-burn agriculture.

Other islands had rich soils but were not high enough to have large permanent streams and hence irrigation. Inhabitants of those islands developed intensive dryland agriculture requiring a heavy input of labor to build terraces, carry out mulching, rotate crops, reduce or eliminate fallow periods, and maintain tree plantations. Dryland agriculture became especially productive on Easter, tiny Anuta, and flat and low Tonga, where Polynesians devoted most of the land area to the growing of food.

The most productive Polynesian agriculture was taro cultivation in irrigated fields. Among the more populous tropical islands, that option was ruled out for Tonga by its low elevation and hence its lack of rivers. Irrigation agriculture reached its peak on the westernmost Hawaiian islands of Kauai, Oahu, and Molokai, which were big and wet enough to support not only large permanent streams but also large human populations available for construction projects. Hawaiian labor corvées built elaborate irrigation systems for taro fields yielding up to 24 tons per acre, the highest crop yields in all of Polynesia. Those yields in turn supported intensive pig production. Hawaii was also unique within Polynesia in using mass labor for aquaculture, by constructing large fishponds in which milkfish and mullet were grown.

As a result of all this environmentally related variation in subsistence, human population densities (measured in people per square mile of arable land) varied greatly over Polynesia. At the lower end were the hunter-gatherers of the Chathams (only 5 people per square mile) and of New Zealand's South Island, and the farmers of the rest of New Zealand (28 people per square mile). In contrast, many islands with intensive agriculture attained population densities exceeding 120 per square mile. Tonga, Samoa, and the Societies achieved 210–250 people per square mile and Hawaii 300. The upper extreme of 1,100 people per square mile was reached on the high island of Anuta, whose population converted essentially all the land to intensive food production, thereby crammed 160 people into the island's 100 acres, and joined the ranks of the densest self-sufficient populations in the world. Anuta's population density exceeded that of modern Holland and even rivaled that of Bangladesh.

Population size is the product of population density (people per square mile) and area (square miles). The relevant area is not the area of an island but that of a political unit, which could be either larger or smaller than a single island. On the one hand, islands near one another might become combined into a single political unit. On the other hand, single large rugged islands were divided into many independent political units. Hence the area of the political unit varied not only with an island's area but also with its fragmentation and isolation.

For small isolated islands without strong barriers to internal communication, the entire island constituted the political unit—as in the case of Anuta, with its 160 people. Many larger islands never did become unified politically, whether because the population consisted of dispersed bands of only a few dozen hunter-gatherers each (the Chathams and New Zealand's southern South Island), or of farmers scattered over large distances (the rest of New Zealand), or of farmers living in dense populations but in rugged terrain precluding political unification. For example, people in neighboring steep-sided valleys of the Marquesas communicated with each other mainly by sea; each valley formed an independent political entity of a few thousand inhabitants, and most individual large Marquesan islands remained divided into many such entities.

The terrains of the Tongan, Samoan, Society, and Hawaiian islands did permit political unification within islands, yielding political units of 10,000 people or more (over 30,000 on the large Hawaiian islands). The distances between islands of the Tongan archipelago, as well as the distances between Tonga and neighboring archipelagoes, were sufficiently modest that a multi-island empire encompassing 40,000 people was eventually established. Thus, Polynesian political units ranged in size from a few dozen to 40,000 people.

A political unit's population size interacted with its population density to influence Polynesian technology and economic, social, and political organization. In general, the larger the size and the higher the density, the more complex and specialized were the technology and organization, for reasons that we shall examine in detail in later chapters. Briefly, at high population densities only a portion of the people came to be farmers, but they were mobilized to devote themselves to intensive food production, thereby yielding surpluses to feed nonproducers. The nonproducers mobilizing them included chiefs, priests, bureaucrats, and warriors. The biggest political units could assemble large labor forces to construct irrigation systems and fishponds that intensified food production even further. These developments were especially apparent on Tonga, Samoa, and the Societies, all of which were fertile, densely populated, and moderately large by

Polynesian standards. The trends reached their zenith on the Hawaiian Archipelago, consisting of the largest tropical Polynesian islands, where high population densities and large land areas meant that very large labor forces were potentially available to individual chiefs.

The variations among Polynesian societies associated with different population densities and sizes were as follows. Economies remained simplest on islands with low population densities (such as the hunter-gatherers of the Chathams), low population numbers (small atolls), or both low densities and low numbers. In those societies each household made what it needed; there was little or no economic specialization. Specialization increased on larger, more densely populated islands, reaching a peak on Samoa, the Societies, and especially Tonga and Hawaii. The latter two islands supported hereditary part-time craft specialists, including canoe builders, navigators, stone masons, bird catchers, and tattooers.

Social complexity was similarly varied. Again, the Chathams and the atolls had the simplest, most egalitarian societies. While those islands retained the original Polynesian tradition of having chiefs, their chiefs wore little or no visible signs of distinction, lived in ordinary huts like those of commoners, and grew or caught their food like everyone else. Social distinctions and chiefly powers increased on high-density islands with large political units, being especially marked on Tonga and the Societies.

Social complexity again reached its peak in the Hawaiian Archipelago, where people of chiefly descent were divided into eight hierarchically ranked lineages. Members of those chiefly lineages did not intermarry with commoners but only with each other, sometimes even with siblings or half-siblings. Commoners had to prostrate themselves before high-ranking chiefs. All the members of chiefly lineages, bureaucrats, and some craft specialists were freed from the work of food production.

Political organization followed the same trends. On the Chathams and atolls, the chiefs had few resources to command, decisions were reached by general discussion, and landownership rested with the community as a whole rather than with the chiefs. Larger, more densely populated political units concentrated more authority with the chiefs. Political complexity was greatest on Tonga and Hawaii, where the powers of hereditary chiefs approximated those of kings elsewhere in the world, and where land was controlled by the chiefs, not by the commoners. Using appointed bureaucrats as agents, chiefs requisitioned food from the commoners and also

conscripted them to work on large construction projects, whose form varied from island to island: irrigation projects and fishponds on Hawaii,
dance and feast centers on the Marquesas, chiefs' tombs on Tonga, and
temples on Hawaii, the Societies, and Easter.

At the time of Europeans' arrival in the 18th century, the Tongan chiefdom or state had already become an inter-archipelagal empire. Because
the Tongan Archipelago itself was geographically close-knit and included
several large islands with unfragmented terrain, each island became unified
under a single chief; then the hereditary chiefs of the largest Tongan island
(Tongatapu) united the whole archipelago, and eventually they conquered
islands outside the archipelago up to 500 miles distant. They engaged in
regular long-distance trade with Fiji and Samoa, established Tongan settlements in Fiji, and began to raid and conquer parts of Fiji. The conquest
and administration of this maritime proto-empire were achieved by navies
of large canoes, each holding up to 150 men.

Like Tonga, Hawaii became a political entity encompassing several
populous islands, but one confined to a single archipelago because of its
extreme isolation. At the time of Hawaii's "discovery" by Europeans in
1778, political unification had already taken place within each Hawaiian
island, and some political fusion between islands had begun. The four
largest islands—Big Island (Hawaii in the narrow sense), Maui, Oahu, and
Kauai—remained independent, controlling (or jockeying with each other
for control of) the smaller islands (Lanai, Molokai, Kahoolawe, and Nii-
hau). After the arrival of Europeans, the Big Island's King Kamehameha I
rapidly proceeded with the consolidation of the largest islands by purchas-
ing European guns and ships to invade and conquer first Maui and then
Oahu. Kamehameha thereupon prepared invasions of the last independent
Hawaiian island, Kauai, whose chief finally reached a negotiated settlement with him, completing the archipelago's unification.

The remaining type of variation among Polynesian societies to be considered involves tools and other aspects of material culture. The differing
availability of raw materials imposed an obvious constraint on material
culture. At the one extreme was Henderson Island, an old coral reef raised
above sea level and devoid of stone other than limestone. Its inhabitants
were reduced to fabricating adzes out of giant clamshells. At the opposite
extreme, the Maori on the minicontinent of New Zealand had access to a
wide range of raw materials and became especially noted for their use of
jade. Between those two extremes fell Polynesia's oceanic volcanic islands,

which lacked granite, flint, and other continental rocks but did at least have volcanic rocks, which Polynesians worked into ground or polished stone adzes used to clear land for farming.

As for the types of artifacts made, the Chatham Islanders required little more than hand-held clubs and sticks to kill seals, birds, and lobsters. Most other islanders produced a diverse array of fishhooks, adzes, jewelry, and other objects. On the atolls, as on the Chathams, those artifacts were small, relatively simple, and individually produced and owned, while architecture consisted of nothing more than simple huts. Large and densely populated islands supported craft specialists who produced a wide range of prestige goods for chiefs—such as the feather capes reserved for Hawaiian chiefs and made of tens of thousands of bird feathers.

The largest products of Polynesia were the immense stone structures of a few islands—the famous giant statues of Easter Island, the tombs of Tongan chiefs, the ceremonial platforms of the Marquesas, and the temples of Hawaii and the Societies. This monumental Polynesian architecture was obviously evolving in the same direction as the pyramids of Egypt, Mesopotamia, Mexico, and Peru. Naturally, Polynesia's structures are not on the scale of those pyramids, but that merely reflects the fact that Egyptian pharaohs could draw conscript labor from a much larger human population than could the chief of any Polynesian island. Even so, the Easter Islanders managed to erect 30-ton stone statues—no mean feat for an island with only 7,000 people, who had no power source other than their own muscles.

THUS, POLYNESIAN ISLAND societies differed greatly in their economic specialization, social complexity, political organization, and material products, related to differences in population size and density, related in turn to differences in island area, fragmentation, and isolation and in opportunities for subsistence and for intensifying food production. All those differences among Polynesian societies developed, within a relatively short time and modest fraction of the Earth's surface, as environmentally related variations on a single ancestral society. Those categories of cultural differences within Polynesia are essentially the same categories that emerged everywhere else in the world.

Of course, the range of variation over the rest of the globe is much greater than that within Polynesia. While modern continental peoples included ones dependent on stone tools, as were Polynesians, South America also spawned societies expert in using precious metals, and Eurasians and Africans went on to utilize iron. Those developments were precluded in Polynesia, because no Polynesian island except New Zealand had significant metal deposits. Eurasia had full-fledged empires before Polynesia was even settled, and South America and Mesoamerica developed empires later, whereas Polynesia produced just two proto-empires, one of which (Hawaii) coalesced only after the arrival of Europeans. Eurasia and Mesoamerica developed indigenous writing, which failed to emerge in Polynesia, except perhaps on Easter Island, whose mysterious script may however have postdated the islanders' contact with Europeans.

That is, Polynesia offers us a small slice, not the full spectrum, of the world's human social diversity. That shouldn't surprise us, since Polynesia provides only a small slice of the world's geographic diversity. In addition, since Polynesia was colonized so late in human history, even the oldest Polynesian societies had only 3,200 years in which to develop, as opposed to at least 13,000 years for societies on even the last-colonized continents (the Americas). Given a few more millennia, perhaps Tonga and Hawaii would have reached the level of full-fledged empires battling each other for control of the Pacific, with indigenously developed writing to administer those empires, while New Zealand's Maori might have added copper and iron tools to their repertoire of jade and other materials.

In short, Polynesia furnishes us with a convincing example of environmentally related diversification of human societies in operation. But we thereby learn only that it can happen, because it happened in Polynesia. Did it also happen on the continents? If so, what were the environmental differences responsible for diversification on the continents, and what were their consequences?

CHAPTER 3

COLLISION AT CAJAMARCA

T HE BIGGEST POPULATION SHIFT OF MODERN TIMES HAS
been the colonization of the New World by Europeans, and the
resulting conquest, numerical reduction, or complete disappearance of
most groups of Native Americans (American Indians). As I explained in
Chapter 1, the New World was initially colonized around or before 11,000
B.C. by way of Alaska, the Bering Strait, and Siberia. Complex agricultural
societies gradually arose in the Americas far to the south of that entry
route, developing in complete isolation from the emerging complex societies of the Old World. After that initial colonization from Asia, the sole
well-attested further contacts between the New World and Asia involved
only hunter-gatherers living on opposite sides of the Bering Strait, plus an
inferred transpacific voyage that introduced the sweet potato from South
America to Polynesia.

As for contacts of New World peoples with Europe, the sole early ones
involved the Norse who occupied Greenland in very small numbers
between A.D. 986 and about 1500. But those Norse visits had no discernible impact on Native American societies. Instead, for practical purposes
the collision of advanced Old World and New World societies began
abruptly in A.D. 1492, with Christopher Columbus's "discovery" of Caribbean islands densely populated by Native Americans.

The most dramatic moment in subsequent European–Native American relations was the first encounter between the Inca emperor Atahuallpa and the Spanish conquistador Francisco Pizarro at the Peruvian highland town of Cajamarca on November 16, 1532. Atahuallpa was absolute monarch of the largest and most advanced state in the New World, while Pizarro represented the Holy Roman Emperor Charles V (also known as King Charles I of Spain), monarch of the most powerful state in Europe. Pizarro, leading a ragtag group of 168 Spanish soldiers, was in unfamiliar terrain, ignorant of the local inhabitants, completely out of touch with the nearest Spaniards (1,000 miles to the north in Panama) and far beyond the reach of timely reinforcements. Atahuallpa was in the middle of his own empire of millions of subjects and immediately surrounded by his army of 80,000 soldiers, recently victorious in a war with other Indians. Nevertheless, Pizarro captured Atahuallpa within a few minutes after the two leaders first set eyes on each other. Pizarro proceeded to hold his prisoner for eight months, while extracting history's largest ransom in return for a promise to free him. After the ransom—enough gold to fill a room 22 feet long by 17 feet wide to a height of over 8 feet—was delivered, Pizarro reneged on his promise and executed Atahuallpa.

Atahuallpa's capture was decisive for the European conquest of the Inca Empire. Although the Spaniards' superior weapons would have assured an ultimate Spanish victory in any case, the capture made the conquest quicker and infinitely easier. Atahuallpa was revered by the Incas as a sun-god and exercised absolute authority over his subjects, who obeyed even the orders he issued from captivity. The months until his death gave Pizarro time to dispatch exploring parties unmolested to other parts of the Inca Empire, and to send for reinforcements from Panama. When fighting between Spaniards and Incas finally did commence after Atahuallpa's execution, the Spanish forces were more formidable.

Thus, Atahuallpa's capture interests us specifically as marking the decisive moment in the greatest collision of modern history. But it is also of more general interest, because the factors that resulted in Pizarro's seizing Atahuallpa were essentially the same ones that determined the outcome of many similar collisions between colonizers and native peoples elsewhere in the modern world. Hence Atahuallpa's capture offers us a broad window onto world history.

WHAT UNFOLDED THAT day at Cajamarca is well known, because it was recorded in writing by many of the Spanish participants. To get a flavor of those events, let us relive them by weaving together excerpts from eyewitness accounts by six of Pizarro's companions, including his brothers Hernando and Pedro:

"The prudence, fortitude, military discipline, labors, perilous naviga-tions, and battles of the Spaniards—vassals of the most invincible Emperor of the Roman Catholic Empire, our natural King and Lord—will cause joy to the faithful and terror to the infidels. For this reason, and for the glory of God our Lord and for the service of the Catholic Imperial Majesty, it has seemed good to me to write this narrative, and to send it to Your Majesty, that all may have a knowledge of what is here related. It will be to the glory of God, because they have conquered and brought to our holy Catholic Faith so vast a number of heathens, aided by His holy guidance. It will be to the honor of our Emperor because, by reason of his great power and good fortune, such events happened in his time. It will give joy to the faithful that such battles have been won, such provinces discovered and conquered, such riches brought home for the King and for themselves; and that such terror has been spread among the infidels, such admiration excited in all mankind.

"For when, either in ancient or modern times, have such great exploits been achieved by so few against so many, over so many climes, across so many seas, over such distances by land, to subdue the unseen and unknown? Whose deeds can be compared with those of Spain? Our Span-iards, being few in number, never having more than 200 or 300 men together, and sometimes only 100 and even fewer, have, in our times, con-quered more territory than has ever been known before, or than all the faithful and infidel princes possess. I will only write, at present, of what befell in the conquest, and I will not write much, in order to avoid pro-lixity.

"Governor Pizarro wished to obtain intelligence from some Indians who had come from Cajamarca, so he had them tortured. They confessed that they had heard that Atahuallpa was waiting for the Governor at Caja-marca. The Governor then ordered us to advance. On reaching the entrance to Cajamarca, we saw the camp of Atahuallpa at a distance of a league, in the skirts of the mountains. The Indians' camp looked like a very beautiful city. They had so many tents that we were all filled with great apprehension. Until then, we had never seen anything like this in the Indies. It filled all our Spaniards with fear and confusion. But we could not show any fear or turn back, for if the Indians had sensed any weakness in us, even the Indians that we were bringing with us as guides would have killed us. So we made a show of good spirits, and after carefully observing the town and the tents, we descended into the valley and entered Cajamarca.

"We talked a lot among ourselves about what to do. All of us were full of fear, because we were so few in number and we had penetrated so far into a land where we could not hope to receive reinforcements. We all met with the Governor to debate what we should undertake the next day. Few of us slept that night, and we kept watch in the square of Cajamarca, looking at the campfires of the Indian army. It was a frightening sight. Most of the campfires were on a hillside and so close to each other that it looked like the sky brightly studded with stars. There was no distinction that night between the mighty and the lowly, or between foot soldiers and horsemen. Everyone carried out sentry duty fully armed. So too did the good old Governor, who went about encouraging his men. The Governor's brother Hernando Pizarro estimated the number of Indian soldiers there at 40,000, but he was telling a lie just to encourage us, for there were actually more than 80,000 Indians.

"On the next morning a messenger from Atahuallpa arrived, and the Governor said to him, 'Tell your lord to come when and how he pleases, and that, in what way soever he may come I will receive him as a friend and brother. I pray that he may come quickly, for I desire to see him. No harm or insult will befall him.'

"The Governor concealed his troops around the square at Cajamarca, dividing the cavalry into two portions of which he gave the command of one to his brother Hernando Pizarro and the command of the other to Hernando de Soto. In like manner he divided the infantry, he himself taking one part and giving the other to his brother Juan Pizarro. At the same time, he ordered Pedro de Candia with two or three infantrymen to go with trumpets to a small fort in the plaza and to station themselves there with a small piece of artillery. When all the Indians, and Atahuallpa with them, had entered the Plaza, the Governor would give a signal to Candia and his men, after which they should start firing the gun, and the trumpets should sound, and at the sound of the trumpets the cavalry should dash out of the large court where they were waiting hidden in readiness.

"At noon Atahuallpa began to draw up his men and to approach. Soon we saw the entire plain full of Indians, halting periodically to wait for more Indians who kept filing out of the camp behind them. They kept filling out in separate detachments into the afternoon. The front detachments were now close to our camp, and still more troops kept issuing from the camp of the Indians. In front of Atahuallpa went 2,000 Indians who swept the road ahead of him, and these were followed by the warriors, half of whom were marching in the fields on one side of him and half on the other side.

"First came a squadron of Indians dressed in clothes of different colors, like a chessboard. They advanced, removing the straws from the ground and sweeping the road. Next came three squadrons in different dresses, dancing and singing. Then came a number of men with armor, large metal plates, and crowns of gold and silver. So great was the amount of furniture of gold and silver which they bore, that it was a marvel to observe how the sun glinted upon it. Among them came the figure of Atahuallpa in a very fine litter with the ends of its timbers covered in silver. Eighty lords carried him on their shoulders, all wearing a very rich blue livery. Atahuallpa himself was very richly dressed, with his crown on his head and a collar of large emeralds around his neck. He sat on a small stool with a rich saddle cushion resting on his litter. The litter was lined with parrot feathers of many colors and decorated with plates of gold and silver.

"Behind Atahuallpa came two other litters and two hammocks, in which were some high chiefs, then several squadrons of Indians with crowns of gold and silver. These Indian squadrons began to enter the plaza to the accompaniment of great songs, and thus entering they occupied every part of the plaza. In the meantime all of us Spaniards were waiting ready, hidden in a courtyard, full of fear. Many of us urinated without noticing it, out of sheer terror. On reaching the center of the plaza, Atahuallpa remained in his litter on high, while his troops continued to file in behind him.

"Governor Pizarro now sent Friar Vicente de Valverde to go speak to Atahuallpa, and to require Atahuallpa in the name of God and of the King of Spain that Atahuallpa subject himself to the law of our Lord Jesus Christ and to the service of His Majesty the King of Spain. Advancing with a cross in one hand and the Bible in the other hand, and going among the Indian troops up to the place where Atahuallpa was, the Friar thus addressed him: 'I am a Priest of God, and I teach Christians the things of God, and in like manner I come to teach you. What I teach is that which God says to us in this Book. Therefore, on the part of God and of the Christians, I beseech you to be their friend, for such is God's will, and it will be for your good.'

"Atahuallpa asked for the Book, that he might look at it, and the Friar gave it to him closed. Atahuallpa did not know how to open the Book, and the Friar was extending his arm to do so, when Atahuallpa, in great anger, gave him a blow on the arm, not wishing that it should be opened. Then he opened it himself, and, without any astonishment at the letters and paper he threw it away from him five or six paces, his face a deep crimson.

"The Friar returned to Pizarro, shouting, 'Come out! Come out, Christians! Come at these enemy dogs who reject the things of God. That tyrant has thrown my book of holy law to the ground! Did you not see what happened? Why remain polite and servile toward this over-proud dog when the plains are full of Indians? March out against him, for I absolve you!'

"The governor then gave the signal to Candia, who began to fire off the guns. At the same time the trumpets were sounded, and the armored Spanish troops, both cavalry and infantry, sallied forth out of their hiding places straight into the mass of unarmed Indians crowding the square, giving the Spanish battle cry, 'Santiago!' We had placed rattles on the horses to terrify the Indians. The booming of the guns, the blowing of the trumpets, and the rattles on the horses threw the Indians into panicked confusion. The Spaniards fell upon them and began to cut them to pieces. The Indians were so filled with fear that they climbed on top of one another, formed mounds, and suffocated each other. Since they were unarmed, they were attacked without danger to any Christian. The cavalry rode them down, killing and wounding, and following in pursuit. The infantry made so good an assault on those that remained that in a short time most of them were put to the sword.

"The Governor himself took his sword and dagger, entered the thick of the Indians with the Spaniards who were with him, and with great bravery reached Atahuallpa's litter. He fearlessly grabbed Atahuallpa's left arm and shouted 'Santiago!,' but he could not pull Atahuallpa out of his litter because it was held up high. Although we killed the Indians who held the litter, others at once took their places and held it aloft, and in this manner we spent a long time in overcoming and killing Indians. Finally seven or eight Spaniards on horseback spurred on their horses, rushed upon the litter from one side, and with great effort they heaved it over on its side. In that way Atahuallpa was captured, and the Governor took Atahuallpa to his lodging. The Indians carrying the litter, and those escorting Atahuallpa, never abandoned him: all died around him.

"The panic-stricken Indians remaining in the square, terrified at the firing of the guns and at the horses—something they had never seen—tried to flee from the square by knocking down a stretch of wall and running out onto the plain outside. Our cavalry jumped the broken wall and charged into the plain, shouting, 'Chase those with the fancy clothes! Don't let any escape! Spear them!' All of the other Indian soldiers whom Atahuallpa had brought were a mile from Cajamarca ready for battle, but not one made a move, and during all this not one Indian raised a weapon against a Spaniard. When the squadrons of Indians who had remained in the plain outside the town saw the other Indians fleeing and shouting, most of them too panicked and fled. It was an astonishing sight, for the whole valley for 15 or 20 miles was completely filled with Indians. Night had already fallen, and our cavalry were continuing to spear Indians in the fields, when we heard a trumpet calling for us to reassemble at camp.

"If night had not come on, few out of the more than 40,000 Indian troops would have been left alive. Six or seven thousand Indians lay dead, and many more had their arms cut off and other wounds. Atahuallpa himself admitted that we had killed 7,000 of his men in that battle. The man killed in one of the litters was his minister, the lord of Chincha, of whom he was very fond. All those Indians who bore Atahuallpa's litter appeared to be high chiefs and councillors. They were all killed, as well as those Indians who were carried in the other litters and hammocks. The lord of Cajamarca was also killed, and others, but their numbers were so great that they could not be counted, for all who came in attendance on Atahuallpa were great lords. It was extraordinary to see so powerful a ruler captured in so short a time, when he had come with such a mighty army. Truly, it was not accomplished by our own forces, for there were so few of us. It was by the grace of God, which is great.

"Atahuallpa's robes had been torn off when the Spaniards pulled him out of his litter. The Governor ordered clothes to be brought to him, and when Atahuallpa was dressed, the Governor ordered Atahuallpa to sit near him and soothed his rage and agitation at finding himself so quickly fallen from his high estate. The Governor said to Atahuallpa, 'Do not take it as an insult that you have been defeated and taken prisoner, for with the Christians who come with me, though so few in number, I have conquered greater kingdoms than yours, and have defeated other more powerful lords than you, imposing upon them the dominion of the Emperor, whose vassal I am, and who is King of Spain and of the universal world. We come to conquer this land by his command, that all may come to a knowledge of God and of His Holy Catholic Faith; and by reason of our good mission, God, the Creator of heaven and earth and of all things in them, permits this, in order that you may know Him and come out from the bestial and diabolical life that you lead. It is for this reason that we, being so few in number, subjugate that vast host. When you have seen the errors in which you live, you will understand the good that we have done you by coming to your land by order of his Majesty the King of Spain. Our Lord permitted that your pride should be brought low and that no Indian should be able to offend a Christian.' "

LET US NOW trace the chain of causation in this extraordinary confrontation, beginning with the immediate events. When Pizarro and Atahuallpa met at Cajamarca, why did Pizarro capture Atahuallpa and kill so many of his followers, instead of Atahuallpa's vastly more numerous forces capturing and killing Pizarro? After all, Pizarro had only 62 soldiers mounted on horses, along with 106 foot soldiers, while Atahuallpa commanded an army of about 80,000. As for the antecedents of those events, how did Atahuallpa come to be at Cajamarca at all? How did Pizarro come to be there to capture him, instead of Atahuallpa's coming to Spain to capture King Charles I? Why did Atahuallpa walk into what seems to us, with the gift of hindsight, to have been such a transparent trap? Did the factors acting in the encounter of Atahuallpa and Pizarro also play a broader role in encounters between Old World and New World peoples and between other peoples?

Why did Pizarro capture Atahuallpa? Pizarro's military advantages lay in the Spaniards' steel swords and other weapons, steel armor, guns, and horses. To those weapons, Atahuallpa's troops, without animals on which to ride into battle, could oppose only stone, bronze, or wooden clubs, maces, and hand axes, plus slingshots and quilted armor. Such imbalances of equipment were decisive in innumerable other confrontations of Europeans with Native Americans and other peoples.

The sole Native Americans able to resist European conquest for many centuries were those tribes that reduced the military disparity by acquiring and mastering both horses and guns. To the average white American, the word "Indian" conjures up an image of a mounted Plains Indian brandishing a rifle, like the Sioux warriors who annihilated General George Custer's U.S. Army battalion at the famous battle of the Little Big Horn in 1876. We easily forget that horses and rifles were originally unknown to Native Americans. They were brought by Europeans and proceeded to transform the societies of Indian tribes that acquired them. Thanks to their mastery of horses and rifles, the Plains Indians of North America, the Araucanian Indians of southern Chile, and the Pampas Indians of Argentina fought off invading whites longer than did any other Native Americans, succumbing only to massive army operations by white governments in the 1870s and 1880s.

Today, it is hard for us to grasp the enormous numerical odds against which the Spaniards' military equipment prevailed. At the battle of Cajamarca recounted above, 168 Spaniards crushed a Native American army 500 times more numerous, killing thousands of natives while not losing a single Spaniard. Time and again, accounts of Pizarro's subsequent battles with the Incas, Cortés's conquest of the Aztecs, and other early European campaigns against Native Americans describe encounters in which a few dozen European horsemen routed thousands of Indians with great slaughter. During Pizarro's march from Cajamarca to the Inca capital of Cuzco after Atahuallpa's death, there were four such battles: at Jauja, Vilcashuaman, Vilcaconga, and Cuzco. Those four battles involved a mere 80, 30, 110, and 40 Spanish horsemen, respectively, in each case ranged against thousands or tens of thousands of Indians.

These Spanish victories cannot be written off as due merely to the help of Native American allies, to the psychological novelty of Spanish weapons and horses, or (as is often claimed) to the Incas' mistaking Spaniards for their returning god Viracocha. The initial successes of both Pizarro and Cortés did attract native allies. However, many of them would not have become allies if they had not already been persuaded, by earlier devastating successes of unassisted Spaniards, that resistance was futile and that they should side with the likely winners. The novelty of horses, steel weapons, and guns undoubtedly paralyzed the Incas at Cajamarca, but the battles after Cajamarca were fought against determined resistance by Inca armies that had already seen Spanish weapons and horses. Within half a dozen years of the initial conquest, Incas mounted two desperate, large-scale, well-prepared rebellions against the Spaniards. All those efforts failed because of the Spaniards' far superior armament.

By the 1700s, guns had replaced swords as the main weapon favoring European invaders over Native Americans and other native peoples. For example, in 1808 a British sailor named Charlie Savage equipped with muskets and excellent aim arrived in the Fiji Islands. The aptly named Savage proceeded single-handedly to upset Fiji's balance of power. Among his many exploits, he paddled his canoe up a river to the Fijian village of Kasavu, halted less than a pistol shot's length from the village fence, and fired away at the undefended inhabitants. His victims were so numerous that surviving villagers piled up the bodies to take shelter behind them, and the stream beside the village was red with blood. Such examples of the power of guns against native peoples lacking guns could be multiplied indefinitely.

In the Spanish conquest of the Incas, guns played only a minor role. The guns of those times (so-called harquebuses) were difficult to load and fire, and Pizarro had only a dozen of them. They did produce a big psychological effect on those occasions when they managed to fire. Far more important were the Spaniards' steel swords, lances, and daggers, strong sharp weapons that slaughtered thinly armored Indians. In contrast, Indian blunt clubs, while capable of battering and wounding Spaniards and their horses, rarely succeeded in killing them. The Spaniards' steel or chain mail armor and, above all, their steel helmets usually provided an effective defense against club blows, while the Indians' quilted armor offered no protection against steel weapons.

The tremendous advantage that the Spaniards gained from their horses leaps out of the eyewitness accounts. Horsemen could easily outride Indian sentries before the sentries had time to warn Indian troops behind them, and could ride down and kill Indians on foot. The shock of a horse's charge, its maneuverability, the speed of attack that it permitted, and the raised and protected fighting platform that it provided left foot soldiers nearly helpless in the open. Nor was the effect of horses due only to the terror that they inspired in soldiers fighting against them for the first time. By the time of the great Inca rebellion of 1536, the Incas had learned how best to defend themselves against cavalry, by ambushing and annihilating Spanish horsemen in narrow passes. But the Incas, like all other foot soldiers, were never able to defeat cavalry in the open. When Quizo Yupanqui, the best general of the Inca emperor Manco, who succeeded Atahuallpa, besieged the Spaniards in Lima in 1536 and tried to storm the city, two squadrons of Spanish cavalry charged a much larger Indian force on flat ground, killed Quizo and all of his commanders in the first charge, and routed his army. A similar cavalry charge of 26 horsemen routed the best troops of Emperor Manco himself, as he was besieging the Spaniards in Cuzco.

The transformation of warfare by horses began with their domestication around 4000 B.C., in the steppes north of the Black Sea. Horses permitted people possessing them to cover far greater distances than was possible on foot, to attack by surprise, and to flee before a superior defending force could be gathered. Their role at Cajamarca thus exemplifies a military weapon that remained potent for 6,000 years, until the early 20th century, and that was eventually applied on all the continents. Not until the First World War did the military dominance of cavalry finally end. When we consider the advantages that Spaniards derived from horses, steel weapons, and armor against foot soldiers without metal, it should no longer surprise us that Spaniards consistently won battles against enormous odds.

How did Atahuallpa come to be at Cajamarca? Atahuallpa and his army came to be at Cajamarca because they had just won decisive battles in a civil war that left the Incas divided and vulnerable. Pizarro quickly appreciated those divisions and exploited them. The reason for the civil war was that an epidemic of smallpox, spreading overland among South American Indians after its arrival with Spanish settlers in Panama and Colombia, had killed the Inca emperor Huayna Capac and most of his court around 1526, and then immediately killed his designated heir, Ninan Cuyuchi. Those deaths precipitated a contest for the throne between Atahuallpa and his half brother Huascar. If it had not been for the epidemic, the Spaniards would have faced a united empire.

Atahuallpa's presence at Cajamarca thus highlights one of the key factors in world history: diseases transmitted to peoples lacking immunity by invading peoples with considerable immunity. Smallpox, measles, influenza, typhus, bubonic plague, and other infectious diseases endemic in Europe played a decisive role in European conquests, by decimating many peoples on other continents. For example, a smallpox epidemic devastated the Aztecs after the failure of the first Spanish attack in 1520 and killed Cuitláhuac, the Aztec emperor who briefly succeeded Montezuma.

Throughout the Americas, diseases introduced with Europeans spread from tribe to tribe far in advance of the Europeans themselves, killing an estimated 95 percent of the pre-Columbian Native American population. The most populous and highly organized native societies of North America, the Mississippian chiefdoms, disappeared in that way between 1492 and the late 1600s, even before Europeans themselves made their first settlement on the Mississippi River. A smallpox epidemic in 1713 was the biggest single step in the destruction of South Africa's native San people by European settlers. Soon after the British settlement of Sydney in 1788, the first of the epidemics that decimated Aboriginal Australians began. A well-documented example from Pacific islands is the epidemic that swept over Fiji in 1806, brought by a few European sailors who struggled ashore from the wreck of the ship *Argo*. Similar epidemics marked the histories of Tonga, Hawaii, and other Pacific islands.

I do not mean to imply, however, that the role of disease in history was confined to paving the way for European expansion. Malaria, yellow fever, and other diseases of tropical Africa, India, Southeast Asia, and New Guinea furnished the most important obstacle to European colonization of those tropical areas.

How did Pizarro come to be at Cajamarca? Why didn't Atahuallpa instead try to conquer Spain? Pizarro came to Cajamarca by means of European maritime technology, which built the ships that took him across the Atlantic from Spain to Panama, and then in the Pacific from Panama to Peru. Lacking such technology, Atahuallpa did not expand overseas out of South America.

In addition to the ships themselves, Pizarro's presence depended on the centralized political organization that enabled Spain to finance, build, staff, and equip the ships. The Inca Empire also had a centralized political organization, but that actually worked to its disadvantage, because Pizarro seized the Inca chain of command intact by capturing Atahuallpa. Since the Inca bureaucracy was so strongly identified with its godlike absolute monarch, it disintegrated after Atahuallpa's death. Maritime technology coupled with political organization was similarly essential for European expansions to other continents, as well as for expansions of many other peoples.

A related factor bringing Spaniards to Peru was the existence of writing. Spain possessed it, while the Inca Empire did not. Information could be spread far more widely, more accurately, and in more detail by writing than it could be transmitted by mouth. That information, coming back to Spain from Columbus's voyages and from Cortés's conquest of Mexico, sent Spaniards pouring into the New World. Letters and pamphlets supplied both the motivation and the necessary detailed sailing directions. The first published report of Pizarro's exploits, by his companion Captain Cristóbal de Mena, was printed in Seville in April 1534, a mere nine months after Atahuallpa's execution. It became a best-seller, was rapidly translated into other European languages, and sent a further stream of Spanish colonists to tighten Pizarro's grip on Peru.

Why did Atahuallpa walk into the trap? In hindsight, we find it astonishing that Atahuallpa marched into Pizarro's obvious trap at Cajamarca. The Spaniards who captured him were equally surprised at their success. The consequences of literacy are prominent in the ultimate explanation.

The immediate explanation is that Atahuallpa had very little information about the Spaniards, their military power, and their intent. He derived that scant information by word of mouth, mainly from an envoy who had visited Pizarro's force for two days while it was en route inland from the coast. That envoy saw the Spaniards at their most disorganized, told Atahuallpa that they were not fighting men, and that he could tie them all up if given 200 Indians. Understandably, it never occurred to Atahuallpa that the Spaniards were formidable and would attack him without provocation.

In the New World the ability to write was confined to small elites among some peoples of modern Mexico and neighboring areas far to the north of the Inca Empire. Although the Spanish conquest of Panama, a mere 600 miles from the Incas' northern boundary, began already in 1510, no knowledge even of the Spaniards' existence appears to have reached the Incas until Pizarro's first landing on the Peruvian coast in 1527. Atahuallpa remained entirely ignorant about Spain's conquests of Central America's most powerful and populous Indian societies.

As surprising to us today as Atahuallpa's behavior leading to his capture is his behavior thereafter. He offered his famous ransom in the naive belief that, once paid off, the Spaniards would release him and depart. He had no way of understanding that Pizarro's men formed the spearhead of a force bent on permanent conquest, rather than an isolated raid.

Atahuallpa was not alone in these fatal miscalculations. Even after Atahuallpa had been captured, Francisco Pizarro's brother Hernando Pizarro deceived Atahuallpa's leading general, Chalcuchima, commanding a large

army, into delivering himself to the Spaniards. Chalcuchima's miscalcula-
tion marked a turning point in the collapse of Inca resistance, a moment
almost as significant as the capture of Atahuallpa himself. The Aztec
emperor Montezuma miscalculated even more grossly when he took Cortés for a returning god and admitted him and his tiny army into the Aztec
capital of Tenochtitlán. The result was that Cortés captured Montezuma,
then went on to conquer Tenochtitlán and the Aztec Empire.

On a mundane level, the miscalculations by Atahuallpa, Chalcuchima,
Montezuma, and countless other Native American leaders deceived by
Europeans were due to the fact that no living inhabitants of the New
World had been to the Old World, so of course they could have had no
specific information about the Spaniards. Even so, we find it hard to avoid
the conclusion that Atahuallpa "should" have been more suspicious, if
only his society had experienced a broader range of human behavior.
Pizarro too arrived at Cajamarca with no information about the Incas
other than what he had learned by interrogating the Inca subjects he
encountered in 1527 and 1531. However, while Pizarro himself happened
to be illiterate, he belonged to a literate tradition. From books, the Spaniards knew of many contemporary civilizations remote from Europe, and
about several thousand years of European history. Pizarro explicitly modeled his ambush of Atahuallpa on the successful strategy of Cortés.

In short, literacy made the Spaniards heirs to a huge body of knowledge
about human behavior and history. By contrast, not only did Atahuallpa
have no conception of the Spaniards themselves, and no personal experience of any other invaders from overseas, but he also had not even heard
(or read) of similar threats to anyone else, anywhere else, anytime previously in history. That gulf of experience encouraged Pizarro to set his
trap and Atahuallpa to walk into it.

THUS, PIZARRO'S CAPTURE of Atahuallpa illustrates the set of proximate factors that resulted in Europeans' colonizing the New World instead
of Native Americans' colonizing Europe. Immediate reasons for Pizarro's
success included military technology based on guns, steel weapons, and
horses; infectious diseases endemic in Eurasia; European maritime technology; the centralized political organization of European states; and writing.
The title of this book will serve as shorthand for those proximate factors,
which also enabled modern Europeans to conquer peoples of other conti-

nents. Long before anyone began manufacturing guns and steel, others of those same factors had led to the expansions of some non-European peoples, as we shall see in later chapters.

But we are still left with the fundamental question why all those immediate advantages came to lie more with Europe than with the New World. Why weren't the Incas the ones to invent guns and steel swords, to be mounted on animals as fearsome as horses, to bear diseases to which European lacked resistance, to develop oceangoing ships and advanced political organization, and to be able to draw on the experience of thousands of years of written history? Those are no longer the questions of proximate causation that this chapter has been discussing, but questions of ultimate causation that will take up the next two parts of this book.

PART TWO

THE RISE AND SPREAD OF FOOD PRODUCTION

CHAPTER 4

FARMER POWER

As a teenager, I spent the summer of 1956 in Montana, working for an elderly farmer named Fred Hirschy. Born in Switzerland, Fred had come to southwestern Montana as a teenager in the 1890s and proceeded to develop one of the first farms in the area. At the time of his arrival, much of the original Native American population of hunter-gatherers was still living there.

My fellow farmhands were, for the most part, tough whites whose normal speech featured strings of curses, and who spent their weekdays working so that they could devote their weekends to squandering their week's wages in the local saloon. Among the farmhands, though, was a member of the Blackfoot Indian tribe named Levi, who behaved very differently from the coarse miners—being polite, gentle, responsible, sober, and well spoken. He was the first Indian with whom I had spent much time, and I came to admire him.

It was therefore a shocking disappointment to me when, one Sunday morning, Levi too staggered in drunk and cursing after a Saturday-night binge. Among his curses, one has stood out in my memory: "Damn you, Fred Hirschy, and damn the ship that brought you from Switzerland!" It poignantly brought home to me the Indians' perspective on what I, like other white schoolchildren, had been taught to view as the heroic conquest of the American West. Fred Hirschy's family was proud of him, as a pioneer farmer who had succeeded under difficult conditions. But Levi's tribe of hunters and famous warriors had been robbed of its lands by the immigrant white farmers. How did the farmers win out over the famous warriors?

For most of the time since the ancestors of modern humans diverged from the ancestors of the living great apes, around 7 million years ago, all humans on Earth fed themselves exclusively by hunting wild animals and gathering wild plants, as the Blackfeet still did in the 19th century. It was only within the last 11,000 years that some peoples turned to what is termed food production: that is, domesticating wild animals and plants and eating the resulting livestock and crops. Today, most people on Earth consume food that they produced themselves or that someone else produced for them. At current rates of change, within the next decade the few remaining bands of hunter-gatherers will abandon their ways, disintegrate, or die out, thereby ending our millions of years of commitment to the hunter-gatherer lifestyle.

Different peoples acquired food production at different times in prehistory. Some, such as Aboriginal Australians, never acquired it at all. Of those who did, some (for example, the ancient Chinese) developed it independently by themselves, while others (including ancient Egyptians) acquired it from neighbors. But, as we'll see, food production was indirectly a prerequisite for the development of guns, germs, and steel. Hence geographic variation in whether, or when, the peoples of different continents became farmers and herders explains to a large extent their subsequent contrasting fates. Before we devote the next six chapters to understanding how geographic differences in food production arose, this chapter will trace the main connections through which food production led to all the advantages that enabled Pizarro to capture Atahuallpa, and Fred Hirschy's people to dispossess Levi's (Figure 4.1).

The first connection is the most direct one: availability of more consum-

Figure 4.1. Schematic overview of the chains of causation leading up to proximate factors (such as guns, horses, and diseases) enabling some peoples to conquer other peoples, from ultimate factors (such as the orientation of continental axes). For example, diverse epidemic diseases of humans evolved in areas with many wild plant and animal species suitable for domestication, partly because the resulting crops and livestock

Factors Underlying the Broadest Pattern of History

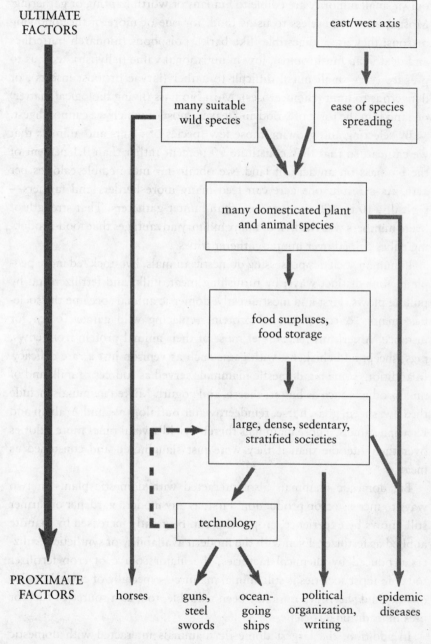

helped feed dense societies in which epidemics could maintain themselves, and partly because the diseases evolved from germs of the domestic animals themselves.

able calories means more people. Among wild plant and animal species, only a small minority are edible to humans or worth hunting or gathering. Most species are useless to us as food, for one or more of the following reasons: they are indigestible (like bark), poisonous (monarch butterflies and death-cap mushrooms), low in nutritional value (jellyfish), tedious to prepare (very small nuts), difficult to gather (larvae of most insects), or dangerous to hunt (rhinoceroses). Most biomass (living biological matter) on land is in the form of wood and leaves, most of which we cannot digest.

By selecting and growing those few species of plants and animals that we can eat, so that they constitute 90 percent rather than 0.1 percent of the biomass on an acre of land, we obtain far more edible calories per acre. As a result, one acre can feed many more herders and farmers—typically, 10 to 100 times more—than hunter-gatherers. That strength of brute numbers was the first of many military advantages that food-producing tribes gained over hunter-gatherer tribes.

In human societies possessing domestic animals, livestock fed more people in four distinct ways: by furnishing meat, milk, and fertilizer and by pulling plows. First and most directly, domestic animals became the societies' major source of animal protein, replacing wild game. Today, for instance, Americans tend to get most of their animal protein from cows, pigs, sheep, and chickens, with game such as venison just a rare delicacy. In addition, some big domestic mammals served as sources of milk and of milk products such as butter, cheese, and yogurt. Milked mammals include the cow, sheep, goat, horse, reindeer, water buffalo, yak, and Arabian and Bactrian camels. Those mammals thereby yield several times more calories over their lifetime than if they were just slaughtered and consumed as meat.

Big domestic mammals also interacted with domestic plants in two ways to increase crop production. First, as any modern gardener or farmer still knows by experience, crop yields can be greatly increased by manure applied as fertilizer. Even with the modern availability of synthetic fertilizers produced by chemical factories, the major source of crop fertilizer today in most societies is still animal manure—especially of cows, but also of yaks and sheep. Manure has been valuable, too, as a source of fuel for fires in traditional societies.

In addition, the largest domestic mammals interacted with domestic plants to increase food production by pulling plows and thereby making it possible for people to till land that had previously been uneconomical for farming. Those plow animals were the cow, horse, water buffalo, Bali cattle, and yak / cow hybrids. Here is one example of their value: the first prehistoric farmers of central Europe, the so-called Linearbandkeramik culture that arose slightly before 5000 B.C., were initially confined to soils light enough to be tilled by means of hand-held digging sticks. Only over a thousand years later, with the introduction of the ox-drawn plow, were those farmers able to extend cultivation to a much wider range of heavy soils and tough sods. Similarly, Native American farmers of the North American Great Plains grew crops in the river valleys, but farming of the tough sods on the extensive uplands had to await 19th-century Europeans and their animal-drawn plows.

All those are direct ways in which plant and animal domestication led to denser human populations by yielding more food than did the hunter-gatherer lifestyle. A more indirect way involved the consequences of the sedentary lifestyle enforced by food production. People of many hunter-gatherer societies move frequently in search of wild foods, but farmers must remain near their fields and orchards. The resulting fixed abode contributes to denser human populations by permitting a shortened birth interval. A hunter-gatherer mother who is shifting camp can carry only one child, along with her few possessions. She cannot afford to bear her next child until the previous toddler can walk fast enough to keep up with the tribe and not hold it back. In practice, nomadic hunter-gatherers space their children about four years apart by means of lactational amenorrhea, sexual abstinence, infanticide, and abortion. By contrast, sedentary people, unconstrained by problems of carrying young children on treks, can bear and raise as many children as they can feed. The birth interval for many farm peoples is around two years, half that of hunter-gatherers. That higher birthrate of food producers, together with their ability to feed more people per acre, lets them achieve much higher population densities than hunter-gatherers.

A separate consequence of a settled existence is that it permits one to store food surpluses, since storage would be pointless if one didn't remain nearby to guard the stored food. While some nomadic hunter-gatherers may occasionally bag more food than they can consume in a few days, such a bonanza is of little use to them because they cannot protect it. But stored food is essential for feeding non-food-producing specialists, and certainly for supporting whole towns of them. Hence nomadic hunter-gatherer societies have few or no such full-time specialists, who instead first appear in sedentary societies.

Two types of such specialists are kings and bureaucrats. Hunter-gatherer societies tend to be relatively egalitarian, to lack full-time bureaucrats and hereditary chiefs, and to have small-scale political organization at the level of the band or tribe. That's because all able-bodied hunter-gatherers are obliged to devote much of their time to acquiring food. In contrast, once food can be stockpiled, a political elite can gain control of food produced by others, assert the right of taxation, escape the need to feed itself, and engage full-time in political activities. Hence moderate-sized agricultural societies are often organized in chiefdoms, and kingdoms are confined to large agricultural societies. Those complex political units are much better able to mount a sustained war of conquest than is an egalitarian band of hunters. Some hunter-gatherers in especially rich environments, such as the Pacific Northwest coast of North America and the coast of Ecuador, also developed sedentary societies, food storage, and nascent chiefdoms, but they did not go farther on the road to kingdoms.

A stored food surplus built up by taxation can support other full-time specialists besides kings and bureaucrats. Of most direct relevance to wars of conquest, it can be used to feed professional soldiers. That was the decisive factor in the British Empire's eventual defeat of New Zealand's well-armed indigenous Maori population. While the Maori achieved some stunning temporary victories, they could not maintain an army constantly in the field and were in the end worn down by 18,000 full-time British troops. Stored food can also feed priests, who provide religious justification for wars of conquest; artisans such as metalworkers, who develop swords, guns, and other technologies; and scribes, who preserve far more information than can be remembered accurately.

So far, I've emphasized direct and indirect values of crops and livestock as food. However, they have other uses, such as keeping us warm and providing us with valuable materials. Crops and livestock yield natural fibers for making clothing, blankets, nets, and rope. Most of the major centers of plant domestication evolved not only food crops but also fiber crops—notably cotton, flax (the source of linen), and hemp. Several domestic animals yielded animal fibers—especially wool from sheep, goats, llamas, and alpacas, and silk from silkworms. Bones of domestic animals were important raw materials for artifacts of Neolithic peoples before the development of metallurgy. Cow hides were used to make leather. One of the earliest cultivated plants in many parts of the Americas was grown for nonfood purposes: the bottle gourd, used as a container.

Big domestic mammals further revolutionized human society by becoming our main means of land transport until the development of railroads in the 19th century. Before animal domestication, the sole means of transporting goods and people by land was on the backs of humans. Large mammals changed that: for the first time in human history, it became possible to move heavy goods in large quantities, as well as people, rapidly overland for long distances. The domestic animals that were ridden were the horse, donkey, yak, reindeer, and Arabian and Bactrian camels. Animals of those same five species, as well as the llama, were used to bear packs. Cows and horses were hitched to wagons, while reindeer and dogs pulled sleds in the Arctic. The horse became the chief means of long-distance transport over most of Eurasia. The three domestic camel species (Arabian camel, Bactrian camel, and llama) played a similar role in areas of North Africa and Arabia, Central Asia, and the Andes, respectively.

The most direct contribution of plant and animal domestication to wars of conquest was from Eurasia's horses, whose military role made them the jeeps and Sherman tanks of ancient warfare on that continent. As I mentioned in Chapter 3, they enabled Cortés and Pizarro, leading only small bands of adventurers, to overthrow the Aztec and Inca Empires. Even much earlier (around 4000 B.C.), at a time when horses were still ridden bareback, they may have been the essential military ingredient behind the westward expansion of speakers of Indo-European languages from the Ukraine. Those languages eventually replaced all earlier western European languages except Basque. When horses later were yoked to wagons and other vehicles, horse-drawn battle chariots (invented around 1800 B.C.) proceeded to revolutionize warfare in the Near East, the Mediterranean region, and China. For example, in 1674 B.C., horses even enabled a foreign people, the Hyksos, to conquer then horseless Egypt and to establish themselves temporarily as pharaohs.

Still later, after the invention of saddles and stirrups, horses allowed the Huns and successive waves of other peoples from the Asian steppes to terrorize the Roman Empire and its successor states, culminating in the Mongol conquests of much of Asia and Russia in the 13th and 14th centuries A.D. Only with the introduction of trucks and tanks in World War I did horses finally become supplanted as the main assault vehicle and means of fast transport in war. Arabian and Bactrian camels played a similar military role within their geographic range. In all these examples, peoples with domestic horses (or camels), or with improved means of using them, enjoyed an enormous military advantage over those without them.

Of equal importance in wars of conquest were the germs that evolved in human societies with domestic animals. Infectious diseases like smallpox, measles, and flu arose as specialized germs of humans, derived by mutations of very similar ancestral germs that had infected animals (Chapter 11). The humans who domesticated animals were the first to fall victim to the newly evolved germs, but those humans then evolved substantial resistance to the new diseases. When such partly immune people came into contact with others who had had no previous exposure to the germs, epidemics resulted in which up to 99 percent of the previously unexposed population was killed. Germs thus acquired ultimately from domestic animals played decisive roles in the European conquests of Native Americans, Australians, South Africans, and Pacific islanders.

In short, plant and animal domestication meant much more food and hence much denser human populations. The resulting food surpluses, and (in some areas) the animal-based means of transporting those surpluses, were a prerequisite for the development of settled, politically centralized, socially stratified, economically complex, technologically innovative societies. Hence the availability of domestic plants and animals ultimately explains why empires, literacy, and steel weapons developed earliest in Eurasia and later, or not at all, on other continents. The military uses of horses and camels, and the killing power of animal-derived germs, complete the list of major links between food production and conquest that we shall be exploring.

CHAPTER 5

HISTORY'S HAVES AND HAVE-NOTS

MUCH OF HUMAN HISTORY HAS CONSISTED OF UNEQUAL conflicts between the haves and the have-nots: between peoples with farmer power and those without it, or between those who acquired it at different times. It should come as no surprise that food production never arose in large areas of the globe, for ecological reasons that still make it difficult or impossible there today. For instance, neither farming nor herding developed in prehistoric times in North America's Arctic, while the sole element of food production to arise in Eurasia's Arctic was reindeer herding. Nor could food production spring up spontaneously in deserts remote from sources of water for irrigation, such as central Australia and parts of the western United States.

Instead, what cries out for explanation is the failure of food production to appear, until modern times, in some ecologically very suitable areas that are among the world's richest centers of agriculture and herding today. Foremost among these puzzling areas, where indigenous peoples were still hunter-gatherers when European colonists arrived, were California and the other Pacific states of the United States, the Argentine pampas, southwestern and southeastern Australia, and much of the Cape region of South Africa. Had we surveyed the world in 4000 B.C., thousands of years after the rise of food production in its oldest sites of origin, we would have been

surprised too at several other modern breadbaskets that were still then
without it—including all the rest of the United States, England and much
of France, Indonesia, and all of subequatorial Africa. When we trace food
production back to its beginnings, the earliest sites provide another surprise. Far from being modern breadbaskets, they include areas ranking
today as somewhat dry or ecologically degraded: Iraq and Iran, Mexico,
the Andes, parts of China, and Africa's Sahel zone. Why did food production develop first in these seemingly rather marginal lands, and only later
in today's most fertile farmlands and pastures?

Geographic differences in the means by which food production arose
are also puzzling. In a few places it developed independently, as a result of
local people domesticating local plants and animals. In most other places
it was instead imported, in the form of crops and livestock that had been
domesticated elsewhere. Since those areas of nonindependent origins were
suitable for prehistoric food production as soon as domesticates had
arrived, why did the peoples of those areas not become farmers and herders without outside assistance, by domesticating local plants and animals?

Among those regions where food production did spring up independently, why did the times at which it appeared vary so greatly—for example, thousands of years earlier in eastern Asia than in the eastern United
States and never in eastern Australia? Among those regions into which it
was imported in the prehistoric era, why did the date of arrival also vary
so greatly—for example, thousands of years earlier in southwestern
Europe than in the southwestern United States? Again among those
regions where it was imported, why in some areas (such as the southwestern United States) did local hunter-gatherers themselves adopt crops and
livestock from neighbors and survive as farmers, while in other areas (such
as Indonesia and much of subequatorial Africa) the importation of food
production involved a cataclysmic replacement of the region's original
hunter-gatherers by invading food producers? All these questions involve
developments that determined which peoples became history's have-nots,
and which became its haves.

BEFORE WE CAN hope to answer these questions, we need to figure out
how to identify areas where food production originated, when it arose
there, and where and when a given crop or animal was first domesticated.
The most unequivocal evidence comes from identification of plant and

animal remains at archaeological sites. Most domesticated plant and animal species differ morphologically from their wild ancestors: for example, in the smaller size of domestic cattle and sheep, the larger size of domestic chickens and apples, the thinner and smoother seed coats of domestic peas, and the corkscrew-twisted rather than scimitar-shaped horns of domestic goats. Hence remains of domesticated plants and animals at a dated archaeological site can be recognized and provide strong evidence of food production at that place and time, whereas finding the remains only of wild species at a site fails to provide evidence of food production and is compatible with hunting-gathering. Naturally, food producers, especially early ones, continued to gather some wild plants and hunt wild animals, so the food remains at their sites often include wild species as well as domesticated ones.

Archaeologists date food production by radiocarbon dating of carbon-containing materials at the site. This method is based on the slow decay of radioactive carbon 14, a very minor component of carbon, the ubiquitous building block of life, into the nonradioactive isotope nitrogen 14. Carbon 14 is continually being generated in the atmosphere by cosmic rays. Plants take up atmospheric carbon, which has a known and approximately constant ratio of carbon 14 to the prevalent isotope carbon 12 (a ratio of about one to a million). That plant carbon goes on to form the body of the herbivorous animals that eat the plants, and of the carnivorous animals that eat those herbivorous animals. Once the plant or animal dies, though, half of its carbon 14 content decays into carbon 12 every 5,700 years, until after about 40,000 years the carbon 14 content is very low and difficult to measure or to distinguish from contamination with small amounts of modern materials containing carbon 14. Hence the age of material from an archaeological site can be calculated from the material's carbon 14 / carbon 12 ratio.

Radiocarbon is plagued by numerous technical problems, of which two deserve mention here. One is that radiocarbon dating until the 1980s required relatively large amounts of carbon (a few grams), much more than the amount in small seeds or bones. Hence scientists instead often had to resort to dating material recovered nearby at the same site and believed to be "associated with" the food remains—that is, to have been deposited simultaneously by the people who left the food. A typical choice of "associated" material is charcoal from fires.

But archaeological sites are not always neatly sealed time capsules of materials all deposited on the same day. Materials deposited at different times can get mixed together, as worms and rodents and other agents churn up the ground. Charcoal residues from a fire can thereby end up close to the remains of a plant or animal that died and was eaten thousands of years earlier or later. Increasingly today, archaeologists are circumventing this problem by a new technique termed accelerator mass spectrometry, which permits radiocarbon dating of tiny samples and thus lets one directly date a single small seed, small bone, or other food residue. In some cases big differences have been found between recent radiocarbon dates based on the direct new methods (which have their own problems) and those based on the indirect older ones. Among the resulting controversies remaining unresolved, perhaps the most important for the purposes of this book concerns the date when food production originated in the Americas: indirect methods of the 1960s and 1970s yielded dates as early as 7000 B.C., but more recent direct dating has been yielding dates no earlier than 3500 B.C.

A second problem in radiocarbon dating is that the carbon 14 / carbon 12 ratio of the atmosphere is in fact not rigidly constant but fluctuates slightly with time, so calculations of radiocarbon dates based on the assumption of a constant ratio are subject to small systematic errors. The magnitude of this error for each past date can in principle be determined with the help of long-lived trees laying down annual growth rings, since the rings can be counted up to obtain an absolute calendar date in the past for each ring, and a carbon sample of wood dated in this manner can then be analyzed for its carbon 14 / carbon 12 ratio. In this way, measured radiocarbon dates can be "calibrated" to take account of fluctuations in the atmospheric carbon ratio. The effect of this correction is that, for materials with apparent (that is, uncalibrated) dates between about 1000 and 6000 B.C., the true (calibrated) date is between a few centuries and a thousand years earlier. Somewhat older samples have more recently begun to be calibrated by an alternative method based on another radioactive decay process and yielding the conclusion that samples apparently dating to about 9000 B.C. actually date to around 11,000 B.C.

Archaeologists often distinguish calibrated from uncalibrated dates by writing the former in upper-case letters and the latter in lower-case letters (for example, 3000 B.C. vs. 3000 b.c., respectively). However, the archaeological literature can be confusing in this respect, because many books and papers report *un*calibrated dates as B.C. and fail to mention that they are

Plate 1. A woman and child from New Guinea's north coastal lowlands
(Siar Island).

Plate 2. Paran, a New Guinea highlander of the Fore people. Plates 2–5 depict four of my New Guinea friends to whom this book is dedicated.

Plate 3. Esa, a New Guinea highlander of the Fore people.

*Plate 4. Kariniga, a south New Guinea lowlander of the Tudawhe
people.*

Plate 5. Sauakari, a New Guinea lowlander from the north coast.

Plate 6. A New Guinea highlander.

Plate 7. An Aboriginal Australian man of the Pintupi people (central Australia).

Plate 8. Aboriginal Australians from Arnhem Land (northern Australia).

Plate 9. An Aboriginal Tasmanian woman, one of the last survivors of those born before European arrival.

Plate 10. A Tungus woman from Siberia.

Plate 11. A Japanese: Emperor Akihito celebrating his 59th birthday.

Plate 12. A Javanese woman harvesting rice. Plates 12 and 13 depict speakers of Austronesian languages.

Plate 13. A Polynesian woman from Rapa Island in the tropical Pacific, 7,000 miles east of Java.

Plate 14. A Chinese girl gathering bamboo shoots.

Plate 15. A Native North American: Spotted Horse Chief of the Pawnee tribe of the Great Plains.

Plate 16. Another Native North American: a Navajo woman of the south-western United States.

actually uncalibrated. The dates that I report in this book for events within the last 15,000 years are calibrated dates. That accounts for some of the discrepancies that readers may note between this book's dates and those quoted in some standard reference books on early food production.

Once one has recognized and dated ancient remains of domestic plants or animals, how does one decide whether the plant or animal was actually domesticated in the vicinity of that site itself, rather than domesticated elsewhere and then spread to the site? One method is to examine a map of the geographic distribution of the crop's or animal's wild ancestor, and to reason that domestication must have taken place in the area where the wild ancestor occurs. For example, chickpeas are widely grown by traditional farmers from the Mediterranean and Ethiopia east to India, with the latter country accounting for 80 percent of the world's chickpea production today. One might therefore have been deceived into supposing that chickpeas were domesticated in India. But it turns out that ancestral wild chickpeas occur only in southeastern Turkey. The interpretation that chickpeas were actually domesticated there is supported by the fact that the oldest finds of possibly domesticated chickpeas in Neolithic archaeological sites come from southeastern Turkey and nearby northern Syria that date to around 8000 B.C.; not until over 5,000 years later does archaeological evidence of chickpeas appear on the Indian subcontinent.

A second method for identifying a crop's or animal's site of domestication is to plot on a map the dates of the domesticated form's first appearance at each locality. The site where it appeared earliest may be its site of initial domestication—especially if the wild ancestor also occurred there, and if the dates of first appearance at other sites become progressively earlier with increasing distance from the putative site of initial domestication, suggesting spread to those other sites. For instance, the earliest known cultivated emmer wheat comes from the Fertile Crescent around 8500 B.C. Soon thereafter, the crop appears progressively farther west, reaching Greece around 6500 B.C. and Germany around 5000 B.C. Those dates suggest domestication of emmer wheat in the Fertile Crescent, a conclusion supported by the fact that ancestral wild emmer wheat is confined to the area extending from Israel to western Iran and Turkey.

However, as we shall see, complications arise in many cases where the same plant or animal was domesticated independently at several different sites. Such cases can often be detected by analyzing the resulting morphological, genetic, or chromosomal differences between specimens of the same crop or domestic animal in different areas. For instance, India's zebu breeds of domestic cattle possess humps lacking in western Eurasian cattle breeds, and genetic analyses show that the ancestors of modern Indian and western Eurasian cattle breeds diverged from each other hundreds of thousands of years ago, long before any animals were domesticated anywhere. That is, cattle were domesticated independently in India and western Eurasia, within the last 10,000 years, starting with wild Indian and western Eurasian cattle subspecies that had diverged hundreds of thousands of years earlier.

LET'S NOW RETURN to our earlier questions about the rise of food production. Where, when, and how did food production develop in different parts of the globe?

At one extreme are areas in which food production arose altogether independently, with the domestication of many indigenous crops (and, in some cases, animals) before the arrival of any crops or animals from other areas. There are only five such areas for which the evidence is at present detailed and compelling: Southwest Asia, also known as the Near East or Fertile Crescent; China; Mesoamerica (the term applied to central and southern Mexico and adjacent areas of Central America); the Andes of South America, and possibly the adjacent Amazon Basin as well; and the eastern United States (Figure 5.1). Some or all of these centers may actually comprise several nearby centers where food production arose more or less independently, such as North China's Yellow River valley and South China's Yangtze River valley.

In addition to these five areas where food production definitely arose de novo, four others—Africa's Sahel zone, tropical West Africa, Ethiopia, and New Guinea—are candidates for that distinction. However, there is some uncertainty in each case. Although indigenous wild plants were undoubtedly domesticated in Africa's Sahel zone just south of the Sahara, cattle herding may have preceded agriculture there, and it is not yet certain whether those were independently domesticated Sahel cattle or, instead, domestic cattle of Fertile Crescent origin whose arrival triggered local plant domestication. It remains similarly uncertain whether the arrival of those Sahel crops then triggered the undoubted local domestication of indigenous wild plants in tropical West Africa, and whether the arrival of Southwest Asian crops is what triggered the local domestication of indige-

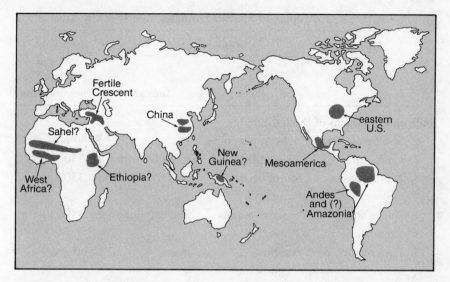

Figure 5.1. Centers of origin of food production. A question mark indicates some uncertainty whether the rise of food production at that center was really uninfluenced by the spread of food production from other centers, or (in the case of New Guinea) what the earliest crops were.

nous wild plants in Ethiopia. As for New Guinea, archaeological studies there have provided evidence of early agriculture well before food production in any adjacent areas, but the crops grown have not been definitely identified.

Table 5.1 summarizes, for these and other areas of local domestication, some of the best-known crops and animals and the earliest known dates of domestication. Among these nine candidate areas for the independent evolution of food production, Southwest Asia has the earliest definite dates for both plant domestication (around 8500 B.C.) and animal domestication (around 8000 B.C.); it also has by far the largest number of accurate radiocarbon dates for early food production. Dates for China are nearly as early, while dates for the eastern United States are clearly about 6,000 years later. For the other six candidate areas, the earliest well-established dates do not rival those for Southwest Asia, but too few early sites have been securely dated in those six other areas for us to be certain that they really lagged behind Southwest Asia and (if so) by how much.

The next group of areas consists of ones that did domesticate at least a

TABLE 5.1 **Examples of Species Domesticated in Each Area**

Area	Domesticated		Earliest Attested Date of Domestication
	Plants	Animals	
Independent Origins of Domestication			
1. Southwest Asia	wheat, pea, olive	sheep, goat	8500 B.C.
2. China	rice, millet	pig, silkworm	by 7500 B.C.
3. Mesoamerica	corn, beans, squash	turkey	by 3500 B.C.
4. Andes and Amazonia	potato, manioc	llama, guinea pig	by 3500 B.C.
5. Eastern United States	sunflower, goosefoot	none	2500 B.C.
? 6. Sahel	sorghum, African rice	guinea fowl	by 5000 B.C.
? 7. Tropical West Africa	African yams, oil palm	none	by 3000 B.C.
? 8. Ethiopia	coffee, teff	none	?
? 9. New Guinea	sugar cane, banana	none	7000 B.C.?
Local Domestication Following Arrival of Founder Crops from Elsewhere			
10. Western Europe	poppy, oat	none	6000–3500 B.C.
11. Indus Valley	sesame, eggplant	humped cattle	7000 B.C.
12. Egypt	sycamore fig, chufa	donkey, cat	6000 B.C.

couple of local plants or animals, but where food production depended mainly on crops and animals that were domesticated elsewhere. Those imported domesticates may be thought of as "founder" crops and animals, because they founded local food production. The arrival of founder domesticates enabled local people to become sedentary, and thereby increased the likelihood of local crops' evolving from wild plants that were gathered, brought home and planted accidentally, and later planted intentionally.

In three or four such areas, the arriving founder package came from Southwest Asia. One of them is western and central Europe, where food production arose with the arrival of Southwest Asian crops and animals between 6000 and 3500 B.C., but at least one plant (the poppy, and probably oats and some others) was then domesticated locally. Wild poppies are confined to coastal areas of the western Mediterranean. Poppy seeds are absent from excavated sites of the earliest farming communities in eastern Europe and Southwest Asia; they first appear in early farming sites in western Europe. In contrast, the wild ancestors of most Southwest Asian crops and animals were absent from western Europe. Thus, it seems clear that food production did not evolve independently in western Europe. Instead, it was triggered there by the arrival of Southwest Asian domesticates. The resulting western European farming societies domesticated the poppy, which subsequently spread eastward as a crop.

Another area where local domestication appears to have followed the arrival of Southwest Asian founder crops is the Indus Valley region of the Indian subcontinent. The earliest farming communities there in the seventh millennium B.C. utilized wheat, barley, and other crops that had been previously domesticated in the Fertile Crescent and that evidently spread to the Indus Valley through Iran. Only later did domesticates derived from indigenous species of the Indian subcontinent, such as humped cattle and sesame, appear in Indus Valley farming communities. In Egypt as well, food production began in the sixth millennium B.C. with the arrival of Southwest Asian crops. Egyptians then domesticated the sycamore fig and a local vegetable called chufa.

The same pattern perhaps applies to Ethiopia, where wheat, barley, and other Southwest Asian crops have been cultivated for a long time. Ethiopians also domesticated many locally available wild species to obtain crops most of which are still confined to Ethiopia, but one of them (the coffee bean) has now spread around the world. However, it is not yet known whether Ethiopians were cultivating these local plants before or only after the arrival of the Southwest Asian package.

In these and other areas where food production depended on the arrival of founder crops from elsewhere, did local hunter-gatherers themselves adopt those founder crops from neighboring farming peoples and thereby become farmers themselves? Or was the founder package instead brought by invading farmers, who were thereby enabled to outbreed the local hunters and to kill, displace, or outnumber them?

In Egypt it seems likely that the former happened: local hunter-gatherers simply added Southwest Asian domesticates and farming and herding techniques to their own diet of wild plants and animals, then gradually phased out the wild foods. That is, what arrived to launch food production in Egypt was foreign crops and animals, not foreign peoples. The same may have been true on the Atlantic coast of Europe, where local hunter-gatherers apparently adopted Southwest Asian sheep and cereals over the course of many centuries. In the Cape of South Africa the local Khoi hunter-gatherers became herders (but not farmers) by acquiring sheep and cows from farther north in Africa (and ultimately from Southwest Asia). Similarly, Native American hunter-gatherers of the U.S. Southwest gradually became farmers by acquiring Mexican crops. In these four areas the onset of food production provides little or no evidence for the domestication of local plant or animal species, but also little or no evidence for the replacement of human population.

At the opposite extreme are regions in which food production certainly began with an abrupt arrival of foreign people as well as of foreign crops and animals. The reason why we can be certain is that the arrivals took place in modern times and involved literate Europeans, who described in innumerable books what happened. Those areas include California, the Pacific Northwest of North America, the Argentine pampas, Australia, and Siberia. Until recent centuries, these areas were still occupied by hunter-gatherers—Native Americans in the first three cases and Aboriginal Australians or Native Siberians in the last two. Those hunter-gatherers were killed, infected, driven out, or largely replaced by arriving European farmers and herders who brought their own crops and did not domesticate any local wild species after their arrival (except for macadamia nuts in Australia). In the Cape of South Africa the arriving Europeans found not only Khoi hunter-gatherers but also Khoi herders who already possessed only domestic animals, not crops. The result was again the start of farming dependent on crops from elsewhere, a failure to domesticate local species, and a massive modern replacement of human population.

Finally, the same pattern of an abrupt start of food production dependent on domesticates from elsewhere, and an abrupt and massive population replacement, seems to have repeated itself in many areas in the prehistoric era. In the absence of written records, the evidence of those prehistoric replacements must be sought in the archaeological record or inferred from linguistic evidence. The best-attested cases are ones in which there can be no doubt about population replacement because the newly arriving food producers differed markedly in their skeletons from the hunter-gatherers whom they replaced, and because the food producers introduced not only crops and animals but also pottery. Later chapters will describe the two clearest such examples: the Austronesian expansion from South China into the Philippines and Indonesia (Chapter 17), and the Bantu expansion over subequatorial Africa (Chapter 19).

Southeastern Europe and central Europe present a similar picture of an abrupt onset of food production (dependent on Southwest Asian crops and animals) and of pottery making. This onset too probably involved replacement of old Greeks and Germans by new Greeks and Germans, just as old gave way to new in the Philippines, Indonesia, and subequatorial Africa. However, the skeletal differences between the earlier hunter-gatherers and the farmers who replaced them are less marked in Europe than in the Philippines, Indonesia, and subequatorial Africa. Hence the case for population replacement in Europe is less strong or less direct.

IN SHORT, ONLY a few areas of the world developed food production independently, and they did so at widely differing times. From those nuclear areas, hunter-gatherers of some neighboring areas learned food production, and peoples of other neighboring areas were replaced by invading food producers from the nuclear areas—again at widely differing times. Finally, peoples of some areas ecologically suitable for food production neither evolved nor acquired agriculture in prehistoric times at all; they persisted as hunter-gatherers until the modern world finally swept upon them. The peoples of areas with a head start on food production thereby gained a head start on the path leading toward guns, germs, and steel. The result was a long series of collisions between the haves and the have-nots of history.

How can we explain these geographic differences in the times and modes of onset of food production? That question, one of the most important problems of prehistory, will be the subject of the next five chapters.

CHAPTER 6

TO FARM OR NOT
TO FARM

F ORMERLY, ALL PEOPLE ON EARTH WERE HUNTER-GATHER-
ers. Why did any of them adopt food production at all? Given that
they must have had some reason, why did they do so around 8500 B.C. in
Mediterranean habitats of the Fertile Crescent, only 3,000 years later in
the climatically and structurally similar Mediterranean habitats of southwestern Europe, and never indigenously in the similar Mediterranean habitats of California, southwestern Australia, and the Cape of South Africa?
Why did even people of the Fertile Crescent wait until 8500 B.C., instead
of becoming food producers already around 18,500 or 28,500 B.C.?

From our modern perspective, all these questions at first seem silly,
because the drawbacks of being a hunter-gatherer appear so obvious. Scientists used to quote a phrase of Thomas Hobbes's in order to characterize
the lifestyle of hunter-gatherers as "nasty, brutish, and short." They
seemed to have to work hard, to be driven by the daily quest for food,
often to be close to starvation, to lack such elementary material comforts
as soft beds and adequate clothing, and to die young.

In reality, only for today's affluent First World citizens, who don't actually do the work of raising food themselves, does food production (by
remote agribusinesses) mean less physical work, more comfort, freedom
from starvation, and a longer expected lifetime. Most peasant farmers and

herders, who constitute the great majority of the world's actual food producers, aren't necessarily better off than hunter-gatherers. Time budget studies show that they may spend more rather than fewer hours per day at work than hunter-gatherers do. Archaeologists have demonstrated that the first farmers in many areas were smaller and less well nourished, suffered from more serious diseases, and died on the average at a younger age than the hunter-gatherers they replaced. If those first farmers could have foreseen the consequences of adopting food production, they might not have opted to do so. Why, unable to foresee the result, did they nevertheless make that choice?

There exist many actual cases of hunter-gatherers who did see food production practiced by their neighbors, and who nevertheless refused to accept its supposed blessings and instead remained hunter-gatherers. For instance, Aboriginal hunter-gatherers of northeastern Australia traded for thousands of years with farmers of the Torres Strait Islands, between Australia and New Guinea. California Native American hunter-gatherers traded with Native American farmers in the Colorado River valley. In addition, Khoi herders west of the Fish River of South Africa traded with Bantu farmers east of the Fish River, and continued to dispense with farming themselves. Why?

Still other hunter-gatherers in contact with farmers did eventually become farmers, but only after what may seem to us like an inordinately long delay. For example, the coastal peoples of northern Germany did not adopt food production until 1,300 years after peoples of the Linearbandkeramik culture introduced it to inland parts of Germany only 125 miles to the south. Why did those coastal Germans wait so long, and what led them finally to change their minds?

BEFORE WE CAN answer these questions, we must dispel some misconceptions about the origins of food production and then reformulate the question. What actually happened was not a *discovery* of food production, nor an *invention,* as we might first assume. There was often not even a conscious choice between food production and hunting-gathering. Specifically, in each area of the globe the first people who adopted food production could obviously not have been making a conscious choice or consciously striving toward farming as a goal, because they had never seen farming and had no way of knowing what it would be like. Instead, as we shall see, food production *evolved* as a by-product of decisions made without awareness of their consequences. Hence the question that we have to ask is why food production did evolve, why it evolved in some places but not others, why at different times in different places, and why not instead at some earlier or later date.

Another misconception is that there is necessarily a sharp divide between nomadic hunter-gatherers and sedentary food producers. In reality, although we frequently draw such a contrast, hunter-gatherers in some productive areas, including North America's Pacific Northwest coast and possibly southeastern Australia, became sedentary but never became food producers. Other hunter-gatherers, in Palestine, coastal Peru, and Japan, became sedentary first and adopted food production much later. Sedentary groups probably made up a much higher fraction of hunter-gatherers 15,000 years ago, when all inhabited parts of the world (including the most productive areas) were still occupied by hunter-gatherers, than they do today, when the few remaining hunter-gatherers survive only in unproductive areas where nomadism is the sole option.

Conversely, there are mobile groups of food producers. Some modern nomads of New Guinea's Lakes Plains make clearings in the jungle, plant bananas and papayas, go off for a few months to live again as hunter-gatherers, return to check on their crops, weed the garden if they find the crops growing, set off again to hunt, return months later to check again, and settle down for a while to harvest and eat if their garden has produced. Apache Indians of the southwestern United States settled down to farm in the summer at higher elevations and toward the north, then withdrew to the south and to lower elevations to wander in search of wild foods during the winter. Many herding peoples of Africa and Asia shift camp along regular seasonal routes to take advantage of predictable seasonal changes in pasturage. Thus, the shift from hunting-gathering to food production did not always coincide with a shift from nomadism to sedentary living.

Another supposed dichotomy that becomes blurred in reality is a distinction between food producers as active managers of their land and hunter-gatherers as mere collectors of the land's wild produce. In reality, some hunter-gatherers intensively manage their land. For example, New Guinea peoples who never domesticated sago palms or mountain pandanus nevertheless increase production of these wild edible plants by clearing away encroaching competing trees, keeping channels in sago swamps clear, and promoting growth of new sago shoots by cutting down mature sago trees. Aboriginal Australians who never reached the stage of farming yams and seed plants nonetheless anticipated several elements of farming. They managed the landscape by burning it, to encourage the growth of edible seed plants that sprout after fires. In gathering wild yams, they cut off most of the edible tuber but replaced the stems and tops of the tubers in the ground so that the tubers would regrow. Their digging to extract the tuber loosened and aerated the soil and fostered regrowth. All that they would have had to do to meet the definition of farmers was to carry the stems and remaining attached tubers home and similarly replace them in soil at their camp.

FROM THOSE PRECURSORS of food production already practiced by hunter-gatherers, it developed stepwise. Not all the necessary techniques were developed within a short time, and not all the wild plants and animals that were eventually domesticated in a given area were domesticated simultaneously. Even in the cases of the most rapid independent development of food production from a hunting-gathering lifestyle, it took thousands of years to shift from complete dependence on wild foods to a diet with very few wild foods. In early stages of food production, people simultaneously collected wild foods *and* raised cultivated ones, and diverse types of collecting activities diminished in importance at different times as reliance on crops increased.

The underlying reason why this transition was piecemeal is that food production systems evolved as a result of the accumulation of many separate decisions about allocating time and effort. Foraging humans, like foraging animals, have only finite time and energy, which they can spend in various ways. We can picture an incipient farmer waking up and asking: Shall I spend today hoeing my garden (predictably yielding a lot of vegetables several months from now), gathering shellfish (predictably yielding a little meat today), or hunting deer (yielding possibly a lot of meat today, but more likely nothing)? Human and animal foragers are constantly prioritizing and making effort-allocation decisions, even if only unconsciously. They concentrate first on favorite foods, or ones that yield the highest payoff. If these are unavailable, they shift to less and less preferred foods.

Many considerations enter into these decisions. People seek food in order to satisfy their hunger and fill their bellies. They also crave specific foods, such as protein-rich foods, fat, salt, sweet fruits, and foods that simply taste good. All other things being equal, people seek to maximize their return of calories, protein, or other specific food categories by foraging in a way that yields the most return with the greatest certainty in the least time for the least effort. Simultaneously, they seek to minimize their risk of starving: moderate but reliable returns are preferable to a fluctuating lifestyle with a high time-averaged rate of return but a substantial likelihood of starving to death. One suggested function of the first gardens of nearly 11,000 years ago was to provide a reliable reserve larder as insurance in case wild food supplies failed.

Conversely, men hunters tend to guide themselves by considerations of prestige: for example, they might rather go giraffe hunting every day, bag a giraffe once a month, and thereby gain the status of great hunter, than bring home twice a giraffe's weight of food in a month by humbling themselves and reliably gathering nuts every day. People are also guided by seemingly arbitrary cultural preferences, such as considering fish either delicacies or taboo. Finally, their priorities are heavily influenced by the relative values they attach to different lifestyles—just as we can see today. For instance, in the 19th-century U.S. West, the cattlemen, sheepmen, and farmers all despised each other. Similarly, throughout human history farmers have tended to despise hunter-gatherers as primitive, hunter-gatherers have despised farmers as ignorant, and herders have despised both. All these elements come into play in people's separate decisions about how to obtain their food.

As we already noted, the first farmers on each continent could not have chosen farming consciously, because there were no other nearby farmers for them to observe. However, once food production had arisen in one part of a continent, neighboring hunter-gatherers could see the result and make conscious decisions. In some cases the hunter-gatherers adopted the neighboring system of food production virtually as a complete package; in others they chose only certain elements of it; and in still others they rejected food production entirely and remained hunter-gatherers.

For example, hunter-gatherers in parts of southeastern Europe had quickly adopted Southwest Asian cereal crops, pulse crops, and livestock simultaneously as a complete package by around 6000 B.C. All three of these elements also spread rapidly through central Europe in the centuries before 5000 B.C. Adoption of food production may have been rapid and wholesale in southeastern and central Europe because the hunter-gatherer lifestyle there was less productive and less competitive. In contrast, food production was adopted piecemeal in southwestern Europe (southern France, Spain, and Italy), where sheep arrived first and cereals later. The adoption of intensive food production from the Asian mainland was also very slow and piecemeal in Japan, probably because the hunter-gatherer lifestyle based on seafood and local plants was so productive there.

Just as a hunting-gathering lifestyle can be traded piecemeal for a food-producing lifestyle, one system of food production can also be traded piecemeal for another. For example, Indians of the eastern United States were domesticating local plants by about 2500 B.C. but had trade connections with Mexican Indians who developed a more productive crop system based on the trinity of corn, squash, and beans. Eastern U.S. Indians adopted Mexican crops, and many of them discarded many of their local domesticates, piecemeal; squash was domesticated independently, corn arrived from Mexico around A.D. 200 but remained a minor crop until around A.D. 900, and beans arrived a century or two later. It even happened that food-production systems were abandoned in favor of hunting-gathering. For instance, around 3000 B.C. the hunter-gatherers of southern Sweden adopted farming based on Southwest Asian crops, but abandoned it around 2700 B.C. and reverted to hunting-gathering for 400 years before resuming farming.

ALL THESE CONSIDERATIONS make it clear that we should not suppose that the decision to adopt farming was made in a vacuum, as if the people had previously had no means to feed themselves. Instead, we must consider food production and hunting-gathering as *alternative strategies* competing with each other. Mixed economies that added certain crops or livestock to hunting-gathering also competed against both types of "pure" economies, and against mixed economies with higher or lower proportions of food production. Nevertheless, over the last 10,000 years, the predominant result has been a shift from hunting-gathering to food production. Hence we must ask: What were the factors that tipped the competitive advantage away from the former and toward the latter?

That question continues to be debated by archaeologists and anthropologists. One reason for its remaining unsettled is that different factors may have been decisive in different parts of the world. Another has been the problem of disentangling cause and effect in the rise of food production. However, five main contributing factors can still be identified; the controversies revolve mainly around their relative importance.

One factor is the decline in the availability of wild foods. The lifestyle of hunter-gatherers has become increasingly less rewarding over the past 13,000 years, as resources on which they depended (especially animal resources) have become less abundant or even disappeared. As we saw in Chapter 1, most large mammal species became extinct in North and South America at the end of the Pleistocene, and some became extinct in Eurasia and Africa, either because of climate changes or because of the rise in skill and numbers of human hunters. While the role of animal extinctions in eventually (after a long lag) nudging ancient Native Americans, Eurasians, and Africans toward food production can be debated, there are numerous incontrovertible cases on islands in more recent times. Only after the first Polynesian settlers had exterminated moas and decimated seal populations on New Zealand, and exterminated or decimated seabirds and land birds on other Polynesian islands, did they intensify their food production. For instance, although the Polynesians who colonized Easter Island around A.D. 500 brought chickens with them, chicken did not become a major food until wild birds and porpoises were no longer readily available as food. Similarly, a suggested contributing factor to the rise of animal domestication in the Fertile Crescent was the decline in abundance of the wild gazelles that had previously been a major source of meat for hunter-gatherers in that area.

A second factor is that, just as the depletion of wild game tended to make hunting-gathering less rewarding, an increased availability of domesticable wild plants made steps leading to plant domestication more rewarding. For instance, climate changes at the end of the Pleistocene in the Fertile Crescent greatly expanded the area of habitats with wild cereals, of which huge crops could be harvested in a short time. Those wild cereal harvests were precursors to the domestication of the earliest crops, the cereals wheat and barley, in the Fertile Crescent.

Still another factor tipping the balance away from hunting-gathering was the cumulative development of technologies on which food production would eventually depend—technologies for collecting, processing, and storing wild foods. What use can would-be farmers make of a ton of wheat grains on the stalk, if they have not first figured out how to harvest, husk, and store them? The necessary methods, implements, and facilities appeared rapidly in the Fertile Crescent after 11,000 B.C., having been invented for dealing with the newly available abundance of wild cereals.

Those inventions included sickles of flint blades cemented into wooden or bone handles, for harvesting wild grains; baskets in which to carry the grains home from the hillsides where they grew; mortars and pestles, or grinding slabs, to remove the husks; the technique of roasting grains so that they could be stored without sprouting; and underground storage pits, some of them plastered to make them waterproof. Evidence for all of these techniques becomes abundant at sites of hunter-gatherers in the Fertile Crescent after 11,000 B.C. All these techniques, though developed for the exploitation of wild cereals, were prerequisites to the planting of cereals as crops. These cumulative developments constituted the unconscious first steps of plant domestication.

A fourth factor was the two-way link between the rise in human population density and the rise in food production. In all parts of the world where adequate evidence is available, archaeologists find evidence of rising densities associated with the appearance of food production. Which was the cause and which the result? This is a long-debated chicken-or-egg problem: did a rise in human population density force people to turn to food production, or did food production permit a rise in human population density?

In principle, one expects the chain of causation to operate in both directions. As I've already discussed, food production tends to lead to increased population densities because it yields more edible calories per acre than does hunting-gathering. On the other hand, human population densities were gradually rising throughout the late Pleistocene anyway, thanks to improvements in human technology for collecting and processing wild foods. As population densities rose, food production became increasingly favored because it provided the increased food outputs needed to feed all those people.

That is, the adoption of food production exemplifies what is termed an autocatalytic process—one that catalyzes itself in a positive feedback cycle, going faster and faster once it has started. A gradual rise in population densities impelled people to obtain more food, by rewarding those who unconsciously took steps toward producing it. Once people began to produce food and become sedentary, they could shorten the birth spacing and produce still more people, requiring still more food. This bidirectional link between food production and population density explains the paradox that food production, while increasing the quantity of edible calories per acre, left the food producers less well nourished than the hunter-gatherers whom they succeeded. That paradox developed because human population densities rose slightly more steeply than did the availability of food.

Taken together, these four factors help us understand why the transition to food production in the Fertile Crescent began around 8500 B.C., not around 18,500 or 28,500 B.C. At the latter two dates hunting-gathering was still much more rewarding than incipient food production, because wild mammals were still abundant; wild cereals were not yet abundant; people had not yet developed the inventions necessary for collecting, processing, and storing cereals efficiently; and human population densities were not yet high enough for a large premium to be placed on extracting more calories per acre.

A final factor in the transition became decisive at geographic boundaries between hunter-gatherers and food producers. The much denser populations of food producers enabled them to displace or kill hunter-gatherers by their sheer numbers, not to mention the other advantages associated with food production (including technology, germs, and professional soldiers). In areas where there were only hunter-gatherers to begin with, those groups of hunter-gatherers who adopted food production outbred those who didn't.

As a result, in most areas of the globe suitable for food production, hunter-gatherers met one of two fates: either they were displaced by neighboring food producers, or else they survived only by adopting food production themselves. In places where they were already numerous or where geography retarded immigration by food producers, local hunter-gatherers did have time to adopt farming in prehistoric times and thus to survive as farmers. This may have happened in the U.S. Southwest, in the western Mediterranean, on the Atlantic coast of Europe, and in parts of Japan. However, in Indonesia, tropical Southeast Asia, most of subequatorial Africa, and probably in parts of Europe, the hunter-gatherers were replaced by farmers in the prehistoric era, whereas a similar replacement took place in modern times in Australia and much of the western United States.

Only where especially potent geographic or ecological barriers made immigration of food producers or diffusion of locally appropriate food-producing techniques very difficult were hunter-gatherers able to persist until modern times in areas suitable for food production. The three outstanding examples are the persistence of Native American hunter-gatherers in California, separated by deserts from the Native American farmers of Arizona; that of Khoisan hunter-gatherers at the Cape of South Africa, in a Mediterranean climate zone unsuitable for the equatorial crops of nearby Bantu farmers; and that of hunter-gatherers throughout the Australian continent, separated by narrow seas from the food producers of Indonesia and New Guinea. Those few peoples who remained hunter-gatherers into the 20th century escaped replacement by food producers because they were confined to areas not fit for food production, especially deserts and Arctic regions. Within the present decade, even they will have been seduced by the attractions of civilization, settled down under pressure from bureaucrats or missionaries, or succumbed to germs.

CHAPTER 7

HOW TO MAKE AN ALMOND

I F YOU'RE A HIKER WHOSE APPETITE IS JADED BY FARM-grown foods, it's fun to try eating wild foods. You know that some wild plants, such as wild strawberries and blueberries, are both tasty and safe to eat. They're sufficiently similar to familiar crops that you can easily recognize the wild berries, even though they're much smaller than those we grow. Adventurous hikers cautiously eat mushrooms, aware that many species can kill us. But not even ardent nut lovers eat wild almonds, of which a few dozen contain enough cyanide (the poison used in Nazi gas chambers) to kill us. The forest is full of many other plants deemed inedible.

Yet all crops arose from wild plant species. How did certain wild plants get turned into crops? That question is especially puzzling in regard to the many crops (like almonds) whose wild progenitors are lethal or bad-tasting, and to other crops (like corn) that look drastically different from their wild ancestors. What cavewoman or caveman ever got the idea of "domesticating" a plant, and how was it accomplished?

Plant domestication may be defined as growing a plant and thereby, consciously or unconsciously, causing it to change genetically from its wild ancestor in ways making it more useful to human consumers. Crop development is today a conscious, highly specialized effort carried out by professional scientists. They already know about the hundreds of existing crops and set out to develop yet another one. To achieve that goal, they plant many different seeds or roots, select the best progeny and plant their seeds, apply knowledge of genetics to develop good varieties that breed true, and perhaps even use the latest techniques of genetic engineering to transfer specific useful genes. At the Davis campus of the University of California, an entire department (the Department of Pomology) is devoted to apples and another (the Department of Viticulture and Enology) to grapes and wine.

But plant domestication goes back over 10,000 years. Early farmers surely didn't use molecular genetic techniques to arrive at their results. The first farmers didn't even have any existing crop as a model to inspire them to develop new ones. Hence they couldn't have known that, whatever they were doing, they would enjoy a tasty treat as a result.

How, then, did early farmers domesticate plants unwittingly? For example, how did they turn poisonous almonds into safe ones without knowing what they were doing? What changes did they actually make in wild plants, besides rendering some of them bigger or less poisonous? Even for valuable crops, the times of domestication vary greatly: for instance, peas were domesticated by 8000 B.C., olives around 4000 B.C., strawberries not until the Middle Ages, and pecans not until 1846. Many valuable wild plants yielding food prized by millions of people, such as oaks sought for their edible acorns in many parts of the world, remain untamed even today. What made some plants so much easier or more inviting to domesticate than others? Why did olive trees yield to Stone Age farmers, whereas oak trees continue to defeat our brightest agronomists?

LET'S BEGIN BY looking at domestication from the plant's point of view. As far as plants are concerned, we're just one of thousands of animal species that unconsciously "domesticate" plants.

Like all animal species (including humans), plants must spread their offspring to areas where they can thrive and pass on their parents' genes. Young animals disperse by walking or flying, but plants don't have that option, so they must somehow hitchhike. While some plant species have seeds adapted for being carried by the wind or for floating on water, many others trick an animal into carrying their seeds, by wrapping the seed in a tasty fruit and advertising the fruit's ripeness by its color or smell. The hungry animal plucks and swallows the fruit, walks or flies off, and then spits out or defecates the seed somewhere far from its parent tree. Seeds can in this manner be carried for thousands of miles.

It may come as a surprise to learn that plant seeds can resist digestion by your gut and nonetheless germinate out of your feces. But any adventurous readers who are not too squeamish can make the test and prove it for themselves. The seeds of many wild plant species actually *must* pass through an animal's gut before they can germinate. For instance, one African melon species is so well adapted to being eaten by a hyena-like animal called the aardwolf that most melons of that species grow on the latrine sites of aardwolves.

As an example of how would-be plant hitchhikers attract animals, consider wild strawberries. When strawberry seeds are still young and not yet ready to be planted, the surrounding fruit is green, sour, and hard. When the seeds finally mature, the berries turn red, sweet, and tender. The change in the berries' color serves as a signal attracting birds like thrushes to pluck the berries and fly off, eventually to spit out or defecate the seeds.

Naturally, strawberry plants didn't set out with a conscious intent of attracting birds when, and only when, their seeds were ready to be dispersed. Neither did thrushes set out with the intent of domesticating strawberries. Instead, strawberry plants evolved through natural selection. The greener and more sour the young strawberry, the fewer the birds that destroyed the seeds by eating berries before the seeds were ready; the sweeter and redder the final strawberry, the more numerous the birds that dispersed its ripe seeds.

Countless other plants have fruits adapted to being eaten and dispersed by particular species of animals. Just as strawberries are adapted to birds, so acorns are adapted to squirrels, mangos to bats, and some sedges to ants. That fulfills part of our definition of plant domestication, as the genetic modification of an ancestral plant in ways that make it more useful to consumers. But no one would seriously describe this evolutionary process as domestication, because birds and bats and other animal consumers don't fulfill the other part of the definition: they don't consciously grow plants. In the same way, the early unconscious stages of crop evolution from wild plants consisted of plants evolving in ways that attracted humans to eat and disperse their fruit without yet intentionally growing them. Human latrines, like those of aardvarks, may have been a testing ground of the first unconscious crop breeders.

LATRINES ARE MERELY one of the many places where we accidentally sow the seeds of wild plants that we eat. When we gather edible wild plants and bring them home, some spill en route or at our houses. Some fruit rots while still containing perfectly good seeds, and gets thrown out uneaten into the garbage. As parts of the fruit that we actually take into our mouths, strawberry seeds are tiny and inevitably swallowed and defecated, but other seeds are large enough to be spat out. Thus, our spittoons and garbage dumps joined our latrines to form the first agricultural research laboratories.

At whichever such "lab" the seeds ended up, they tended to come from only certain individuals of edible plants—namely, those that we preferred to eat for one reason or another. From your berry-picking days, you know that you select particular berries or berry bushes. Eventually, when the first farmers began to sow seeds deliberately, they would inevitably sow those from the plants they had chosen to gather, even though they didn't understand the genetic principle that big berries have seeds likely to grow into bushes yielding more big berries.

So, when you wade into a thorny thicket amid the mosquitoes on a hot, humid day, you don't do it for just any strawberry bush. Even if unconsciously, you decide which bush looks most promising, and whether it's worth it at all. What are your unconscious criteria?

One criterion, of course, is size. You prefer large berries, because it's not worth your while to get sunburned and mosquito bitten for some lousy little berries. That provides part of the explanation why many crop plants have much bigger fruits than their wild ancestors do. It's especially familiar to us that supermarket strawberries and blueberries are gigantic compared with wild ones; those differences arose only in recent centuries.

Such size differences in other plants go back to the very beginnings of agriculture, when cultivated peas evolved through human selection to be 10 times heavier than wild peas. The little wild peas had been collected by hunter-gatherers for thousands of years, just as we collect little wild blueberries today, before the preferential harvesting and planting of the most appealing largest wild peas—that is, what we call farming—began automatically to contribute to increases in average pea size from generation to generation. Similarly, supermarket apples are typically around three inches in diameter, wild apples only one inch. The oldest corn cobs are barely more than half an inch long, but Mexican Indian farmers of A.D. 1500 already had developed six-inch cobs, and some modern cobs are one and a half feet long.

Another obvious difference between seeds that we grow and many of their wild ancestors is in bitterness. Many wild seeds evolved to be bitter, bad-tasting, or actually poisonous, in order to deter animals from eating them. Thus, natural selection acts oppositely on seeds and on fruits. Plants whose fruits are tasty get their seeds dispersed by animals, but the seed itself within the fruit has to be bad-tasting. Otherwise, the animal would also chew up the seed, and it couldn't sprout.

Almonds provide a striking example of bitter seeds and their change under domestication. Most wild almond seeds contain an intensely bitter chemical called amygdalin, which (as was already mentioned) breaks down to yield the poison cyanide. A snack of wild almonds can kill a person foolish enough to ignore the warning of the bitter taste. Since the first stage in unconscious domestication involves gathering seeds to eat, how on earth did domestication of wild almonds ever reach that first stage?

The explanation is that occasional individual almond trees have a mutation in a single gene that prevents them from synthesizing the bitter-tasting amygdalin. Such trees die out in the wild without leaving any progeny, because birds discover and eat all their seeds. But curious or hungry children of early farmers, nibbling wild plants around them, would eventually have sampled and noticed those nonbitter almond trees. (In the same way, European peasants today still recognize and appreciate occasional individual oak trees whose acorns are sweet rather than bitter.) Those nonbitter almond seeds are the only ones that ancient farmers would have planted, at first unintentionally in their garbage heaps and later intentionally in their orchards.

Already by 8000 B.C. wild almonds show up in excavated archaeological sites in Greece. By 3000 B.C. they were being domesticated in lands of the eastern Mediterranean. When the Egyptian king Tutankhamen died, around 1325 B.C., almonds were one of the foods left in his famous tomb to nourish him in the afterlife. Lima beans, watermelons, potatoes, eggplants, and cabbages are among the many other familiar crops whose wild ancestors were bitter or poisonous, and of which occasional sweet individuals must have sprouted around the latrines of ancient hikers.

While size and tastiness are the most obvious criteria by which human hunter-gatherers select wild plants, other criteria include fleshy or seedless fruits, oily seeds, and long fibers. Wild squashes and pumpkins have little or no fruit around their seeds, but the preferences of early farmers selected for squashes and pumpkins consisting of far more flesh than seeds. Cultivated bananas were selected long ago to be all flesh and no seed, thereby inspiring modern agricultural scientists to develop seedless oranges, grapes, and watermelons as well. Seedlessness provides a good example of how human selection can completely reverse the original evolved function of a wild fruit, which in nature serves as a vehicle for dispersing seeds.

In ancient times many plants were similarly selected for oily fruits or seeds. Among the earliest fruit trees domesticated in the Mediterranean world were olives, cultivated since around 4000 B.C. for their oil. Crop olives are not only bigger but also oilier than wild ones. Ancient farmers selected sesame, mustard, poppies, and flax as well for oily seeds, while modern plant scientists have done the same for sunflower, safflower, and cotton.

Before that recent development of cotton for oil, it was of course selected for its fibers, used to weave textiles. The fibers (termed lint) are hairs on the cotton seeds, and early farmers of both the Americas and the Old World independently selected different species of cotton for long lint. In flax and hemp, two other plants grown to supply the textiles of antiquity, the fibers come instead from the stem, and plants were selected for long, straight stems. While we think of most crops as being grown for food, flax is one of our oldest crops (domesticated by around 7000 B.C.). It furnished linen, which remained the chief textile of Europe until it became supplanted by cotton and synthetics after the Industrial Revolution.

SO FAR, ALL the changes that I've described in the evolution of wild plants into crops involve characters that early farmers could actually notice—such as fruit size, bitterness, fleshiness, and oiliness, and fiber length. By harvesting those individual wild plants possessing these desirable qualities to an exceptional degree, ancient peoples unconsciously dispersed the plants and set them on the road to domestication.

In addition, though, there were at least four other major types of change that did not involve berry pickers making visible choices. In these cases the berry pickers caused changes either by harvesting available plants while other plants remained unavailable for invisible reasons, or by changing the selective conditions acting on plants.

The first such change affected wild mechanisms for the dispersal of seeds. Many plants have specialized mechanisms that scatter seeds (and thereby prevent humans from gathering them efficiently). Only mutant seeds lacking those mechanisms would have been harvested and would thus have become the progenitors of crops.

A clear example involves peas, whose seeds (the peas we eat) come enclosed in a pod. Wild peas have to get out of the pod if they are to germinate. To achieve that result, pea plants evolved a gene that makes the pod explode, shooting out the peas onto the ground. Pods of occasional mutant peas don't explode. In the wild the mutant peas would die entombed in their pod on their parent plants, and only the popping pods would pass on their genes. But, conversely, the only pods available to humans to harvest would be the nonpopping ones left on the plant. Thus, once humans began bringing wild peas home to eat, there was immediate selection for that single-gene mutant. Similar nonpopping mutants were selected in lentils, flax, and poppies.

Instead of being enclosed in a poppable pod, wild wheat and barley seeds grow at the top of a stalk that spontaneously shatters, dropping the seeds to the ground where they can germinate. A single-gene mutation prevents the stalks from shattering. In the wild that mutation would be lethal to the plant, since the seeds would remain suspended in the air, unable to germinate and take root. But those mutant seeds would have been the ones waiting conveniently on the stalk to be harvested and brought home by humans. When humans then planted those harvested mutant seeds, any mutant seeds among the progeny again became available to the farmers to harvest and sow, while normal seeds among the progeny fell to the ground and became unavailable. Thus, human farmers reversed the direction of natural selection by 180 degrees: the formerly successful gene suddenly became lethal, and the lethal mutant became successful. Over 10,000 years ago, that unconscious selection for nonshattering wheat and barley stalks was apparently the first major human "improvement" in any plant. That change marked the beginning of agriculture in the Fertile Crescent.

The second type of change was even less visible to ancient hikers. For annual plants growing in an area with a very unpredictable climate, it could be lethal if all the seeds sprouted quickly and simultaneously. Were that to happen, the seedlings might all be killed by a single drought or frost, leaving no seeds to propagate the species. Hence many annual plants have evolved to hedge their bets by means of germination inhibitors, which make seeds initially dormant and spread out their germination over several years. In that way, even if most seedlings are killed by a bout of bad weather, some seeds will be left to germinate later.

A common bet-hedging adaptation by which wild plants achieve that result is to enclose their seeds in a thick coat or armor. The many wild plants with such adaptations include wheat, barley, peas, flax, and sunflowers. While such late-sprouting seeds still have the opportunity to germinate in the wild, consider what must have happened as farming developed. Early farmers would have discovered by trial and error that they could obtain higher yields by tilling and watering the soil and then sowing seeds. When that happened, seeds that immediately sprouted grew into plants whose seeds were harvested and planted in the next year. But many of the wild seeds did not immediately sprout, and they yielded no harvest.

Occasional mutant individuals among wild plants lacked thick seed coats or other inhibitors of germination. All such mutants promptly sprouted and yielded harvested mutant seeds. Early farmers wouldn't have noticed the difference, in the way that they did notice and selectively harvest big berries. But the cycle of sow / grow / harvest / sow would have selected immediately and unconsciously for the mutants. Like the changes in seed dispersal, these changes in germination inhibition characterize wheat, barley, peas, and many other crops compared with their wild ancestors.

The remaining major type of change invisible to early farmers involved plant reproduction. A general problem in crop development is that occasional mutant plant individuals are more useful to humans (for example, because of bigger or less bitter seeds) than are normal individuals. If those desirable mutants proceeded to interbreed with normal plants, the mutation would immediately be diluted or lost. Under what circumstances would it remain preserved for early farmers?

For plants that reproduce themselves, the mutant would automatically be preserved. That's true of plants that reproduce vegetatively (from a tuber or root of the parent plant), or that are hermaphrodites capable of fertilizing themselves. But the vast majority of wild plants don't reproduce that way. They're either hermaphrodites incapable of fertilizing themselves and forced to interbreed with other hermaphrodite individuals (my male part fertilizes your female part, your male part fertilizes my female part), or else they occur as separate male and female individuals, like all normal mammals. The former plants are termed self-incompatible hermaphrodites; the latter, dioecious species. Both were bad news for ancient farmers, who would thereby have promptly lost any favorable mutants without understanding why.

The solution involved another type of invisible change. Numerous plant mutations affect the reproductive system itself. Some mutant individuals developed fruit without even having to be pollinated, resulting in our seedless bananas, grapes, oranges, and pineapples. Some mutant hermaphrodites lost their self-incompatibility and became able to fertilize themselves—a process exemplified by many fruit trees such as plums, peaches, apples, apricots, and cherries. Some mutant grapes that normally would have had separate male and female individuals also became self-fertilizing hermaphrodites. By all these means, ancient farmers, who didn't understand plant reproductive biology, still ended up with useful crops that bred true and were worth replanting, instead of initially promising mutants whose worthless progeny were consigned to oblivion.

Thus, farmers selected from among individual plants on the basis not only of perceptible qualities like size and taste, but also of invisible features like seed dispersal mechanisms, germination inhibition, and reproductive biology. As a result, different plants became selected for quite different or even opposite features. Some plants (like sunflowers) were selected for much bigger seeds, while others (like bananas) were selected for tiny or even nonexistent seeds. Lettuce was selected for luxuriant leaves at the expense of seeds or fruit; wheat and sunflowers, for seeds at the expense of leaves; and squash, for fruit at the expense of leaves. Especially instructive are cases in which a single wild plant species was variously selected for different purposes and thereby gave rise to quite different-looking crops. Beets, grown already in Babylonian times for their leaves (like the modern beet varieties called chards), were then developed for their edible roots and finally (in the 18th century) for their sugar content (sugar beets). Ancestral cabbage plants, possibly grown originally for their oily seeds, underwent even greater diversification as they became variously selected for leaves (modern cabbage and kale), stems (kohlrabi), buds (brussels sprouts), or flower shoots (cauliflower and broccoli).

So far, we have been discussing transformations of wild plants into crops as a result of selection by farmers, consciously or unconsciously. That is, farmers initially selected seeds of certain wild plant individuals to bring into their gardens and then chose certain progeny seeds each year to grow in the next year's garden. But much of the transformation was also effected as a result of plants' selecting themselves. Darwin's phrase "natural selection" refers to certain individuals of a species surviving better, and / or reproducing more successfully, than competing individuals of the same species under natural conditions. In effect, the natural processes of differential survival and reproduction do the selecting. If the conditions change, different types of individuals may now survive or reproduce better and become "naturally selected," with the result that the population undergoes evolutionary change. A classic example is the development of industrial melanism in British moths: darker moth individuals became relatively commoner than paler individuals as the environment became dirtier during the 19th century, because dark moths resting on a dark, dirty tree were more likely than contrasting pale moths to escape the attention of predators.

Much as the Industrial Revolution changed the environment for moths, farming changed the environment for plants. A tilled, fertilized, watered, weeded garden provides growing conditions very different from those on a dry, unfertilized hillside. Many changes of plants under domestication resulted from such changes in conditions and hence in the favored types of individuals. For example, when a farmer sows seeds densely in a garden, there is intense competition among the seeds. Big seeds that can take advantage of the good conditions to grow quickly will now be favored over small seeds that were previously favored on dry, unfertilized hillsides where seeds were sparser and competition less intense. Such increased competition among plants themselves made a major contribution to larger seed size and to many other changes developing during the transformation of wild plants into ancient crops.

WHAT ACCOUNTS FOR the great differences among plants in ease of domestication, such that some species were domesticated long ago and others not until the Middle Ages, whereas still other wild plants have proved immune to all our activities? We can deduce many of the answers by examining the well-established sequence in which various crops developed in Southwest Asia's Fertile Crescent.

It turns out that the earliest Fertile Crescent crops, such as the wheat and barley and peas domesticated around 10,000 years ago, arose from wild ancestors offering many advantages. They were already edible and gave high yields in the wild. They were easily grown, merely by being sown or planted. They grew quickly and could be harvested within a few months of sowing, a big advantage for incipient farmers still on the borderline between nomadic hunters and settled villagers. They could be readily stored, unlike many later crops such as strawberries and lettuce. They were mostly self-pollinating: that is, the crop varieties could pollinate themselves and pass on their own desirable genes unchanged, instead of having to hybridize with other varieties less useful to humans. Finally, their wild ancestors required very little genetic change to be converted into crops—for instance, in wheat, just the mutations for nonshattering stalks and uniform quick germination.

A next stage of crop development included the first fruit and nut trees, domesticated around 4000 B.C. They comprised olives, figs, dates, pomegranates, and grapes. Compared with cereals and legumes, they had the drawback of not starting to yield food until at least three years after planting, and not reaching full production until after as much as a decade. Thus, growing these crops was possible only for people already fully committed to the settled village life. However, these early fruit and nut trees were still the easiest such crops to cultivate. Unlike later tree domesticates, they could be grown directly by being planted as cuttings or even seeds. Cuttings have the advantage that, once ancient farmers had found or developed a productive tree, they could be sure that all its descendants would remain identical to it.

A third stage involved fruit trees that proved much harder to cultivate, including apples, pears, plums, and cherries. These trees cannot be grown from cuttings. It's also a waste of effort to grow them from seed, since the offspring even of an outstanding individual tree of those species are highly variable and mostly yield worthless fruit. Instead, those trees must be grown by the difficult technique of grafting, developed in China long after the beginnings of agriculture. Not only is grafting hard work even once you know the principle, but the principle itself could have been discovered only through conscious experimentation. The invention of grafting was hardly just a matter of some nomad relieving herself at a latrine and returning later to be pleasantly surprised by the resulting crop of fine fruit.

Many of these late-stage fruit trees posed a further problem in that their wild progenitors were the opposite of self-pollinating. They had to be cross-pollinated by another plant belonging to a genetically different variety of their species. Hence early farmers either had to find mutant trees not requiring cross-pollination, or had consciously to plant genetically different varieties or else male and female individuals nearby in the same orchard. All those problems delayed the domestication of apples, pears, plums, and cherries until around classical times. At about the same time, though, another group of late domesticates arose with much less effort, as wild plants that established themselves initially as weeds in fields of intentionally cultivated crops. Crops starting out as weeds included rye and oats, turnips and radishes, beets and leeks, and lettuce.

ALTHOUGH THE DETAILED sequence that I've just described applies to the Fertile Crescent, partly similar sequences also appeared elsewhere in the world. In particular, the Fertile Crescent's wheat and barley exemplify the class of crops termed cereals or grains (members of the grass family), while Fertile Crescent peas and lentils exemplify pulses (members of the legume family, which includes beans). Cereal crops have the virtues of being fast growing, high in carbohydrates, and yielding up to a ton of edible food per hectare cultivated. As a result, cereals today account for over half of all calories consumed by humans and include five of the modern world's 12 leading crops (wheat, corn, rice, barley, and sorghum). Many cereal crops are low in protein, but that deficit is made up by pulses, which are often 25 percent protein (38 percent in the case of soybeans). Cereals and pulses together thus provide many of the ingredients of a balanced diet.

As Table 7.1 (next page) summarizes, the domestication of local cereal / pulse combinations launched food production in many areas. The most familiar examples are the combination of wheat and barley with peas and lentils in the Fertile Crescent, the combination of corn with several bean species in Mesoamerica, and the combination of rice and millets with soybeans and other beans in China. Less well known are Africa's combination of sorghum, African rice, and pearl millet with cowpeas and groundnuts, and the Andes' combination of the noncereal grain quinoa with several bean species.

Table 7.1 also shows that the Fertile Crescent's early domestication of flax for fiber was paralleled elsewhere. Hemp, four cotton species, yucca, and agave variously furnished fiber for rope and woven clothing in China,

TABLE 7.1. **Examples of Early Major Crop Types around the Ancient World**

Area	Crop Type	
	Cereals, Other Grasses	Pulses
Fertile Crescent	emmer wheat, einkorn wheat, barley	pea, lentil, chickpea
China	foxtail millet, broomcorn millet, rice	soybean, adzuki bean, mung bean
Mesoamerica	corn	common bean, tepary bean, scarlet runner bean
Andes, Amazonia	quinoa, [corn]	lima bean, common bean, peanut
West Africa and Sahel	sorghum, pearl millet, African rice	cowpea, groundnut
India	[wheat, barley, rice, sorghum, millets]	hyacinth bean, black gram, green gram
Ethiopia	teff, finger millet, [wheat, barley]	[pea, lentil]
Eastern United States	maygrass, little barley, knotweed, goosefoot	—
New Guinea	sugar cane	—

Mesoamerica, India, Ethiopia, sub-Saharan Africa, and South America, supplemented in several of those areas by wool from domestic animals. Of the centers of early food production, only the eastern United States and New Guinea remained without a fiber crop.

Alongside these parallels, there were also some major differences in food production systems around the world. One is that agriculture in much of the Old World came to involve broadcast seeding and monoculture fields, and eventually plowing. That is, seeds were sown by being

Crop Type		
Fiber	Roots, Tubers	Melons
flax	—	muskmelon
hemp	—	[muskmelon]
cotton (G. hirsutum), yucca, agave	jicama	squashes (C. pepo, etc.)
cotton (G. barbadense)	manioc, sweet potato, potato, oca	squashes (C. maxima, etc.)
cotton G. herbaceum)	African yams	watermelon, bottle gourd
cotton (G. arboreum), flax	—	cucumber
[flax]	—	—
—	Jerusalem artichoke	squash (C. pepo)
—	yams, taro	—

The table gives major crops, of five crop classes, from early agricultural sites in various parts of the world. Square brackets enclose names of crops first domesticated elsewhere; names not enclosed in brackets refer to local domesticates. Omitted are crops that arrived or became important only later, such as bananas in Africa, corn and beans in the eastern United States, and sweet potato in New Guinea. Cottons are four species of the genus *Gossypium*, each species being native to a particular part of the world; squashes are five species of the genus *Cucurbita*. Note that cereals, pulses, and fiber crops launched agriculture in most areas, but that root and tuber crops and melons were of early importance in only some areas.

thrown in handfuls, resulting in a whole field devoted to a single crop. Once cows, horses, and other large mammals were domesticated, they were hitched to plows, and fields were tilled by animal power. In the New World, however, no animal was ever domesticated that could be hitched to a plow. Instead, fields were always tilled by hand-held sticks or hoes, and seeds were planted individually by hand and not scattered as whole handfuls. Most New World fields thus came to be mixed gardens of many crops planted together, rather than monoculture.

Another major difference among agricultural systems involved the main sources of calories and carbohydrates. As we have seen, these were cereals in many areas. In other areas, though, that role of cereals was taken over or shared by roots and tubers, which were of negligible importance in the ancient Fertile Crescent and China. Manioc (alias cassava) and sweet potato became staples in tropical South America, potato and oca in the Andes, African yams in Africa, and Indo-Pacific yams and taro in Southeast Asia and New Guinea. Tree crops, notably bananas and breadfruit, also furnished carbohydrate-rich staples in Southeast Asia and New Guinea.

THUS, BY ROMAN times, almost all of today's leading crops were being cultivated somewhere in the world. Just as we shall see for domestic animals too (Chapter 9), ancient hunter-gatherers were intimately familiar with local wild plants, and ancient farmers evidently discovered and domesticated almost all of those worth domesticating. Of course, medieval monks did begin to cultivate strawberries and raspberries, and modern plant breeders are still improving ancient crops and have added new minor crops, notably some berries (like blueberries, cranberries, and kiwifruit) and nuts (macadamias, pecans, and cashews). But these few modern additions have remained of modest importance compared with ancient staples like wheat, corn, and rice.

Still, our list of triumphs lacks many wild plants that, despite their value as food, we never succeeded in domesticating. Notable among these failures of ours are oak trees, whose acorns were a staple food of Native Americans in California and the eastern United States as well as a fallback food for European peasants in famine times of crop failure. Acorns are nutritionally valuable, being rich in starch and oil. Like many otherwise edible wild foods, most acorns do contain bitter tannins, but acorn lovers learned to deal with tannins in the same way that they dealt with bitter chemicals in almonds and other wild plants: either by grinding and leaching the acorns to remove the tannins, or by harvesting acorns from the occasional mutant individual oak tree low in tannins.

Why have we failed to domesticate such a prized food source as acorns? Why did we take so long to domesticate strawberries and raspberries? What is it about those plants that kept their domestication beyond the reach of ancient farmers capable of mastering such difficult techniques as grafting?

It turns out that oak trees have three strikes against them. First, their slow growth would exhaust the patience of most farmers. Sown wheat yields a crop within a few months; a planted almond grows into a nut-bearing tree in three or four years; but a planted acorn may not become productive for a decade or more. Second, oak trees evolved to make nuts of a size and taste suitable for squirrels, which we've all seen burying, digging up, and eating acorns. Oaks grow from the occasional acorn that a squirrel forgets to dig up. With billions of squirrels each spreading hundreds of acorns every year to virtually any spot suitable for oak trees to grow, we humans didn't stand a chance of selecting oaks for the acorns that *we* wanted. Those same problems of slow growth and fast squirrels probably also explain why beech and hickory trees, heavily exploited as wild trees for their nuts by Europeans and Native Americans, respectively, were also not domesticated.

Finally, perhaps the most important difference between almonds and acorns is that bitterness is controlled by a single dominant gene in almonds but appears to be controlled by many genes in oaks. If ancient farmers planted almonds or acorns from the occasional nonbitter mutant tree, the laws of genetics dictate that half of the nuts from the resulting tree growing up would also be nonbitter in the case of almonds, but almost all would still be bitter in the case of oaks. That alone would kill the enthusiasm of any would-be acorn farmer who had defeated the squirrels and remained patient.

As for strawberries and raspberries, we had similar trouble competing with thrushes and other berry-loving birds. Yes, the Romans did tend wild strawberries in their gardens. But with billions of European thrushes defecating wild strawberry seeds in every possible place (including Roman gardens), strawberries remained the little berries that thrushes wanted, not the big berries that humans wanted. Only with the recent development of protective nets and greenhouses were we finally able to defeat the thrushes, and to redesign strawberries and raspberries according to our own standards.

WE'VE THUS SEEN that the difference between gigantic supermarket strawberries and tiny wild ones is just one example of the various features distinguishing cultivated plants from their wild ancestors. Those differences arose initially from natural variation among the wild plants themselves. Some of it, such as the variation in berry size or in nut bitterness, would have been readily noticed by ancient farmers. Other variation, such as that in seed dispersal mechanisms or seed dormancy, would have gone unrecognized by humans before the rise of modern botany. But whether or not the selection of wild edible plants by ancient hikers relied on conscious or unconscious criteria, the resulting evolution of wild plants into crops was at first an unconscious process. It followed inevitably from our *selecting* among wild plant individuals, and from competition among plant individuals in gardens favoring individuals different from those favored in the wild.

That's why Darwin, in his great book *On the Origin of Species,* didn't start with an account of natural selection. His first chapter is instead a lengthy account of how our domesticated plants and animals arose through artificial selection by humans. Rather than discussing the Galápagos Island birds that we usually associate with him, Darwin began by discussing—how farmers develop varieties of gooseberries! He wrote, "I have seen great surprise expressed in horticultural works at the wonderful skill of gardeners, in having produced such splendid results from such poor materials; but the art has been simple, and as far as the final result is concerned, has been followed almost unconsciously. It has consisted in always cultivating the best-known variety, sowing its seeds, and, when a slightly better variety chanced to appear, selecting it, and so onwards." Those principles of crop development by artificial selection still serve as our most understandable model of the origin of species by natural selection.

CHAPTER 8

APPLES OR INDIANS

W E HAVE JUST SEEN HOW PEOPLES OF SOME REGIONS began to cultivate wild plant species, a step with momentous unforeseen consequences for their lifestyle and their descendants' place in history. Let us now return to our questions: Why did agriculture never arise independently in some fertile and highly suitable areas, such as California, Europe, temperate Australia, and subequatorial Africa? Why, among the areas where agriculture did arise independently, did it develop much earlier in some than in others?

Two contrasting explanations suggest themselves: problems with the local people, or problems with the locally available wild plants. On the one hand, perhaps almost any well-watered temperate or tropical area of the globe offers enough species of wild plants suitable for domestication. In that case, the explanation for agriculture's failure to develop in some of those areas would lie with cultural characteristics of their peoples. On the other hand, perhaps at least some humans in any large area of the globe would have been receptive to the experimentation that led to domestication. Only the lack of suitable wild plants might then explain why food production did not evolve in some areas.

As we shall see in the next chapter, the corresponding problem for domestication of big wild mammals proves easier to solve, because there are many fewer species of them than of plants. The world holds only about 148 species of large wild mammalian terrestrial herbivores or omnivores, the large mammals that could be considered candidates for domestication. Only a modest number of factors determines whether a mammal is suitable for domestication. It's thus straightforward to review a region's big mammals and to test whether the lack of mammal domestication in some regions was due to the unavailability of suitable wild species, rather than to local peoples.

That approach would be much more difficult to apply to plants because of the sheer number—200,000—of species of wild flowering plants, the plants that dominate vegetation on the land and that have furnished almost all of our crops. We can't possibly hope to examine all the wild plant species of even a circumscribed area like California, and to assess how many of them would have been domesticable. But we shall now see how to get around that problem.

WHEN ONE HEARS that there are so many species of flowering plants, one's first reaction might be as follows: surely, with all those wild plant species on Earth, any area with a sufficiently benign climate must have had more than enough species to provide plenty of candidates for crop development.

But then reflect that the vast majority of wild plants are unsuitable for obvious reasons: they are woody, they produce no edible fruit, and their leaves and roots are also inedible. Of the 200,000 wild plant species, only a few thousand are eaten by humans, and just a few hundred of these have been more or less domesticated. Even of these several hundred crops, most provide minor supplements to our diet and would not by themselves have sufficed to support the rise of civilizations. A mere dozen species account for over 80 percent of the modern world's annual tonnage of all crops. Those dozen blockbusters are the cereals wheat, corn, rice, barley, and sorghum; the pulse soybean; the roots or tubers potato, manioc, and sweet potato; the sugar sources sugarcane and sugar beet; and the fruit banana. Cereal crops alone now account for more than half of the calories consumed by the world's human populations. With so few major crops in the world, all of them domesticated thousands of years ago, it's less surprising that many areas of the world had no wild native plants at all of outstanding potential. Our failure to domesticate even a single major new food plant in modern times suggests that ancient peoples really may have explored virtually all useful wild plants and domesticated all the ones worth domesticating.

Yet some of the world's failures to domesticate wild plants remain hard to explain. The most flagrant cases concern plants that were domesticated in one area but not in another. We can thus be sure that it was indeed possible to develop the wild plant into a useful crop, and we have to ask why that wild species was not domesticated in certain areas.

A typical puzzling example comes from Africa. The important cereal sorghum was domesticated in Africa's Sahel zone, just south of the Sahara. It also occurs as a wild plant as far south as southern Africa, yet neither it nor any other plant was cultivated in southern Africa until the arrival of the whole crop package that Bantu farmers brought from Africa north of the equator 2,000 years ago. Why did the native peoples of southern Africa not domesticate sorghum for themselves?

Equally puzzling is the failure of people to domesticate flax in its wild range in western Europe and North Africa, or einkorn wheat in its wild range in the southern Balkans. Since these two plants were among the first eight crops of the Fertile Crescent, they were presumably among the most readily domesticated of all wild plants. They were adopted for cultivation in those areas of their wild range outside the Fertile Crescent as soon as they arrived with the whole package of food production from the Fertile Crescent. Why, then, had peoples of those outlying areas not already begun to grow them of their own accord?

Similarly, the four earliest domesticated fruits of the Fertile Crescent all had wild ranges stretching far beyond the eastern Mediterranean, where they appear to have been first domesticated: the olive, grape, and fig occurred west to Italy and Spain and Northwest Africa, while the date palm extended to all of North Africa and Arabia. These four were evidently among the easiest to domesticate of all wild fruits. Why did peoples outside the Fertile Crescent fail to domesticate them, and begin to grow them only when they had already been domesticated in the eastern Mediterranean and arrived thence as crops?

Other striking examples involve wild species that were not domesticated in areas where food production never arose spontaneously, even though those wild species had close relatives domesticated elsewhere. For example, the olive *Olea europea* was domesticated in the eastern Mediterranean. There are about 40 other species of olives in tropical and southern

Africa, southern Asia, and eastern Australia, some of them closely related to *Olea europea,* but none of them was ever domesticated. Similarly, while a wild apple species and a wild grape species were domesticated in Eurasia, there are many related wild apple and grape species in North America, some of which have in modern times been hybridized with the crops derived from their wild Eurasian counterparts in order to improve those crops. Why, then, didn't Native Americans domesticate those apparently useful apples and grapes themselves?

One can go on and on with such examples. But there is a fatal flaw in this reasoning: plant domestication is not a matter of hunter-gatherers' domesticating a single plant and otherwise carrying on unchanged with their nomadic lifestyle. Suppose that North American wild apples really would have evolved into a terrific crop if only Indian hunter-gatherers had settled down and cultivated them. But nomadic hunter-gatherers would not throw over their traditional way of life, settle in villages, and start tending apple orchards unless many other domesticable wild plants and animals were available to make a sedentary food-producing existence competitive with a hunting-gathering existence.

How, in short, do we assess the potential of an entire local flora for domestication? For those Native Americans who failed to domesticate North American apples, did the problem really lie with the Indians or with the apples?

In order to answer this question, we shall now compare three regions that lie at opposite extremes among centers of independent domestication. As we have seen, one of them, the Fertile Crescent, was perhaps the earliest center of food production in the world, and the site of origin of several of the modern world's major crops and almost all of its major domesticated animals. The other two regions, New Guinea and the eastern United States, did domesticate local crops, but these crops were very few in variety, only one of them gained worldwide importance, and the resulting food package failed to support extensive development of human technology and political organization as in the Fertile Crescent. In the light of this comparison, we shall ask: Did the flora and environment of the Fertile Crescent have clear advantages over those of New Guinea and the eastern United States?

ONE OF THE central facts of human history is the early importance of the part of Southwest Asia known as the Fertile Crescent (because of the crescent-like shape of its uplands on a map: see Figure 8.1). That area appears to have been the earliest site for a whole string of developments, including cities, writing, empires, and what we term (for better or worse) civilization. All those developments sprang, in turn, from the dense human populations, stored food surpluses, and feeding of nonfarming specialists made possible by the rise of food production in the form of crop cultivation and animal husbandry. Food production was the first of those major innovations to appear in the Fertile Crescent. Hence any attempt to understand the origins of the modern world must come to grips with the question why the Fertile Crescent's domesticated plants and animals gave it such a potent head start.

Fortunately, the Fertile Crescent is by far the most intensively studied and best understood part of the globe as regards the rise of agriculture. For most crops domesticated in or near the Fertile Crescent, the wild plant ancestor has been identified; its close relationship to the crop has been proven by genetic and chromosomal studies; its wild geographic range is known; its changes under domestication have been identified and are often understood at the level of single genes; those changes can be observed in

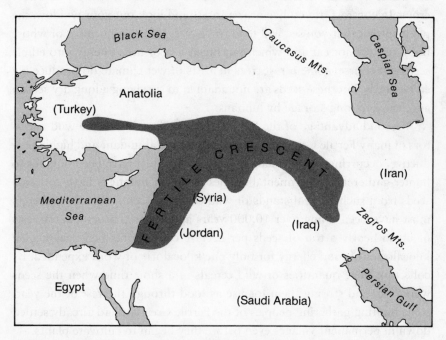

Figure 8.1. The Fertile Crescent, encompassing sites of food production before 7000 B.C.

successive layers of the archaeological record; and the approximate place and time of domestication are known. I don't deny that other areas, notably China, also had advantages as early sites of domestication, but those advantages and the resulting development of crops can be specified in much more detail for the Fertile Crescent.

One advantage of the Fertile Crescent is that it lies within a zone of so-called Mediterranean climate, a climate characterized by mild, wet winters and long, hot, dry summers. That climate selects for plant species able to survive the long dry season and to resume growth rapidly upon the return of the rains. Many Fertile Crescent plants, especially species of cereals and pulses, have adapted in a way that renders them useful to humans: they are annuals, meaning that the plant itself dries up and dies in the dry season.

Within their mere one year of life, annual plants inevitably remain small herbs. Many of them instead put much of their energy into producing big seeds, which remain dormant during the dry season and are then ready to sprout when the rains come. Annual plants therefore waste little energy on making inedible wood or fibrous stems, like the body of trees and bushes. But many of the big seeds, notably those of the annual cereals and pulses, are edible by humans. They constitute 6 of the modern world's 12 major crops. In contrast, if you live near a forest and look out your window, the plant species that you see will tend to be trees and shrubs, most of whose body you cannot eat and which put much less of their energy into edible seeds. Of course, some forest trees in areas of wet climate do produce big edible seeds, but these seeds are not adapted to surviving a long dry season and hence to long storage by humans.

A second advantage of the Fertile Crescent flora is that the wild ancestors of many Fertile Crescent crops were already abundant and highly productive, occurring in large stands whose value must have been obvious to hunter-gatherers. Experimental studies in which botanists have collected seeds from such natural stands of wild cereals, much as hunter-gatherers must have been doing over 10,000 years ago, show that annual harvests of up to nearly a ton of seeds per hectare can be obtained, yielding 50 kilocalories of food energy for only one kilocalorie of work expended. By collecting huge quantities of wild cereals in a short time when the seeds were ripe, and storing them for use as food through the rest of the year, some hunting-gathering peoples of the Fertile Crescent had already settled down in permanent villages even before they began to cultivate plants.

Since Fertile Crescent cereals were so productive in the wild, few additional changes had to be made in them under cultivation. As we discussed in the preceding chapter, the principal changes—the breakdown of the natural systems of seed dispersal and of germination inhibition—evolved automatically and quickly as soon as humans began to cultivate the seeds in fields. The wild ancestors of our wheat and barley crops look so similar to the crops themselves that the identity of the ancestor has never been in doubt. Because of this ease of domestication, big-seeded annuals were the first, or among the first, crops developed not only in the Fertile Crescent but also in China and the Sahel.

Contrast this quick evolution of wheat and barley with the story of corn, the leading cereal crop of the New World. Corn's probable ancestor, a wild plant known as teosinte, looks so different from corn in its seed and flower structures that even its role as ancestor has been hotly debated by botanists for a long time. Teosinte's value as food would not have impressed hunter-gatherers: it was less productive in the wild than wild wheat, it produced much less seed than did the corn eventually developed from it, and it enclosed its seeds in inedible hard coverings. For teosinte to become a useful crop, it had to undergo drastic changes in its reproductive biology, to increase greatly its investment in seeds, and to lose those rock-like coverings of its seeds. Archaeologists are still vigorously debating how many centuries or millennia of crop development in the Americas were required for ancient corn cobs to progress from a tiny size up to the size of a human thumb, but it seems clear that several thousand more years were then required for them to reach modern sizes. That contrast between the immediate virtues of wheat and barley and the difficulties posed by teosinte may have been a significant factor in the differing developments of New World and Eurasian human societies.

A third advantage of the Fertile Crescent flora is that it includes a high percentage of hermaphroditic "selfers"—that is, plants that usually pollinate themselves but that are occasionally cross-pollinated. Recall that most wild plants either are regularly cross-pollinated hermaphrodites or consist of separate male and female individuals that inevitably depend on another individual for pollination. Those facts of reproductive biology vexed early farmers, because, as soon as they had located a productive mutant plant, its offspring would cross-breed with other plant individuals and thereby lose their inherited advantage. As a result, most crops belong to the small percentage of wild plants that either are hermaphrodites usually pollinating themselves or else reproduce without sex by propagating vegetatively (for example, by a root that genetically duplicates the parent plant). Thus, the high percentage of hermaphroditic selfers in the Fertile Crescent flora aided early farmers, because it meant that a high percentage of the wild flora had a reproductive biology convenient for humans.

Selfers were also convenient for early farmers in that they occasionally did become cross-pollinated, thereby generating new varieties among which to select. That occasional cross-pollination occurred not only between individuals of the same species, but also between related species to produce interspecific hybrids. One such hybrid among Fertile Crescent selfers, bread wheat, became the most valuable crop in the modern world.

Of the first eight significant crops to have been domesticated in the Fertile Crescent, all were selfers. Of the three selfer cereals among them—einkorn wheat, emmer wheat, and barley—the wheats offered the additional advantage of a high protein content, 8–14 percent. In contrast, the most important cereal crops of eastern Asia and of the New World—rice and corn, respectively—had a lower protein content that posed significant nutritional problems.

THOSE WERE SOME of the advantages that the Fertile Crescent's flora afforded the first farmers: it included an unusually high percentage of wild plants suitable for domestication. However, the Mediterranean climate zone of the Fertile Crescent extends westward through much of southern Europe and northwestern Africa. There are also zones of similar Mediterranean climates in four other parts of the world: California, Chile, southwestern Australia, and South Africa (Figure 8.2). Yet those other Mediterranean zones not only failed to rival the Fertile Crescent as early sites of food production; they never gave rise to indigenous agriculture at all. What advantage did that particular Mediterranean zone of western Eurasia enjoy?

It turns out that it, and especially its Fertile Crescent portion, possessed at least five advantages over other Mediterranean zones. First, western Eurasia has by far the world's largest zone of Mediterranean climate. As a result, it has a high diversity of wild plant and animal species, higher than in the comparatively tiny Mediterranean zones of southwestern Australia and Chile. Second, among Mediterranean zones, western Eurasia's experiences the greatest climatic variation from season to season and year to year. That variation favored the evolution, among the flora, of an espe-

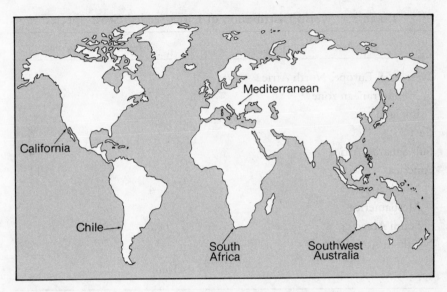

Figure 8.2. The world's zones of Mediterranean climate.

cially high percentage of annual plants. The combination of these two factors—a high diversity of species and a high percentage of annuals—means that western Eurasia's Mediterranean zone is the one with by far the highest diversity of annuals.

The significance of that botanical wealth for humans is illustrated by the geographer Mark Blumler's studies of wild grass distributions. Among the world's thousands of wild grass species, Blumler tabulated the 56 with the largest seeds, the cream of nature's crop: the grass species with seeds at least 10 times heavier than the median grass species (see Table 8.1). Virtually all of them are native to Mediterranean zones or other seasonally dry environments. Furthermore, they are overwhelmingly concentrated in the Fertile Crescent or other parts of western Eurasia's Mediterranean zone, which offered a huge selection to incipient farmers: about 32 of the world's 56 prize wild grasses! Specifically, barley and emmer wheat, the two earliest important crops of the Fertile Crescent, rank respectively 3rd and 13th in seed size among those top 56. In contrast, the Mediterranean zone of Chile offered only two of those species, California and southern Africa just one each, and southwestern Australia none at all. That fact alone goes a long way toward explaining the course of human history.

A third advantage of the Fertile Crescent's Mediterranean zone is that

TABLE 8.1 **World Distribution of Large-Seeded Grass Species**

Area		Number of Species
West Asia, Europe, North Africa		33
Mediterranean zone	32	
England	1	
East Asia		6
Sub-Saharan Africa		4
Americas		11
North America	4	
Mesoamerica	5	
South America	2	
Northern Australia		2
	Total:	56

Table 12.1 of Mark Blumler's Ph.D. dissertation, "Seed Weight and Environment in Mediterranean-type Grasslands in California and Israel" (University of California, Berkeley, 1992), listed the world's 56 heaviest-seeded wild grass species (excluding bamboos) for which data were available. Grain weight in those species ranged from 10 milligrams to over 40 milligrams, about 10 times greater than the median value for all of the world's grass species. Those 56 species make up less than 1 percent of the world's grass species. This table shows that these prize grasses are overwhelmingly concentrated in the Mediterranean zone of western Eurasia.

it provides a wide range of altitudes and topographies within a short distance. Its range of elevations, from the lowest spot on Earth (the Dead Sea) to mountains of 18,000 feet (near Teheran), ensures a corresponding variety of environments, hence a high diversity of the wild plants serving as potential ancestors of crops. Those mountains are in proximity to gentle lowlands with rivers, flood plains, and deserts suitable for irrigation agriculture. In contrast, the Mediterranean zones of southwestern Australia and, to a lesser degree, of South Africa and western Europe offer a narrower range of altitudes, habitats, and topographies.

The range of altitudes in the Fertile Crescent meant staggered harvest seasons: plants at higher elevations produced seeds somewhat later than plants at lower elevations. As a result, hunter-gatherers could move up a mountainside harvesting grain seeds as they matured, instead of being overwhelmed by a concentrated harvest season at a single altitude, where all grains matured simultaneously. When cultivation began, it was a simple matter for the first farmers to take the seeds of wild cereals growing on hillsides and dependent on unpredictable rains, and to plant those seeds in the damp valley bottoms, where they would grow reliably and be less dependent on rain.

The Fertile Crescent's biological diversity over small distances contributed to a fourth advantage—its wealth in ancestors not only of valuable crops but also of domesticated big mammals. As we shall see, there were few or no wild mammal species suitable for domestication in the other Mediterranean zones of California, Chile, southwestern Australia, and South Africa. In contrast, four species of big mammals—the goat, sheep, pig, and cow—were domesticated very early in the Fertile Crescent, possibly earlier than any other animal except the dog anywhere else in the world. Those species remain today four of the world's five most important domesticated mammals (Chapter 9). But their wild ancestors were commonest in slightly different parts of the Fertile Crescent, with the result that the four species were domesticated in different places: sheep possibly in the central part, goats either in the eastern part at higher elevations (the Zagros Mountains of Iran) or in the southwestern part (the Levant), pigs in the north-central part, and cows in the western part, including Anatolia. Nevertheless, even though the areas of abundance of these four wild progenitors thus differed, all four lived in sufficiently close proximity that they were readily transferred after domestication from one part of the Fertile Crescent to another, and the whole region ended up with all four species.

Agriculture was launched in the Fertile Crescent by the early domestication of eight crops, termed "founder crops" (because they founded agriculture in the region and possibly in the world). Those eight founders were the cereals emmer wheat, einkorn wheat, and barley; the pulses lentil, pea, chickpea, and bitter vetch; and the fiber crop flax. Of these eight, only two, flax and barley, range in the wild at all widely outside the Fertile Crescent and Anatolia. Two of the founders had very small ranges in the wild, chickpea being confined to southeastern Turkey and emmer wheat to the Fertile Crescent itself. Thus, agriculture could arise in the Fertile Crescent from domestication of locally available wild plants, without having to wait for the arrival of crops derived from wild plants domesticated elsewhere. Conversely, two of the eight founder crops could not have been domesticated anywhere in the world except in the Fertile Crescent, since they did not occur wild elsewhere.

Thanks to this availability of suitable wild mammals and plants, early peoples of the Fertile Crescent could quickly assemble a potent and balanced biological package for intensive food production. That package comprised three cereals, as the main carbohydrate sources; four pulses, with 20–25 percent protein, and four domestic animals, as the main protein sources, supplemented by the generous protein content of wheat; and flax as a source of fiber and oil (termed linseed oil: flax seeds are about 40 percent oil). Eventually, thousands of years after the beginnings of animal domestication and food production, the animals also began to be used for milk, wool, plowing, and transport. Thus, the crops and animals of the Fertile Crescent's first farmers came to meet humanity's basic economic needs: carbohydrate, protein, fat, clothing, traction, and transport.

A final advantage of early food production in the Fertile Crescent is that it may have faced less competition from the hunter-gatherer lifestyle than that in some other areas, including the western Mediterranean. Southwest Asia has few large rivers and only a short coastline, providing relatively meager aquatic resources (in the form of river and coastal fish and shellfish). One of the important mammal species hunted for meat, the gazelle, originally lived in huge herds but was overexploited by the growing human population and reduced to low numbers. Thus, the food production package quickly became superior to the hunter-gatherer package. Sedentary villages based on cereals were already in existence before the rise of food production and predisposed those hunter-gatherers to agriculture and herding. In the Fertile Crescent the transition from hunting-gathering to food production took place relatively fast: as late as 9000 B.C. people still had no crops and domestic animals and were entirely dependent on wild foods, but by 6000 B.C. some societies were almost completely dependent on crops and domestic animals.

The situation in Mesoamerica contrasts strongly: that area provided only two domesticable animals (the turkey and the dog), whose meat yield was far lower than that of cows, sheep, goats, and pigs; and corn, Mesoamerica's staple grain, was, as I've already explained, difficult to domesticate and perhaps slow to develop. As a result, domestication may not have begun in Mesoamerica until around 3500 B.C. (the date remains very uncertain); those first developments were undertaken by people who were still nomadic hunter-gatherers; and settled villages did not arise there until around 1500 B.C.

IN ALL THIS discussion of the Fertile Crescent's advantages for the early rise of food production, we have not had to invoke any supposed advantages of Fertile Crescent peoples themselves. Indeed, I am unaware of anyone's even seriously suggesting any supposed distinctive biological features of the region's peoples that might have contributed to the potency of its food production package. Instead, we have seen that the many distinctive features of the Fertile Crescent's climate, environment, wild plants, and animals together provide a convincing explanation.

Since the food production packages arising indigenously in New Guinea and in the eastern United States were considerably less potent, might the explanation there lie with the peoples of those areas? Before turning to those regions, however, we must consider two related questions arising in regard to any area of the world where food production never developed independently or else resulted in a less potent package. First, do hunter-gatherers and incipient farmers really know well all locally available wild species and their uses, or might they have overlooked potential ancestors of valuable crops? Second, if they do know their local plants and animals, do they exploit that knowledge to domesticate the most useful available species, or do cultural factors keep them from doing so?

As regards the first question, an entire field of science, termed ethnobiology, studies peoples' knowledge of the wild plants and animals in their environment. Such studies have concentrated especially on the world's few surviving hunting-gathering peoples, and on farming peoples who still depend heavily on wild foods and natural products. The studies generally show that such peoples are walking encyclopedias of natural history, with individual names (in their local language) for as many as a thousand or more plant and animal species, and with detailed knowledge of those species' biological characteristics, distribution, and potential uses. As people become increasingly dependent on domesticated plants and animals, this traditional knowledge gradually loses its value and becomes lost, until one arrives at modern supermarket shoppers who could not distinguish a wild grass from a wild pulse.

Here's a typical example. For the last 33 years, while conducting biological exploration in New Guinea, I have been spending my field time there constantly in the company of New Guineans who still use wild plants and animals extensively. One day, when my companions of the Foré tribe and I were starving in the jungle because another tribe was blocking our return to our supply base, a Foré man returned to camp with a large rucksack full of mushrooms he had found, and started to roast them. Dinner at last! But then I had an unsettling thought: what if the mushrooms were poisonous?

I patiently explained to my Foré companions that I had read about some mushrooms' being poisonous, that I had heard of even expert American mushroom collectors' dying because of the difficulty of distinguishing safe from dangerous mushrooms, and that although we were all hungry, it just wasn't worth the risk. At that point my companions got angry and told me to shut up and listen while they explained some things to me. After I had been quizzing them for years about names of hundreds of trees and birds, how could I insult them by assuming they didn't have names for different mushrooms? Only Americans could be so stupid as to confuse poisonous mushrooms with safe ones. They went on to lecture me about 29 types of edible mushroom species, each species' name in the Foré language, and where in the forest one should look for it. This one, the *tánti*, grew on trees, and it was delicious and perfectly edible.

Whenever I have taken New Guineans with me to other parts of their island, they regularly talk about local plants and animals with other New Guineans whom they meet, and they gather potentially useful plants and bring them back to their home villages to try planting them. My experiences with New Guineans are paralleled by those of ethnobiologists studying traditional peoples elsewhere. However, all such peoples either practice at least some food production or are the partly acculturated last remnants of the world's former hunter-gatherer societies. Knowledge of wild species was presumably even more detailed before the rise of food production, when everyone on Earth still depended entirely on wild species for food. The first farmers were heirs to that knowledge, accumulated through tens of thousands of years of nature observation by biologically modern humans living in intimate dependence on the natural world. It therefore seems extremely unlikely that wild species of potential value would have escaped the notice of the first farmers.

The other, related question is whether ancient hunter-gatherers and farmers similarly put their ethnobiological knowledge to good use in selecting wild plants to gather and eventually to cultivate. One test comes from an archaeological site at the edge of the Euphrates Valley in Syria, called Tell Abu Hureyra. Between 10,000 and 9000 B.C. the people living there may already have been residing year-round in villages, but they were still hunter-gatherers; crop cultivation began only in the succeeding millennium. The archaeologists Gordon Hillman, Susan Colledge, and David Harris retrieved large quantities of charred plant remains from the site, probably representing discarded garbage of wild plants gathered elsewhere and brought to the site by its residents. The scientists analyzed over 700 samples, each containing an average of over 500 identifiable seeds belonging to over 70 plant species. It turned out that the villagers were collecting a prodigious variety (157 species!) of plants identified by their charred seeds, not to mention other plants that cannot now be identified.

Were those naive villagers collecting every type of seed plant that they found, bringing it home, poisoning themselves on most of the species, and nourishing themselves from only a few species? No, they were not so silly. While 157 species sounds like indiscriminate collecting, many more species growing wild in the vicinity were absent from the charred remains. The 157 selected species fall into three categories. Many of them have seeds that are nonpoisonous and immediately edible. Others, such as pulses and members of the mustard family, have toxic seeds, but the toxins are easily removed, leaving the seeds edible. A few seeds belong to species traditionally used as sources of dyes or medicine. The many wild species not represented among the 157 selected are ones that would have been useless or harmful to people, including all of the most toxic weed species in the environment.

Thus, the hunter-gatherers of Tell Abu Hureyra were not wasting time and endangering themselves by collecting wild plants indiscriminately. Instead, they evidently knew the local wild plants as intimately as do modern New Guineans, and they used that knowledge to select and bring home only the most useful available seed plants. But those gathered seeds would have constituted the material for the unconscious first steps of plant domestication.

My other example of how ancient peoples apparently used their ethnobiological knowledge to good effect comes from the Jordan Valley in the ninth millennium B.C., the period of the earliest crop cultivation there. The valley's first domesticated cereals were barley and emmer wheat, which are still among the world's most productive crops today. But, as at Tell Abu Hureyra, hundreds of other seed-bearing wild plant species must have grown in the vicinity, and a hundred or more of them would have been edible and gathered before the rise of plant domestication. What was it about barley and emmer wheat that caused them to be the first crops? Were those first Jordan Valley farmers botanical ignoramuses who didn't know what they were doing? Or were barley and emmer wheat actually the best of the local wild cereals that they could have selected?

Two Israeli scientists, Ofer Bar-Yosef and Mordechai Kislev, tackled this question by examining the wild grass species still growing wild in the valley today. Leaving aside species with small or unpalatable seeds, they picked out 23 of the most palatable and largest-seeded wild grasses. Not surprisingly, barley and emmer wheat were on that list.

But it wasn't true that the 21 other candidates would have been equally useful. Among those 23, barley and emmer wheat proved to be the best by many criteria. Emmer wheat has the biggest seeds and barley the second biggest. In the wild, barley is one of the 4 most abundant of the 23 species, while emmer wheat is of medium abundance. Barley has the further advantage that its genetics and morphology permit it to evolve quickly the useful changes in seed dispersal and germination inhibition that we discussed in the preceding chapter. Emmer wheat, however, has compensating virtues: it can be gathered more efficiently than barley, and it is unusual among cereals in that its seeds do not adhere to husks. As for the other 21 species, their drawbacks include smaller seeds, in many cases lower abundance, and in some cases their being perennial rather than annual plants, with the consequence that they would have evolved only slowly under domestication.

Thus, the first farmers in the Jordan Valley selected the 2 very best of the 23 best wild grass species available to them. Of course, the evolutionary changes (following cultivation) in seed dispersal and germination inhibition would have been unforeseen consequences of what those first farmers were doing. But their initial selection of barley and emmer wheat rather than other cereals to collect, bring home, and cultivate would have been conscious and based on the easily detected criteria of seed size, palatability, and abundance.

This example from the Jordan Valley, like that from Tell Abu Hureyra, illustrates that the first farmers used their detailed knowledge of local species to their own benefit. Knowing far more about local plants than all but a handful of modern professional botanists, they would hardly have failed to cultivate any useful wild plant species that was comparably suitable for domestication.

WE CAN NOW examine what local farmers, in two parts of the world (New Guinea and the eastern United States) with indigenous but apparently deficient food production systems compared to that of the Fertile Crescent, actually did when more-productive crops arrived from elsewhere. If it turned out that such crops did not become adopted for cultural or other reasons, we would be left with a nagging doubt. Despite all our reasoning so far, we would still have to suspect that the local wild flora harbored some ancestor of a potential valuable crop that local farmers failed to exploit because of similar cultural factors. These two examples will also demonstrate in detail a fact critical to history: that indigenous crops from different parts of the globe were not equally productive.

New Guinea, the largest island in the world after Greenland, lies just north of Australia and near the equator. Because of its tropical location and great diversity in topography and habitats, New Guinea is rich in both plant and animal species, though less so than continental tropical areas because it is an island. People have been living in New Guinea for at least 40,000 years—much longer than in the Americas, and slightly longer than anatomically modern peoples have been living in western Europe. Thus, New Guineans have had ample opportunity to get to know their local flora and fauna. Were they motivated to apply this knowledge to developing food production?

I mentioned already that the adoption of food production involved a *competition* between the food producing and the hunting-gathering life-styles. Hunting-gathering is not so rewarding in New Guinea as to remove the motivation to develop food production. In particular, modern New Guinea hunters suffer from the crippling disadvantage of a dearth of wild game: there is no native land animal larger than a 100-pound flightless bird (the cassowary) and a 50-pound kangaroo. Lowland New Guineans on the coast do obtain much fish and shellfish, and some lowlanders in the interior still live today as hunter-gatherers, subsisting especially on wild sago palms. But no peoples still live as hunter-gatherers in the New Guinea highlands; all modern highlanders are instead farmers who use wild foods only to supplement their diets. When highlanders go into the forest on hunting trips, they take along garden-grown vegetables to feed themselves. If they have the misfortune to run out of those provisions, even they starve to death despite their detailed knowledge of locally available wild foods. Since the hunting-gathering lifestyle is thus nonviable in much of modern New Guinea, it comes as no surprise that all New Guinea highlanders and most lowlanders today are settled farmers with sophisticated systems of food production. Extensive, formerly forested areas of the highlands were converted by traditional New Guinea farmers to fenced, drained, inten-sively managed field systems supporting dense human populations.

Archaeological evidence shows that the origins of New Guinea agriculture are ancient, dating to around 7000 B.C. At those early dates all the landmasses surrounding New Guinea were still occupied exclusively by hunter-gatherers, so this ancient agriculture must have developed independently in New Guinea. While unequivocal remains of crops have not been recovered from those early fields, they are likely to have included some of the same crops that were being grown in New Guinea at the time of European colonization and that are now known to have been domesticated locally from wild New Guinea ancestors. Foremost among these local domesticates is the modern world's leading crop, sugarcane, of which the annual tonnage produced today nearly equals that of the number two and number three crops combined (wheat and corn). Other crops of undoubted New Guinea origin are a group of bananas known as *Australimusa* bananas, the nut tree *Canarium indicum,* and giant swamp taro, as well as various edible grass stems, roots, and green vegetables. The breadfruit tree and the root crops yams and (ordinary) taro may also be New Guinean domesticates, although that conclusion remains uncertain because their wild ancestors are not confined to New Guinea but are distributed from New Guinea to Southeast Asia. At present we lack evidence that could resolve the question whether they were domesticated in Southeast Asia, as traditionally assumed, or independently or even only in New Guinea.

However, it turns out that New Guinea's biota suffered from three severe limitations. First, no cereal crops were domesticated in New Guinea, whereas several vitally important ones were domesticated in the Fertile Crescent, Sahel, and China. In its emphasis instead on root and tree crops, New Guinea carries to an extreme a trend seen in agricultural systems in other wet tropical areas (the Amazon, tropical West Africa, and Southeast Asia), whose farmers also emphasized root crops but did manage to come up with at least two cereals (Asian rice and a giant-seeded Asian cereal called Job's tears). A likely reason for the failure of cereal agriculture to arise in New Guinea is a glaring deficiency of the wild starting material: not one of the world's 56 largest-seeded wild grasses is native there.

Second, the New Guinea fauna included no domesticable large mammal species whatsoever. The sole domestic animals of modern New Guinea, the pig and chicken and dog, arrived from Southeast Asia by way of Indonesia within the last several thousand years. As a result, while New Guinea lowlanders obtain protein from the fish they catch, New Guinea highland farmer populations suffer from severe protein limitation, because the staple crops that provide most of their calories (taro and sweet potato) are low in protein. Taro, for example, consists of barely 1 percent protein, much worse than even white rice, and far below the levels of the Fertile Crescent's wheats and pulses (8–14 percent and 20–25 percent protein, respectively).

Children in the New Guinea highlands have the swollen bellies characteristic of a high-bulk but protein-deficient diet. New Guineans old and young routinely eat mice, spiders, frogs, and other small animals that peoples elsewhere with access to large domestic mammals or large wild game species do not bother to eat. Protein starvation is probably also the ultimate reason why cannibalism was widespread in traditional New Guinea highland societies.

Finally, in former times New Guinea's available root crops were limiting for calories as well as for protein, because they do not grow well at the high elevations where many New Guineans live today. Many centuries ago, however, a new root crop of ultimately South American origin, the sweet potato, reached New Guinea, probably by way of the Philippines, where it had been introduced by Spaniards. Compared with taro and other presumably older New Guinea root crops, the sweet potato can be grown up to higher elevations, grows more quickly, and gives higher yields per acre cultivated and per hour of labor. The result of the sweet potato's arrival was a highland population explosion. That is, even though people had been farming in the New Guinea highlands for many thousands of years before sweet potatoes were introduced, the available local crops had limited them in the population densities they could attain, and in the elevations they could occupy.

In short, New Guinea offers an instructive contrast to the Fertile Crescent. Like hunter-gatherers of the Fertile Crescent, those of New Guinea did evolve food production independently. However, their indigenous food production was restricted by the local absence of domesticable cereals, pulses, and animals, by the resulting protein deficiency in the highlands, and by limitations of the locally available root crops at high elevations. Yet New Guineans themselves know as much about the wild plants and animals available to them as any peoples on Earth today. They can be expected to have discovered and tested any wild plant species worth domesticating. They are perfectly capable of recognizing useful additions to their crop larder, as is shown by their exuberant adoption of the sweet potato when it arrived. That same lesson is being driven home again in New Guinea today, as those tribes with preferential access to introduced new crops and livestock (or with the cultural willingness to adopt them) expand at the expense of tribes without that access or willingness. Thus, the limits on indigenous food production in New Guinea had nothing to do with New Guinea peoples, and everything with the New Guinea biota and environment.

OUR OTHER EXAMPLE of indigenous agriculture apparently constrained by the local flora comes from the eastern United States. Like New Guinea, that area supported independent domestication of local wild plants. However, early developments are much better understood for the eastern United States than for New Guinea: the crops grown by the earliest farmers have been identified, and the dates and crop sequences of local domestication are known. Well before other crops began to arrive from elsewhere, Native Americans settled in eastern U.S. river valleys and developed intensified food production based on local crops. Hence they were in a position to take advantage of the most promising wild plants. Which ones did they actually cultivate, and how did the resulting local crop package compare with the Fertile Crescent's founder package?

It turns out that the eastern U.S. founder crops were four plants domesticated in the period 2500–1500 B.C., a full 6,000 years after wheat and barley domestication in the Fertile Crescent. A local species of squash provided small containers, as well as yielding edible seeds. The remaining three founders were grown solely for their edible seeds (sunflower, a daisy relative called sumpweed, and a distant relative of spinach called goosefoot).

But four seed crops and a container fall far short of a complete food production package. For 2,000 years those founder crops served only as minor dietary supplements while eastern U.S. Native Americans continued to depend mainly on wild foods, especially wild mammals and waterbirds, fish, shellfish, and nuts. Farming did not supply a major part of their diet until the period 500–200 B.C., after three more seed crops (knotweed, maygrass, and little barley) had been brought into cultivation.

A modern nutritionist would have applauded those seven eastern U.S.

crops. All of them were high in protein—17–32 percent, compared with 8–14 percent for wheat, 9 percent for corn, and even lower for barley and white rice. Two of them, sunflower and sumpweed, were also high in oil (45–47 percent). Sumpweed, in particular, would have been a nutritionist's ultimate dream, being 32 percent protein and 45 percent oil. Why aren't we still eating those dream foods today?

Alas, despite their nutritional advantage, most of these eastern U.S. crops suffered from serious disadvantages in other respects. Goosefoot, knotweed, little barley, and maygrass had tiny seeds, with volumes only one-tenth that of wheat and barley seeds. Worse yet, sumpweed is a wind-pollinated relative of ragweed, the notorious hayfever-causing plant. Like ragweed's, sumpweed's pollen can cause hayfever where the plant occurs in abundant stands. If that doesn't kill your enthusiasm for becoming a sumpweed farmer, be aware that it has a strong odor objectionable to some people and that handling it can cause skin irritation.

Mexican crops finally began to reach the eastern United States by trade routes after A.D. 1. Corn arrived around A.D. 200, but its role remained very minor for many centuries. Finally, around A.D. 900 a new variety of corn adapted to North America's short summers appeared, and the arrival of beans around A.D. 1100 completed Mexico's crop trinity of corn, beans, and squash. Eastern U.S. farming became greatly intensified, and densely populated chiefdoms developed along the Mississippi River and its tributaries. In some areas the original local domesticates were retained along-side the far more productive Mexican trinity, but in other areas the trinity replaced them completely. No European ever saw sumpweed growing in Indian gardens, because it had disappeared as a crop by the time that European colonization of the Americas began, in A.D. 1492. Among all those ancient eastern U.S. crop specialties, only two (sunflower and eastern squash) have been able to compete with crops domesticated elsewhere and are still grown today. Our modern acorn squashes and summer squashes are derived from those American squashes domesticated thousands of years ago.

Thus, like the case of New Guinea, that of the eastern United States is instructive. A priori, the region might have seemed a likely one to support productive indigenous agriculture. It has rich soils, reliable moderate rainfall, and a suitable climate that sustains bountiful agriculture today. The flora is a species-rich one that includes productive wild nut trees (oak and hickory). Local Native Americans did develop an agriculture based on local domesticates, did thereby support themselves in villages, and even developed a cultural florescence (the Hopewell culture centered on what is today Ohio) around 200 B.C.–A.D. 400. They were thus in a position for several thousand years to exploit as potential crops the most useful available wild plants, whatever those should be.

Nevertheless, the Hopewell florescence sprang up nearly 9,000 years after the rise of village living in the Fertile Crescent. Still, it was not until after A.D. 900 that the assembly of the Mexican crop trinity triggered a larger population boom, the so-called Mississippian florescence, which produced the largest towns and most complex societies achieved by Native Americans north of Mexico. But that boom came much too late to prepare Native Americans of the United States for the impending disaster of European colonization. Food production based on eastern U.S. crops alone had been insufficient to trigger the boom, for reasons that are easy to specify. The area's available wild cereals were not nearly as useful as wheat and barley. Native Americans of the eastern United States domesticated no locally available wild pulse, no fiber crop, no fruit or nut tree. They had no domesticated animals at all except for dogs, which were probably domesticated elsewhere in the Americas.

It's also clear that Native Americans of the eastern United States were not overlooking potential major crops among the wild species around them. Even 20th-century plant breeders, armed with all the power of modern science, have had little success in exploiting North American wild plants. Yes, we have now domesticated pecans as a nut tree and blueberries as a fruit, and we have improved some Eurasian fruit crops (apples, plums, grapes, raspberries, blackberries, strawberries) by hybridizing them with North American wild relatives. However, those few successes have changed our food habits far less than Mexican corn changed food habits of Native Americans in the eastern United States after A.D. 900.

The farmers most knowledgeable about eastern U.S. domesticates, the region's Native Americans themselves, passed judgment on them by discarding or deemphasizing them when the Mexican trinity arrived. That outcome also demonstrates that Native Americans were not constrained by cultural conservativism and were quite able to appreciate a good plant when they saw it. Thus, as in New Guinea, the limitations on indigenous food production in the eastern United States were not due to Native American peoples themselves, but instead depended entirely on the American biota and environment.

WE HAVE NOW considered examples of three contrasting areas, in all of which food production did arise indigenously. The Fertile Crescent lies at one extreme; New Guinea and the eastern United States lie at the opposite extreme. Peoples of the Fertile Crescent domesticated local plants much earlier. They domesticated far more species, domesticated far more productive or valuable species, domesticated a much wider range of types of crops, developed intensified food production and dense human populations more rapidly, and as a result entered the modern world with more advanced technology, more complex political organization, and more epidemic diseases with which to infect other peoples.

We found that these differences between the Fertile Crescent, New Guinea, and the eastern United States followed straightforwardly from the differing suites of wild plant and animal species available for domestication, not from limitations of the peoples themselves. When more-productive crops arrived from elsewhere (the sweet potato in New Guinea, the Mexican trinity in the eastern United States), local peoples promptly took advantage of them, intensified food production, and increased greatly in population. By extension, I suggest that areas of the globe where food production never developed indigenously at all—California, Australia, the Argentine pampas, western Europe, and so on—may have offered even less in the way of wild plants and animals suitable for domestication than did New Guinea and the eastern United States, where at least a limited food production did arise. Indeed, Mark Blumler's worldwide survey of locally available large-seeded wild grasses mentioned in this chapter, and the worldwide survey of locally available big mammals to be presented in the next chapter, agree in showing that all those areas of nonexistent or limited indigenous food production were deficient in wild ancestors of domesticable livestock and cereals.

Recall that the rise of food production involved a competition between food production and hunting-gathering. One might therefore wonder whether all these cases of slow or nonexistent rise of food production might instead have been due to an exceptional local richness of resources to be hunted and gathered, rather than to an exceptional availability of species suitable for domestication. In fact, most areas where indigenous food production arose late or not at all offered exceptionally poor rather than rich resources to hunter-gatherers, because most large mammals of Australia and the Americas (but not of Eurasia and Africa) had become extinct toward the end of the Ice Ages. Food production would have faced even less competition from hunting-gathering in these areas than it did in the Fertile Crescent. Hence these local failures or limitations of food production cannot be attributed to competition from bountiful hunting opportunities.

LEST THESE CONCLUSIONS be misinterpreted, we should end this chapter with caveats against exaggerating two points: peoples' readiness to accept better crops and livestock, and the constraints imposed by locally available wild plants and animals. Neither that readiness nor those constraints are absolute.

We've already discussed many examples of local peoples' adopting more-productive crops domesticated elsewhere. Our broad conclusion is that people can recognize useful plants, would therefore have probably recognized better local ones suitable for domestication if any had existed, and aren't barred from doing so by cultural conservatism or taboos. *But* a big qualifier must be added to this sentence: "in the long run and over large areas." Anyone knowledgeable about human societies can cite innumerable examples of societies that refused crops, livestock, and other innovations that would have been productive.

Naturally, I don't subscribe to the obvious fallacy that every society promptly adopts every innovation that would be useful for it. The fact is that, over entire continents and other large areas containing hundreds of competing societies, some societies will be more open to innovation, and some will be more resistant. The ones that do adopt new crops, livestock, or technology may thereby be enabled to nourish themselves better and to outbreed, displace, conquer, or kill off societies resisting innovation. That's an important phenomenon whose manifestations extend far beyond the adoption of new crops, and to which we shall return in Chapter 13.

Our other caveat concerns the limits that locally available wild species set on the rise of food production. I'm not saying that food production could never, in any amount of time, have arisen in all those areas where it actually had not arisen indigenously by modern times. Europeans today who note that Aboriginal Australians entered the modern world as Stone Age hunter-gatherers often assume that the Aborigines would have gone on that way forever.

To appreciate the fallacy, consider a visitor from Outer Space who dropped in on Earth in the year 3000 B.C. The spaceling would have observed no food production in the eastern United States, because food production did not begin there until around 2500 B.C. Had the visitor of 3000 B.C. drawn the conclusion that limitations posed by the wild plants and animals of the eastern United States foreclosed food production there forever, events of the subsequent millennium would have proved the visitor wrong. Even a visitor to the Fertile Crescent in 9500 B.C. rather than in 8500 B.C. could have been misled into supposing the Fertile Crescent permanently unsuitable for food production.

That is, my thesis is not that California, Australia, western Europe, and all the other areas without indigenous food production were devoid of domesticable species and would have continued to be occupied just by hunter-gatherers indefinitely if foreign domesticates or peoples had not arrived. Instead, I note that regions differed greatly in their available pool of domesticable species, that they varied correspondingly in the date when local food production arose, and that food production had not yet arisen independently in some fertile regions as of modern times.

Australia, supposedly the most "backward" continent, illustrates this point well. In southeastern Australia, the well-watered part of the continent most suitable for food production, Aboriginal societies in recent millennia appear to have been evolving on a trajectory that would eventually have led to indigenous food production. They had already built winter villages. They had begun to manage their environment intensively for fish production by building fish traps, nets, and even long canals. Had Europeans not colonized Australia in 1788 and aborted that independent trajectory, Aboriginal Australians might within a few thousand years have become food producers, tending ponds of domesticated fish and growing domesticated Australian yams and small-seeded grasses.

In that light, we can now answer the question implicit in the title of this chapter. I asked whether the reason for the failure of North American Indians to domesticate North American apples lay with the Indians or with the apples.

I'm not thereby implying that apples could never have been domesticated in North America. Recall that apples were historically among the most difficult fruit trees to cultivate and among the last major ones to be domesticated in Eurasia, because their propagation requires the difficult technique of grafting. There is no evidence for large-scale cultivation of apples even in the Fertile Crescent and in Europe until classical Greek times, 8,000 years after the rise of Eurasian food production began. If Native Americans had proceeded at the same rate in inventing or acquiring grafting techniques, they too would eventually have domesticated apples—around the year A.D. 5500, some 8,000 years after the rise of domestication in North America around 2500 B.C.

Thus, the reason for the failure of Native Americans to domesticate North American apples by the time Europeans arrived lay neither with the people nor with the apples. As far as biological prerequisites for apple domestication were concerned, North American Indian farmers were like Eurasian farmers, and North American wild apples were like Eurasian wild apples. Indeed, some of the supermarket apple varieties now being munched by readers of this chapter have been developed recently by crossing Eurasian apples with wild North American apples. Instead, the reason Native Americans did not domesticate apples lay with the entire suite of wild plant and animal species available to Native Americans. That suite's modest potential for domestication was responsible for the late start of food production in North America.

CHAPTER 9

ZEBRAS, UNHAPPY MARRIAGES, AND THE *ANNA KARENINA* PRINCIPLE

DOMESTICABLE ANIMALS ARE ALL ALIKE; EVERY UNDOmesticable animal is undomesticable in its own way.

If you think you've already read something like that before, you're right. Just make a few changes, and you have the famous first sentence of Tolstoy's great novel *Anna Karenina*: "Happy families are all alike; every unhappy family is unhappy in its own way." By that sentence, Tolstoy meant that, in order to be happy, a marriage must succeed in many different respects: sexual attraction, agreement about money, child discipline, religion, in-laws, and other vital issues. Failure in any one of those essential respects can doom a marriage even if it has all the other ingredients needed for happiness.

This principle can be extended to understanding much else about life besides marriage. We tend to seek easy, single-factor explanations of success. For most important things, though, success actually requires avoiding many separate possible causes of failure. The *Anna Karenina* principle explains a feature of animal domestication that had heavy consequences for human history—namely, that so many seemingly suitable big wild mammal species, such as zebras and peccaries, have never been domesticated and that the successful domesticates were almost exclusively Eurasian. Having in the preceding two chapters discussed why so many wild plant species seemingly suitable for domestication were never domesticated, we shall now tackle the corresponding question for domestic mammals. Our former question about apples or Indians becomes a question of zebras or Africans.

IN CHAPTER 4 we reminded ourselves of the many ways in which big domestic mammals were crucial to those human societies possessing them. Most notably, they provided meat, milk products, fertilizer, land transport, leather, military assault vehicles, plow traction, and wool, as well as germs that killed previously unexposed peoples.

In addition, of course, small domestic mammals and domestic birds and insects have also been useful to humans. Many birds were domesticated for meat, eggs, and feathers: the chicken in China, various duck and goose species in parts of Eurasia, turkeys in Mesoamerica, guinea fowl in Africa, and the Muscovy duck in South America. Wolves were domesticated in Eurasia and North America to become our dogs used as hunting companions, sentinels, pets, and, in some societies, food. Rodents and other small mammals domesticated for food included the rabbit in Europe, the guinea pig in the Andes, a giant rat in West Africa, and possibly a rodent called the hutia on Caribbean islands. Ferrets were domesticated in Europe to hunt rabbits, and cats were domesticated in North Africa and Southwest Asia to hunt rodent pests. Small mammals domesticated as recently as the 19th and 20th centuries include foxes, mink, and chinchillas grown for fur and hamsters kept as pets. Even some insects have been domesticated, notably Eurasia's honeybee and China's silkworm moth, kept for honey and silk, respectively.

Many of these small animals thus yielded food, clothing, or warmth. But none of them pulled plows or wagons, none bore riders, none except dogs pulled sleds or became war machines, and none of them have been as important for food as have big domestic mammals. Hence the rest of this chapter will confine itself to the big mammals.

THE IMPORTANCE OF domesticated mammals rests on surprisingly few species of big terrestrial herbivores. (Only terrestrial mammals have been domesticated, for the obvious reason that aquatic mammals were difficult to maintain and breed until the development of modern Sea World facilities.) If one defines "big" as "weighing over 100 pounds," then only 14 such species were domesticated before the twentieth century (see Table 9.1 for a list). Of those Ancient Fourteen, 9 (the "Minor Nine" of Table 9.1) became important livestock for people in only limited areas of the globe: the Arabian camel, Bactrian camel, llama / alpaca (distinct breeds of the same ancestral species), donkey, reindeer, water buffalo, yak, banteng, and gaur. Only 5 species became widespread and important around the world. Those Major Five of mammal domestication are the cow, sheep, goat, pig, and horse.

This list may at first seem to have glaring omissions. What about the African elephants with which Hannibal's armies crossed the Alps? What about the Asian elephants still used as work animals in Southeast Asia today? No, I didn't forget them, and that raises an important distinction. Elephants have been tamed, but never domesticated. Hannibal's elephants were, and Asian work elephants are, just wild elephants that were captured and tamed; they were not bred in captivity. In contrast, a domesticated animal is defined as an animal selectively bred in captivity and thereby modified from its wild ancestors, for use by humans who control the animal's breeding and food supply.

That is, domestication involves wild animals' being transformed into something more useful to humans. Truly domesticated animals differ in various ways from their wild ancestors. These differences result from two processes: human selection of those individual animals more useful to humans than other individuals of the same species, and automatic evolutionary responses of animals to the altered forces of natural selection operating in human environments as compared with wild environments. We already saw in Chapter 7 that all of these statements also apply to plant domestication.

The ways in which domesticated animals have diverged from their wild ancestors include the following. Many species changed in size: cows, pigs, and sheep became smaller under domestication, while guinea pigs became larger. Sheep and alpacas were selected for retention of wool and reduction or loss of hair, while cows have been selected for high milk yields. Several species of domestic animals have smaller brains and less developed sense organs than their wild ancestors, because they no longer need the bigger brains and more developed sense organs on which their ancestors depended to escape from wild predators.

To appreciate the changes that developed under domestication, just

TABLE 9.1 **The Ancient Fourteen Species of Big Herbivorous Domestic Mammals**

The Major Five

1. *Sheep.* Wild ancestor: the Asiatic mouflon sheep of West and Central Asia. Now worldwide.

2. *Goat.* Wild ancestor: the bezoar goat of West Asia. Now worldwide.

3. *Cow, alias ox or cattle.* Wild ancestor: the now extinct aurochs, formerly distributed over Eurasia and North Africa. Now worldwide.

4. *Pig.* Wild ancestor: the wild boar, distributed over Eurasia and North Africa. Now worldwide. Actually an omnivore (regularly eats both animal and plant food), whereas the other 13 of the Ancient Fourteen are more strictly herbivores.

5. *Horse.* Wild ancestor: now extinct wild horses of southern Russia; a different subspecies of the same species survived in the wild to modern times as Przewalski's horse of Mongolia. Now worldwide.

The Minor Nine

6. *Arabian (one-humped) camel.* Wild ancestor: now extinct, formerly lived in Arabia and adjacent areas. Still largely restricted to Arabia and northern Africa, though feral in Australia.

7. *Bactrian (two-humped) camel:* Wild ancestor: now extinct, lived in Central Asia. Still largely confined to Central Asia.

8. *Llama and alpaca.* These appear to be well-differentiated breeds of the same species, rather than different species. Wild ancestor: the guanaco of the Andes. Still largely confined to the Andes, although some are bred as pack animals in North America.

9. *Donkey.* Wild ancestor: the African wild ass of North Africa and formerly perhaps the adjacent area of Southwest Asia. Originally confined as a domestic animal to North Africa and western Eurasia, more recently also used elsewhere.

10. *Reindeer.* Wild ancestor: the reindeer of northern Eurasia. Still largely confined as a domestic animal to that area, though now some are also used in Alaska.

11. *Water buffalo.* Wild ancestor lives in Southeast Asia. Still used as a domestic animal mainly in that area, though many are also used in Brazil and others have escaped to the wild in Australia and other places.

12. *Yak.* Wild ancestor: the wild yak of the Himalayas and Tibetan plateau. Still confined as a domestic animal to that area.

13. *Bali cattle.* Wild ancestor: the banteng (a relative of the aurochs) of Southeast Asia. Still confined as a domestic animal to that area.

14. *Mithan.* Wild ancestor: the gaur (another relative of the aurochs) of Indian and Burma. Still confined as a domestic animal to that area.

---

compare wolves, the wild ancestors of domestic dogs, with the many breeds of dogs. Some dogs are much bigger than wolves (Great Danes), while others are much smaller (Pekingese). Some are slimmer and built for racing (greyhounds), while others are short-legged and useless for racing (dachshunds). They vary enormously in hair form and color, and some are even hairless. Polynesians and Aztecs developed dog breeds specifically raised for food. Comparing a dachshund with a wolf, you wouldn't even suspect that the former had been derived from the latter if you didn't already know it.

THE WILD ANCESTORS of the Ancient Fourteen were spread unevenly over the globe. South America had only one such ancestor, which gave rise to the llama and alpaca. North America, Australia, and sub-Saharan Africa had none at all. The lack of domestic mammals indigenous to sub-Saharan Africa is especially astonishing, since a main reason why tourists visit Africa today is to see its abundant and diverse wild mammals. In contrast, the wild ancestors of 13 of the Ancient Fourteen (including all of the Major Five) were confined to Eurasia. (As elsewhere in this book, my use of the term "Eurasia" includes in several cases North Africa, which biogeographically and in many aspects of human culture is more closely related to Eurasia than to sub-Saharan Africa.)

Of course, not all 13 of these wild ancestral species occurred together throughout Eurasia. No area had all 13, and some of the wild ancestors were quite local, such as the yak, confined in the wild to Tibet and adjacent highland areas. However, many parts of Eurasia did have quite a few of these 13 species living together in the same area: for example, seven of the wild ancestors occurred in Southwest Asia.

This very unequal distribution of wild ancestral species among the continents became an important reason why Eurasians, rather than peoples of other continents, were the ones to end up with guns, germs, and steel. How can we explain the concentration of the Ancient Fourteen in Eurasia?

One reason is simple. Eurasia has the largest number of big terrestrial wild mammal species, whether or not ancestral to a domesticated species. Let's define a "candidate for domestication" as any terrestrial herbivorous or omnivorous mammal species (one not predominantly a carnivore) weighing on the average over 100 pounds (45 kilograms). Table 9.2 shows that Eurasia has the most candidates, 72 species, just as it has the most species in many other plant and animal groups. That's because Eurasia is the world's largest landmass, and it's also very diverse ecologically, with habitats ranging from extensive tropical rain forests, through temperate forests, deserts, and marshes, to equally extensive tundras. Sub-Saharan Africa has fewer candidates, 51 species, just as it has fewer species in most other plant and animal groups—because it's smaller and ecologically less diverse than Eurasia. Africa has smaller areas of tropical rain forest than does Southeast Asia, and no temperate habitats at all beyond latitude 37 degrees. As I discussed in Chapter 1, the Americas may formerly have had almost as many candidates as Africa, but most of America's big wild mammals (including its horses, most of its camels, and other species likely to have been domesticated had they survived) became extinct about 13,000 years ago. Australia, the smallest and most isolated continent, has always had far fewer species of big wild mammals than has Eurasia, Africa, or the Americas. Just as in the Americas, in Australia all of those few candidates

TABLE 9.2 **Mammalian Candidates for Domestication**

	Continent			
	Eurasia	Sub-Saharan Africa	The Americas	Australia
Candidates	72	51	24	1
Domesticated species	13	0	1	0
Percentage of candidates domesticated	18%	0%	4%	0%

A "candidate" is defined as a species of terrestrial, herbivorous or omnivorous, wild mammal weighing on the average over 100 pounds.

except the red kangaroo became extinct around the time of the continent's first colonization by humans.

Thus, part of the explanation for Eurasia's having been the main site of big mammal domestication is that it was the continent with the most candidate species of wild mammals to start out with, and lost the fewest candidates to extinction in the last 40,000 years. But the numbers in Table 9.2 warn us that that's not the whole explanation. It's also true that the *percentage* of candidates actually domesticated is highest in Eurasia (18 percent), and is especially low in sub-Saharan Africa (no species domesticated out of 51 candidates!). Particularly surprising is the large number of species of African and American mammals that were never domesticated, despite their having Eurasian close relatives or counterparts that were domesticated. Why were Eurasia's horses domesticated, but not Africa's zebras? Why Eurasia's pigs, but not American peccaries or Africa's three species of true wild pigs? Why Eurasia's five species of wild cattle (aurochs, water buffalo, yak, gaur, banteng), but not the African buffalo or American bison? Why the Asian mouflon sheep (ancestor of our domestic sheep), but not North American bighorn sheep?

DID ALL THOSE peoples of Africa, the Americas, and Australia, despite their enormous diversity, nonetheless share some cultural obstacles to domestication not shared with Eurasian peoples? For example, did Africa's abundance of big wild mammals, available to kill by hunting, make it superfluous for Africans to go to the trouble of tending domestic stock?

The answer to that question is unequivocal: No! The interpretation is refuted by five types of evidence: rapid acceptance of Eurasian domesticates by non-Eurasian peoples, the universal human penchant for keeping pets, the rapid domestication of the Ancient Fourteen, the repeated independent domestications of some of them, and the limited successes of modern efforts at further domestications.

First, when Eurasia's Major Five domestic mammals reached sub-Saharan Africa, they were adopted by the most diverse African peoples wherever conditions permitted. Those African herders thereby achieved a huge advantage over African hunter-gatherers and quickly displaced them. In particular, Bantu farmers who acquired cows and sheep spread out of their homeland in West Africa and within a short time overran the former hunter-gatherers in most of the rest of sub-Saharan Africa. Even without acquiring crops, Khoisan peoples who acquired cows and sheep around 2,000 years ago displaced Khoisan hunter-gatherers over much of southern Africa. The arrival of the domestic horse in West Africa transformed warfare there and turned the area into a set of kingdoms dependent on cavalry. The only factor that prevented horses from spreading beyond West Africa was trypanosome diseases borne by tsetse flies.

The same pattern repeated itself elsewhere in the world, whenever peoples lacking native wild mammal species suitable for domestication finally had the opportunity to acquire Eurasian domestic animals. European horses were eagerly adopted by Native Americans in both North and South America, within a generation of the escape of horses from European settlements. For example, by the 19th century North America's Great Plains Indians were famous as expert horse-mounted warriors and bison hunters, but they did not even obtain horses until the late 17th century. Sheep acquired from Spaniards similarly transformed Navajo Indian society and led to, among other things, the weaving of the beautiful woolen blankets for which the Navajo have become renowned. Within a decade of Tasmania's settlement by Europeans with dogs, Aboriginal Tasmanians, who had never before seen dogs, began to breed them in large numbers for use in hunting. Thus, among the thousands of culturally diverse native peoples of Australia, the Americas, and Africa, no universal cultural taboo stood in the way of animal domestication.

Surely, if some local wild mammal species of those continents had been domesticable, some Australian, American, and African peoples would have domesticated them and gained great advantage from them, just as they benefited from the Eurasian domestic animals that they immediately adopted when those became available. For instance, consider all the peoples of sub-Saharan Africa living within the range of wild zebras and buffalo. Why wasn't there at least one African hunter-gatherer tribe that domesticated those zebras and buffalo and that thereby gained sway over other Africans, without having to await the arrival of Eurasian horses and cattle? All these facts indicate that the explanation for the lack of native mammal domestication outside Eurasia lay with the locally available wild mammals themselves, not with the local peoples.

A SECOND TYPE of evidence for the same interpretation comes from pets. Keeping wild animals as pets, and taming them, constitute an initial stage in domestication. But pets have been reported from virtually all traditional human societies on all continents. The variety of wild animals thus tamed is far greater than the variety eventually domesticated, and includes some species that we would scarcely have imagined as pets.

For example, in the New Guinea villages where I work, I often see people with pet kangaroos, possums, and birds ranging from flycatchers to ospreys. Most of these captives are eventually eaten, though some are kept just as pets. New Guineans even regularly capture chicks of wild cassowaries (an ostrich–like large, flightless bird) and raise them to eat as a delicacy—even though captive adult cassowaries are extremely dangerous and now and then disembowel village people. Some Asian peoples tame eagles for use in hunting, although those powerful pets have also been known on occasion to kill their human handlers. Ancient Egyptians and Assyrians, and modern Indians, tamed cheetahs for use in hunting. Paintings made by ancient Egyptians show that they further tamed (not surprisingly) hoofed mammals such as gazelles and hartebeests, birds such as cranes, more surprisingly giraffes (which can be dangerous), and most astonishingly hyenas. African elephants were tamed in Roman times despite the obvious danger, and Asian elephants are still being tamed today. Perhaps the most unlikely pet is the European brown bear (the same species as the American grizzly bear), which the Ainu people of Japan *regularly* captured as young animals, tamed, and reared to kill and eat in a ritual ceremony.

Thus, many wild animal species reached the first stage in the sequence of animal-human relations leading to domestication, but only a few emerged at the other end of that sequence as domestic animals. Over a century ago, the British scientist Francis Galton summarized this discrepancy succinctly: "It would appear that every wild animal has had its chance of being domesticated, that [a] few . . . were domesticated long ago, but that the large remainder, who failed sometimes in only one small particular, are destined to perpetual wildness."

DATES OF DOMESTICATION provide a third line of evidence confirming Galton's view that early herding peoples quickly domesticated all big mammal species suitable for being domesticated. All species for whose dates of domestication we have archaeological evidence were domesticated between about 8000 and 2500 B.C.—that is, within the first few thousand years of the sedentary farming-herding societies that arose after the end of the last Ice Age. As summarized in Table 9.3, the era of big mammal domestication began with the sheep, goat, and pig and ended with camels. Since 2500 B.C. there have been no significant additions.

It's true, of course, that some small mammals were first domesticated long after 2500 B.C. For example, rabbits were not domesticated for food until the Middle Ages, mice and rats for laboratory research not until the 20th century, and hamsters for pets not until the 1930s. The continuing development of domesticated small mammals isn't surprising, because there are literally thousands of wild species as candidates, and because they were of too little value to traditional societies to warrant the effort of raising them. But big mammal domestication virtually ended 4,500 years ago. By then, all of the world's 148 candidate big species must have been tested innumerable times, with the result that only a few passed the test and no other suitable ones remained.

STILL A FOURTH line of evidence that some mammal species are much more suitable than others is provided by the repeated independent domestications of the same species. Genetic evidence based on the portions of our genetic material known as mitochondrial DNA recently confirmed, as had long been suspected, that humped cattle of India and humpless European cattle were derived from two separate populations of wild ancestral cattle that had diverged hundreds of thousands of years ago. That is, Indian peoples domesticated the local Indian subspecies of wild aurochs, Southwest Asians independently domesticated their own Southwest Asian subspecies of aurochs, and North Africans may have independently domesticated the North African aurochs.

Similarly, wolves were independently domesticated to become dogs in the Americas and probably in several different parts of Eurasia, including China and Southwest Asia. Modern pigs are derived from independent sequences of domestication in China, western Eurasia, and possibly other areas as well. These examples reemphasize that the same few suitable wild species attracted the attention of many different human societies.

THE FAILURES OF modern efforts provide a final type of evidence that past failures to domesticate the large residue of wild candidate species arose from shortcomings of those species, rather than from shortcomings

TABLE 9.3 **Approximate Dates of First Attested Evidence for Domestication of Large Mammal Species**

Species	Date (B.C.)	Place
Dog	10,000	Southwest Asia, China, North America
Sheep	8,000	Southwest Asia
Goat	8,000	Southwest Asia
Pig	8,000	China, Southwest Asia
Cow	6,000	Southwest Asia, India, (?)North Africa
Horse	4,000	Ukraine
Donkey	4,000	Egypt
Water buffalo	4,000	China?
Llama / alpaca	3,500	Andes
Bactrian camel	2,500	Central Asia
Arabian camel	2,500	Arabia

For the other four domesticated large mammal species—reindeer, yak, gaur, and banteng—there is as yet little evidence concerning the date of domestication. Dates and places shown are merely the earliest ones attested to date; domestication may actually have begun earlier and at a different location.

of ancient humans. Europeans today are heirs to one of the longest traditions of animal domestication on Earth—that which began in Southwest Asia around 10,000 years ago. Since the fifteenth century, Europeans have spread around the globe and encountered wild mammal species not found in Europe. European settlers, such as those that I encounter in New Guinea with pet kangaroos and possums, have tamed or made pets of many local mammals, just as have indigenous peoples. European herders and farmers emigrating to other continents have also made serious efforts to domesticate some local species.

In the 19th and 20th centuries at least six large mammals—the eland, elk, moose, musk ox, zebra, and American bison—have been the subjects of especially well-organized projects aimed at domestication, carried out by modern scientific animal breeders and geneticists. For example, eland, the largest African antelope, have been undergoing selection for meat quality and milk quantity in the Askaniya-Nova Zoological Park in the

Ukraine, as well as in England, Kenya, Zimbabwe, and South Africa; an experimental farm for elk (red deer, in British terminology) has been operated by the Rowett Research Institute at Aberdeen, Scotland; and an experimental farm for moose has operated in the Pechero-Ilych National Park in Russia. Yet these modern efforts have achieved only very limited successes. While bison meat occasionally appears in some U.S. supermarkets, and while moose have been ridden, milked, and used to pull sleds in Sweden and Russia, none of these efforts has yielded a result of sufficient economic value to attract many ranchers. It is especially striking that recent attempts to domesticate eland within Africa itself, where its disease resistance and climate tolerance would give it a big advantage over introduced Eurasian wild stock susceptible to African diseases, have not caught on.

Thus, neither indigenous herders with access to candidate species over thousands of years, nor modern geneticists, have succeeded in making useful domesticates of large mammals beyond the Ancient Fourteen, which were domesticated by at least 4,500 years ago. Yet scientists today could undoubtedly, if they wished, fulfill for many species that part of the definition of domestication that specifies the control of breeding and food supply. For example, the San Diego and Los Angeles zoos are now subjecting the last surviving California condors to a more draconian control of breeding than that imposed upon any domesticated species. All individual condors have been genetically identified, and a computer program determines which male shall mate with which female in order to achieve human goals (in this case, to maximize genetic diversity and thereby preserve this endangered bird). Zoos are conducting similar breeding programs for many other threatened species, including gorillas and rhinos. But the zoos' rigorous selection of California condors shows no prospects of yielding an economically useful product. Nor do zoos' efforts with rhinos, although rhinos offer up to over three tons of meat on the hoof. As we shall now see, rhinos (and most other big mammals) present insuperable obstacles to domestication.

In all, of the world's 148 big wild terrestrial herbivorous mammals— the candidates for domestication—only 14 passed the test. Why did the other 134 species fail? To which conditions was Francis Galton referring, when he spoke of those other species as "destined to perpetual wildness"?

The answer follows from the *Anna Karenina* principle. To be domesticated, a candidate wild species must possess many different characteristics. Lack of any single required characteristic dooms efforts at domestication, just as it dooms efforts at building a happy marriage. Playing marriage counselor to the zebra / human couple and other ill-sorted pairs, we can recognize at least six groups of reasons for failed domestication.

Diet. Every time that an animal eats a plant or another animal, the conversion of food biomass into the consumer's biomass involves an efficiency of much less than 100 percent: typically around 10 percent. That is, it takes around 10,000 pounds of corn to grow a 1,000-pound cow. If instead you want to grow 1,000 pounds of carnivore, you have to feed it 10,000 pounds of herbivore grown on 100,000 pounds of corn. Even among herbivores and omnivores, many species, like koalas, are too finicky in their plant preferences to recommend themselves as farm animals.

. As a result of this fundamental inefficiency, no mammalian carnivore has ever been domesticated for food. (No, it's not because its meat would be tough or tasteless: we eat carnivorous wild fish all the time, and I can personally attest to the delicious flavor of lion burger.) The nearest thing to an exception is the dog, originally domesticated as a sentinel and hunting companion, but breeds of dogs were developed and raised for food in Aztec Mexico, Polynesia, and ancient China. However, regular dog eating has been a last resort of meat-deprived human societies: the Aztecs had no other domestic mammal, and the Polynesians and ancient Chinese had only pigs and dogs. Human societies blessed with domestic herbivorous mammals have not bothered to eat dogs, except as an uncommon delicacy (as in parts of Southeast Asia today). In addition, dogs are not strict carnivores but omnivores: if you are so naive as to think that your beloved pet dog is really a meat eater, just read the list of ingredients on your bag of dog food. The dogs that the Aztecs and Polynesians reared for food were efficiently fattened on vegetables and garbage.

Growth Rate. To be worth keeping, domesticates must also grow quickly. That eliminates gorillas and elephants, even though they are vegetarians with admirably nonfinicky food preferences and represent a lot of meat. What would-be gorilla or elephant rancher would wait 15 years for his herd to reach adult size? Modern Asians who want work elephants find it much cheaper to capture them in the wild and tame them.

Problems of Captive Breeding. We humans don't like to have sex under the watchful eyes of others; some potentially valuable animal species don't like to, either. That's what derailed attempts to domesticate cheetahs, the swiftest of all land animals, despite our strong motivation to do so for thousands of years.

As I already mentioned, tame cheetahs were prized by ancient Egyptians and Assyrians and modern Indians as hunting animals infinitely superior to dogs. One Mogul emperor of India kept a stable of a thousand cheetahs. But despite those large investments that many wealthy princes made, all of their cheetahs were tamed ones caught in the wild. The princes' efforts to breed cheetahs in captivity failed, and not until 1960 did even biologists in modern zoos achieve their first successful cheetah birth. In the wild, several cheetah brothers chase a female for several days, and that rough courtship over large distances seems to be required to get the female to ovulate or to become sexually receptive. Cheetahs usually refuse to carry out that elaborate courtship ritual inside a cage.

A similar problem has frustrated schemes to breed the vicuña, an Andean wild camel whose wool is prized as the finest and lightest of any animal's. The ancient Incas obtained vicuña wool by driving wild vicuñas into corrals, shearing them, and then releasing them alive. Modern merchants wanting this luxury wool have had to resort either to this same method or simply to killing wild vicuñas. Despite strong incentives of money and prestige, all attempts to breed vicuñas for wool production in captivity have failed, for reasons that include vicuñas' long and elaborate courtship ritual before mating, a ritual inhibited in captivity; male vicuñas' fierce intolerance of each other; and their requirement for both a year-round feeding territory and a separate year-round sleeping territory.

Nasty Disposition. Naturally, almost any mammal species that is sufficiently large is capable of killing a human. People have been killed by pigs, horses, camels, and cattle. Nevertheless, some large animals have much nastier dispositions and are more incurably dangerous than are others. Tendencies to kill humans have disqualified many otherwise seemingly ideal candidates for domestication.

One obvious example is the grizzly bear. Bear meat is an expensive delicacy, grizzlies weigh up to 1,700 pounds, they are mainly vegetarians (though also formidable hunters), their vegetable diet is very broad, they thrive on human garbage (thereby creating big problems in Yellowstone and Glacier National Parks), and they grow relatively fast. If they would behave themselves in captivity, grizzlies would be a fabulous meat production animal. The Ainu people of Japan made the experiment by routinely rearing grizzly cubs as part of a ritual. For understandable reasons, though, the Ainu found it prudent to kill and eat the cubs at the age of one year. Keeping grizzly bears for longer would be suicidal; I am not aware of any adult that has been tamed.

Another otherwise suitable candidate that disqualifies itself for equally obvious reasons is the African buffalo. It grows quickly up to a weight of a ton and lives in herds that have a well-developed dominance hierarchy, a trait whose virtues will be discussed below. But the African buffalo is considered the most dangerous and unpredictable large mammal of Africa. Anyone insane enough to try to domesticate it either died in the effort or was forced to kill the buffalo before it got too big and nasty. Similarly, hippos, as four-ton vegetarians, would be great barnyard animals if they weren't so dangerous. They kill more people each year than do any other African mammals, including even lions.

Few people would be surprised at the disqualification of those notoriously ferocious candidates. But there are other candidates whose dangers are not so well known. For instance, the eight species of wild equids (horses and their relatives) vary greatly in disposition, even though all eight are genetically so close to each other that they will interbreed and produce healthy (though usually sterile) offspring. Two of them, the horse and the North African ass (ancestor of the donkey), were successfully domesticated. Closely related to the North African ass is the Asiatic ass, also known as the onager. Since its homeland includes the Fertile Crescent, the cradle of Western civilization and animal domestication, ancient peoples must have experimented extensively with onagers. We know from Sumerian and later depictions that onagers were regularly hunted, as well as captured and hybridized with donkeys and horses. Some ancient depictions of horselike animals used for riding or for pulling carts may refer to onagers. However, all writers about them, from Romans to modern zookeepers, decry their irascible temper and their nasty habit of biting people. As a result, although similar in other respects to ancestral donkeys, onagers have never been domesticated.

Africa's four species of zebras are even worse. Efforts at domestication went as far as hitching them to carts: they were tried out as draft animals in 19th-century South Africa, and the eccentric Lord Walter Rothschild drove through the streets of London in a carriage pulled by zebras. Alas, zebras become impossibly dangerous as they grow older. (That's not to deny that many individual horses are also nasty, but zebras and onagers are much more uniformly so.) Zebras have the unpleasant habit of biting a person and not letting go. They thereby injure even more American zoo-keepers each year than do tigers! Zebras are also virtually impossible to lasso with a rope—even for cowboys who win rodeo championships by lassoing horses—because of their unfailing ability to watch the rope noose fly toward them and then to duck their head out of the way.

Hence it has rarely (if ever) been possible to saddle or ride a zebra, and South Africans' enthusiasm for their domestication waned. Unpredictably aggressive behavior on the part of a large and potentially dangerous mammal is also part of the reason why the initially so promising modern experiments in domesticating elk and eland have not been more successful.

Tendency to Panic. Big mammalian herbivore species react to danger from predators or humans in different ways. Some species are nervous, fast, and programmed for instant flight when they perceive a threat. Other species are slower, less nervous, seek protection in herds, stand their ground when threatened, and don't run until necessary. Most species of deer and antelope (with the conspicuous exception of reindeer) are of the former type, while sheep and goats are of the latter.

Naturally, the nervous species are difficult to keep in captivity. If put into an enclosure, they are likely to panic, and either die of shock or batter themselves to death against the fence in their attempts to escape. That's true, for example, of gazelles, which for thousands of years were the most frequently hunted game species in some parts of the Fertile Crescent. There is no mammal species that the first settled peoples of that area had more opportunity to domesticate than gazelles. But no gazelle species has ever been domesticated. Just imagine trying to herd an animal that bolts, blindly bashes itself against walls, can leap up to nearly 30 feet, and can run at a speed of 50 miles per hour!

Social Structure. Almost all species of domesticated large mammals prove to be ones whose wild ancestors share three social characteristics: they live in herds; they maintain a well-developed dominance hierarchy among herd members; and the herds occupy overlapping home ranges rather than mutually exclusive territories. For example, herds of wild horses consist of one stallion, up to half a dozen mares, and their foals. Mare A is dominant over mares B, C, D, and E; mare B is submissive to A but dominant over C, D, and E; C is submissive to B and A but dominant over D and E; and so on. When the herd is on the move, its members maintain a stereotyped order: in the rear, the stallion; in the front, the top-ranking female, followed by her foals in order of age, with the youngest first; and behind her, the other mares in order of rank, each followed by her foals in order of age. In that way, many adults can coexist in the herd without constant fighting and with each knowing its rank.

That social structure is ideal for domestication, because humans in effect take over the dominance hierarchy. Domestic horses of a pack line follow the human leader as they would normally follow the top-ranking female. Herds or packs of sheep, goats, cows, and ancestral dogs (wolves) have a similar hierarchy. As young animals grow up in such a herd, they imprint on the animals that they regularly see nearby. Under wild conditions those are members of their own species, but captive young herd animals also see humans nearby and imprint on humans as well.

Such social animals lend themselves to herding. Since they are tolerant of each other, they can be bunched up. Since they instinctively follow a dominant leader and will imprint on humans as that leader, they can readily be driven by a shepherd or sheepdog. Herd animals do well when penned in crowded conditions, because they are accustomed to living in densely packed groups in the wild.

In contrast, members of most solitary territorial animal species cannot be herded. They do not tolerate each other, they do not imprint on humans, and they are not instinctively submissive. Who ever saw a line of cats (solitary and territorial in the wild) following a human or allowing themselves to be herded by a human? Every cat lover knows that cats are not submissive to humans in the way dogs instinctively are. Cats and ferrets are the sole territorial mammal species that were domesticated, because our motive for doing so was not to herd them in large groups raised for food but to keep them as solitary hunters or pets.

While most solitary territorial species thus haven't been domesticated, it's not conversely the case that most herd species can be domesticated. Most can't, for one of several additional reasons.

First, herds of many species don't have overlapping home ranges but instead maintain exclusive territories against other herds. It's no more possible to pen two such herds together than to pen two males of a solitary species.

Second, many species that live in herds for part of the year are territorial in the breeding season, when they fight and do not tolerate each other's presence. That's true of most deer and antelope species (again with the exception of reindeer), and it's one of the main factors that has disqualified all the social antelope species for which Africa is famous from being domesticated. While one's first association to African antelope is "vast dense herds spreading across the horizon," in fact the males of those herds space themselves into territories and fight fiercely with each other when breeding. Hence those antelope cannot be maintained in crowded enclosures in captivity, as can sheep or goats or cattle. Territorial behavior similarly combines with a fierce disposition and a slow growth rate to banish rhinos from the farmyard.

Finally, many herd species, including again most deer and antelope, do not have a well-defined dominance hierarchy and are not instinctively prepared to become imprinted on a dominant leader (hence to become misimprinted on humans). As a result, though many deer and antelope species have been tamed (think of all those true Bambi stories), one never sees such tame deer and antelope driven in herds like sheep. That problem also derailed domestication of North American bighorn sheep, which belong to the same genus as Asiatic mouflon sheep, ancestor of our domestic sheep. Bighorn sheep are suitable to us and similar to mouflons in most respects except a crucial one: they lack the mouflon's stereotypical behavior whereby some individuals behave submissively toward other individuals whose dominance they acknowledge.

LET'S NOW RETURN to the problem I posed at the outset of this chapter. Initially, one of the most puzzling features of animal domestication is the seeming arbitrariness with which some species have been domesticated while their close relatives have not. It turns out that all but a few candidates for domestication have been eliminated by the *Anna Karenina* principle. Humans and most animal species make an unhappy marriage, for one or more of many possible reasons: the animal's diet, growth rate, mating habits, disposition, tendency to panic, and several distinct features of social organization. Only a small percentage of wild mammal species ended up in happy marriages with humans, by virtue of compatibility on all those separate counts.

Eurasian peoples happened to inherit many more species of domesticable large wild mammalian herbivores than did peoples of the other continents. That outcome, with all of its momentous advantages for Eurasian societies, stemmed from three basic facts of mammalian geography, history, and biology. First, Eurasia, befitting its large area and ecological diversity, started out with the most candidates. Second, Australia and the Americas, but not Eurasia or Africa, lost most of their candidates in a massive wave of late-Pleistocene extinctions—possibly because the mammals of the former continents had the misfortune to be first exposed to humans suddenly and late in our evolutionary history, when our hunting skills were already highly developed. Finally, a higher percentage of the surviving candidates proved suitable for domestication on Eurasia than on the other continents. An examination of the candidates that were never domesticated, such as Africa's big herd-forming mammals, reveals particular reasons that disqualified each of them. Thus, Tolstoy would have approved of the insight offered in another context by an earlier author, Saint Matthew: "Many are called, but few are chosen."

CHAPTER 10

SPACIOUS SKIES AND
TILTED AXES

O N THE MAP OF THE WORLD ON PAGE 177 (FIGURE 10.1),
compare the shapes and orientations of the continents. You'll be
struck by an obvious difference. The Americas span a much greater distance north–south (9,000 miles) than east–west: only 3,000 miles at the
widest, narrowing to a mere 40 miles at the Isthmus of Panama. That is,
the major axis of the Americas is north–south. The same is also true,
though to a less extreme degree, for Africa. In contrast, the major axis of
Eurasia is east–west. What effect, if any, did those differences in the orientation of the continents' axes have on human history?

This chapter will be about what I see as their enormous, sometimes
tragic, consequences. Axis orientations affected the rate of spread of crops
and livestock, and possibly also of writing, wheels, and other inventions.
That basic feature of geography thereby contributed heavily to the very
different experiences of Native Americans, Africans, and Eurasians in the
last 500 years.

FOOD PRODUCTION'S SPREAD proves as crucial to understanding
geographic differences in the rise of guns, germs, and steel as did its origins, which we considered in the preceding chapters. That's because, as we

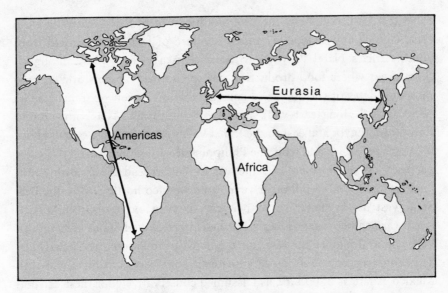

Figure 10.1. Major axes of the continents.

saw in Chapter 5, there were no more than nine areas of the globe, perhaps as few as five, where food production arose independently. Yet, already in prehistoric times, food production became established in many other regions besides those few areas of origins. All those other areas became food producing as a result of the spread of crops, livestock, and knowledge of how to grow them and, in some cases, as a result of migrations of farmers and herders themselves.

The main such spreads of food production were from Southwest Asia to Europe, Egypt and North Africa, Ethiopia, Central Asia, and the Indus Valley; from the Sahel and West Africa to East and South Africa; from China to tropical Southeast Asia, the Philippines, Indonesia, Korea, and Japan; and from Mesoamerica to North America. Moreover, food production even in its areas of origin became enriched by the addition of crops, livestock, and techniques from other areas of origin.

Just as some regions proved much more suitable than others for the origins of food production, the ease of its spread also varied greatly around the world. Some areas that are ecologically very suitable for food production never acquired it in prehistoric times at all, even though areas of prehistoric food production existed nearby. The most conspicuous such examples are the failure of both farming and herding to reach Native

American California from the U.S. Southwest or to reach Australia from New Guinea and Indonesia, and the failure of farming to spread from South Africa's Natal Province to South Africa's Cape. Even among all those areas where food production did spread in the prehistoric era, the rates and dates of spread varied considerably. At the one extreme was its rapid spread along east–west axes: from Southwest Asia both west to Europe and Egypt and east to the Indus Valley (at an average rate of about 0.7 miles per year); and from the Philippines east to Polynesia (at 3.2 miles per year). At the opposite extreme was its slow spread along north–south axes: at less than 0.5 miles per year, from Mexico northward to the U.S. Southwest; at less than 0.3 miles per year, for corn and beans from Mexico northward to become productive in the eastern United States around A.D. 900; and at 0.2 miles per year, for the llama from Peru north to Ecuador. These differences could be even greater if corn was not domesticated in Mexico as late as 3500 B.C., as I assumed conservatively for these calculations, and as some archaeologists now assume, but if it was instead domesticated considerably earlier, as most archaeologists used to assume (and many still do).

There were also great differences in the completeness with which suites of crops and livestock spread, again implying stronger or weaker barriers to their spreading. For instance, while most of Southwest Asia's founder crops and livestock did spread west to Europe and east to the Indus Valley, neither of the Andes' domestic mammals (the llama / alpaca and the guinea pig) ever reached Mesoamerica in pre-Columbian times. That astonishing failure cries out for explanation. After all, Mesoamerica did develop dense farming populations and complex societies, so there can be no doubt that Andean domestic animals (if they had been available) would have been valuable for food, transport, and wool. Except for dogs, Mesoamerica was utterly without indigenous mammals to fill those needs. Some South American crops nevertheless did succeed in reaching Mesoamerica, such as manioc, sweet potatoes, and peanuts. What selective barrier let those crops through but screened out llamas and guinea pigs?

A subtler expression of this geographically varying ease of spread is the phenomenon termed preemptive domestication. Most of the wild plant species from which our crops were derived vary genetically from area to area, because alternative mutations had become established among the wild ancestral populations of different areas. Similarly, the changes required to transform wild plants into crops can in principle be brought

about by alternative new mutations or alternative courses of selection to
yield equivalent results. In this light, one can examine a crop widespread
in prehistoric times and ask whether all of its varieties show the same wild
mutation or same transforming mutation. The purpose of this examination is to try to figure out whether the crop was developed in just one area
or else independently in several areas.

If one carries out such a genetic analysis for major ancient New World
crops, many of them prove to include two or more of those alternative
wild variants, or two or more of those alternative transforming mutations.
This suggests that the crop was domesticated independently in at least two
different areas, and that some varieties of the crop inherited the particular
mutation of one area while other varieties of the same crop inherited the
mutation of another area. On this basis, botanists conclude that lima
beans (*Phaseolus lunatus*), common beans (*Phaseolus vulgaris*), and chili
peppers of the *Capsicum annuum / chinense* group were all domesticated
on at least two separate occasions, once in Mesoamerica and once in South
America; and that the squash *Cucurbita pepo* and the seed plant goosefoot
were also domesticated independently at least twice, once in Mesoamerica
and once in the eastern United States. In contrast, most ancient Southwest
Asian crops exhibit just one of the alternative wild variants or alternative
transforming mutations, suggesting that all modern varieties of that particular crop stem from only a single domestication.

What does it imply if the same crop has been repeatedly and independently domesticated in several different parts of its wild range, and not
just once and in a single area? We have already seen that plant domestication involves the modification of wild plants so that they become more
useful to humans by virtue of larger seeds, a less bitter taste, or other
qualities. Hence if a productive crop is already available, incipient farmers
will surely proceed to grow it rather than start all over again by gathering
its not yet so useful wild relative and redomesticating it. Evidence for just
a single domestication thus suggests that, once a wild plant had been
domesticated, the crop spread quickly to other areas throughout the wild
plant's range, preempting the need for other independent domestications
of the same plant. However, when we find evidence that the same wild
ancestor was domesticated independently in different areas, we infer that
the crop spread too slowly to preempt its domestication elsewhere. The
evidence for predominantly single domestications in Southwest Asia, but
frequent multiple domestications in the Americas, might thus provide

more subtle evidence that crops spread more easily out of Southwest Asia than in the Americas.

Rapid spread of a crop may preempt domestication not only of the same wild ancestral species somewhere else but also of related wild species. If you're already growing good peas, it's of course pointless to start from scratch to domesticate the same wild ancestral pea again, but it's also pointless to domesticate closely related wild pea species that for farmers are virtually equivalent to the already domesticated pea species. All of Southwest Asia's founder crops preempted domestication of any of their close relatives throughout the whole expanse of western Eurasia. In contrast, the New World presents many cases of equivalent and closely related, but nevertheless distinct, species having been domesticated in Mesoamerica and South America. For instance, 95 percent of the cotton grown in the world today belongs to the cotton species *Gossypium hirsutum,* which was domesticated in prehistoric times in Mesoamerica. However, prehistoric South American farmers instead grew the related cotton *Gossypium barbadense.* Evidently, Mesoamerican cotton had such difficulty reaching South America that it failed in the prehistoric era to preempt the domestication of a different cotton species there (and vice versa). Chili peppers, squashes, amaranths, and chenopods are other crops of which different but related species were domesticated in Mesoamerica and South America, since no species was able to spread fast enough to preempt the others.

We thus have many different phenomena converging on the same conclusion: that food production spread more readily out of Southwest Asia than in the Americas, and possibly also than in sub-Saharan Africa. Those phenomena include food production's complete failure to reach some ecologically suitable areas; the differences in its rate and selectivity of spread; and the differences in whether the earliest domesticated crops preempted redomestications of the same species or domestications of close relatives. What was it about the Americas and Africa that made the spread of food production more difficult there than in Eurasia?

To ANSWER THIS question, let's begin by examining the rapid spread of food production out of Southwest Asia (the Fertile Crescent). Soon after food production arose there, somewhat before 8000 B.C., a centrifugal wave of it appeared in other parts of western Eurasia and North Africa farther and farther removed from the Fertile Crescent, to the west and east. On this page I have redrawn the striking map (Figure 10.2) assembled by the geneticist Daniel Zohary and botanist Maria Hopf, in which they illustrate how the wave had reached Greece and Cyprus and the Indian subcontinent by 6500 B.C., Egypt soon after 6000 B.C., central Europe by 5400 B.C., southern Spain by 5200 B.C., and Britain around 3500 B.C. In each of those areas, food production was initiated by some of the same suite of domestic plants and animals that launched it in the Fertile Crescent. In addition, the Fertile Crescent package penetrated Africa southward to Ethiopia at some still-uncertain date. However, Ethiopia also developed many indigenous crops, and we do not yet know whether it was these crops or the arriving Fertile Crescent crops that launched Ethiopian food production.

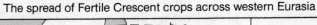

The spread of Fertile Crescent crops across western Eurasia

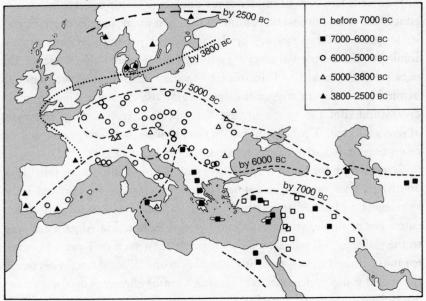

Figure 10.2. *The symbols show early radiocarbon-dated sites where remains of Fertile Crescent crops have been found.* □ = *the Fertile Crescent itself (sites before 7000 B.C.). Note that dates become progressively later as one gets farther from the Fertile Crescent. This map is based on Map 20 of Zohary and Hopf's* Domestication of Plants in the Old World *but substitutes calibrated radiocarbon dates for their uncalibrated dates.*

Of course, not all pieces of the package spread to all those outlying areas: for example, Egypt was too warm for einkorn wheat to become established. In some outlying areas, elements of the package arrived at different times: for instance, sheep preceded cereals in southwestern Europe. Some outlying areas went on to domesticate a few local crops of their own, such as poppies in western Europe and watermelons possibly in Egypt. But most food production in outlying areas depended initially on Fertile Crescent domesticates. Their spread was soon followed by that of other innovations originating in or near the Fertile Crescent, including the wheel, writing, metalworking techniques, milking, fruit trees, and beer and wine production.

Why did the same plant package launch food production throughout western Eurasia? Was it because the same set of plants occurred in the wild in many areas, were found useful there just as in the Fertile Crescent, and were independently domesticated? No, that's not the reason. First, many of the Fertile Crescent's founder crops don't even occur in the wild outside Southwest Asia. For instance, none of the eight main founder crops except barley grows wild in Egypt. Egypt's Nile Valley provides an environment similar to the Fertile Crescent's Tigris and Euphrates Valleys. Hence the package that worked well in the latter valleys also worked well enough in the Nile Valley to trigger the spectacular rise of indigenous Egyptian civilization. But the foods to fuel that spectacular rise were originally absent in Egypt. The sphinx and pyramids were built by people fed on crops originally native to the Fertile Crescent, not to Egypt.

Second, even for those crops whose wild ancestor does occur outside of Southwest Asia, we can be confident that the crops of Europe and India were mostly obtained from Southwest Asia and were not local domesticates. For example, wild flax occurs west to Britain and Algeria and east to the Caspian Sea, while wild barley occurs east even to Tibet. However, for most of the Fertile Crescent's founding crops, all cultivated varieties in the world today share only one arrangement of chromosomes out of the multiple arrangements found in the wild ancestor; or else they share only a single mutation (out of many possible mutations) by which the cultivated varieties differ from the wild ancestor in characteristics desirable to humans. For instance, all cultivated peas share the same recessive gene that prevents ripe pods of cultivated peas from spontaneously popping open and spilling their peas, as wild pea pods do.

Evidently, most of the Fertile Crescent's founder crops were never domesticated again elsewhere after their initial domestication in the Fertile Crescent. Had they been repeatedly domesticated independently, they would exhibit legacies of those multiple origins in the form of varied chromosomal arrangements or varied mutations. Hence these are typical examples of the phenomenon of preemptive domestication that we discussed above. The quick spread of the Fertile Crescent package preempted any possible other attempts, within the Fertile Crescent or elsewhere, to domesticate the same wild ancestors. Once the crop had become available, there was no further need to gather it from the wild and thereby set it on the path to domestication again.

The ancestors of most of the founder crops have wild relatives, in the Fertile Crescent and elsewhere, that would also have been suitable for domestication. For example, peas belong to the genus *Pisum*, which consists of two wild species: *Pisum sativum,* the one that became domesticated to yield our garden peas, and *Pisum fulvum,* which was never domesticated. Yet wild peas of *Pisum fulvum* taste good, either fresh or dried, and are common in the wild. Similarly, wheats, barley, lentil, chickpea, beans, and flax all have numerous wild relatives besides the ones that became domesticated. Some of those related beans and barleys were indeed domesticated independently in the Americas or China, far from the early site of domestication in the Fertile Crescent. But in western Eurasia only one of several potentially useful wild species was domesticated—probably because that one spread so quickly that people soon stopped gathering the other wild relatives and ate only the crop. Again as we discussed above, the crop's rapid spread preempted any possible further attempts to domesticate its relatives, as well as to redomesticate its ancestor.

WHY WAS THE spread of crops from the Fertile Crescent so rapid? The answer depends partly on that east–west axis of Eurasia with which I opened this chapter. Localities distributed east and west of each other at the same latitude share exactly the same day length and its seasonal variations. To a lesser degree, they also tend to share similar diseases, regimes of temperature and rainfall, and habitats or biomes (types of vegetation). For example, Portugal, northern Iran, and Japan, all located at about the same latitude but lying successively 4,000 miles east or west of each other, are more similar to each other in climate than each is to a location lying even a mere 1,000 miles due south. On all the continents the habitat type known as tropical rain forest is confined to within about 10 degrees latitude of the equator, while Mediterranean scrub habitats (such as California's chaparral and Europe's maquis) lie between about 30 and 40 degrees of latitude.

But the germination, growth, and disease resistance of plants are adapted to precisely those features of climate. Seasonal changes of day length, temperature, and rainfall constitute signals that stimulate seeds to germinate, seedlings to grow, and mature plants to develop flowers, seeds, and fruit. Each plant population becomes genetically programmed, through natural selection, to respond appropriately to signals of the seasonal regime under which it has evolved. Those regimes vary greatly with latitude. For example, day length is constant throughout the year at the equator, but at temperate latitudes it increases as the months advance from the winter solstice to the summer solstice, and it then declines again through the next half of the year. The growing season—that is, the months with temperatures and day lengths suitable for plant growth—is shortest at high latitudes and longest toward the equator. Plants are also adapted to the diseases prevalent at their latitude.

Woe betide the plant whose genetic program is mismatched to the latitude of the field in which it is planted! Imagine a Canadian farmer foolish enough to plant a race of corn adapted to growing farther south, in Mexico. The unfortunate corn plant, following its Mexico-adapted genetic program, would prepare to thrust up its shoots in March, only to find itself still buried under 10 feet of snow. Should the plant become genetically reprogrammed so as to germinate at a time more appropriate to Canada— say, late June—the plant would still be in trouble for other reasons. Its genes would be telling it to grow at a leisurely rate, sufficient only to bring it to maturity in five months. That's a perfectly safe strategy in Mexico's mild climate, but in Canada a disastrous one that would guarantee the plant's being killed by autumn frosts before it had produced any mature corn cobs. The plant would also lack genes for resistance to diseases of northern climates, while uselessly carrying genes for resistance to diseases of southern climates. All those features make low-latitude plants poorly adapted to high-latitude conditions, and vice versa. As a consequence, most Fertile Crescent crops grow well in France and Japan but poorly at the equator.

Animals too are adapted to latitude-related features of climate. In that respect we are typical animals, as we know by introspection. Some of us can't stand cold northern winters with their short days and characteristic germs, while others of us can't stand hot tropical climates with their own characteristic diseases. In recent centuries overseas colonists from cool northern Europe have preferred to emigrate to the similarly cool climates of North America, Australia, and South Africa, and to settle in the cool highlands within equatorial Kenya and New Guinea. Northern Europeans who were sent out to hot tropical lowland areas used to die in droves of diseases such as malaria, to which tropical peoples had evolved some genetic resistance.

That's part of the reason why Fertile Crescent domesticates spread west and east so rapidly: they were already well adapted to the climates of the regions to which they were spreading. For instance, once farming crossed from the plains of Hungary into central Europe around 5400 B.C., it spread so quickly that the sites of the first farmers in the vast area from Poland west to Holland (marked by their characteristic pottery with linear decorations) were nearly contemporaneous. By the time of Christ, cereals of Fertile Crescent origin were growing over the 8,000-mile expanse from the Atlantic coast of Ireland to the Pacific coast of Japan. That west–east expanse of Eurasia is the largest land distance on Earth.

Thus, Eurasia's west–east axis allowed Fertile Crescent crops quickly to launch agriculture over the band of temperate latitudes from Ireland to the Indus Valley, and to enrich the agriculture that arose independently in eastern Asia. Conversely, Eurasian crops that were first domesticated far from the Fertile Crescent but at the same latitudes were able to diffuse back to the Fertile Crescent. Today, when seeds are transported over the whole globe by ship and plane, we take it for granted that our meals are a geographic mishmash. A typical American fast-food restaurant meal would include chicken (first domesticated in China) and potatoes (from the Andes) or corn (from Mexico), seasoned with black pepper (from India) and washed down with a cup of coffee (of Ethiopian origin). Already, though, by 2,000 years ago, Romans were also nourishing themselves with their own hodgepodge of foods that mostly originated elsewhere. Of Roman crops, only oats and poppies were native to Italy. Roman staples were the Fertile Crescent founder package, supplemented by quince (originating in the Caucasus); millet and cumin (domesticated in Central Asia); cucumber, sesame, and citrus fruit (from India); and chicken, rice, apricots, peaches, and foxtail millet (originally from China). Even though Rome's apples were at least native to western Eurasia, they were grown by means of grafting techniques that had developed in China and spread westward from there.

While Eurasia provides the world's widest band of land at the same latitude, and hence the most dramatic example of rapid spread of domesticates, there are other examples as well. Rivaling in speed the spread of the Fertile Crescent package was the eastward spread of a subtropical package that was initially assembled in South China and that received additions on reaching tropical Southeast Asia, the Philippines, Indonesia, and New Guinea. Within 1,600 years that resulting package of crops (including bananas, taro, and yams) and domestic animals (chickens, pigs, and dogs) had spread more than 5,000 miles eastward into the tropical Pacific to reach the islands of Polynesia. A further likely example is the east-west spread of crops within Africa's wide Sahel zone, but paleobotanists have yet to work out the details.

CONTRAST THE EASE of east–west diffusion in Eurasia with the difficulties of diffusion along Africa's north–south axis. Most of the Fertile Crescent founder crops reached Egypt very quickly and then spread as far south as the cool highlands of Ethiopia, beyond which they didn't spread. South Africa's Mediterranean climate would have been ideal for them, but the 2,000 miles of tropical conditions between Ethiopia and South Africa posed an insuperable barrier. Instead, African agriculture south of the Sahara was launched by the domestication of wild plants (such as sorghum and African yams) indigenous to the Sahel zone and to tropical West Africa, and adapted to the warm temperatures, summer rains, and relatively constant day lengths of those low latitudes.

Similarly, the spread southward of Fertile Crescent domestic animals through Africa was stopped or slowed by climate and disease, especially by trypanosome diseases carried by tsetse flies. The horse never became established farther south than West Africa's kingdoms north of the equator. The advance of cattle, sheep, and goats halted for 2,000 years at the northern edge of the Serengeti Plains, while new types of human economies and livestock breeds were being developed. Not until the period A.D. 1–200, some 8,000 years after livestock were domesticated in the Fertile Crescent, did cattle, sheep, and goats finally reach South Africa. Tropical African crops had their own difficulties spreading south in Africa, arriving in South Africa with black African farmers (the Bantu) just after those

Fertile Crescent livestock did. However, those tropical African crops could never be transmitted across South Africa's Fish River, beyond which they were stopped by Mediterranean conditions to which they were not adapted.

The result was the all-too-familiar course of the last two millennia of South African history. Some of South Africa's indigenous Khoisan peoples (otherwise known as Hottentots and Bushmen) acquired livestock but remained without agriculture. They became outnumbered and were replaced northeast of the Fish River by black African farmers, whose southward spread halted at that river. Only when European settlers arrived by sea in 1652, bringing with them their Fertile Crescent crop package, could agriculture thrive in South Africa's Mediterranean zone. The collisions of all those peoples produced the tragedies of modern South Africa: the quick decimation of the Khoisan by European germs and guns; a century of wars between Europeans and blacks; another century of racial oppression; and now, efforts by Europeans and blacks to seek a new mode of coexistence in the former Khoisan lands.

CONTRAST ALSO THE ease of diffusion in Eurasia with its difficulties along the Americas' north–south axis. The distance between Mesoamerica and South America—say, between Mexico's highlands and Ecuador's—is only 1,200 miles, approximately the same as the distance in Eurasia sepa-rating the Balkans from Mesopotamia. The Balkans provided ideal grow-ing conditions for most Mesopotamian crops and livestock, and received those domesticates as a package within 2,000 years of its assembly in the Fertile Crescent. That rapid spread preempted opportunities for domesti-cating those and related species in the Balkans. Highland Mexico and the Andes would similarly have been suitable for many of each other's crops and domestic animals. A few crops, notably Mexican corn, did indeed spread to the other region in the pre-Columbian era.

But other crops and domestic animals failed to spread between Meso-america and South America. The cool highlands of Mexico would have provided ideal conditions for raising llamas, guinea pigs, and potatoes, all domesticated in the cool highlands of the South American Andes. Yet the northward spread of those Andean specialties was stopped completely by the hot intervening lowlands of Central America. Five thousand years after llamas had been domesticated in the Andes, the Olmecs, Maya, Aztecs, and all other native societies of Mexico remained without pack animals and without any edible domestic mammals except for dogs.

Conversely, domestic turkeys of Mexico and domestic sunflowers of the eastern United States might have thrived in the Andes, but their southward spread was stopped by the intervening tropical climates. The mere 700 miles of north–south distance prevented Mexican corn, squash, and beans from reaching the U.S. Southwest for several thousand years after their domestication in Mexico, and Mexican chili peppers and chenopods never did reach it in prehistoric times. For thousands of years after corn was domesticated in Mexico, it failed to spread northward into eastern North America, because of the cooler climates and shorter growing season prevailing there. At some time between A.D. 1 and A.D. 200, corn finally appeared in the eastern United States but only as a very minor crop. Not until around A.D. 900, after hardy varieties of corn adapted to northern climates had been developed, could corn-based agriculture contribute to the flowering of the most complex Native American society of North America, the Mississippian culture—a brief flowering ended by European-introduced germs arriving with and after Columbus.

Recall that most Fertile Crescent crops prove, upon genetic study, to derive from only a single domestication process, whose resulting crop spread so quickly that it preempted any other incipient domestications of the same or related species. In contrast, many apparently widespread Native American crops prove to consist of related species or even of genetically distinct varieties of the same species, independently domesticated in Mesoamerica, South America, and the eastern United States. Closely related species replace each other geographically among the amaranths, beans, chenopods, chili peppers, cottons, squashes, and tobaccos. Different varieties of the same species replace each other among the kidney beans, lima beans, the chili pepper *Capsicum annuum / chinense,* and the squash *Cucurbita pepo.* Those legacies of multiple independent domestications may provide further testimony to the slow diffusion of crops along the Americas' north–south axis.

Africa and the Americas are thus the two largest landmasses with a predominantly north–south axis and resulting slow diffusion. In certain other parts of the world, slow north–south diffusion was important on a smaller scale. These other examples include the snail's pace of crop exchange between Pakistan's Indus Valley and South India, the slow spread of South Chinese food production into Peninsular Malaysia, and the failure of tropical Indonesian and New Guinean food production to arrive in prehistoric times in the modern farmlands of southwestern and southeastern Australia, respectively. Those two corners of Australia are now the continent's breadbaskets, but they lie more than 2,000 miles south of the equator. Farming there had to await the arrival from faraway Europe, on European ships, of crops adapted to Europe's cool climate and short growing season.

I HAVE BEEN dwelling on latitude, readily assessed by a glance at a map, because it is a major determinant of climate, growing conditions, and ease of spread of food production. However, latitude is of course not the only such determinant, and it is not always true that adjacent places at the same latitude have the same climate (though they do necessarily have the same day length). Topographic and ecological barriers, much more pronounced on some continents than on others, were locally important obstacles to diffusion.

For instance, crop diffusion between the U.S. Southeast and Southwest was very slow and selective although these two regions are at the same latitude. That's because much of the intervening area of Texas and the southern Great Plains was dry and unsuitable for agriculture. A corresponding example within Eurasia involved the eastern limit of Fertile Crescent crops, which spread rapidly westward to the Atlantic Ocean and eastward to the Indus Valley without encountering a major barrier. However, farther eastward in India the shift from predominantly winter rainfall to predominantly summer rainfall contributed to a much more delayed extension of agriculture, involving different crops and farming techniques, into the Ganges plain of northeastern India. Still farther east, temperate areas of China were isolated from western Eurasian areas with similar climates by the combination of the Central Asian desert, Tibetan plateau, and Himalayas. The initial development of food production in China was therefore independent of that at the same latitude in the Fertile Crescent, and gave rise to entirely different crops. However, even those barriers between China and western Eurasia were at least partly overcome during the second millennium B.C., when West Asian wheat, barley, and horses reached China.

By the same token, the potency of a 2,000-mile north–south shift as a barrier also varies with local conditions. Fertile Crescent food production spread southward over that distance to Ethiopia, and Bantu food production spread quickly from Africa's Great Lakes region south to Natal, because in both cases the intervening areas had similar rainfall regimes and were suitable for agriculture. In contrast, crop diffusion from Indonesia south to southwestern Australia was completely impossible, and diffusion over the much shorter distance from Mexico to the U.S. Southwest and Southeast was slow, because the intervening areas were deserts hostile to agriculture. The lack of a high-elevation plateau in Mesoamerica south of Guatemala, and Mesoamerica's extreme narrowness south of Mexico and especially in Panama, were at least as important as the latitudinal gradient in throttling crop and livestock exchanges between the highlands of Mexico and the Andes.

Continental differences in axis orientation affected the diffusion not only of food production but also of other technologies and inventions. For example, around 3,000 B.C. the invention of the wheel in or near Southwest Asia spread rapidly west and east across much of Eurasia within a few centuries, whereas the wheels invented independently in prehistoric Mexico never spread south to the Andes. Similarly, the principle of alphabetic writing, developed in the western part of the Fertile Crescent by 1500 B.C., spread west to Carthage and east to the Indian subcontinent within about a thousand years, but the Mesoamerican writing systems that flourished in prehistoric times for at least 2,000 years never reached the Andes.

Naturally, wheels and writing aren't directly linked to latitude and day length in the way crops are. Instead, the links are indirect, especially via food production systems and their consequences. The earliest wheels were parts of ox-drawn carts used to transport agricultural produce. Early writing was restricted to elites supported by food-producing peasants, and it served purposes of economically and socially complex food-producing societies (such as royal propaganda, goods inventories, and bureaucratic record keeping). In general, societies that engaged in intense exchanges of crops, livestock, and technologies related to food production were more likely to become involved in other exchanges as well.

America's patriotic song "America the Beautiful" invokes our spacious skies, our amber waves of grain, from sea to shining sea. Actually, that song reverses geographic realities. As in Africa, in the Americas the spread of native crops and domestic animals was slowed by constricted skies and environmental barriers. No waves of native grain ever stretched from the Atlantic to the Pacific coast of North America, from Canada to Patagonia, or from Egypt to South Africa, while amber waves of wheat and barley came to stretch from the Atlantic to the Pacific across the spacious skies of Eurasia. That faster spread of Eurasian agriculture, compared with that of Native American and sub-Saharan African agriculture, played a role (as the next part of this book will show) in the more rapid diffusion of Eurasian writing, metallurgy, technology, and empires.

To bring up all those differences isn't to claim that widely distributed crops are admirable, or that they testify to the superior ingenuity of early Eurasian farmers. They reflect, instead, the orientation of Eurasia's axis compared with that of the Americas or Africa. Around those axes turned the fortunes of history.

PART THREE

FROM FOOD TO GUNS, GERMS, AND STEEL

CHAPTER 11

LETHAL GIFT OF
LIVESTOCK

W E HAVE NOW TRACED HOW FOOD PRODUCTION AROSE
in a few centers, and how it spread at unequal rates from there
to other areas. Those geographic differences constitute important ultimate
answers to Yali's question about why different peoples ended up with disparate degrees of power and affluence. However, food production itself is
not a proximate cause. In a one-on-one fight, a naked farmer would have
no advantage over a naked hunter-gatherer.

Instead, one part of the explanation for farmer power lies in the much
denser populations that food production could support: ten naked farmers
certainly would have an advantage over one naked hunter-gatherer in a
fight. The other part is that neither farmers nor hunter-gatherers are
naked, at least not figuratively. Farmers tend to breathe out nastier germs,
to own better weapons and armor, to own more-powerful technology in
general, and to live under centralized governments with literate elites better able to wage wars of conquest. Hence the next four chapters will
explore how the ultimate cause of food production led to the proximate
causes of germs, literacy, technology, and centralized government.

The links connecting livestock and crops to germs were unforgettably
illustrated for me by a hospital case about which I learned through a physician friend. When my friend was an inexperienced young doctor, he was

called into a hospital room to deal with a married couple stressed-out by a mysterious illness. It did not help that the couple was also having difficulty communicating with each other, and with my friend. The husband was a small, timid man, sick with pneumonia caused by an unidentified microbe, and with only limited command of the English language. Acting as translator was his beautiful wife, worried about her husband's condition and frightened by the unfamiliar hospital environment. My friend was also stressed-out from a long week of hospital work, and from trying to figure out what unusual risk factors might have brought on the strange illness. The stress caused my friend to forget everything he had been taught about patient confidentiality: he committed the awful blunder of requesting the woman to ask her husband whether he'd had any sexual experiences that could have caused the infection.

As the doctor watched, the husband turned red, pulled himself together so that he seemed even smaller, tried to disappear under his bedsheets, and stammered out words in a barely audible voice. His wife suddenly screamed in rage and drew herself up to tower over him. Before the doctor could stop her, she grabbed a heavy metal bottle, slammed it with full force onto her husband's head, and stormed out of the room. It took a while for the doctor to revive her husband and even longer to elicit, through the man's broken English, what he'd said that so enraged his wife. The answer slowly emerged: he had confessed to repeated intercourse with sheep on a recent visit to the family farm; perhaps that was how he had contracted the mysterious microbe.

This incident sounds bizarrely one-of-a-kind and of no possible broader significance. In fact, it illustrates an enormous subject of great importance: human diseases of animal origins. Very few of us love sheep in the carnal sense that this patient did. But most of us platonically love our pet animals, such as our dogs and cats. As a society, we certainly appear to have an inordinate fondness for sheep and other livestock, to judge from the vast numbers of them that we keep. For example, at the time of a recent census, Australia's 17,085,400 people thought so highly of sheep that they kept 161,600,000 of them.

Some of us adults, and even more of our children, pick up infectious diseases from our pets. Usually they remain no more than a nuisance, but a few have evolved into something far more serious. The major killers of humanity throughout our recent history—smallpox, flu, tuberculosis, malaria, plague, measles, and cholera—are infectious diseases that evolved from diseases of animals, even though most of the microbes responsible for our own epidemic illnesses are paradoxically now almost confined to humans. Because diseases have been the biggest killers of people, they have also been decisive shapers of history. Until World War II, more victims of war died of war-borne microbes than of battle wounds. All those military histories glorifying great generals oversimplify the ego-deflating truth: the winners of past wars were not always the armies with the best generals and weapons, but were often merely those bearing the nastiest germs to transmit to their enemies.

The grimmest examples of germs' role in history come from the European conquest of the Americas that began with Columbus's voyage of 1492. Numerous as were the Native American victims of the murderous Spanish conquistadores, they were far outnumbered by the victims of murderous Spanish microbes. Why was the exchange of nasty germs between the Americas and Europe so unequal? Why didn't Native American diseases instead decimate the Spanish invaders, spread back to Europe, and wipe out 95 percent of Europe's population? Similar questions arise for the decimation of many other native peoples by Eurasian germs, as well as for the decimation of would-be European conquistadores in the tropics of Africa and Asia.

Thus, questions of the animal origins of human disease lie behind the broadest pattern of human history, and behind some of the most important issues in human health today. (Think of AIDS, an explosively spreading human disease that appears to have evolved from a virus resident in wild African monkeys.) This chapter will begin by considering what a "disease" is, and why some microbes have evolved so as to "make us sick," whereas most other species of living things don't make us sick. We'll examine why many of our most familiar infectious diseases run in epidemics, such as our current AIDS epidemic and the Black Death (bubonic plague) epidemics of the Middle Ages. We'll then consider how the ancestors of microbes now confined to us transferred themselves from their original animal hosts. Finally, we'll see how insight into the animal origins of our infectious diseases helps explain the momentous, almost one-way exchange of germs between Europeans and Native Americans.

NATURALLY, WE'RE DISPOSED to think about diseases just from our own point of view: what can we do to save ourselves and to kill the microbes? Let's stamp out the scoundrels, and never mind what *their* motives are! In life in general, though, one has to understand the enemy in order to beat him, and that's especially true in medicine.

Hence let's begin by temporarily setting aside our human bias and considering disease from the microbes' point of view. After all, microbes are as much a product of natural selection as we are. What evolutionary benefit does a microbe derive from making us sick in bizarre ways, like giving us genital sores or diarrhea? And why should microbes evolve so as to kill us? That seems especially puzzling and self-defeating, since a microbe that kills its host kills itself.

Basically, microbes evolve like other species. Evolution selects for those individuals most effective at producing babies and at helping them spread to suitable places to live. For a microbe, spread may be defined mathematically as the number of new victims infected per each original patient. That number depends on how long each victim remains capable of infecting new victims, and how efficiently the microbe is transferred from one victim to the next.

Microbes have evolved diverse ways of spreading from one person to another, and from animals to people. The germ that spreads better leaves more babies and ends up favored by natural selection. Many of our "symptoms" of disease actually represent ways in which some damned clever microbe modifies our bodies or our behavior such that we become enlisted to spread microbes.

The most effortless way a germ could spread is by just waiting to be transmitted passively to the next victim. That's the strategy practiced by microbes that wait for one host to be eaten by the next host: for instance, salmonella bacteria, which we contract by eating already infected eggs or meat; the worm responsible for trichinosis, which gets from pigs to us by waiting for us to kill the pig and eat it without proper cooking; and the worm causing anisakiasis, with which sushi-loving Japanese and Americans occasionally infect themselves by consuming raw fish. Those parasites pass to a person from an eaten animal, but the virus causing laughing sickness (kuru) in the New Guinea highlands used to pass to a person from another person who was eaten. It was transmitted by cannibalism, when highland babies made the fatal mistake of licking their fingers after playing with raw brains that their mothers had just cut out of dead kuru victims awaiting cooking.

Some microbes don't wait for the old host to die and get eaten, but instead hitchhike in the saliva of an insect that bites the old host and flies off to find a new host. The free ride may be provided by mosquitoes, fleas, lice, or tsetse flies that spread malaria, plague, typhus, or sleeping sickness, respectively. The dirtiest of all tricks for passive carriage is perpetrated by microbes that pass from a woman to her fetus and thereby infect babies already at birth. By playing that trick, the microbes responsible for syphilis, rubella, and now AIDS pose ethical dilemmas with which believers in a fundamentally just universe have had to struggle desperately.

Other germs take matters into their own hands, figuratively speaking. They modify the anatomy or habits of their host in such a way as to accelerate their transmission. From our perspective, the open genital sores caused by venereal diseases like syphilis are a vile indignity. From the microbes' point of view, however, they're just a useful device to enlist a host's help in inoculating microbes into a body cavity of a new host. The skin lesions caused by smallpox similarly spread microbes by direct or indirect body contact (occasionally very indirect, as when U.S. whites bent on wiping out "belligerent" Native Americans sent them gifts of blankets previously used by smallpox patients).

More vigorous yet is the strategy practiced by the influenza, common cold, and pertussis (whooping cough) microbes, which induce the victim to cough or sneeze, thereby launching a cloud of microbes toward prospective new hosts. Similarly, the cholera bacterium induces in its victim a massive diarrhea that delivers bacteria into the water supplies of potential new victims, while the virus responsible for Korean hemorrhagic fever broadcasts itself in the urine of mice. For modification of a host's behavior, nothing matches rabies virus, which not only gets into the saliva of an infected dog but drives the dog into a frenzy of biting and thus infecting many new victims. But for physical effort on the bug's own part, the prize still goes to worms such as hookworms and schistosomes, which actively burrow through a host's skin from the water or soil into which their larvae had been excreted in a previous victim's feces.

Thus, from our point of view, genital sores, diarrhea, and coughing are "symptoms of disease." From a germ's point of view, they're clever evolutionary strategies to broadcast the germ. That's why it's in the germ's interests to "make us sick." But why should a germ evolve the apparently self-defeating strategy of killing its host?

From the germ's perspective, that's just an unintended by-product (fat consolation to us!) of host symptoms promoting efficient transmission of microbes. Yes, an untreated cholera patient may eventually die from producing diarrheal fluid at a rate of several gallons per day. At least for a while, though, as long as the patient is still alive, the cholera bacterium profits from being massively broadcast into the water supplies of its next victims. Provided that each victim thereby infects on the average more than one new victim, the bacterium will spread, even though the first host happens to die.

So MUCH FOR our dispassionate examination of the germ's interests. Now let's get back to considering our own selfish interests: to stay alive and healthy, best done by killing the damned germs. One common response of ours to infection is to develop a fever. Again, we're used to considering fever as a "symptom of disease," as if it developed inevitably without serving any function. But regulation of body temperature is under our genetic control and doesn't just happen by accident. A few microbes are more sensitive to heat than our own bodies are. By raising our body temperature, we in effect try to bake the germs to death before we get baked ourselves.

Another common response of ours is to mobilize our immune system. White blood cells and other cells of ours actively seek out and kill foreign microbes. The specific antibodies that we gradually build up against a particular microbe infecting us make us less likely to get reinfected once we become cured. As we all know from experience, there are some illnesses, such as flu and the common cold, to which our resistance is only temporary; we can eventually contract the illness again. Against other illnesses, though—including measles, mumps, rubella, pertussis, and the now defeated smallpox—our antibodies stimulated by one infection confer lifelong immunity. That's the principle of vaccination: to stimulate our antibody production without our having to go through the actual experience of the disease, by inoculating us with a dead or weakened strain of microbe.

Alas, some clever microbes don't just cave in to our immune defenses. Some have learned to trick us by changing those molecular pieces of the microbe (its so-called antigens) that our antibodies recognize. The constant evolution or recycling of new strains of flu, with differing antigens, explains why your having gotten flu two years ago didn't protect you against the different strain that arrived this year. Malaria and sleeping sickness are even more slippery customers in their ability rapidly to change their antigens. Among the slipperiest of all is AIDS, which evolves new antigens even as it sits within an individual patient, thereby eventually overwhelming his or her immune system.

Our slowest defensive response is through natural selection, which changes our gene frequencies from generation to generation. For almost any disease, some people prove to be genetically more resistant than are others. In an epidemic those people with genes for resistance to that particular microbe are more likely to survive than are people lacking such genes. As a result, over the course of history, human populations repeatedly exposed to a particular pathogen have come to consist of a higher proportion of individuals with those genes for resistance—just because unfortunate individuals without the genes were less likely to survive to pass their genes on to babies.

Fat consolation, you may be thinking again. This evolutionary response is not one that does the genetically susceptible dying individual any good. It does mean, though, that a human population as a whole becomes better protected against the pathogen. Examples of those genetic defenses include the protections (at a price) that the sickle-cell gene, Tay-Sachs gene, and cystic fibrosis gene may confer on African blacks, Ashkenazi Jews, and northern Europeans against malaria, tuberculosis, and bacterial diarrheas, respectively.

In short, our interaction with most species, as exemplified by hummingbirds, doesn't make us or the hummingbird "sick." Neither we nor hummingbirds have had to evolve defenses against each other. That peaceful relationship was able to persist because hummingbirds don't count on us to spread their babies or to offer our bodies for food. Hummingbirds evolved instead to feed on nectar and insects, which they find by using their own wings.

But microbes evolved to feed on the nutrients within our own bodies, and they don't have wings to let them reach a new victim's body once the original victim is dead or resistant. Hence many germs have had to evolve tricks to let them spread between potential victims, and many of those tricks are what we experience as "symptoms of disease." We've evolved countertricks of our own, to which the germs have responded by evolving counter-countertricks. We and our pathogens are now locked in an escalating evolutionary contest, with the death of one contestant the price of defeat, and with natural selection playing the role of umpire. Now let's consider the form of the contest: blitzkrieg or guerrilla war?

SUPPOSE THAT ONE counts the number of cases of some particular infectious disease in some geographic area, and watches how the numbers change with time. The resulting patterns differ greatly among diseases. For certain diseases, like malaria or hookworm, new cases appear any month of any year in an affected area. So-called epidemic diseases, though, produce no cases for a long time, then a whole wave of cases, then no more cases again for a while.

Among such epidemic diseases, influenza is one personally familiar to most Americans, certain years being particularly bad years for us (but great years for the influenza virus). Cholera epidemics come at longer intervals, the 1991 Peruvian epidemic being the first one to reach the New World during the 20th century. Although today's influenza and cholera epidemics make front-page stories, epidemics used to be far more terrifying before the rise of modern medicine. The greatest single epidemic in human history was the one of influenza that killed 21 million people at the end of the First World War. The Black Death (bubonic plague) killed one-quarter of Europe's population between 1346 and 1352, with death tolls ranging up to 70 percent in some cities. When the Canadian Pacific Railroad was being built through Saskatchewan in the early 1880s, that province's Native Americans, who had previously had little exposure to whites and their germs, died of tuberculosis at the incredible rate of 9 percent per year.

The infectious diseases that visit us as epidemics, rather than as a steady trickle of cases, share several characteristics. First, they spread quickly and efficiently from an infected person to nearby healthy people, with the result that the whole population gets exposed within a short time. Second, they're "acute" illnesses: within a short time, you either die or recover completely. Third, the fortunate ones of us who do recover develop antibodies that leave us immune against a recurrence of the disease for a long time, possibly for the rest of our life. Finally, these diseases tend to be restricted to humans; the microbes causing them tend not to live in the soil or in other animals. All four of these traits apply to what Americans think of as the familiar acute epidemic diseases of childhood, including measles, rubella, mumps, pertussis, and smallpox.

The reason why the combination of those four traits tends to make a disease run in epidemics is easy to understand. In simplified form, here's what happens. The rapid spread of microbes, and the rapid course of symptoms, mean that everybody in a local human population is quickly infected and soon thereafter is either dead or else recovered and immune. No one is left alive who could still be infected. But since the microbe can't survive except in the bodies of living people, the disease dies out, until a new crop of babies reaches the susceptible age—and until an infectious person arrives from the outside to start a new epidemic.

A classic illustration of how such diseases occur as epidemics is the history of measles on the isolated Atlantic islands called the Faeroes. A severe epidemic of measles reached the Faeroes in 1781 and then died out, leaving the islands measles free until an infected carpenter arrived on a ship from Denmark in 1846. Within three months, almost the whole Faeroes population (7,782 people) had gotten measles and then either died or recovered, leaving the measles virus to disappear once again until the next epidemic. Studies show that measles is likely to die out in any human population numbering fewer than half a million people. Only in larger populations can the disease shift from one local area to another, thereby persisting until enough babies have been born in the originally infected area that measles can return there.

What's true for measles in the Faeroes is true of our other familiar acute infectious diseases throughout the world. To sustain themselves, they need a human population that is sufficiently numerous, and sufficiently densely packed, that a numerous new crop of susceptible children is available for infection by the time the disease would otherwise be waning. Hence measles and similar diseases are also known as crowd diseases.

OBVIOUSLY, CROWD DISEASES could not sustain themselves in small bands of hunter-gatherers and slash-and-burn farmers. As tragic modern experience with Amazonian Indians and Pacific Islanders confirms, almost an entire tribelet may be wiped out by an epidemic brought by an outside visitor—because no one in the tribelet had any antibodies against the microbe. For example, in the winter of 1902 a dysentery epidemic brought by a sailor on the whaling ship *Active* killed 51 out of the 56 Sadlermiut Eskimos, a very isolated band of people living on Southampton Island in the Canadian Arctic. In addition, measles and some of our other "childhood" diseases are more likely to kill infected adults than children, and all adults in the tribelet are susceptible. (In contrast, modern Americans rarely contract measles as adults, because most of them get either measles or the vaccine against it as children.) Having killed most of the tribelet, the epidemic then disappears. The small population size of tribelets explains not only why they can't sustain epidemics introduced from the outside, but also why they never could evolve epidemic diseases of their own to give back to visitors.

That's not to say, though, that small human populations are free from all infectious diseases. They do have infections, but only of certain types. Some are caused by microbes capable of maintaining themselves in animals or in the soil, with the result that the disease doesn't die out but remains constantly available to infect people. For example, the yellow fever virus is carried by African wild monkeys, whence it can always infect rural human populations of Africa, whence it was carried by the transatlantic slave trade to infect New World monkeys and people.

Still other infections of small human populations are chronic diseases such as leprosy and yaws. Since the disease may take a very long time to kill its victim, the victim remains alive as a reservoir of microbes to infect other members of the tribelet. For instance, the Karimui Basim of the New Guinea highlands, where I worked in the 1960s, was occupied by an isolated population of a few thousand people, suffering from the world's highest incidence of leprosy—about 40 percent! Finally, small human populations are also susceptible to nonfatal infections against which we don't develop immunity, with the result that the same person can become reinfected after recovering. That happens with hookworm and many other parasites.

All these types of diseases, characteristic of small isolated populations, must be the oldest diseases of humanity. They were the ones we could evolve and sustain through the early millions of years of our evolutionary history, when the total human population was tiny and fragmented. These diseases are also shared with, or similar to the diseases of, our closest wild relatives, the African great apes. In contrast, the crowd diseases, which we discussed earlier, could have arisen only with the buildup of large, dense human populations. That buildup began with the rise of agriculture starting about 10,000 years ago and then accelerated with the rise of cities starting several thousand years ago. In fact, the first attested dates for many familiar infectious diseases are surprisingly recent: around 1600 B.C. for smallpox (as deduced from pockmarks on an Egyptian mummy), 400 B.C. for mumps, 200 B.C. for leprosy, A.D. 1840 for epidemic polio, and 1959 for AIDS.

WHY DID THE rise of agriculture launch the evolution of our crowd infectious diseases? One reason just mentioned is that agriculture sustains much higher human population densities than does the hunting-gathering lifestyle—on the average, 10 to 100 times higher. In addition, hunter-gatherers frequently shift camp and leave behind their own piles of feces with accumulated microbes and worm larvae. But farmers are sedentary and live amid their own sewage, thus providing microbes with a short path from one person's body into another's drinking water.

Some farming populations make it even easier for their own fecal bacteria and worms to infect new victims, by gathering their feces and urine and spreading them as fertilizer on the fields where people work. Irrigation agriculture and fish farming provide ideal living conditions for the snails carrying schistosomiasis and for flukes that burrow through our skin as we wade through the feces-laden water. Sedentary farmers become surrounded not only by their feces but also by disease transmitting rodents, attracted by the farmers' stored food. The forest clearings made by African farmers also provide ideal breeding habitats for malaria-transmitting mosquitoes.

If the rise of farming was thus a bonanza for our microbes, the rise of cities was a greater one, as still more densely packed human populations festered under even worse sanitation conditions. Not until the beginning of the 20th century did Europe's urban populations finally become self-sustaining: before then, constant immigration of healthy peasants from the countryside was necessary to make up for the constant deaths of city dwellers from crowd diseases. Another bonanza was the development of world trade routes, which by Roman times effectively joined the populations of Europe, Asia, and North Africa into one giant breeding ground for microbes. That's when smallpox finally reached Rome, as the Plague of Antoninus, which killed millions of Roman citizens between A.D. 165 and 180.

Similarly, bubonic plague first appeared in Europe as the Plague of Justinian (A.D. 542–43). But plague didn't begin to hit Europe with full force as the Black Death epidemics until A.D. 1346, when a new route for overland trade with China provided rapid transit, along Eurasia's east–west axis, for flea-infested furs from plague-ridden areas of Central Asia to Europe. Today, our jet planes have made even the longest intercontinental flights briefer than the duration of any human infectious disease. That's how an Aerolineas Argentinas airplane, stopping in Lima (Peru) in 1991, managed to deliver dozens of cholera-infected people that same day to my city of Los Angeles, over 3,000 miles from Lima. The explosive increase in world travel by Americans, and in immigration to the United States, is turning us into another melting pot—this time, of microbes that we previously dismissed as just causing exotic diseases in far-off countries.

THUS, WHEN THE human population became sufficiently large and concentrated, we reached the stage in our history at which we could at last evolve and sustain crowd diseases confined to our own species. But that conclusion presents a paradox: such diseases could never have existed before then! Instead, they had to evolve as new diseases. Where did those new diseases come from?

Evidence has recently been emerging from molecular studies of the disease-causing microbes themselves. For many of the microbes responsible for our unique diseases, molecular biologists can now identify the microbe's closest relatives. These also prove to be agents of crowd infectious diseases—but ones confined to various species of our domestic animals and pets! Among animals, too, epidemic diseases require large, dense populations and don't afflict just any animal: they're confined mainly to social animals providing the necessary large populations. Hence when we domesticated social animals, such as cows and pigs, they were already afflicted by epidemic diseases just waiting to be transferred to us.

For example, measles virus is most closely related to the virus causing rinderpest. That nasty epidemic disease affects cattle and many wild cud-chewing mammals, but not humans. Measles in turn doesn't afflict cattle. The close similarity of the measles virus to the rinderpest virus suggests that the latter transferred from cattle to humans and then evolved into the measles virus by changing its properties to adapt to us. That transfer is not at all surprising, considering that many peasant farmers live and sleep close to cows and their feces, urine, breath, sores, and blood. Our intimacy with cattle has been going on for the 9,000 years since we domesticated them—ample time for the rinderpest virus to discover us nearby. As Table 11.1 illustrates, others of our familiar infectious diseases can similarly be traced back to diseases of our animal friends.

GIVEN OUR PROXIMITY to the animals we love, we must be getting constantly bombarded by their microbes. Those invaders get winnowed by natural selection, and only a few of them succeed in establishing themselves as human diseases. A quick survey of current diseases lets us trace out four stages in the evolution of a specialized human disease from an animal precursor.

The first stage is illustrated by dozens of diseases that we now and then pick up directly from our pets and domestic animals. They include cat-scratch fever from our cats, leptospirosis from our dogs, psittacosis from our chickens and parrots, and brucellosis from our cattle. We're similarly liable to pick up diseases from wild animals, such as the tularemia that hunters can get from skinning wild rabbits. All those microbes are still at an early stage in their evolution into specialized human pathogens. They still don't get transmitted directly from one person to another, and even their transfer to us from animals remains uncommon.

In the second stage a former animal pathogen evolves to the point where it does get transmitted directly between people and causes epidemics.

TABLE 11.1 **Deadly Gifts from Our Animal Friends**

Human Disease	Animal with Most Closely Related Pathogen
Measles	cattle (rinderpest)
Tuberculosis	cattle
Smallpox	cattle (cowpox) or other livestock with related pox viruses
Flu	pigs and ducks
Pertussis	pigs, dogs
Falciparum malaria	birds (chickens and ducks?)

However, the epidemic dies out for any of several reasons, such as being cured by modern medicine, or being stopped when everybody around has already been infected and either becomes immune or dies. For example, a previously unknown fever termed O'nyong-nyong fever appeared in East Africa in 1959 and proceeded to infect several million Africans. It probably arose from a virus of monkeys and was transmitted to humans by mosquitoes. The fact that patients recovered quickly and became immune to further attack helped the new disease die out quickly. Closer to home for Americans, Fort Bragg fever was the name applied to a new leptospiral disease that broke out in the United States in the summer of 1942 and soon disappeared.

A fatal disease vanishing for another reason was New Guinea's laughing sickness, transmitted by cannibalism and caused by a slow-acting virus from which no one has ever recovered. Kuru was on its way to exterminating New Guinea's Foré tribe of 20,000 people, until the establishment of Australian government control around 1959 ended cannibalism and thereby the transmission of kuru. The annals of medicine are full of accounts of diseases that sound like no disease known today, but that once caused terrifying epidemics and then disappeared as mysteriously as they had come. The "English sweating sickness," which swept and terrified Europe between 1485 and 1552, and the "Picardy sweats" of 18th- and 19th-century France, are just two of the many epidemic illnesses that vanished long before modern medicine had devised methods for identifying the responsible microbes.

A third stage in the evolution of our major diseases is represented by former animal pathogens that did establish themselves in humans, that have not (not yet?) died out, and that may or may not still become major killers of humanity. The future remains very uncertain for Lassa fever, caused by a virus derived probably from rodents. Lassa fever was first observed in 1969 in Nigeria, where it causes a fatal illness so contagious that Nigerian hospitals have been closed down if even a single case appears. Better established is Lyme disease, caused by a spirochete that we get from the bite of ticks carried by mice and deer. Although the first known human cases in the United States appeared only as recently as 1962, Lyme disease is already reaching epidemic proportions in many parts of our country. The future of AIDS, derived from monkey viruses and first documented in humans around 1959, is even more secure (from the virus's perspective).

The final stage of this evolution is represented by the major, long-established epidemic diseases confined to humans. These diseases must have been the evolutionary survivors of far more pathogens that tried to make the jump to us from animals—and mostly failed.

What is actually going on in those stages, as an exclusive disease of animals transforms itself into an exclusive disease of humans? One transformation involves a change of intermediate vector: when a microbe relying on some arthropod vector for transmission switches to a new host, the microbe may be forced to find a new arthropod as well. For example, typhus was initially transmitted between rats by rat fleas, which sufficed for a while to transfer typhus from rats to humans. Eventually, typhus microbes discovered that human body lice offered a much more efficient method of traveling directly between humans. Now that Americans have mostly deloused themselves, typhus has discovered a new route into us: by infecting eastern North American flying squirrels and then transferring to people whose attics harbor flying squirrels.

In short, diseases represent evolution in progress, and microbes adapt by natural selection to new hosts and vectors. But compared with cows' bodies, ours offer different immune defenses, lice, feces, and chemistries. In that new environment, a microbe must evolve new ways to live and to propagate itself. In several instructive cases doctors or veterinarians have actually been able to observe microbes evolving those new ways.

The best-studied case involves what happened when myxomatosis hit Australian rabbits. The myxo virus, native to a wild species of Brazilian rabbit, had been observed to cause a lethal epidemic in European domestic rabbits, which are a different species. Hence the virus was intentionally introduced to Australia in 1950 in the hopes of ridding the continent of its plague of European rabbits, foolishly introduced in the nineteenth century. In the first year, myxo produced a gratifying (to Australian farmers) 99.8 percent mortality rate in infected rabbits. Unfortunately for the farmers, the death rate then dropped in the second year to 90 percent and eventually to 25 percent, frustrating hopes of eradicating rabbits completely from Australia. The problem was that the myxo virus evolved to serve its own interests, which differed from ours as well as from those of the rabbits. The virus changed so as to kill fewer rabbits and to permit lethally infected ones to live longer before dying. As a result, a less lethal myxo virus spreads baby viruses to more rabbits than did the original, highly virulent myxo.

For a similar example in humans, we have only to consider the surprising evolution of syphilis. Today, our two immediate associations to syphilis are genital sores and a very slowly developing disease, leading to the death of many untreated victims only after many years. However, when syphilis was first definitely recorded in Europe in 1495, its pustules often covered the body from the head to the knees, caused flesh to fall off people's faces, and led to death within a few months. By 1546, syphilis had evolved into the disease with the symptoms so well known to us today. Apparently, just as with myxomatosis, those syphilis spirochetes that evolved so as to keep their victims alive for longer were thereby able to transmit their spirochete offspring into more victims.

THE IMPORTANCE OF lethal microbes in human history is well illustrated by Europeans' conquest and depopulation of the New World. Far more Native Americans died in bed from Eurasian germs than on the battlefield from European guns and swords. Those germs undermined Indian resistance by killing most Indians and their leaders and by sapping the survivors' morale. For instance, in 1519 Cortés landed on the coast of Mexico with 600 Spaniards, to conquer the fiercely militaristic Aztec Empire with a population of many millions. That Cortés reached the Aztec capital of Tenochtitlán, escaped with the loss of "only" two-thirds of his force, and managed to fight his way back to the coast demonstrates both Spanish military advantages and the initial naïveté of the Aztecs. But when Cortés's next onslaught came, the Aztecs were no longer naive and fought street by street with the utmost tenacity. What gave the Spaniards a decisive advantage was smallpox, which reached Mexico in 1520 with one infected slave arriving from Spanish Cuba. The resulting epidemic proceeded to kill nearly half of the Aztecs, including Emperor Cuitláhuac. Aztec survivors were demoralized by the mysterious illness that killed Indians and spared Spaniards, as if advertising the Spaniards' invincibility. By 1618, Mexico's initial population of about 20 million had plummeted to about 1.6 million.

Pizarro had similarly grim luck when he landed on the coast of Peru in 1531 with 168 men to conquer the Inca Empire of millions. Fortunately for Pizarro and unfortunately for the Incas, smallpox had arrived overland around 1526, killing much of the Inca population, including both the emperor Huayna Capac and his designated successor. As we saw in Chapter 3, the result of the throne's being left vacant was that two other sons of Huayna Capac, Atahuallpa and Huascar, became embroiled in a civil war that Pizarro exploited to conquer the divided Incas.

When we in the United States think of the most populous New World societies existing in 1492, only those of the Aztecs and the Incas tend to come to our minds. We forget that North America also supported populous Indian societies in the most logical place, the Mississippi Valley, which contains some of our best farmland today. In that case, however, conquistadores contributed nothing directly to the societies' destruction; Eurasian germs, spreading in advance, did everything. When Hernando de Soto became the first European conquistador to march through the southeastern United States, in 1540, he came across Indian town sites abandoned two years earlier because the inhabitants had died in epidemics. These epidemics had been transmitted from coastal Indians infected by Spaniards visiting the coast. The Spaniards' microbes spread to the interior in advance of the Spaniards themselves.

De Soto was still able to see some of the densely populated Indian towns lining the lower Mississippi. After the end of his expedition, it was a long time before Europeans again reached the Mississippi Valley, but Eurasian microbes were now established in North America and kept spreading. By the time of the next appearance of Europeans on the lower Mississippi, that of French settlers in the late 1600s, almost all of those big Indian towns had vanished. Their relics are the great mound sites of the Mississippi Valley. Only recently have we come to realize that many of the mound-building societies were still largely intact when Columbus reached the New World, and that they collapsed (probably as a result of disease) between 1492 and the systematic European exploration of the Mississippi.

When I was young, American schoolchildren were taught that North America had originally been occupied by only about one million Indians. That low number was useful in justifying the white conquest of what could be viewed as an almost empty continent. However, archaeological excavations, and scrutiny of descriptions left by the very first European explorers on our coasts, now suggest an initial number of around 20 million Indians. For the New World as a whole, the Indian population decline in the century or two following Columbus's arrival is estimated to have been as large as 95 percent.

The main killers were Old World germs to which Indians had never been exposed, and against which they therefore had neither immune nor genetic resistance. Smallpox, measles, influenza, and typhus competed for top rank among the killers. As if these had not been enough, diphtheria, malaria, mumps, pertussis, plague, tuberculosis, and yellow fever came up close behind. In countless cases, whites were actually there to witness the destruction occurring when the germs arrived. For example, in 1837 the Mandan Indian tribe, with one of the most elaborate cultures in our Great Plains, contracted smallpox from a steamboat traveling up the Missouri River from St. Louis. The population of one Mandan village plummeted from 2,000 to fewer than 40 within a few weeks.

WHILE OVER A dozen major infectious diseases of Old World origins became established in the New World, perhaps not a single major killer reached Europe from the Americas. The sole possible exception is syphilis, whose area of origin remains controversial. The one-sidedness of that exchange of germs becomes even more striking when we recall that large, dense human populations are a prerequisite for the evolution of our crowd infectious diseases. If recent reappraisals of the pre-Columbian New World population are correct, it was not far below the contemporary population of Eurasia. Some New World cities like Tenochtitlán were among the world's most populous cities at the time. Why didn't Tenochtitlán have awful germs waiting for the Spaniards?

One possible contributing factor is that the rise of dense human populations began somewhat later in the New World than in the Old World. Another is that the three most densely populated American centers—the Andes, Mesoamerica, and the Mississippi Valley—never became connected by regular fast trade into one huge breeding ground for microbes, in the way that Europe, North Africa, India, and China became linked in Roman times. Those factors still don't explain, though, why the New World apparently ended up with no lethal crowd epidemics at all. (Tuberculosis DNA has been reported from the mummy of a Peruvian Indian who died 1,000 years ago, but the identification procedure used did not distinguish human tuberculosis from a closely related pathogen (*Mycobacterium bovis*) that is widespread in wild animals.)

Instead, what must be the main reason for the failure of lethal crowd epidemics to arise in the Americas becomes clear when we pause to ask a simple question. From what microbes could they conceivably have evolved? We've seen that Eurasian crowd diseases evolved out of diseases of Eurasian herd animals that became domesticated. Whereas many such animals existed in Eurasia, only five animals of any sort became domesticated in the Americas: the turkey in Mexico and the U.S. Southwest, the llama / alpaca and the guinea pig in the Andes, the Muscovy duck in tropical South America, and the dog throughout the Americas.

In turn, we also saw that this extreme paucity of domestic animals in the New World reflects the paucity of wild starting material. About 80 percent of the big wild mammals of the Americas became extinct at the end of the last Ice Age, around 13,000 years ago. The few domesticates that remained to Native Americans were not likely sources of crowd diseases, compared with cows and pigs. Muscovy ducks and turkeys don't live in enormous flocks, and they're not cuddly species (like young lambs) with which we have much physical contact. Guinea pigs may have contributed a trypanosome infection like Chagas' disease or leishmaniasis to our catalog of woes, but that's uncertain. Initially, most surprising is the absence of any human disease derived from llamas (or alpacas), which it's tempting to consider the Andean equivalent of Eurasian livestock. However, llamas had four strikes against them as a source of human pathogens: they were kept in smaller herds than were sheep and goats and pigs; their total numbers were never remotely as large as those of the Eurasian populations of domestic livestock, since llamas never spread beyond the Andes; people don't drink (and get infected by) llama milk; and llamas aren't kept indoors, in close association with people. In contrast, human mothers in the New Guinea highlands often nurse piglets, and pigs as well as cows are frequently kept inside the huts of peasant farmers.

THE HISTORICAL IMPORTANCE of animal-derived diseases extends far beyond the collision of the Old and the New Worlds. Eurasian germs played a key role in decimating native peoples in many other parts of the world, including Pacific islanders, Aboriginal Australians, and the Khoisan peoples (Hottentots and Bushmen) of southern Africa. Cumulative mortalities of these previously unexposed peoples from Eurasian germs ranged from 50 percent to 100 percent. For instance, the Indian population of Hispaniola declined from around 8 million, when Columbus arrived in A.D. 1492, to zero by 1535. Measles reached Fiji with a Fijian chief returning from a visit to Australia in 1875, and proceeded to kill about one-quarter of all Fijians then alive (after most Fijians had already been killed by epidemics beginning with the first European visit, in 1791). Syphilis, gonorrhea, tuberculosis, and influenza arriving with Captain Cook in 1779, followed by a big typhoid epidemic in 1804 and numerous "minor" epidemics, reduced Hawaii's population from around half a million in 1779 to 84,000 in 1853, the year when smallpox finally reached Hawaii and killed around 10,000 of the survivors. These examples could be multiplied almost indefinitely.

However, germs did not act solely to Europeans' advantage. While the New World and Australia did not harbor native epidemic diseases awaiting Europeans, tropical Asia, Africa, Indonesia, and New Guinea certainly did. Malaria throughout the tropical Old World, cholera in tropical Southeast Asia, and yellow fever in tropical Africa were (and still are) the most notorious of the tropical killers. They posed the most serious obstacle to European colonization of the tropics, and they explain why the European colonial partitioning of New Guinea and most of Africa was not accomplished until nearly 400 years after European partitioning of the New World began. Furthermore, once malaria and yellow fever did become transmitted to the Americas by European ship traffic, they emerged as the major impediment to colonization of the New World tropics as well. A familiar example is the role of those two diseases in aborting the French effort, and nearly aborting the ultimately successful American effort, to construct the Panama Canal.

Bearing all these facts in mind, let's try to regain our sense of perspective about the role of germs in answering Yali's question. There is no doubt that Europeans developed a big advantage in weaponry, technology, and political organization over most of the non-European peoples that they conquered. But that advantage alone doesn't fully explain how initially so few European immigrants came to supplant so much of the native population of the Americas and some other parts of the world. That might not have happened without Europe's sinister gift to other continents—the germs evolving from Eurasians' long intimacy with domestic animals.

CHAPTER 12

BLUEPRINTS AND
BORROWED LETTERS

N INETEENTH-CENTURY AUTHORS TENDED TO INTERPRET history as a progression from savagery to civilization. Key hallmarks of this transition included the development of agriculture, metallurgy, complex technology, centralized government, and writing. Of these, writing was traditionally the one most restricted geographically: until the expansions of Islam and of colonial Europeans, it was absent from Australia, Pacific islands, subequatorial Africa, and the whole New World except for a small part of Mesoamerica. As a result of that confined distribution, peoples who pride themselves on being civilized have always viewed writing as the sharpest distinction raising them above "barbarians" or "savages."

Knowledge brings power. Hence writing brings power to modern societies, by making it possible to transmit knowledge with far greater accuracy and in far greater quantity and detail, from more distant lands and more remote times. Of course, some peoples (notably the Incas) managed to administer empires without writing, and "civilized" peoples don't always defeat "barbarians," as Roman armies facing the Huns learned. But the European conquests of the Americas, Siberia, and Australia illustrate the typical recent outcome.

Writing marched together with weapons, microbes, and centralized political organization as a modern agent of conquest. The commands of the monarchs and merchants who organized colonizing fleets were conveyed in writing. The fleets set their courses by maps and written sailing directions prepared by previous expeditions. Written accounts of earlier expeditions motivated later ones, by describing the wealth and fertile lands awaiting the conquerors. The accounts taught subsequent explorers what conditions to expect, and helped them prepare themselves. The resulting empires were administered with the aid of writing. While all those types of information were also transmitted by other means in preliterate societies, writing made the transmission easier, more detailed, more accurate, and more persuasive.

Why, then, did only some peoples and not others develop writing, given its overwhelming value? For example, why did no traditional hunters-gatherers evolve or adopt writing? Among island empires, why did writing arise in Minoan Crete but not in Polynesian Tonga? How many separate times did writing evolve in human history, under what circumstances, and for what uses? Of those peoples who did develop it, why did some do so much earlier than others? For instance, today almost all Japanese and Scandinavians are literate but most Iraqis are not: why did writing nevertheless arise nearly four thousand years earlier in Iraq?

The diffusion of writing from its sites of origin also raises important questions. Why, for instance, did it spread to Ethiopia and Arabia from the Fertile Crescent, but not to the Andes from Mexico? Did writing systems spread by being copied, or did existing systems merely inspire neighboring peoples to invent their own systems? Given a writing system that works well for one language, how do you devise a system for a different language? Similar questions arise whenever one tries to understand the origins and spread of many other aspects of human culture—such as technology, religion, and food production. The historian interested in such questions about writing has the advantage that they can often be answered in unique detail by means of the written record itself. We shall therefore trace writing's development not only because of its inherent importance, but also for the general insights into cultural history that it provides.

THE THREE BASIC strategies underlying writing systems differ in the size of the speech unit denoted by one written sign: either a single basic sound, a whole syllable, or a whole word. Of these, the one employed today by most peoples is the alphabet, which ideally would provide a unique sign (termed a letter) for each basic sound of the language (a phoneme). Actually, most alphabets consist of only about 20 or 30 letters, and most languages have more phonemes than their alphabets have letters. For example, English transcribes about 40 phonemes with a mere 26 letters. Hence most alphabetically written languages, including English, are forced to assign several different phonemes to the same letter and to represent some phonemes by combinations of letters, such as the English two-letter combinations *sh* and *th* (each represented by a single letter in the Russian and Greek alphabets, respectively).

The second strategy uses so-called logograms, meaning that one written sign stands for a whole word. That's the function of many signs of Chinese writing and of the predominant Japanese writing system (termed kanji). Before the spread of alphabetic writing, systems making much use of logograms were more common and included Egyptian hieroglyphs, Maya glyphs, and Sumerian cuneiform.

The third strategy, least familiar to most readers of this book, uses a sign for each syllable. In practice, most such writing systems (termed syllabaries) provide distinct signs just for syllables of one consonant followed by one vowel (like the syllables of the word "fa-mi-ly"), and resort to various tricks in order to write other types of syllables by means of those signs. Syllabaries were common in ancient times, as exemplified by the Linear B writing of Mycenaean Greece. Some syllabaries persist today, the most important being the kana syllabary that the Japanese use for telegrams, bank statements, and texts for blind readers.

I've intentionally termed these three approaches strategies rather than writing systems. No actual writing system employs one strategy exclusively. Chinese writing is not purely logographic, nor is English writing purely alphabetic. Like all alphabetic writing systems, English uses many logograms, such as numerals, $, %, and + : that is, arbitrary signs, not made up of phonetic elements, representing whole words. "Syllabic" Linear B had many logograms, and "logographic" Egyptian hieroglyphs included many syllabic signs as well as a virtual alphabet of individual letters for each consonant.

INVENTING A WRITING system from scratch must have been incomparably more difficult than borrowing and adapting one. The first scribes had to settle on basic principles that we now take for granted. For example, they had to figure out how to decompose a continuous utterance into speech units, regardless of whether those units were taken as words, syllables, or phonemes. They had to learn to recognize the same sound or speech unit through all our normal variations in speech volume, pitch, speed, emphasis, phrase grouping, and individual idiosyncrasies of pronunciation. They had to decide that a writing system should ignore all of that variation. They then had to devise ways to represent sounds by symbols.

Somehow, the first scribes solved all those problems, without having in front of them any example of the final result to guide their efforts. That task was evidently so difficult that there have been only a few occasions in history when people invented writing entirely on their own. The two indisputably independent inventions of writing were achieved by the Sumerians of Mesopotamia somewhat before 3000 B.C. and by Mexican Indians before 600 B.C. (Figure 12.1); Egyptian writing of 3000 B.C. and Chinese writing (by 1300 B.C.) may also have arisen independently. Probably all other peoples who have developed writing since then have borrowed, adapted, or at least been inspired by existing systems.

The independent invention that we can trace in greatest detail is history's oldest writing system, Sumerian cuneiform (Figure 12.1). For thousands of years before it jelled, people in some farming villages of the Fertile Crescent had been using clay tokens of various simple shapes for accounting purposes, such as recording numbers of sheep and amounts of grain. In the last centuries before 3000 B.C., developments in accounting technology, format, and signs rapidly led to the first system of writing. One such technological innovation was the use of flat clay tablets as a convenient writing surface. Initially, the clay was scratched with pointed tools, which gradually yielded to reed styluses for neatly pressing a mark into the tablet. Developments in format included the gradual adoption of conventions whose necessity is now universally accepted: that writing should be organized into ruled rows or columns (horizontal rows for the Sumerians, as for modern Europeans); that the lines should be read in a constant direction (left to right for Sumerians, as for modern Europeans); and that the lines should be read from top to bottom of the tablet rather than vice versa.

But the crucial change involved the solution of the problem basic to

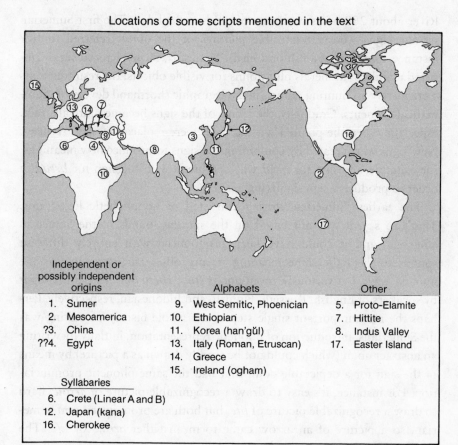

Locations of some scripts mentioned in the text

Independent or possibly independent origins
1. Sumer
2. Mesoamerica
?3. China
??4. Egypt

Syllabaries
6. Crete (Linear A and B)
12. Japan (kana)
16. Cherokee

Alphabets
9. West Semitic, Phoenician
10. Ethiopian
11. Korea (han'gŭl)
13. Italy (Roman, Etruscan)
14. Greece
15. Ireland (ogham)

Other
5. Proto-Elamite
7. Hittite
8. Indus Valley
17. Easter Island

Figure 12.1. The question marks next to China and Egypt denote some doubt whether early writing in those areas arose completely independently or was stimulated by writing systems that arose elsewhere earlier. "Other" refers to scripts that were neither alphabets nor syllabaries and that probably arose under the influence of earlier scripts.

virtually all writing systems: how to devise agreed-on visible marks that represent actual spoken sounds, rather than only ideas or else words independent of their pronunciation. Early stages in the development of the solution have been detected especially in thousands of clay tablets excavated from the ruins of the former Sumerian city of Uruk, on the Euphrates

River about 200 miles southeast of modern Baghdad. The first Sumerian writing signs were recognizable pictures of the object referred to (for instance, a picture of a fish or a bird). Naturally, those pictorial signs consisted mainly of numerals plus nouns for visible objects; the resulting texts were merely accounting reports in a telegraphic shorthand devoid of grammatical elements. Gradually, the forms of the signs became more abstract, especially when the pointed writing tools were replaced by reed styluses. New signs were created by combining old signs to produce new meanings: for example, the sign for *head* was combined with the sign for *bread* in order to produce a sign signifying *eat*.

The earliest Sumerian writing consisted of nonphonetic logograms. That's to say, it was not based on the specific sounds of the Sumerian language, and it could have been pronounced with entirely different sounds to yield the same meaning in any other language—just as the numeral sign 4 is variously pronounced *four, chetwíre, neljä,* and *empat* by speakers of English, Russian, Finnish, and Indonesian, respectively. Perhaps the most important single step in the whole history of writing was the Sumerians' introduction of phonetic representation, initially by writing an abstract noun (which could not be readily drawn as a picture) by means of the sign for a depictable noun that had the same phonetic pronunciation. For instance, it's easy to draw a recognizable picture of *arrow,* hard to draw a recognizable picture of *life,* but both are pronounced *ti* in Sumerian, so a picture of an arrow came to mean either *arrow* or *life.* The resulting ambiguity was resolved by the addition of a silent sign called a determinative, to indicate the category of nouns to which the intended object belonged. Linguists term this decisive innovation, which also underlies puns today, the rebus principle.

Once Sumerians had hit upon this phonetic principle, they began to use it for much more than just writing abstract nouns. They employed it to write syllables or letters constituting grammatical endings. For instance, in English it's not obvious how to draw a picture of the common syllable -*tion,* but we could instead draw a picture illustrating the verb *shun,* which has the same pronunciation. Phonetically interpreted signs were also used to "spell out" longer words, as a series of pictures each depicting the sound of one syllable. That's as if an English speaker were to write the word *believe* as a picture of a bee followed by a picture of a leaf. Phonetic signs also permitted scribes to use the same pictorial sign for a set of related words (such as *tooth, speech,* and *speaker*), but to resolve the ambiguity

An example of Babylonian cuneiform writing, derived ultimately from Sumerian cuneiform.

with an additional phonetically interpreted sign (such as selecting the sign for *two, each,* or *peak*).

Thus, Sumerian writing came to consist of a complex mixture of three types of signs: logograms, referring to a whole word or name; phonetic signs, used in effect for spelling syllables, letters, grammatical elements, or parts of words; and determinatives, which were not pronounced but were used to resolve ambiguities. Nevertheless, the phonetic signs in Sumerian writing fell far short of a complete syllabary or alphabet. Some Sumerian syllables lacked any written signs; the same sign could be pronounced in different ways; and the same sign could variously be read as a word, a syllable, or a letter.

Besides Sumerian cuneiform, the other certain instance of independent origins of writing in human history comes from Native American societies of Mesoamerica, probably southern Mexico. Mesoamerican writing is believed to have arisen independently of Old World writing, because there is no convincing evidence for pre-Norse contact of New World societies with Old World societies possessing writing. In addition, the forms of Mesoamerican writing signs were entirely different from those of any Old World script. About a dozen Mesoamerican scripts are known, all or most of them apparently related to each other (for example, in their numerical and calendrical systems), and most of them still only partially deciphered. At the moment, the earliest preserved Mesoamerican script is from the Zapotec area of southern Mexico around 600 B.C., but by far the best-understood one is of the Lowland Maya region, where the oldest known written date corresponds to A.D. 292.

Despite its independent origins and distinctive sign forms, Maya writing is organized on principles basically similar to those of Sumerian writing and other western Eurasian writing systems that Sumerian inspired. Like Sumerian, Maya writing used both logograms and phonetic signs. Logograms for abstract words were often derived by the rebus principle. That is, an abstract word was written with the sign for another word pronounced similarly but with a different meaning that could be readily depicted. Like the signs of Japan's kana and Mycenaean Greece's Linear B syllabaries, Maya phonetic signs were mostly signs for syllables of one consonant plus one vowel (such as *ta, te, ti, to, tu*). Like letters of the early Semitic alphabet, Maya syllabic signs were derived from pictures of the object whose pronunciation began with that syllable (for example, the Maya syllabic sign "*ne*" resembles a tail, for which the Maya word is *neh*).

All of these parallels between Mesoamerican and ancient western Eurasian writing testify to the underlying universality of human creativity. While Sumerian and Mesoamerican languages bear no special relation to each other among the world's languages, both raised similar basic issues in reducing them to writing. The solutions that Sumerians invented before

A painting of the Rajasthani or Gujarati school, from the Indian subcontinent in the early 17th century. The script, like most other modern Indian scripts, is derived from ancient India's Brahmi script, which was probably derived in turn by idea diffusion from the Aramaic alphabet around the seventh century B.C. Indian scripts incorporated the alphabetic principle but independently devised letter forms, letter sequence, and vowel treatment without resort to blueprint copying.

3000 B.C. were reinvented, halfway around the world, by early Mesoamerican Indians before 600 B.C.

WITH THE POSSIBLE exceptions of the Egyptian, Chinese, and Easter Island writing to be considered later, all other writing systems devised anywhere in the world, at any time, appear to have been descendants of systems modified from or at least inspired by Sumerian or early Mesoamerican writing. One reason why there were so few independent origins of writing is the great difficulty of inventing it, as we have already discussed. The other reason is that other opportunities for the independent invention of writing were preempted by Sumerian or early Mesoamerican writing and their derivatives.

We know that the development of Sumerian writing took at least hundreds, possibly thousands, of years. As we shall see, the prerequisites for those developments consisted of several features of human society that determined whether a society would find writing useful, and whether the society could support the necessary specialist scribes. Many other human societies besides those of the Sumerians and early Mexicans—such as those of ancient India, Crete, and Ethiopia—evolved these prerequisites. However, the Sumerians and early Mexicans happened to have been the first to evolve them in the Old World and the New World, respectively. Once the Sumerians and early Mexicans had invented writing, the details or principles of their writing spread rapidly to other societies, before they could go through the necessary centuries or millennia of independent experimentation with writing themselves. Thus, that potential for other, independent experiments was preempted or aborted.

The spread of writing has occurred by either of two contrasting methods, which find parallels throughout the history of technology and ideas. Someone invents something and puts it to use. How do you, another would-be user, then design something similar for your own use, knowing that other people have already got their own model built and working?

Such transmission of inventions assumes a whole spectrum of forms. At the one end lies "blueprint copying," when you copy or modify an available detailed blueprint. At the opposite end lies "idea diffusion," when you receive little more than the basic idea and have to reinvent the details. Knowing that it can be done stimulates you to try to do it yourself, but your eventual specific solution may or may not resemble that of the first inventor.

To take a recent example, historians are still debating whether blueprint copying or idea diffusion contributed more to Russia's building of an atomic bomb. Did Russia's bomb-building efforts depend critically on blueprints of the already constructed American bomb, stolen and transmitted to Russia by spies? Or was it merely that the revelation of America's A-bomb at Hiroshima at last convinced Stalin of the feasibility of building such a bomb, and that Russian scientists then reinvented the principles in an independent crash program, with little detailed guidance from the earlier American effort? Similar questions arise for the history of the development of wheels, pyramids, and gunpowder. Let's now examine how blueprint copying and idea diffusion contributed to the spread of writing systems.

TODAY, PROFESSIONAL LINGUISTS design writing systems for unwritten languages by the method of blueprint copying. Most such tailor-made systems modify existing alphabets, though some instead design syllabaries. For example, missionary linguists are working on modified Roman alphabets for hundreds of New Guinea and Native American languages. Government linguists devised the modified Roman alphabet adopted in 1928 by Turkey for writing Turkish, as well as the modified Cyrillic alphabets designed for many tribal languages of Russia.

In a few cases, we also know something about the individuals who designed writing systems by blueprint copying in the remote past. For instance, the Cyrillic alphabet itself (the one still used today in Russia) is descended from an adaptation of Greek and Hebrew letters devised by Saint Cyril, a Greek missionary to the Slavs in the ninth century A.D. The first preserved texts for any Germanic language (the language family that includes English) are in the Gothic alphabet created by Bishop Ulfilas, a missionary living with the Visigoths in what is now Bulgaria in the fourth century A.D. Like Saint Cyril's invention, Ulfilas's alphabet was a mishmash of letters borrowed from different sources: about 20 Greek letters, about five Roman letters, and two letters either taken from the runic alphabet or invented by Ulfilas himself. Much more often, we know nothing about the individuals responsible for devising famous alphabets of the past. But it's still possible to compare newly emerged alphabets of the past with previously existing ones, and to deduce from letter forms which existing ones served as models. For the same reason, we can be sure that the Linear B syllabary of Mycenaean Greece had been adapted by around 1400 B.C. from the Linear A syllabary of Minoan Crete.

At all of the hundreds of times when an existing writing system of one language has been used as a blueprint to adapt to a different language, some problems have arisen, because no two languages have exactly the same sets of sounds. Some inherited letters or signs may simply be dropped, when the sounds that those letters represent in the lending language do not exist in the borrowing language. For example, Finnish lacks the sounds that many other European languages express by the letters *b, c, f, g, w, x,* and *z,* so the Finns dropped these letters from their version of the Roman alphabet. There has also been a frequent reverse problem, of devising letters to represent "new" sounds present in the borrowing language but absent in the lending language. That problem has been solved in several different ways: such as using an arbitrary combination of two or more letters (like the English *th* to represent a sound for which the Greek and runic alphabets used a single letter); adding a small distinguishing mark to an existing letter (like the Spanish tilde *ñ,* the German umlaut *ö,* and the proliferation of marks dancing around Polish and Turkish letters); co-opting existing letters for which the borrowing language had no use (such as modern Czechs recycling the letter *c* of the Roman alphabet to express the Czech sound *ts*); or just inventing a new letter (as our medieval ancestors did when they created the new letters *j, u,* and *w*).

The Roman alphabet itself was the end product of a long sequence of blueprint copying. Alphabets apparently arose only once in human history: among speakers of Semitic languages, in the area from modern Syria to the Sinai, during the second millennium B.C. All of the hundreds of historical and now existing alphabets were ultimately derived from that ancestral Semitic alphabet, in a few cases (such as the Irish ogham alphabet) by idea diffusion, but in most by actual copying and modification of letter forms.

That evolution of the alphabet can be traced back to Egyptian hieroglyphs, which included a complete set of 24 signs for the 24 Egyptian consonants. The Egyptians never took the logical (to us) next step of discarding all their logograms, determinatives, and signs for pairs and trios of consonants, and using just their consonantal alphabet. Starting around

1700 B.C., though, Semites familiar with Egyptian hieroglyphs did begin to experiment with that logical step.

Restricting signs to those for single consonants was only the first of three crucial innovations that distinguished alphabets from other writing systems. The second was to help users memorize the alphabet by placing the letters in a fixed sequence and giving them easy-to-remember names. Our English names are mostly meaningless monosyllables ("a," "bee," "cee," "dee," and so on). But the Semitic names did possess meaning in Semitic languages: they were the words for familiar objects ('aleph = ox, beth = house, gimel = camel, daleth = door, and so on). These Semitic words were related "acrophonically" to the Semitic consonants to which they refer: that is, the first letter of the word for the object was also the letter named for the object ('a, b, g, d, and so on). In addition, the earliest forms of the Semitic letters appear in many cases to have been pictures of those same objects. All these features made the forms, names, and sequence of Semitic alphabet letters easy to remember. Many modern alphabets, including ours, retain with minor modifications that original sequence (and, in the case of Greek, even the letters' original names: alpha, beta, gamma, delta, and so on) over 3,000 years later. One minor modification that readers will already have noticed is that the Semitic and Greek g became the Roman and English c, while the Romans invented a new g in its present position.

The third and last innovation leading to modern alphabets was to provide for vowels. Already in the early days of the Semitic alphabet, experiments began with methods for writing vowels by adding small extra letters to indicate selected vowels, or else by dots, lines, or hooks sprinkled over the consonantal letters. In the eighth century B.C. the Greeks became the first people to indicate all vowels systematically by the same types of letters used for consonants. Greeks derived the forms of their vowel letters α - ϵ - η - ι - o by "co-opting" five letters used in the Phoenician alphabet for consonantal sounds lacking in Greek.

From those earliest Semitic alphabets, one line of blueprint copying and evolutionary modification led via early Arabian alphabets to the modern Ethiopian alphabet. A far more important line evolved by way of the Aramaic alphabet, used for official documents of the Persian Empire, into the modern Arabic, Hebrew, Indian, and Southeast Asian alphabets. But the line most familiar to European and American readers is the one that led via the Phoenicians to the Greeks by the early eighth century B.C., thence to the Etruscans in the same century, and in the next century to the Romans, whose alphabet with slight modifications is the one used to print this book. Thanks to their potential advantage of combining precision with simplicity, alphabets have now been adopted in most areas of the modern world.

WHILE BLUEPRINT COPYING and modification are the most straight-forward option for transmitting technology, that option is sometimes unavailable. Blueprints may be kept secret, or they may be unreadable to someone not already steeped in the technology. Word may trickle through about an invention made somewhere far away, but the details may not get transmitted. Perhaps only the basic idea is known: someone has succeeded, somehow, in achieving a certain final result. That knowledge may never-theless inspire others, by idea diffusion, to devise their own routes to such a result.

A striking example from the history of writing is the origin of the sylla-bary devised in Arkansas around 1820 by a Cherokee Indian named Sequoyah, for writing the Cherokee language. Sequoyah observed that white people made marks on paper, and that they derived great advantage by using those marks to record and repeat lengthy speeches. However, the detailed operations of those marks remained a mystery to him, since (like most Cherokees before 1820) Sequoyah was illiterate and could neither speak nor read English. Because he was a blacksmith, Sequoyah began by devising an accounting system to help him keep track of his customers' debts. He drew a picture of each customer; then he drew circles and lines of various sizes to represent the amount of money owed.

Around 1810, Sequoyah decided to go on to design a system for writing the Cherokee language. He again began by drawing pictures, but gave them up as too complicated and too artistically demanding. He next started to invent separate signs for each word, and again became dissatis-fied when he had coined thousands of signs and still needed more.

Finally, Sequoyah realized that words were made up of modest numbers of different sound bites that recurred in many different words—what we would call syllables. He initially devised 200 syllabic signs and gradually reduced them to 85, most of them for combinations of one consonant and one vowel.

As one source of the signs themselves, Sequoyah practiced copying the

a	e	i	o	u	v
a	e	i	o	u	v
ga, ka	ge	gi	go	gu	gv
ha	he	hi	ho	hu	hv
la	le	li	lo	lu	lv
ma	me	mi	mo	mu	
na, hna, nah	ne	ni	no	nu	nv
qua	que	qui	quo	quu	quv
sa, s	se	si	so	su	sv
da, ta	de, te	di, ti	do	du	dv
dla, tla	tle	tli	tlo	tlu	tlv
tsa	tse	tsi	tso	tsu	tsv
wa	we	wi	wo	wu	wv
ya	ye	yi	yo	yu	yv

The set of signs that Sequoyah devised to represent syllables of the Chero-kee language.

letters from an English spelling book given to him by a schoolteacher. About two dozen of his Cherokee syllabic signs were taken directly from those letters, though of course with completely changed meanings, since Sequoyah did not know the English meanings. For example, he chose the shapes D, R, b, h to represent the Cherokee syllables *a, e, si,* and *ni,* respectively, while the shape of the numeral 4 was borrowed for the syllable *se.* He coined other signs by modifying English letters, such as designing the signs $\tilde{G}$, ⊌, and θ to represent the syllables *yu, sa,* and *na,* respectively.

Still other signs were entirely of his creation, such as Ⱶ, ℔, and ꝑ for *ho, li,* and *nu,* respectively. Sequoyah's syllabary is widely admired by professional linguists for its good fit to Cherokee sounds, and for the ease with which it can be learned. Within a short time, the Cherokees achieved almost 100 percent literacy in the syllabary, bought a printing press, had Sequoyah's signs cast as type, and began printing books and newspapers.

Cherokee writing remains one of the best-attested examples of a script that arose through idea diffusion. We know that Sequoyah received paper and other writing materials, the idea of a writing system, the idea of using separate marks, and the forms of several dozen marks. Since, however, he could neither read nor write English, he acquired no details or even principles from the existing scripts around him. Surrounded by alphabets he could not understand, he instead independently reinvented a syllabary, unaware that the Minoans of Crete had already invented another syllabary 3,500 years previously.

SEQUOYAH'S EXAMPLE CAN serve as a model for how idea diffusion probably led to many writing systems of ancient times as well. The han'gul alphabet devised by Korea's King Sejong in A.D. 1446 for the Korean language was evidently inspired by the block format of Chinese characters and by the alphabetic principle of Mongol or Tibetan Buddhist writing. However, King Sejong invented the forms of han'gul letters and several unique features of his alphabet, including the grouping of letters by syllables into square blocks, the use of related letter shapes to represent related vowel or consonant sounds, and shapes of consonant letters that depict the position in which the lips or tongue are held to pronounce that consonant. The ogham alphabet used in Ireland and parts of Celtic Britain from around the fourth century A.D. similarly adopted the alphabetic principle (in this case, from existing European alphabets) but again devised unique letter forms, apparently based on a five-finger system of hand signals.

We can confidently attribute the han'gul and ogham alphabets to idea diffusion rather than to independent invention in isolation, because we know that both societies were in close contact with societies possessing writing and because it is clear which foreign scripts furnished the inspiration. In contrast, we can confidently attribute Sumerian cuneiform and the earliest Mesoamerican writing to independent invention, because at the times of their first appearances there existed no other script in their respective hemispheres that could have inspired them. Still debatable are the origins of writing on Easter Island, in China, and in Egypt.

The Polynesians living on Easter Island, in the Pacific Ocean, had a unique script of which the earliest preserved examples date back only to about A.D. 1851, long after Europeans reached Easter in 1722. Perhaps writing arose independently on Easter before the arrival of Europeans, although no examples have survived. But the most straightforward interpretation is to take the facts at face value, and to assume that Easter

산 유 화

산에는 꽃피네
꽃이 피네
갈 봄 여름 없이
꽃이 피네

산에
산에
피는 꽃은
저만치 혼자서 피어있네

산에서 우는 작은 새요
꽃이 좋아
산에서
사노라네

산에는 꽃지네
꽃이 지네
갈 봄 여름 없이
꽃이 지네

김 소 월

A Korean text (the poem "Flowers on the Hills" by So-Wol Kim), illustrating the remarkable Han'gul writing system. Each square block represents a syllable, but each component sign within the block represents a letter.

Islanders were stimulated to devise a script after seeing the written proclamation of annexation that a Spanish expedition handed to them in the year 1770.

As for Chinese writing, first attested around 1300 B.C. but with possible earlier precursors, it too has unique local signs and some unique principles, and most scholars assume that it evolved independently. Writing had developed before 3000 B.C. in Sumer, 4,000 miles west of early Chinese urban centers, and appeared by 2200 B.C. in the Indus Valley, 2,600 miles west, but no early writing systems are known from the whole area between the Indus Valley and China. Thus, there is no evidence that the earliest Chinese scribes could have had knowledge of any other writing system to inspire them.

Egyptian hieroglyphics, the most famous of all ancient writing systems, are also usually assumed to be the product of independent invention, but the alternative interpretation of idea diffusion is more feasible than in the case of Chinese writing. Hieroglyphic writing appeared rather suddenly, in nearly full-blown form, around 3000 B.C. Egypt lay only 800 miles west of Sumer, with which Egypt had trade contacts. I find it suspicious that no evidence of a gradual development of hieroglyphs has come down to us, even though Egypt's dry climate would have been favorable for preserving earlier experiments in writing, and though the similarly dry climate of Sumer has yielded abundant evidence of the development of Sumerian cuneiform for at least several centuries before 3000 B.C. Equally suspicious is the appearance of several other, apparently independently designed, writing systems in Iran, Crete, and Turkey (so-called proto-Elamite writing, Cretan pictographs, and Hieroglyphic Hittite, respectively), after the rise of Sumerian and Egyptian writing. Although each of those systems used distinctive sets of signs not borrowed from Egypt or Sumer, the peoples involved could hardly have been unaware of the writing of their neighboring trade partners.

It would be a remarkable coincidence if, after millions of years of human existence without writing, all those Mediterranean and Near Eastern societies had just happened to hit independently on the idea of writing within a few centuries of each other. Hence a possible interpretation seems to me idea diffusion, as in the case of Sequoyah's syllabary. That is, Egyptians and other peoples may have learned from Sumerians about the idea

An example of Chinese writing: a handscroll by Wu Li, from A.D. *1679.*

An example of Egyptian hieroglyphs: the funerary papyrus of Princess Entiu-ny.

of writing and possibly about some of the principles, and then devised other principles and all the specific forms of the letters for themselves.

LET US NOW return to the main question with which we began this chapter: why did writing arise in and spread to some societies, but not to many others? Convenient starting points for our discussion are the limited capabilities, uses, and users of early writing systems.

Early scripts were incomplete, ambiguous, or complex, or all three. For example, the oldest Sumerian cuneiform writing could not render normal prose but was a mere telegraphic shorthand, whose vocabulary was restricted to names, numerals, units of measure, words for objects counted, and a few adjectives. That's as if a modern American court clerk were forced to write "John 27 fat sheep," because English writing lacked the necessary words and grammar to write "We order John to deliver the 27 fat sheep that he owes to the government." Later Sumerian cuneiform did become capable of rendering prose, but it did so by the messy system that I've already described, with mixtures of logograms, phonetic signs, and unpronounced determinatives totaling hundreds of separate signs. Linear B, the writing of Mycenaean Greece, was at least simpler, being based on a syllabary of about 90 signs plus logograms. Offsetting that virtue, Linear B was quite ambiguous. It omitted any consonant at the end of a word, and it used the same sign for several related consonants (for instance, one sign for both *l* and *r,* another for *p* and *b* and *ph,* and still another for *g* and *k* and *kh*). We know how confusing we find it when native-born Japanese people speak English without distinguishing *l* and *r:* imagine the confusion if our alphabet did the same while similarly homogenizing the other consonants that I mentioned! It's as if we were to spell the words "rap," "lap," "lab," and "laugh" identically.

A related limitation is that few people ever learned to write these early scripts. Knowledge of writing was confined to professional scribes in the employ of the king or temple. For instance, there is no hint that Linear B was used or understood by any Mycenaean Greek beyond small cadres of palace bureaucrats. Since individual Linear B scribes can be distinguished by their handwriting on preserved documents, we can say that all preserved Linear B documents from the palaces of Knossos and Pylos are the work of a mere 75 and 40 scribes, respectively.

The uses of these telegraphic, clumsy, ambiguous early scripts were as restricted as the number of their users. Anyone hoping to discover how Sumerians of 3000 B.C. thought and felt is in for a disappointment. Instead, the first Sumerian texts are emotionless accounts of palace and temple bureaucrats. About 90 percent of the tablets in the earliest known Sumerian archives, from the city of Uruk, are clerical records of goods paid in, workers given rations, and agricultural products distributed. Only later, as Sumerians progressed beyond logograms to phonetic writing, did they begin to write prose narratives, such as propaganda and myths.

Mycenaean Greeks never even reached that propaganda-and-myths stage. One-third of all Linear B tablets from the palace of Knossos are accountants' records of sheep and wool, while an inordinate proportion of writing at the palace of Pylos consists of records of flax. Linear B was inherently so ambiguous that it remained restricted to palace accounts, whose context and limited word choices made the interpretation clear. Not a trace of its use for literature has survived. The *Iliad* and *Odyssey* were composed and transmitted by nonliterate bards for nonliterate listeners, and not committed to writing until the development of the Greek alphabet hundreds of years later.

Similarly restricted uses characterize early Egyptian, Mesoamerican, and Chinese writing. Early Egyptian hieroglyphs recorded religious and state propaganda and bureaucratic accounts. Preserved Maya writing was similarly devoted to propaganda, births and accessions and victories of kings, and astronomical observations of priests. The oldest preserved Chinese writing of the late Shang Dynasty consists of religious divination about dynastic affairs, incised into so-called oracle bones. A sample Shang text: "The king, reading the meaning of the crack [in a bone cracked by heating], said: 'If the child is born on a keng day, it will be extremely auspicious.' "

To us today, it is tempting to ask why societies with early writing systems accepted the ambiguities that restricted writing to a few functions and a few scribes. But even to pose that question is to illustrate the gap between ancient perspectives and our own expectations of mass literacy. The *intended* restricted uses of early writing provided a positive disincentive for devising less ambiguous writing systems. The kings and priests of ancient Sumer wanted writing to be used by professional scribes to record numbers of sheep owed in taxes, not by the masses to write poetry and hatch plots. As the anthropologist Claude Lévi-Strauss put it, ancient writing's main function was "to facilitate the enslavement of other human beings." Personal uses of writing by nonprofessionals came only much later, as writing systems grew simpler and more expressive.

For instance, with the fall of Mycenaean Greek civilization, around 1200 B.C., Linear B disappeared, and Greece returned to an age of preliteracy. When writing finally returned to Greece, in the eighth century B.C., the new Greek writing, its users, and its uses were very different. The writing was no longer an ambiguous syllabary mixed with logograms but an alphabet borrowed from the Phoenician consonantal alphabet and improved by the Greek invention of vowels. In place of lists of sheep, legible only to scribes and read only in palaces, Greek alphabetic writing from the moment of its appearance was a vehicle of poetry and humor, to be read in private homes. For instance, the first preserved example of Greek alphabetic writing, scratched onto an Athenian wine jug of about 740 B.C., is a line of poetry announcing a dancing contest: "Whoever of all dancers performs most nimbly will win this vase as a prize." The next example is three lines of dactylic hexameter scratched onto a drinking cup: "I am Nestor's delicious drinking cup. Whoever drinks from this cup swiftly will the desire of fair-crowned Aphrodite seize him." The earliest preserved examples of the Etruscan and Roman alphabets are also inscriptions on drinking cups and wine containers. Only later did the alphabet's easily learned vehicle of private communication become co-opted for public or bureaucratic purposes. Thus, the developmental sequence of uses for alphabetic writing was the reverse of that for the earlier systems of logograms and syllabaries.

THE LIMITED USES and users of early writing suggest why writing appeared so late in human evolution. All of the likely or possible independent inventions of writing (in Sumer, Mexico, China, and Egypt), and all of the early adaptations of those invented systems (for example, those in Crete, Iran, Turkey, the Indus Valley, and the Maya area), involved socially stratified societies with complex and centralized political institutions, whose necessary relation to food production we shall explore in a later chapter. Early writing served the needs of those political institutions (such as record keeping and royal propaganda), and the users were full-time bureaucrats nourished by stored food surpluses grown by food-producing peasants. Writing was never developed or even adopted by hunter-gatherer societies, because they lacked both the institutional uses of early writing and the social and agricultural mechanisms for generating the food surpluses required to feed scribes.

Thus, food production and thousands of years of societal evolution following its adoption were as essential for the evolution of writing as for the evolution of microbes causing human epidemic diseases. Writing arose independently only in the Fertile Crescent, Mexico, and probably China precisely because those were the first areas where food production emerged in their respective hemispheres. Once writing had been invented by those few societies, it then spread, by trade and conquest and religion, to other societies with similar economies and political organizations.

While food production was thus a necessary condition for the evolution or early adoption of writing, it was not a sufficient condition. At the beginning of this chapter, I mentioned the failure of some food-producing societies with complex political organization to develop or adopt writing before modern times. Those cases, initially so puzzling to us moderns accustomed to viewing writing as indispensable to a complex society, included one of the world's largest empires as of A.D. 1520, the Inca Empire of South America. They also included Tonga's maritime proto-empire, the Hawaiian state emerging in the late 18th century, all of the states and chiefdoms of subequatorial Africa and sub-Saharan West Africa before the arrival of Islam, and the largest native North American societies, those of the Mississippi Valley and its tributaries. Why did all those societies fail to acquire writing, despite their sharing prerequisites with societies that did do so?

Here we have to remind ourselves that the vast majority of societies with writing acquired it by borrowing it from neighbors or by being inspired by them to develop it, rather than by independently inventing it themselves. The societies without writing that I just mentioned are ones that got a later start on food production than did Sumer, Mexico, and China. (The only uncertainty in this statement concerns the relative dates for the onset of food production in Mexico and in the Andes, the eventual Inca realm.) Given enough time, the societies lacking writing might also have eventually developed it on their own. Had they been located nearer to Sumer, Mexico, and China, they might instead have acquired writing or the idea of writing from those centers, just as did India, the Maya, and most other societies with writing. But they were too far from the first centers of writing to have acquired it before modern times.

The importance of isolation is most obvious for Hawaii and Tonga, both of which were separated by at least 4,000 miles of ocean from the nearest societies with writing. The other societies illustrate the important point that distance as the crow flies is not an appropriate measure of isolation for humans. The Andes, West Africa's kingdoms, and the mouth of the Mississippi River lay only about 1,200, 1,500, and 700 miles, respectively, from societies with writing in Mexico, North Africa, and Mexico, respectively. These distances are considerably less than the distances the alphabet had to travel from its homeland on the eastern shores of the Mediterranean to reach Ireland, Ethiopia, and Southeast Asia within 2,000 years of its invention. But humans are slowed by ecological and water barriers that crows can fly over. The states of North Africa (with writing) and West Africa (without writing) were separated from each other by Saharan desert unsuitable for agriculture and cities. The deserts of northern Mexico similarly separated the urban centers of southern Mexico from the chiefdoms of the Mississippi Valley. Communication between southern Mexico and the Andes required either a sea voyage or else a long chain of overland contacts via the narrow, forested, never urbanized Isthmus of Darien. Hence the Andes, West Africa, and the Mississippi Valley were effectively rather isolated from societies with writing.

That's not to say that those societies without writing were *totally* isolated. West Africa eventually did receive Fertile Crescent domestic animals across the Sahara, and later accepted Islamic influence, including Arabic writing. Corn diffused from Mexico to the Andes and, more slowly, from Mexico to the Mississippi Valley. But we already saw in Chapter 10 that the north–south axes and ecological barriers within Africa and the Americas retarded the diffusion of crops and domestic animals. The history of writing illustrates strikingly the similar ways in which geography and ecology influenced the spread of human inventions.

CHAPTER 13

NECESSITY'S MOTHER

O N JULY 3, 1908, ARCHAEOLOGISTS EXCAVATING THE ancient Minoan palace at Phaistos, on the island of Crete, chanced upon one of the most remarkable objects in the history of technology. At first glance it seemed unprepossessing: just a small, flat, unpainted, circular disk of hard-baked clay, 6½ inches in diameter. Closer examination showed each side to be covered with writing, resting on a curved line that spiraled clockwise in five coils from the disk's rim to its center. A total of 241 signs or letters was neatly divided by etched vertical lines into groups of several signs, possibly constituting words. The writer must have planned and executed the disk with care, so as to start writing at the rim and fill up all the available space along the spiraling line, yet not run out of space on reaching the center (page 240).

Ever since it was unearthed, the disk has posed a mystery for historians of writing. The number of distinct signs (45) suggests a syllabary rather than an alphabet, but it is still undeciphered, and the forms of the signs are unlike those of any other known writing system. Not another scrap of the strange script has turned up in the 89 years since its discovery. Thus, it remains unknown whether it represents an indigenous Cretan script or a foreign import to Crete.

For historians of technology, the Phaistos disk is even more baffling; its

One side of the two-sided Phaistos Disk.

estimated date of 1700 B.C. makes it by far the earliest printed document in the world. Instead of being etched by hand, as were all texts of Crete's later Linear A and Linear B scripts, the disk's signs were punched into soft clay (subsequently baked hard) by stamps that bore a sign as raised type. The printer evidently had a set of at least 45 stamps, one for each sign appearing on the disk. Making these stamps must have entailed a great deal of work, and they surely weren't manufactured just to print this single document. Whoever used them was presumably doing a lot of writing. With those stamps, their owner could make copies much more quickly and neatly than if he or she had written out each of the script's complicated signs at each appearance.

The Phaistos disk anticipates humanity's next efforts at printing, which similarly used cut type or blocks but applied them to paper with ink, not to clay without ink. However, those next efforts did not appear until 2,500 years later in China and 3,100 years later in medieval Europe. Why was the disk's precocious technology not widely adopted in Crete or elsewhere in the ancient Mediterranean? Why was its printing method invented around 1700 B.C. in Crete and not at some other time in Mesopotamia, Mexico, or any other ancient center of writing? Why did it then take thousands of years to add the ideas of ink and a press and arrive at a printing press? The disk thus constitutes a threatening challenge to historians. If inventions are as idiosyncratic and unpredictable as the disk seems to suggest, then efforts to generalize about the history of technology may be doomed from the outset.

Technology, in the form of weapons and transport, provides the direct means by which certain peoples have expanded their realms and conquered other peoples. That makes it the leading cause of history's broadest pattern. But why were Eurasians, rather than Native Americans or sub-Saharan Africans, the ones to invent firearms, oceangoing ships, and steel equipment? The differences extend to most other significant technological advances, from printing presses to glass and steam engines. Why were all those inventions Eurasian? Why were all New Guineans and Native Australians in A.D. 1800 still using stone tools like ones discarded thousands of years ago in Eurasia and most of Africa, even though some of the world's richest copper and iron deposits are in New Guinea and Australia, respectively? All those facts explain why so many laypeople assume that Eurasians are superior to other peoples in inventiveness and intelligence.

If, on the other hand, no such difference in human neurobiology exists to account for continental differences in technological development, what does account for them? An alternative view rests on the heroic theory of invention. Technological advances seem to come disproportionately from a few very rare geniuses, such as Johannes Gutenberg, James Watt, Thomas Edison, and the Wright brothers. They were Europeans, or descendants of European emigrants to America. So were Archimedes and other rare geniuses of ancient times. Could such geniuses have equally well been born in Tasmania or Namibia? Does the history of technology depend on nothing more than accidents of the birthplaces of a few inventors?

Still another alternative view holds that it is a matter not of individual inventiveness but of the receptivity of whole societies to innovation. Some societies seem hopelessly conservative, inward looking, and hostile to change. That's the impression of many Westerners who have attempted to help Third World peoples and ended up discouraged. The people seem perfectly intelligent as individuals; the problem seems instead to lie with their societies. How else can one explain why the Aborigines of northeastern Australia failed to adopt bows and arrows, which they saw being used by Torres Straits islanders with whom they traded? Might all the societies of an entire continent be unreceptive, thereby explaining technology's slow pace of development there? In this chapter we shall finally come to grips with a central problem of this book: the question of why technology did evolve at such different rates on different continents.

THE STARTING POINT for our discussion is the common view expressed in the saying "Necessity is the mother of invention." That is, inventions supposedly arise when a society has an unfulfilled need: some technology is widely recognized to be unsatisfactory or limiting. Would-be inventors, motivated by the prospect of money or fame, perceive the need and try to meet it. Some inventor finally comes up with a solution superior to the existing, unsatisfactory technology. Society adopts the solution if it is compatible with the society's values and other technologies.

Quite a few inventions do conform to this commonsense view of necessity as invention's mother. In 1942, in the middle of World War II, the U.S. government set up the Manhattan Project with the explicit goal of inventing the technology required to build an atomic bomb before Nazi Germany could do so. That project succeeded in three years, at a cost of $2 billion (equivalent to over $20 billion today). Other instances are Eli Whitney's 1794 invention of his cotton gin to replace laborious hand cleaning of cotton grown in the U.S. South, and James Watt's 1769 invention of his steam engine to solve the problem of pumping water out of British coal mines.

These familiar examples deceive us into assuming that other major inventions were also responses to perceived needs. In fact, many or most inventions were developed by people driven by curiosity or by a love of tinkering, in the absence of any initial demand for the product they had in mind. Once a device had been invented, the inventor then had to find an application for it. Only after it had been in use for a considerable time did consumers come to feel that they "needed" it. Still other devices, invented to serve one purpose, eventually found most of their use for other, unanticipated purposes. It may come as a surprise to learn that these inventions in search of a use include most of the major technological breakthroughs of modern times, ranging from the airplane and automobile, through the internal combustion engine and electric light bulb, to the phonograph and transistor. Thus, invention is often the mother of necessity, rather than vice versa.

A good example is the history of Thomas Edison's phonograph, the most original invention of the greatest inventor of modern times. When Edison built his first phonograph in 1877, he published an article proposing ten uses to which his invention might be put. They included preserving the last words of dying people, recording books for blind people to hear, announcing clock time, and teaching spelling. Reproduction of music was not high on Edison's list of priorities. A few years later Edison told his assistant that his invention had no commercial value. Within another few years he changed his mind and did enter business to sell phonographs— but for use as office dictating machines. When other entrepreneurs created jukeboxes by arranging for a phonograph to play popular music at the drop of a coin, Edison objected to this debasement, which apparently detracted from serious office use of his invention. Only after about 20 years did Edison reluctantly concede that the main use of his phonograph was to record and play music.

The motor vehicle is another invention whose uses seem obvious today. However, it was not invented in response to any demand. When Nikolaus Otto built his first gas engine, in 1866, horses had been supplying people's land transportation needs for nearly 6,000 years, supplemented increasingly by steam-powered railroads for several decades. There was no crisis in the availability of horses, no dissatisfaction with railroads.

Because Otto's engine was weak, heavy, and seven feet tall, it did not recommend itself over horses. Not until 1885 did engines improve to the point that Gottfried Daimler got around to installing one on a bicycle to create the first motorcycle; he waited until 1896 to build the first truck.

In 1905, motor vehicles were still expensive, unreliable toys for the rich. Public contentment with horses and railroads remained high until World War I, when the military concluded that it really did need trucks. Intensive postwar lobbying by truck manufacturers and armies finally convinced the public of its own needs and enabled trucks to begin to supplant horse-drawn wagons in industrialized countries. Even in the largest American cities, the changeover took 50 years.

Inventors often have to persist at their tinkering for a long time in the absence of public demand, because early models perform too poorly to be useful. The first cameras, typewriters, and television sets were as awful as Otto's seven-foot-tall gas engine. That makes it difficult for an inventor to foresee whether his or her awful prototype might eventually find a use and thus warrant more time and expense to develop it. Each year, the United States issues about 70,000 patents, only a few of which ultimately reach the stage of commercial production. For each great invention that ultimately found a use, there are countless others that did not. Even inventions that meet the need for which they were initially designed may later prove more valuable at meeting unforeseen needs. While James Watt designed his steam engine to pump water from mines, it soon was supplying power to cotton mills, then (with much greater profit) propelling locomotives and boats.

THUS, THE COMMONSENSE view of invention that served as our starting point reverses the usual roles of invention and need. It also overstates the importance of rare geniuses, such as Watt and Edison. That "heroic theory of invention," as it is termed, is encouraged by patent law, because an applicant for a patent must prove the novelty of the invention submitted. Inventors thereby have a financial incentive to denigrate or ignore previous work. From a patent lawyer's perspective, the ideal invention is one that arises without any precursors, like Athene springing fully formed from the forehead of Zeus.

In reality, even for the most famous and apparently decisive modern inventions, neglected precursors lurked behind the bald claim "X invented Y." For instance, we are regularly told, "James Watt invented the steam engine in 1769," supposedly inspired by watching steam rise from a teakettle's spout. Unfortunately for this splendid fiction, Watt actually got the idea for his particular steam engine while repairing a model of Thomas Newcomen's steam engine, which Newcomen had invented 57 years earlier and of which over a hundred had been manufactured in England by the time of Watt's repair work. Newcomen's engine, in turn, followed the steam engine that the Englishman Thomas Savery patented in 1698, which followed the steam engine that the Frenchman Denis Papin designed (but did not build) around 1680, which in turn had precursors in the ideas of the Dutch scientist Christiaan Huygens and others. All this is not to deny that Watt greatly improved Newcomen's engine (by incorporating a separate steam condenser and a double-acting cylinder), just as Newcomen had greatly improved Savery's.

Similar histories can be related for all modern inventions that are adequately documented. The hero customarily credited with the invention followed previous inventors who had had similar aims and had already produced designs, working models, or (as in the case of the Newcomen steam engine) commercially successful models. Edison's famous "invention" of the incandescent light bulb on the night of October 21, 1879, improved on many other incandescent light bulbs patented by other inventors between 1841 and 1878. Similarly, the Wright brothers' manned powered airplane was preceded by the manned unpowered gliders of Otto Lilienthal and the unmanned powered airplane of Samuel Langley; Samuel Morse's telegraph was preceded by those of Joseph Henry, William Cooke, and Charles Wheatstone; and Eli Whitney's gin for cleaning short-staple (inland) cotton extended gins that had been cleaning long-staple (Sea Island) cotton for thousands of years.

All this is not to deny that Watt, Edison, the Wright brothers, Morse, and Whitney made big improvements and thereby increased or inaugurated commercial success. The form of the invention eventually adopted might have been somewhat different without the recognized inventor's contribution. But the question for our purposes is whether the broad pattern of world history would have been altered significantly if some genius inventor had not been born at a particular place and time. The answer is clear: there has never been any such person. All recognized famous inventors had capable predecessors and successors and made their improvements at a time when society was capable of using their product. As we shall see, the tragedy of the hero who perfected the stamps used for the Phaistos disk was that he or she devised something that the society of the time could not exploit on a large scale.

My examples so far have been drawn from modern technologies, because their histories are well known. My two main conclusions are that technology develops cumulatively, rather than in isolated heroic acts, and that it finds most of its uses after it has been invented, rather than being invented to meet a foreseen need. These conclusions surely apply with much greater force to the undocumented history of ancient technology. When Ice Age hunter-gatherers noticed burned sand and limestone residues in their hearths, it was impossible for them to foresee the long, serendipitous accumulation of discoveries that would lead to the first Roman glass windows (around A.D. 1), by way of the first objects with surface glazes (around 4000 B.C.), the first free-standing glass objects of Egypt and Mesopotamia (around 2500 B.C.), and the first glass vessels (around 1500 B.C.).

We know nothing about how those earliest known surface glazes themselves were developed. Nevertheless, we can infer the methods of prehistoric invention by watching technologically "primitive" people today, such as the New Guineans with whom I work. I already mentioned their knowledge of hundreds of local plant and animal species and each species' edibility, medical value, and other uses. New Guineans told me similarly about dozens of rock types in their environment and each type's hardness, color, behavior when struck or flaked, and uses. All of that knowledge is acquired by observation and by trial and error. I see that process of "invention" going on whenever I take New Guineans to work with me in an area away from their homes. They constantly pick up unfamiliar things in the forest, tinker with them, and occasionally find them useful enough to bring home. I see the same process when I am abandoning a campsite, and local people come to scavenge what is left. They play with my discarded objects and try to figure out whether they might be useful in New Guinea society. Discarded tin cans are easy: they end up reused as containers. Other objects are tested for purposes very different from the one for which they were manufactured. How would that yellow number 2 pencil look as an ornament, inserted through a pierced ear-lobe or nasal septum? Is that piece of broken glass sufficiently sharp and strong to be useful as a knife? Eureka!

The raw substances available to ancient peoples were natural materials such as stone, wood, bone, skins, fiber, clay, sand, limestone, and minerals, all existing in great variety. From those materials, people gradually learned to work particular types of stone, wood, and bone into tools; to convert particular clays into pottery and bricks; to convert certain mixtures of sand, limestone, and other "dirt" into glass; and to work available pure soft metals such as copper and gold, then to extract metals from ores, and finally to work hard metals such as bronze and iron.

A good illustration of the histories of trial and error involved is furnished by the development of gunpowder and gasoline from raw materials. Combustible natural products inevitably make themselves noticed, as when a resinous log explodes in a campfire. By 2000 B.C., Mesopotamians were extracting tons of petroleum by heating rock asphalt. Ancient Greeks discovered the uses of various mixtures of petroleum, pitch, resins, sulfur, and quicklime as incendiary weapons, delivered by catapults, arrows, firebombs, and ships. The expertise at distillation that medieval Islamic alchemists developed to produce alcohols and perfumes also let them distill petroleum into fractions, some of which proved to be even more powerful incendiaries. Delivered in grenades, rockets, and torpedoes, those incendiaries played a key role in Islam's eventual defeat of the Crusaders. By then, the Chinese had observed that a particular mixture of sulfur, charcoal, and saltpeter, which became known as gunpowder, was especially explosive. An Islamic chemical treatise of about A.D. 1100 describes seven gunpowder recipes, while a treatise from A.D. 1280 gives more than 70 recipes that had proved suitable for diverse purposes (one for rockets, another for cannons).

As for postmedieval petroleum distillation, 19th-century chemists found the middle distillate fraction useful as fuel for oil lamps. The chemists discarded the most volatile fraction (gasoline) as an unfortunate waste product—until it was found to be an ideal fuel for internal-combustion engines. Who today remembers that gasoline, the fuel of modern civilization, originated as yet another invention in search of a use?

ONCE AN INVENTOR has discovered a use for a new technology, the next step is to persuade society to adopt it. Merely having a bigger, faster, more powerful device for doing something is no guarantee of ready acceptance. Innumerable such technologies were either not adopted at all or adopted only after prolonged resistance. Notorious examples include the U.S. Congress's rejection of funds to develop a supersonic transport in 1971, the world's continued rejection of an efficiently designed typewriter keyboard, and Britain's long reluctance to adopt electric lighting. What is it that promotes an invention's acceptance by a society?

Let's begin by comparing the acceptability of different inventions within the same society. It turns out that at least four factors influence acceptance. The first and most obvious factor is relative economic advantage compared with existing technology. While wheels are very useful in modern industrial societies, that has not been so in some other societies. Ancient Native Mexicans invented wheeled vehicles with axles for use as toys, but not for transport. That seems incredible to us, until we reflect that ancient Mexicans lacked domestic animals to hitch to their wheeled vehicles, which therefore offered no advantage over human porters.

A second consideration is social value and prestige, which can override economic benefit (or lack thereof). Millions of people today buy designer jeans for double the price of equally durable generic jeans—because the social cachet of the designer label counts for more than the extra cost. Similarly, Japan continues to use its horrendously cumbersome kanji writing system in preference to efficient alphabets or Japan's own efficient kana syllabary—because the prestige attached to kanji is so great.

Still another factor is compatibility with vested interests. This book, like probably every other typed document you have ever read, was typed with a QWERTY keyboard, named for the left-most six letters in its upper row. Unbelievable as it may now sound, that keyboard layout was designed in 1873 as a feat of anti-engineering. It employs a whole series of perverse tricks designed to force typists to type as slowly as possible, such as scattering the commonest letters over all keyboard rows and concentrating them on the left side (where right-handed people have to use their weaker hand). The reason behind all of those seemingly counterproductive features is that the typewriters of 1873 jammed if adjacent keys were struck in quick succession, so that manufacturers had to slow down typists. When improvements in typewriters eliminated the problem of jamming, trials in 1932 with an efficiently laid-out keyboard showed that it would let us double our typing speed and reduce our typing effort by 95 percent. But QWERTY keyboards were solidly entrenched by then. The vested interests of hundreds of millions of QWERTY typists, typing teachers, typewriter and computer salespeople, and manufacturers have crushed all moves toward keyboard efficiency for over 60-years.

While the story of the QWERTY keyboard may sound funny, many similar cases have involved much heavier economic consequences. Why does Japan now dominate the world market for transistorized electronic consumer products, to a degree that damages the United States's balance of payments with Japan, even though transistors were invented and patented in the United States? Because Sony bought transistor licensing rights from Western Electric at a time when the American electronics consumer industry was churning out vacuum tube models and reluctant to compete with its own products. Why were British cities still using gas street lighting into the 1920s, long after U.S. and German cities had converted to electric street lighting? Because British municipal governments had invested heavily in gas lighting and placed regulatory obstacles in the way of the competing electric light companies.

The remaining consideration affecting acceptance of new technologies is the ease with which their advantages can be observed. In A.D. 1340, when firearms had not yet reached most of Europe, England's earl of Derby and earl of Salisbury happened to be present in Spain at the battle of Tarifa, where Arabs used cannons against the Spaniards. Impressed by what they saw, the earls introduced cannons to the English army, which adopted them enthusiastically and already used them against French soldiers at the battle of Crécy six years later.

THUS, WHEELS, DESIGNER jeans, and QWERTY keyboards illustrate the varied reasons why the same society is not equally receptive to all inventions. Conversely, the same invention's reception also varies greatly among contemporary societies. We are all familiar with the supposed generalization that rural Third World societies are less receptive to innovation than are Westernized industrial societies. Even within the industrialized world, some areas are much more receptive than others. Such differences, if they existed on a continental scale, might explain why technology developed faster on some continents than on others. For instance, if all Aboriginal Australian societies were for some reason uniformly resistant to change, that might account for their continued use of stone tools after metal tools had appeared on every other continent. How do differences in receptivity among societies arise?

A laundry list of at least 14 explanatory factors has been proposed by historians of technology. One is long life expectancy, which in principle should give prospective inventors the years necessary to accumulate technical knowledge, as well as the patience and security to embark on long development programs yielding delayed rewards. Hence the greatly increased life expectancy brought by modern medicine may have contributed to the recently accelerating pace of invention.

The next five factors involve economics or the organization of society: (1) The availability of cheap slave labor in classical times supposedly discouraged innovation then, whereas high wages or labor scarcity now stimulate the search for technological solutions. For example, the prospect of changed immigration policies that would cut off the supply of cheap Mexican seasonal labor to Californian farms was the immediate incentive for the development of a machine-harvestable variety of tomatoes in California. (2) Patents and other property laws, protecting ownership rights of inventors, reward innovation in the modern West, while the lack of such protection discourages it in modern China. (3) Modern industrial societies provide extensive opportunities for technical training, as medieval Islam did and modern Zaire does not. (4) Modern capitalism is, and the ancient Roman economy was not, organized in a way that made it potentially rewarding to invest capital in technological development. (5) The strong individualism of U.S. society allows successful inventors to keep earnings for themselves, whereas strong family ties in New Guinea ensure that someone who begins to earn money will be joined by a dozen relatives expecting to move in and be fed and supported.

Another four suggested explanations are ideological, rather than economic or organizational: (1) Risk-taking behavior, essential for efforts at innovation, is more widespread in some societies than in others. (2) The scientific outlook is a unique feature of post-Renaissance European society that has contributed heavily to its modern technological preeminence. (3) Tolerance of diverse views and of heretics fosters innovation, whereas a strongly traditional outlook (as in China's emphasis on ancient Chinese classics) stifles it. (4) Religions vary greatly in their relation to technological innovation: some branches of Judaism and Christianity are claimed to be especially compatible with it, while some branches of Islam, Hinduism, and Brahmanism may be especially incompatible with it.

All ten of these hypotheses are plausible. But none of them has any necessary association with geography. If patent rights, capitalism, and certain religions do promote technology, what selected for those factors in postmedieval Europe but not in contemporary China or India?

At least the direction in which those ten factors influence technology seems clear. The remaining four proposed factors—war, centralized government, climate, and resource abundance—appear to act inconsistently: sometimes they stimulate technology, sometimes they inhibit it. (1) Throughout history, war has often been a leading stimulant of technological innovation. For instance, the enormous investments made in nuclear weapons during World War II and in airplanes and trucks during World

War I launched whole new fields of technology. But wars can also deal devastating setbacks to technological development. (2) Strong centralized government boosted technology in late-19th-century Germany and Japan, and crushed it in China after A.D. 1500. (3) Many northern Europeans assume that technology thrives in a rigorous climate where survival is impossible without technology, and withers in a benign climate where clothing is unnecessary and bananas supposedly fall off the trees. An opposite view is that benign environments leave people free from the constant struggle for existence, free to devote themselves to innovation. (4) There has also been debate over whether technology is stimulated by abundance or by scarcity of environmental resources. Abundant resources might stimulate the development of inventions utilizing those resources, such as water mill technology in rainy northern Europe, with its many rivers—but why didn't water mill technology progress more rapidly in even rainier New Guinea? The destruction of Britain's forests has been suggested as the reason behind its early lead in developing coal technology, but why didn't deforestation have the same effect in China?

This discussion does not exhaust the list of reasons proposed to explain why societies differ in their receptivity to new technology. Worse yet, all of these proximate explanations bypass the question of the ultimate factors behind them. This may seem like a discouraging setback in our attempt to understand the course of history, since technology has undoubtedly been one of history's strongest forces. However, I shall now argue that the diversity of independent factors behind technological innovation actually makes it easier, not harder, to understand history's broad pattern.

FOR THE PURPOSES of this book, the key question about the laundry list is whether such factors differed systematically from continent to continent and thereby led to continental differences in technological development. Most laypeople and many historians assume, expressly or tacitly, that the answer is yes. For example, it is widely believed that Australian Aborigines as a group shared ideological characteristics contributing to their technological backwardness: they were (or are) supposedly conservative, living in an imagined past Dreamtime of the world's creation, and not focused on practical ways to improve the present. A leading historian of Africa characterized Africans as inward looking and lacking Europeans' drive for expansion.

But all such claims are based on pure speculation. There has never been a study of many societies under similar socioeconomic conditions on each of two continents, demonstrating systematic ideological differences between the two continents' peoples. The usual reasoning is instead circular: because technological differences exist, the existence of corresponding ideological differences is inferred.

In reality, I regularly observe in New Guinea that native societies there differ greatly from each other in their prevalent outlooks. Just like industrialized Europe and America, traditional New Guinea has conservative societies that resist new ways, living side by side with innovative societies that selectively adopt new ways. The result, with the arrival of Western technology, is that the more entrepreneurial societies are now exploiting Western technology to overwhelm their conservative neighbors.

For example, when Europeans first reached the highlands of eastern New Guinea, in the 1930s, they "discovered" dozens of previously uncontacted Stone Age tribes, of which the Chimbu tribe proved especially aggressive in adopting Western technology. When Chimbus saw white settlers planting coffee, they began growing coffee themselves as a cash crop. In 1964 I met a 50-year-old Chimbu man, unable to read, wearing a traditional grass skirt, and born into a society still using stone tools, who had become rich by growing coffee, used his profits to buy a sawmill for $100,000 cash, and bought a fleet of trucks to transport his coffee and timber to market. In contrast, a neighboring highland people with whom I worked for eight years, the Daribi, are especially conservative and uninterested in new technology. When the first helicopter landed in the Daribi area, they briefly looked at it and just went back to what they had been doing; the Chimbus would have been bargaining to charter it. As a result, Chimbus are now moving into the Daribi area, taking it over for plantations, and reducing the Daribi to working for them.

On every other continent as well, certain native societies have proved very receptive, adopted foreign ways and technology selectively, and integrated them successfully into their own society. In Nigeria the Ibo people became the local entrepreneurial equivalent of New Guinea's Chimbus. Today the most numerous Native American tribe in the United States is the Navajo, who on European arrival were just one of several hundred tribes. But the Navajo proved especially resilient and able to deal selectively with innovation. They incorporated Western dyes into their weaving, became silversmiths and ranchers, and now drive trucks while continuing to live in traditional dwellings.

Among the supposedly conservative Aboriginal Australians as well, there are receptive societies along with conservative ones. At the one extreme, the Tasmanians continued to use stone tools superseded tens of thousands of years earlier in Europe and replaced in most of mainland Australia too. At the opposite extreme, some aboriginal fishing groups of southeastern Australia devised elaborate technologies for managing fish populations, including the construction of canals, weirs, and standing traps.

Thus, the development and reception of inventions vary enormously from society to society on the same continent. They also vary over time within the same society. Nowadays, Islamic societies in the Middle East are relatively conservative and not at the forefront of technology. But medieval Islam in the same region was technologically advanced and open to innovation. It achieved far higher literacy rates than contemporary Europe; it assimilated the legacy of classical Greek civilization to such a degree that many classical Greek books are now known to us only through Arabic copies; it invented or elaborated windmills, tidal mills, trigonometry, and lateen sails; it made major advances in metallurgy, mechanical and chemical engineering, and irrigation methods; and it adopted paper and gunpowder from China and transmitted them to Europe. In the Middle Ages the flow of technology was overwhelmingly from Islam to Europe, rather than from Europe to Islam as it is today. Only after around A.D. 1500 did the net direction of flow begin to reverse.

Innovation in China too fluctuated markedly with time. Until around A.D. 1450, China was technologically much more innovative and advanced than Europe, even more so than medieval Islam. The long list of Chinese inventions includes canal lock gates, cast iron, deep drilling, efficient animal harnesses, gunpowder, kites, magnetic compasses, movable type, paper, porcelain, printing (except for the Phaistos disk), sternpost rudders, and wheelbarrows. China then ceased to be innovative for reasons about which we shall speculate in the Epilogue. Conversely, we think of western Europe and its derived North American societies as leading the modern world in technological innovation, but technology was less advanced in western Europe than in any other "civilized" area of the Old World until the late Middle Ages.

Thus, it is untrue that there are continents whose societies have tended to be innovative and continents whose societies have tended to be conservative. On any continent, at any given time, there are innovative societies and also conservative ones. In addition, receptivity to innovation fluctuates in time within the same region.

On reflection, these conclusions are precisely what one would expect if a society's innovativeness is determined by many independent factors. Without a detailed knowledge of all of those factors, innovativeness becomes unpredictable. Hence social scientists continue to debate the specific reasons why receptivity changed in Islam, China, and Europe, and why the Chimbus, Ibos, and Navajo were more receptive to new technology than were their neighbors. To the student of broad historical patterns, though, it makes no difference what the specific reasons were in each of those cases. The myriad factors affecting innovativeness make the historian's task paradoxically easier, by converting societal variation in innovativeness into essentially a random variable. That means that, over a large enough area (such as a whole continent) at any particular time, some proportion of societies is likely to be innovative.

WHERE DO INNOVATIONS actually come from? For all societies except the few past ones that were completely isolated, much or most new technology is not invented locally but is instead borrowed from other societies. The relative importance of local invention and of borrowing depends mainly on two factors: the ease of invention of the particular technology, and the proximity of the particular society to other societies.

Some inventions arose straightforwardly from a handling of natural raw materials. Such inventions developed on many independent occasions in world history, at different places and times. One example, which we have already considered at length, is plant domestication, with at least nine independent origins. Another is pottery, which may have arisen from observations of the behavior of clay, a very widespread natural material, when dried or heated. Pottery appeared in Japan around 14,000 years ago, in the Fertile Crescent and China by around 10,000 years ago, and in Amazonia, Africa's Sahel zone, the U.S. Southeast, and Mexico thereafter.

An example of a much more difficult invention is writing, which does not suggest itself by observation of any natural material. As we saw in Chapter 12, it had only a few independent origins, and the alphabet arose apparently only once in world history. Other difficult inventions include the water wheel, rotary quern, tooth gearing, magnetic compass, windmill, and camera obscura, all of which were invented only once or twice in the Old World and never in the New World.

Such complex inventions were usually acquired by borrowing, because they spread more rapidly than they could be independently invented locally. A clear example is the wheel, which is first attested around 3400 B.C. near the Black Sea, and then turns up within the next few centuries over much of Europe and Asia. All those early Old World wheels are of a peculiar design: a solid wooden circle constructed of three planks fastened together, rather than a rim with spokes. In contrast, the sole wheels of Native American societies (depicted on Mexican ceramic vessels) consisted of a single piece, suggesting a second independent invention of the wheel—as one would expect from other evidence for the isolation of New World from Old World civilizations.

No one thinks that that same peculiar Old World wheel design appeared repeatedly by chance at many separate sites of the Old World within a few centuries of each other, after 7 million years of wheelless human history. Instead, the utility of the wheel surely caused it to diffuse rapidly east and west over the Old World from its sole site of invention. Other examples of complex technologies that diffused east and west in the ancient Old World, from a single West Asian source, include door locks, pulleys, rotary querns, windmills—and the alphabet. A New World example of technological diffusion is metallurgy, which spread from the Andes via Panama to Mesoamerica.

When a widely useful invention does crop up in one society, it then tends to spread in either of two ways. One way is that other societies see or learn of the invention, are receptive to it, and adopt it. The second is that societies lacking the invention find themselves at a disadvantage vis-à-vis the inventing society, and they become overwhelmed and replaced if the disadvantage is sufficiently great. A simple example is the spread of muskets among New Zealand's Maori tribes. One tribe, the Ngapuhi, adopted muskets from European traders around 1818. Over the course of the next 15 years, New Zealand was convulsed by the so-called Musket Wars, as musketless tribes either acquired muskets or were subjugated by tribes already armed with them. The outcome was that musket technology had spread throughout the whole of New Zealand by 1833: all surviving Maori tribes now had muskets.

When societies do adopt a new technology from the society that invented it, the diffusion may occur in many different contexts. They include peaceful trade (as in the spread of transistors from the United States to Japan in 1954), espionage (the smuggling of silkworms from Southeast Asia to the Mideast in A.D. 552), emigration (the spread of French glass and clothing manufacturing techniques over Europe by the 200,000 Huguenots expelled from France in 1685), and war. A crucial case of the last was the transfer of Chinese papermaking techniques to Islam, made possible when an Arab army defeated a Chinese army at the battle of Talas River in Central Asia in A.D. 751, found some papermakers among the prisoners of war, and brought them to Samarkand to set up paper manufacture.

In Chapter 12 we saw that cultural diffusion can involve either detailed "blueprints" or just vague ideas stimulating a reinvention of details. While Chapter 12 illustrated those alternatives for the spread of writing, they also apply to the diffusion of technology. The preceding paragraph gave examples of blueprint copying, whereas the transfer of Chinese porcelain technology to Europe provides an instance of long-drawn-out idea diffusion. Porcelain, a fine-grained translucent pottery, was invented in China around the 7th century A.D. When it began to reach Europe by the Silk Road in the 14th century (with no information about how it was manufactured), it was much admired, and many unsuccessful attempts were made to imitate it. Not until 1707 did the German alchemist Johann Böttger, after lengthy experiments with processes and with mixing various minerals and clays together, hit upon the solution and establish the now famous Meissen porcelain works. More or less independent later experiments in France and England led to Sèvres, Wedgwood, and Spode porcelains. Thus, European potters had to reinvent Chinese manufacturing methods for themselves, but they were stimulated to do so by having models of the desired product before them.

DEPENDING ON THEIR geographic location, societies differ in how readily they can receive technology by diffusion from other societies. The most isolated people on Earth in recent history were the Aboriginal Tasmanians, living without oceangoing watercraft on an island 100 miles from Australia, itself the most isolated continent. The Tasmanians had no contact with other societies for 10,000 years and acquired no new technology other than what they invented themselves. Australians and New Guineans, separated from the Asian mainland by the Indonesian island chain, received only a trickle of inventions from Asia. The societies most accessible to receiving inventions by diffusion were those embedded in the major continents. In these societies technology developed most rapidly, because they accumulated not only their own inventions but also those of other societies. For example, medieval Islam, centrally located in Eurasia, acquired inventions from India and China and inherited ancient Greek learning.

The importance of diffusion, and of geographic location in making it possible, is strikingly illustrated by some otherwise incomprehensible cases of societies that abandoned powerful technologies. We tend to assume that useful technologies, once acquired, inevitably persist until superseded by better ones. In reality, technologies must be not only acquired but also maintained, and that too depends on many unpredictable factors. Any society goes through social movements or fads, in which economically useless things become valued or useful things devalued temporarily. Nowadays, when almost all societies on Earth are connected to each other, we cannot imagine a fad's going so far that an important technology would actually be discarded. A society that temporarily turned against a powerful technology would continue to see it being used by neighboring societies and would have the opportunity to reacquire it by diffusion (or would be conquered by neighbors if it failed to do so). But such fads can persist in isolated societies.

A famous example involves Japan's abandonment of guns. Firearms reached Japan in A.D. 1543, when two Portuguese adventurers armed with harquebuses (primitive guns) arrived on a Chinese cargo ship. The Japanese were so impressed by the new weapon that they commenced indigenous gun production, greatly improved gun technology, and by A.D. 1600 owned more and better guns than any other country in the world.

But there were also factors working against the acceptance of firearms in Japan. The country had a numerous warrior class, the samurai, for whom swords rated as class symbols and works of art (and as means for subjugating the lower classes). Japanese warfare had previously involved single combats between samurai swordsmen, who stood in the open, made ritual speeches, and then took pride in fighting gracefully. Such behavior became lethal in the presence of peasant soldiers ungracefully blasting away with guns. In addition, guns were a foreign invention and grew to be despised, as did other things foreign in Japan after 1600. The samurai-controlled government began by restricting gun production to a few cities, then introduced a requirement of a government license for producing a gun, then issued licenses only for guns produced for the government, and finally reduced government orders for guns, until Japan was almost without functional guns again.

Contemporary European rulers also included some who despised guns and tried to restrict their availability. But such measures never got far in Europe, where any country that temporarily swore off firearms would be promptly overrun by gun-toting neighboring countries. Only because Japan was a populous, isolated island could it get away with its rejection of the powerful new military technology. Its safety in isolation came to an end in 1853, when the visit of Commodore Perry's U.S. fleet bristling with cannons convinced Japan of its need to resume gun manufacture.

That rejection and China's abandonment of oceangoing ships (as well as of mechanical clocks and water-driven spinning machines) are well-known historical instances of technological reversals in isolated or semi-isolated societies. Other such reversals occurred in prehistoric times. The extreme case is that of Aboriginal Tasmanians, who abandoned even bone tools and fishing to become the society with the simplest technology in the modern world (Chapter 15). Aboriginal Australians may have adopted and then abandoned bows and arrows. Torres Islanders abandoned canoes, while Gaua Islanders abandoned and then readopted them. Pottery was abandoned throughout Polynesia. Most Polynesians and many Melanesians abandoned the use of bows and arrows in war. Polar Eskimos lost the bow and arrow and the kayak, while Dorset Eskimos lost the bow and arrow, bow drill, and dogs.

These examples, at first so bizarre to us, illustrate well the roles of geography and of diffusion in the history of technology. Without diffusion, fewer technologies are acquired, and more existing technologies are lost.

BECAUSE TECHNOLOGY BEGETS more technology, the importance of an invention's diffusion potentially exceeds the importance of the original invention. Technology's history exemplifies what is termed an autocatalytic process: that is, one that speeds up at a rate that increases with time, because the process catalyzes itself. The explosion of technology since the Industrial Revolution impresses us today, but the medieval explosion was equally impressive compared with that of the Bronze Age, which in turn dwarfed that of the Upper Paleolithic.

One reason why technology tends to catalyze itself is that advances depend upon previous mastery of simpler problems. For example, Stone Age farmers did not proceed directly to extracting and working iron, which requires high-temperature furnaces. Instead, iron ore metallurgy grew out of thousands of years of human experience with natural outcrops of pure metals soft enough to be hammered into shape without heat (copper and gold). It also grew out of thousands of years of development of simple furnaces to make pottery, and then to extract copper ores and work copper alloys (bronzes) that do not require as high temperatures as does iron. In both the Fertile Crescent and China, iron objects became common only after about 2,000 years of experience of bronze metallurgy. New World societies had just begun making bronze artifacts and had not yet started making iron ones at the time when the arrival of Europeans truncated the New World's independent trajectory.

The other main reason for autocatalysis is that new technologies and materials make it possible to generate still other new technologies by recombination. For instance, why did printing spread explosively in medieval Europe after Gutenberg printed his Bible in A.D. 1455, but not after that unknown printer printed the Phaistos disk in 1700 B.C.? The explanation is partly that medieval European printers were able to combine six technological advances, most of which were unavailable to the maker of the Phaistos disk. Of those advances—in paper, movable type, metallurgy, presses, inks, and scripts—paper and the idea of movable type reached Europe from China. Gutenberg's development of typecasting from metal dies, to overcome the potentially fatal problem of nonuniform type size, depended on many metallurgical developments: steel for letter punches, brass or bronze alloys (later replaced by steel) for dies, lead for molds, and a tin-zinc-lead alloy for type. Gutenberg's press was derived from screw presses in use for making wine and olive oil, while his ink was an oil-based improvement on existing inks. The alphabetic scripts that medieval Europe inherited from three millennia of alphabet development lent themselves to printing with movable type, because only a few dozen letter forms had to be cast, as opposed to the thousands of signs required for Chinese writing.

In all six respects, the maker of the Phaistos disk had access to much less powerful technologies to combine into a printing system than did Gutenberg. The disk's writing medium was clay, which is much bulkier and heavier than paper. The metallurgical skills, inks, and presses of 1700 B.C. Crete were more primitive than those of A.D. 1455 Germany, so the disk had to be punched by hand rather than by cast movable type locked into a metal frame, inked, and pressed. The disk's script was a syllabary with more signs, of more complex form, than the Roman alphabet used by Gutenberg. As a result, the Phaistos disk's printing technology was much clumsier, and offered fewer advantages over writing by hand, than Gutenberg's printing press. In addition to all those technological drawbacks, the Phaistos disk was printed at a time when knowledge of writing was confined to a few palace or temple scribes. Hence there was little demand for the disk maker's beautiful product, and little incentive to invest in making the dozens of hand punches required. In contrast, the potential mass market for printing in medieval Europe induced numerous investors to lend money to Gutenberg.

HUMAN TECHNOLOGY DEVELOPED from the first stone tools, in use by two and a half million years ago, to the 1996 laser printer that replaced my already outdated 1992 laser printer and that was used to print this book's manuscript. The rate of development was undetectably slow at the beginning, when hundreds of thousands of years passed with no discernible change in our stone tools and with no surviving evidence for artifacts made of other materials. Today, technology advances so rapidly that it is reported in the daily newspaper.

In this long history of accelerating development, one can single out two especially significant jumps. The first, occurring between 100,000 and 50,000 years ago, probably was made possible by genetic changes in our bodies: namely, by evolution of the modern anatomy permitting modern speech or modern brain function, or both. That jump led to bone tools, single-purpose stone tools, and compound tools. The second jump resulted from our adoption of a sedentary lifestyle, which happened at different times in different parts of the world, as early as 13,000 years ago in some areas and not even today in others. For the most part, that adoption was linked to our adoption of food production, which required us to remain close to our crops, orchards, and stored food surpluses.

Sedentary living was decisive for the history of technology, because it enabled people to accumulate nonportable possessions. Nomadic hunter-gatherers are limited to technology that can be carried. If you move often and lack vehicles or draft animals, you confine your possessions to babies, weapons, and a bare minimum of other absolute necessities small enough to carry. You can't be burdened with pottery and printing presses as you shift camp. That practical difficulty probably explains the tantalizingly early appearance of some technologies, followed by a long delay in their further development. For example, the earliest attested precursors of ceramics are fired clay figurines made in the area of modern Czechoslovakia 27,000 years ago, long before the oldest known fired clay vessels (from Japan 14,000 years ago). The same area of Czechoslovakia at the same time has yielded the earliest evidence for weaving, otherwise not attested until the oldest known basket appears around 13,000 years ago and the oldest known woven cloth around 9,000 years ago. Despite these very early first steps, neither pottery nor weaving took off until people became sedentary and thereby escaped the problem of transporting pots and looms.

Besides permitting sedentary living and hence the accumulation of possessions, food production was decisive in the history of technology for another reason. It became possible, for the first time in human evolution, to develop economically specialized societies consisting of non-food-producing specialists fed by food-producing peasants. But we already saw, in Part 2 of this book, that food production arose at different times in different continents. In addition, as we've seen in this chapter, local technology depends, for both its origin and its maintenance, not only on local invention but also on the diffusion of technology from elsewhere. That consideration tended to cause technology to develop most rapidly on continents with few geographic and ecological barriers to diffusion, either within that continent or on other continents. Finally, each society on a continent represents one more opportunity to invent and adopt a technology, because societies vary greatly in their innovativeness for many separate reasons. Hence, all other things being equal, technology develops fastest in large productive regions with large human populations, many potential inventors, and many competing societies.

Let us now summarize how variations in these three factors—time of onset of food production, barriers to diffusion, and human population size—led straightforwardly to the observed intercontinental differences in the development of technology. Eurasia (effectively including North

Africa) is the world's largest landmass, encompassing the largest number of competing societies. It was also the landmass with the two centers where food production began the earliest: the Fertile Crescent and China. Its east–west major axis permitted many inventions adopted in one part of Eurasia to spread relatively rapidly to societies at similar latitudes and climates elsewhere in Eurasia. Its breadth along its minor axis (north–south) contrasts with the Americas' narrowness at the Isthmus of Panama. It lacks the severe ecological barriers transecting the major axes of the Americas and Africa. Thus, geographic and ecological barriers to diffusion of technology were less severe in Eurasia than in other continents. Thanks to all these factors, Eurasia was the continent on which technology started its post-Pleistocene acceleration earliest and resulted in the greatest local accumulation of technologies.

North and South America are conventionally regarded as separate continents, but they have been connected for several million years, pose similar historical problems, and may be considered together for comparison with Eurasia. The Americas form the world's second-largest landmass, significantly smaller than Eurasia. However, they are fragmented by geography and by ecology: the Isthmus of Panama, only 40 miles wide, virtually transects the Americas geographically, as do the isthmus's Darien rain forests and the northern Mexican desert ecologically. The latter desert separated advanced human societies of Mesoamerica from those of North America, while the isthmus separated advanced societies of Mesoamerica from those of the Andes and Amazonia. In addition, the main axis of the Americas is north–south, forcing most diffusion to go against a gradient of latitude (and climate) rather than to operate within the same latitude. For example, wheels were invented in Mesoamerica, and llamas were domesticated in the central Andes by 3000 B.C., but 5,000 years later the Americas' sole beast of burden and sole wheels had still not encountered each other, even though the distance separating Mesoamerica's Maya societies from the northern border of the Inca Empire (1,200 miles) was far less than the 6,000 miles separating wheel- and horse-sharing France and China. Those factors seem to me to account for the Americas' technological lag behind Eurasia.

Sub-Saharan Africa is the world's third largest landmass, considerably smaller than the Americas. Throughout most of human history it was far more accessible to Eurasia than were the Americas, but the Saharan desert is still a major ecological barrier separating sub-Saharan Africa from

Eurasia plus North Africa. Africa's north–south axis posed a further obstacle to the diffusion of technology, both between Eurasia and sub-Saharan Africa and within the sub-Saharan region itself. As an illustration of the latter obstacle, pottery and iron metallurgy arose in or reached sub-Saharan Africa's Sahel zone (north of the equator) at least as early as they reached western Europe. However, pottery did not reach the southern tip of Africa until around A.D. 1, and metallurgy had not yet diffused overland to the southern tip by the time that it arrived there from Europe on ships.

Finally, Australia is the smallest continent. The very low rainfall and productivity of most of Australia makes it effectively even smaller as regards its capacity to support human populations. It is also the most isolated continent. In addition, food production never arose indigenously in Australia. Those factors combined to leave Australia the sole continent still without metal artifacts in modern times.

Table 13.1 translates these factors into numbers, by comparing the continents with respect to their areas and their modern human populations. The continents' populations 10,000 years ago, just before the rise of food production, are not known but surely stood in the same sequence, since many of the areas producing the most food today would also have been productive areas for hunter-gatherers 10,000 years ago. The differences in population are glaring: Eurasia's (including North Africa's) is nearly 6 times that of the Americas, nearly 8 times that of Africa's, and 230 times that of Australia's. Larger populations mean more inventors and more competing societies. Table 13.1 by itself goes a long way toward explaining the origins of guns and steel in Eurasia.

All these effects that continental differences in area, population, ease of

TABLE 13.1 **Human Populations of the Continents**

Continent	1990 Population	Area (square miles)
Eurasia and North Africa	4,120,000,000	24,200,000
(Eurasia)	(4,000,000,000)	(21,500,000)
(North Africa)	(120,000,000)	(2,700,000)
North America and South America	736,000,000	16,400,000
Sub-Saharan Africa	535,000,000	9,100,000
Australia	18,000,000	3,000,000

diffusion, and onset of food production exerted on the rise of technology became exaggerated, because technology catalyzes itself. Eurasia's considerable initial advantage thereby was translated into a huge lead as of A.D. 1492—for reasons of Eurasia's distinctive geography rather than of distinctive human intellect. The New Guineans whom I know include potential Edisons. But they directed their ingenuity toward technological problems appropriate to their situations: the problems of surviving without any imported items in the New Guinea jungle, rather than the problem of inventing phonographs.

CHAPTER 14

FROM EGALITARIANISM TO KLEPTOCRACY

I N 1979, WHILE I WAS FLYING WITH MISSIONARY FRIENDS over a remote swamp-filled basin of New Guinea, I noticed a few huts many miles apart. The pilot explained to me that, somewhere in that muddy expanse below us, a group of Indonesian crocodile hunters had recently come across a group of New Guinea nomads. Both groups had panicked, and the encounter had ended with the Indonesians shooting several of the nomads.

My missionary friends guessed that the nomads belonged to an uncontacted group called the Fayu, known to the outside world only through accounts by their terrified neighbors, a missionized group of erstwhile nomads called the Kirikiri. First contacts between outsiders and New Guinea groups are always potentially dangerous, but this beginning was especially inauspicious. Nevertheless, my friend Doug flew in by helicopter to try to establish friendly relations with the Fayu. He returned, alive but shaken, to tell a remarkable story.

It turned out that the Fayu normally lived as single families, scattered through the swamp and coming together once or twice each year to negotiate exchanges of brides. Doug's visit coincided with such a gathering, of a few dozen Fayu. To us, a few dozen people constitute a small, ordinary gathering, but to the Fayu it was a rare, frightening event. Murderers suddenly found themselves face-to-face with their victim's relatives. For example, one Fayu man spotted the man who had killed his father. The son raised his ax and rushed at the murderer but was wrestled to the ground by friends; then the murderer came at the prostrate son with an ax and was also wrestled down. Both men were held, screaming in rage, until they seemed sufficiently exhausted to be released. Other men periodically shouted insults at each other, shook with anger and frustration, and pounded the ground with their axes. That tension continued for the several days of the gathering, while Doug prayed that the visit would not end in violence.

The Fayu consist of about 400 hunter-gatherers, divided into four clans and wandering over a few hundred square miles. According to their own account, they had formerly numbered about 2,000, but their population had been greatly reduced as a result of Fayu killing Fayu. They lacked political and social mechanisms, which we take for granted, to achieve peaceful resolution of serious disputes. Eventually, as a result of Doug's visit, one group of Fayu invited a courageous husband-and-wife missionary couple to live with them. The couple has now resided there for a dozen years and gradually persuaded the Fayu to renounce violence. The Fayu are thereby being brought into the modern world, where they face an uncertain future.

Many other previously uncontacted groups of New Guineans and Amazonian Indians have similarly owed to missionaries their incorporation into modern society. After the missionaries come teachers and doctors, bureaucrats and soldiers. The spreads of government and of religion have thus been linked to each other throughout recorded history, whether the spread has been peaceful (as eventually with the Fayu) or by force. In the latter case it is often government that organizes the conquest, and religion that justifies it. While nomads and tribespeople occasionally defeat organized governments and religions, the trend over the past 13,000 years has been for the nomads and tribespeople to lose.

At the end of the last Ice Age, much of the world's population lived in societies similar to that of the Fayu today, and no people then lived in a much more complex society. As recently as A.D. 1500, less than 20 percent of the world's land area was marked off by boundaries into states run by bureaucrats and governed by laws. Today, all land except Antarctica's is so divided. Descendants of those societies that achieved centralized government and organized religion earliest ended up dominating the modern world. The combination of government and religion has thus functioned, together with germs, writing, and technology, as one of the four main sets of proximate agents leading to history's broadest pattern. How did government and religion arise?

FAYU BANDS AND modern states represent opposite extremes along the spectrum of human societies. Modern American society and the Fayu differ in the presence or absence of a professional police force, cities, money, distinctions between rich and poor, and many other political, economic, and social institutions. Did all of those institutions arise together, or did some arise before others? We can infer the answer to this question by comparing modern societies at different levels of organization, by examining written accounts or archaeological evidence about past societies, and by observing how a society's institutions change over time.

Cultural anthropologists attempting to describe the diversity of human societies often divide them into as many as half a dozen categories. Any such attempt to define stages of any evolutionary or developmental continuum—whether of musical styles, human life stages, or human societies—is doubly doomed to imperfection. First, because each stage grows out of some previous stage, the lines of demarcation are inevitably arbitrary. (For example, is a 19-year-old person an adolescent or a young adult?) Second, developmental sequences are not invariant, so examples pigeonholed under the same stage are inevitably heterogeneous. (Brahms and Liszt would turn in their graves to know that they are now grouped together as composers of the romantic period.) Nevertheless, arbitrarily delineated stages provide a useful shorthand for discussing the diversity of music and of human societies, provided one bears in mind the above caveats. In that spirit, we shall use a simple classification based on just four categories—band, tribe, chiefdom, and state (see Table 14.1)—to understand societies.

Bands are the tiniest societies, consisting typically of 5 to 80 people, most or all of them close relatives by birth or by marriage. In effect, a band is an extended family or several related extended families. Today, bands still living autonomously are almost confined to the most remote parts of New Guinea and Amazonia, but within modern times there were many others that have only recently fallen under state control or been assimilated or exterminated. They include many or most African Pygmies, southern African San hunter-gatherers (so-called Bushmen), Aboriginal

TABLE 14.1 **Types of Societies**

	Band	*Tribe*	*Chiefdom*	*State*
Membership				
Number of people	dozens	hundreds	thousands	over 50,000
Settlement pattern	nomadic	fixed: 1 village	fixed: 1 or more villages	fixed: many villages and cities
Basis of relation-ships	kin	kin-based clans	class and resi-dence	class and residence
Ethnicities and languages	1	1	1	1 or more
Government				
Decision making, leadership	"egalitarian"	"egalitarian" or big-man	centralized, hereditary	centralized
Bureaucracy	none	none	none, or 1 or 2 levels	many levels
Monopoly of force and information	no	no	yes	yes
Conflict resolu-tion	informal	informal	centralized	laws, judges
Hierarchy of settlement	no	no	no → para-mount village	capital

Australians, Eskimos (Inuit), and Indians of some resource-poor areas of the Americas such as Tierra del Fuego and the northern boreal forests. All those modern bands are or were nomadic hunter-gatherers rather than settled food producers. Probably all humans lived in bands until at least 40,000 years ago, and most still did as recently as 11,000 years ago.

Bands lack many institutions that we take for granted in our own society. They have no permanent single base of residence. The band's land is used jointly by the whole group, instead of being partitioned among sub-groups or individuals. There is no regular economic specialization, except by age and sex: all able-bodied individuals forage for food. There are no formal institutions, such as laws, police, and treaties, to resolve conflicts within and between bands. Band organization is often described as

	Band	*Tribe*	*Chiefdom*	*State*
Religion				
Justifies klepto-cracy?	no	no	yes	yes → no
Economy				
Food production	no	no → yes	yes → intensive	intensive
Division of labor	no	no	no → yes	yes
Exchanges	reciprocal	reciprocal	redistributive ("tribute")	redistribu-tive ("taxes")
Control of land	band	clan	chief	various
Society				
Stratified	no	no	yes, by kin	yes, not by kin
Slavery	no	no	small-scale	large-scale
Luxury goods for elite	no	no	yes	yes
Public architec-ture	no	no	no → yes	yes
Indigenous lit-eracy	no	no	no	often

A horizontal arrow indicates that the attribute varies between less and more complex societies of that type.

"egalitarian": there is no formalized social stratification into upper and lower classes, no formalized or hereditary leadership, and no formalized monopolies of information and decision making. However, the term "egalitarian" should not be taken to mean that all band members are equal in prestige and contribute equally to decisions. Rather, the term merely means that any band "leadership" is informal and acquired through qualities such as personality, strength, intelligence, and fighting skills.

My own experience with bands comes from the swampy lowland area of New Guinea where the Fayu live, a region known as the Lakes Plains. There, I still encounter extended families of a few adults with their dependent children and elderly, living in crude temporary shelters along streams and traveling by canoe and on foot. Why do peoples of the Lakes Plains continue to live as nomadic bands, when most other New Guinea peoples, and almost all other peoples elsewhere in the world, now live in settled larger groups? The explanation is that the region lacks dense local concentrations of resources that would permit many people to live together, and that (until the arrival of missionaries bringing crop plants) it also lacked native plants that could have permitted productive farming. The bands' food staple is the sago palm tree, whose core yields a starchy pith when the palm reaches maturity. The bands are nomadic, because they must move when they have cut the mature sago trees in an area. Band numbers are kept low by diseases (especially malaria), by the lack of raw materials in the swamp (even stone for tools must be obtained by trade), and by the limited amount of food that the swamp yields for humans. Similar limitations on the resources accessible to existing human technology prevail in the regions of the world recently occupied by other bands.

Our closest animal relatives, the gorillas and chimpanzees and bonobos of Africa, also live in bands. All humans presumably did so too, until improved technology for extracting food allowed some hunter-gatherers to settle in permanent dwellings in some resource-rich areas. The band is the political, economic, and social organization that we inherited from our millions of years of evolutionary history. Our developments beyond it all took place within the last few tens of thousands of years.

THE FIRST OF those stages beyond the band is termed the tribe, which differs in being larger (typically comprising hundreds rather than dozens of people) and usually having fixed settlements. However, some tribes and even chiefdoms consist of herders who move seasonally.

Tribal organization is exemplified by New Guinea highlanders, whose political unit before the arrival of colonial government was a village or else a close-knit cluster of villages. This political definition of "tribe" is thus often much smaller than what linguists and cultural anthropologists would define as a tribe—namely, a group that shares language and culture. For example, in 1964 I began to work among a group of highlanders known as the Foré. By linguistic and cultural standards, there were then 12,000 Foré, speaking two mutually intelligible dialects and living in 65 villages of several hundred people each. But there was no political unity whatsoever among villages of the Foré language group. Each hamlet was involved in a kaleidoscopically changing pattern of war and shifting alliances with all neighboring hamlets, regardless of whether the neighbors were Foré or speakers of a different language.

Tribes, recently independent and now variously subordinated to national states, still occupy much of New Guinea, Melanesia, and Amazonia. Similar tribal organization in the past is inferred from archaeological evidence of settlements that were substantial but lacked the archaeological hallmarks of chiefdoms that I shall explain below. That evidence suggests that tribal organization began to emerge around 13,000 years ago in the Fertile Crescent and later in some other areas. A prerequisite for living in settlements is either food production or else a productive environment with especially concentrated resources that can be hunted and gathered within a small area. That's why settlements, and by inference tribes, began to proliferate in the Fertile Crescent at that time, when climate changes and improved technology combined to permit abundant harvests of wild cereals.

Besides differing from a band by virtue of its settled residence and its larger numbers, a tribe also differs in that it consists of more than one formally recognized kinship group, termed clans, which exchange marriage partners. Land belongs to a particular clan, not to the whole tribe. However, the number of people in a tribe is still low enough that everyone knows everyone else by name and relationships.

For other types of human groups as well, "a few hundred" seems to be an upper limit for group size compatible with everyone's knowing everybody. In our state society, for instance, school principals are likely to know all their students by name if the school contains a few hundred children, but not if it contains a few thousand children. One reason why the organization of human government tends to change from that of a tribe to that of a chiefdom in societies with more than a few hundred members is that the difficult issue of conflict resolution between strangers becomes increasingly acute in larger groups. A fact further diffusing potential problems of conflict resolution in tribes is that almost everyone is related to everyone else, by blood or marriage or both. Those ties of relationships binding all tribal members make police, laws, and other conflict-resolving institutions of larger societies unnecessary, since any two villagers getting into an argument will share many kin, who apply pressure on them to keep it from becoming violent. In traditional New Guinea society, if a New Guinean happened to encounter an unfamiliar New Guinean while both were away from their respective villages, the two engaged in a long discussion of their relatives, in an attempt to establish some relationship and hence some reason why the two should not attempt to kill each other.

Despite all of these differences between bands and tribes, many similarities remain. Tribes still have an informal, "egalitarian" system of government. Information and decision making are both communal. In the New Guinea highlands, I have watched village meetings where all adults in the village were present, sitting on the ground, and individuals made speeches, without any appearance of one person's "chairing" the discussion. Many highland villages do have someone known as the "big-man," the most influential man of the village. But that position is not a formal office to be filled and carries only limited power. The big-man has no independent decision-making authority, knows no diplomatic secrets, and can do no more than attempt to sway communal decisions. Big-men achieve that status by their own attributes; the position is not inherited.

Tribes also share with bands an "egalitarian" social system, without ranked lineages or classes. Not only is status not inherited; no member of a traditional tribe or band can become disproportionately wealthy by his or her own efforts, because each individual has debts and obligations to many others. It is therefore impossible for an outsider to guess, from appearances, which of all the adult men in a village is the big-man: he lives in the same type of hut, wears the same clothes or ornaments, or is as naked, as everyone else.

Like bands, tribes lack a bureaucracy, police force, and taxes. Their economy is based on reciprocal exchanges between individuals or families, rather than on a redistribution of tribute paid to some central authority. Economic specialization is slight: full-time crafts specialists are lacking, and every able-bodied adult (including the big-man) participates in growing, gathering, or hunting food. I recall one occasion when I was walking past a garden in the Solomon Islands, saw a man digging and waving at me in the distance, and realized to my astonishment that it was a friend of mine named Faletau. He was the most famous wood carver of the Solomons, an artist of great originality—but that did not free him of the necessity to grow his own sweet potatoes. Since tribes thus lack economic specialists, they also lack slaves, because there are no specialized menial jobs for a slave to perform.

Just as musical composers of the classical period range from C. P. E. Bach to Schubert and thereby cover the whole spectrum from baroque composers to romantic composers, tribes also shade into bands at one extreme and into chiefdoms at the opposite extreme. In particular, a tribal big-man's role in dividing the meat of pigs slaughtered for feasts points to the role of chiefs in collecting and redistributing food and goods—now reconstrued as tribute—in chiefdoms. Similarly, presence or absence of public architecture is supposedly one of the distinctions between tribes and chiefdoms, but large New Guinea villages often have cult houses (known as *haus tamburan,* on the Sepik River) that presage the temples of chiefdoms.

ALTHOUGH A FEW bands and tribes survive today on remote and ecologically marginal lands outside state control, fully independent chiefdoms had disappeared by the early twentieth century, because they tended to occupy prime land coveted by states. However, as of A.D. 1492, chiefdoms were still widespread over much of the eastern United States, in productive areas of South and Central America and sub-Saharan Africa that had not yet been subsumed under native states, and in all of Polynesia. The archaeological evidence discussed below suggests that chiefdoms arose by around 5500 B.C. in the Fertile Crescent and by around 1000 B.C. in Mesoamerica and the Andes. Let us consider the distinctive features of chiefdoms, very different from modern European and American states and, at the same time, from bands and simple tribal societies.

As regards population size, chiefdoms were considerably larger than tribes, ranging from several thousand to several tens of thousands of people. That size created serious potential for internal conflict because, for any person living in a chiefdom, the vast majority of other people in the chiefdom were neither closely related by blood or marriage nor known by name. With the rise of chiefdoms around 7,500 years ago, people had to learn, for the first time in history, how to encounter strangers regularly without attempting to kill them.

Part of the solution to that problem was for one person, the chief, to exercise a monopoly on the right to use force. In contrast to a tribe's big-man, a chief held a recognized office, filled by hereditary right. Instead of the decentralized anarchy of a village meeting, the chief was a permanent centralized authority, made all significant decisions, and had a monopoly on critical information (such as what a neighboring chief was privately threatening, or what harvest the gods had supposedly promised). Unlike big-men, chiefs could be recognized from afar by visible distinguishing features, such as a large fan worn over the back on Rennell Island in the Southwest Pacific. A commoner encountering a chief was obliged to perform ritual marks of respect, such as (on Hawaii) prostrating oneself. The chief's orders might be transmitted through one or two levels of bureaucrats, many of whom were themselves low-ranked chiefs. However, in contrast to state bureaucrats, chiefdom bureaucrats had generalized rather than specialized roles. In Polynesian Hawaii the same bureaucrats (termed *konohiki*) extracted tribute *and* oversaw irrigation *and* organized labor corvées for the chief, whereas state societies have separate tax collectors, water district managers, and draft boards.

A chiefdom's large population in a small area required plenty of food, obtained by food production in most cases, by hunting-gathering in a few especially rich areas. For example, American Indians of the Pacific Northwest coast, such as the Kwakiutl, Nootka, and Tlingit Indians, lived under chiefs in villages without any agriculture or domestic animals, because the rivers and sea were so rich in salmon and halibut. The food surpluses generated by some people, relegated to the rank of commoners, went to feed the chiefs, their families, bureaucrats, and crafts specialists, who variously made canoes, adzes, or spittoons or worked as bird catchers or tattooers.

Luxury goods, consisting of those specialized crafts products or else rare objects obtained by long-distance trade, were reserved for chiefs. For example, Hawaiian chiefs had feather cloaks, some of them consisting of tens of thousands of feathers and requiring many human generations for their manufacture (by commoner cloak makers, of course). That concentration of luxury goods often makes it possible to recognize chiefdoms archaeologically, by the fact that some graves (those of chiefs) contain much richer goods than other graves (those of commoners), in contrast to the egalitarian burials of earlier human history. Some ancient complex chiefdoms can also be distinguished from tribal villages by the remains of elaborate public architecture (such as temples) and by a regional hierarchy of settlements, with one site (the site of the paramount chief) being obviously larger and having more administrative buildings and artifacts than other sites.

Like tribes, chiefdoms consisted of multiple hereditary lineages living at one site. However, whereas the lineages of tribal villages are equal-ranked clans, in a chiefdom all members of the chief's lineage had hereditary perquisites. In effect, the society was divided into hereditary chief and commoner classes, with Hawaiian chiefs themselves subdivided into eight hierarchically ranked lineages, each concentrating its marriages within its own lineage. Furthermore, since chiefs required menial servants as well as specialized craftspeople, chiefdoms differed from tribes in having many jobs that could be filled by slaves, typically obtained by capture in raids.

The most distinctive economic feature of chiefdoms was their shift from reliance solely on the reciprocal exchanges characteristic of bands and tribes, by which A gives B a gift while expecting that B at some unspecified future time will give a gift of comparable value to A. We modern state dwellers indulge in such behavior on birthdays and holidays, but most of our flow of goods is achieved instead by buying and selling for money according to the law of supply and demand. While continuing reciprocal exchanges and without marketing or money, chiefdoms developed an additional new system termed a redistributive economy. A simple example would involve a chief receiving wheat at harvest time from every farmer in the chiefdom, then throwing a feast for everybody and serving bread or else storing the wheat and gradually giving it out again in the months between harvests. When a large portion of the goods received from commoners was not redistributed to them but was retained and consumed by the chiefly lineages and craftspeople, the redistribution became tribute, a precursor of taxes that made its first appearance in chiefdoms. From the commoners the chiefs claimed not only goods but also labor for construction of public works, which again might return to benefit the commoners (for example, irrigation systems to help feed everybody) or instead benefited mainly the chiefs (for instance, lavish tombs).

We have been talking about chiefdoms generically, as if they were all the same. In fact, chiefdoms varied considerably. Larger ones tended to have more powerful chiefs, more ranks of chiefly lineages, greater distinctions between chiefs and commoners, more retention of tribute by the chiefs, more layers of bureaucrats, and grander public architecture. For instance, societies on small Polynesian islands were effectively rather similar to tribal societies with a big-man, except that the position of chief was hereditary. The chief's hut looked like any other hut, there were no bureaucrats or public works, the chief redistributed most goods he received back to the commoners, and land was controlled by the community. But on the largest Polynesian islands, such as Hawaii, Tahiti, and Tonga, chiefs were recognizable at a glance by their ornaments, public works were erected by large labor forces, most tribute was retained by the chiefs, and all land was controlled by them. A further gradation among societies with ranked lineages was from those where the political unit was a single autonomous village, to those consisting of a regional assemblage of villages in which the largest village with a paramount chief controlled the smaller villages with lesser chiefs.

By NOW, IT should be obvious that chiefdoms introduced the dilemma fundamental to all centrally governed, nonegalitarian societies. At best, they do good by providing expensive services impossible to contract for on an individual basis. At worst, they function unabashedly as kleptocracies, transferring net wealth from commoners to upper classes. These noble and selfish functions are inextricably linked, although some governments emphasize much more of one function than of the other. The difference between a kleptocrat and a wise statesman, between a robber baron and a public benefactor, is merely one of degree: a matter of just how large a percentage of the tribute extracted from producers is retained by the elite, and how much the commoners like the public uses to which the redistributed tribute is put. We consider President Mobutu of Zaire a kleptocrat because he keeps too much tribute (the equivalent of billions of dollars) and redistributes too little tribute (no functioning telephone system in Zaire). We consider George Washington a statesman because he spent tax money on widely admired programs and did not enrich himself as president. Nevertheless, George Washington was born into wealth, which is much more unequally distributed in the United States than in New Guinea villages.

For any ranked society, whether a chiefdom or a state, one thus has to ask: why do the commoners tolerate the transfer of the fruits of their hard labor to kleptocrats? This question, raised by political theorists from Plato to Marx, is raised anew by voters in every modern election. Kleptocracies with little public support run the risk of being overthrown, either by downtrodden commoners or by upstart would-be replacement kleptocrats seeking public support by promising a higher ratio of services rendered to fruits stolen. For example, Hawaiian history was repeatedly punctuated by revolts against repressive chiefs, usually led by younger brothers promising less oppression. This may sound funny to us in the context of old Hawaii, until we reflect on all the misery still being caused by such struggles in the modern world.

What should an elite do to gain popular support while still maintaining a more comfortable lifestyle than commoners? Kleptocrats throughout the ages have resorted to a mixture of four solutions:

1. Disarm the populace, and arm the elite. That's much easier in these days of high-tech weaponry, produced only in industrial plants and easily monopolized by an elite, than in ancient times of spears and clubs easily made at home.

2. Make the masses happy by redistributing much of the tribute received, in popular ways. This principle was as valid for Hawaiian chiefs as it is for American politicians today.

3. Use the monopoly of force to promote happiness, by maintaining public order and curbing violence. This is potentially a big and underappreciated advantage of centralized societies over noncentralized ones. Anthropologists formerly idealized band and tribal societies as gentle and nonviolent, because visiting anthropologists observed no murder in a band of 25 people in the course of a three-year study. Of course they didn't: it's easy to calculate that a band of a dozen adults and a dozen children, subject to the inevitable deaths occurring anyway for the usual reasons other than murder, could not perpetuate itself if in addition one of its dozen adults murdered another adult every three years. Much more extensive long-term information about band and tribal societies reveals that murder is a leading cause of death. For example, I happened to be visiting New Guinea's Iyau people at a time when a woman anthropologist was interviewing Iyau women about their life histories. Woman after woman, when asked to name her husband, named several sequential husbands who had died violent deaths. A typical answer went like this: "My first husband was killed by Elopi raiders. My second husband was killed by a man who wanted me, and who became my third husband. That husband was killed by the brother of my second husband, seeking to avenge his murder." Such biographies prove common for so-called gentle tribespeople and contributed to the acceptance of centralized authority as tribal societies grew larger.

4. The remaining way for kleptocrats to gain public support is to construct an ideology or religion justifying kleptocracy. Bands and tribes already had supernatural beliefs, just as do modern established religions. But the supernatural beliefs of bands and tribes did not serve to justify central authority, justify transfer of wealth, or maintain peace between unrelated individuals. When supernatural beliefs gained those functions and became institutionalized, they were thereby transformed into what we

term a religion. Hawaiian chiefs were typical of chiefs elsewhere, in asserting divinity, divine descent, or at least a hotline to the gods. The chief claimed to serve the people by interceding for them with the gods and reciting the ritual formulas required to obtain rain, good harvests, and success in fishing.

Chiefdoms characteristically have an ideology, precursor to an institutionalized religion, that buttresses the chief's authority. The chief may either combine the offices of political leader and priest in a single person, or may support a separate group of kleptocrats (that is, priests) whose function is to provide ideological justification for the chiefs. That is why chiefdoms devote so much collected tribute to constructing temples and other public works, which serve as centers of the official religion and visible signs of the chief's power.

Besides justifying the transfer of wealth to kleptocrats, institutionalized religion brings two other important benefits to centralized societies. First, shared ideology or religion helps solve the problem of how unrelated individuals are to live together without killing each other—by providing them with a bond not based on kinship. Second, it gives people a motive, other than genetic self-interest, for sacrificing their lives on behalf of others. At the cost of a few society members who die in battle as soldiers, the whole society becomes much more effective at conquering other societies or resisting attacks.

THE POLITICAL, ECONOMIC, and social institutions most familiar to us today are those of states, which now rule all of the world's land area except for Antarctica. Many early states and all modern ones have had literate elites, and many modern states have literate masses as well. Vanished states tended to leave visible archaeological hallmarks, such as ruins of temples with standardized designs, at least four levels of settlement sizes, and pottery styles covering tens of thousands of square miles. We thereby know that states arose around 3700 B.C. in Mesopotamia and around 300 B.C. in Mesoamerica, over 2,000 years ago in the Andes, China, and Southeast Asia, and over 1,000 years ago in West Africa. In modern times the formation of states out of chiefdoms has been observed repeatedly. Thus, we possess much more information about past states and their formation than about past chiefdoms, tribes, and bands.

Protostates extend many features of large paramount (multivillage) chiefdoms. They continue the increase in size from bands to tribes to chiefdoms. Whereas chiefdoms' populations range from a few thousand to a few tens of thousands, the populations of most modern states exceed one million, and China's exceeds one billion. The paramount chief's location may become the state's capital city. Other population centers of states outside the capital may also qualify as true cities, which are lacking in chiefdoms. Cities differ from villages in their monumental public works, palaces of rulers, accumulation of capital from tribute or taxes, and concentration of people other than food producers.

Early states had a hereditary leader with a title equivalent to king, like a super paramount chief and exercising an even greater monopoly of information, decision making, and power. Even in democracies today, crucial knowledge is available to only a few individuals, who control the flow of information to the rest of the government and consequently control decisions. For instance, in the Cuban Missile Crisis of 1963, information and discussions that determined whether nuclear war would engulf half a billion people were initially confined by President Kennedy to a ten-member executive committee of the National Security Council that he himself appointed; then he limited final decisions to a four-member group consisting of himself and three of his cabinet ministers.

Central control is more far-reaching, and economic redistribution in the form of tribute (renamed taxes) more extensive, in states than in chiefdoms. Economic specialization is more extreme, to the point where today not even farmers remain self-sufficient. Hence the effect on society is catastrophic when state government collapses, as happened in Britain upon the removal of Roman troops, administrators, and coinage between A.D. 407 and 411. Even the earliest Mesopotamian states exercised centralized control of their economies. Their food was produced by four specialist groups (cereal farmers, herders, fishermen, and orchard and garden growers), from each of which the state took the produce and to each of which it gave out the necessary supplies, tools, and foods other than the type of food that this group produced. The state supplied seeds and plow animals to the cereal farmers, took wool from the herders, exchanged the wool by long-distance trade for metal and other essential raw materials, and paid out food rations to the laborers who maintained the irrigation systems on which the farmers depended.

Many, perhaps most, early states adopted slavery on a much larger scale than did chiefdoms. That was not because chiefdoms were more kindly disposed toward defeated enemies but because the greater economic specialization of states, with more mass production and more public works, provided more uses for slave labor. In addition, the larger scale of state warfare made more captives available.

A chiefdom's one or two levels of administration are greatly multiplied in states, as anyone who has seen an organizational chart of any government knows. Along with the proliferation of vertical levels of bureaucrats, there is also horizontal specialization. Instead of konohiki carrying out every aspect of administration for a Hawaiian district, state governments have several separate departments, each with its own hierarchy, to handle water management, taxes, military draft, and so on. Even small states have more complex bureaucracies than large chiefdoms. For instance, the West African state of Maradi had a central administration with over 130 titled offices.

Internal conflict resolution within states has become increasingly formalized by laws, a judiciary, and police. The laws are often written, because many states (with conspicuous exceptions, such as that of the Incas) have had literate elites, writing having been developed around the same time as the formation of the earliest states in both Mesopotamia and Mesoamerica. In contrast, no early chiefdom not on the verge of statehood developed writing.

Early states had state religions and standardized temples. Many early kings were considered divine and were accorded special treatment in innumerable respects. For example, the Aztec and Inca emperors were both carried about in litters; servants went ahead of the Inca emperor's litter and swept the ground clear; and the Japanese language includes special forms of the pronoun "you" for use only in addressing the emperor. Early kings were themselves the head of the state religion or else had separate high priests. The Mesopotamian temple was the center not only of religion but also of economic redistribution, writing, and crafts technology.

All these features of states carry to an extreme the developments that led from tribes to chiefdoms. In addition, though, states have diverged from chiefdoms in several new directions. The most fundamental such distinction is that states are organized on political and territorial lines, not on the kinship lines that defined bands, tribes, and simple chiefdoms. Furthermore, bands and tribes always, and chiefdoms usually, consist of a single ethnic and linguistic group. States, though—especially so-called empires formed by amalgamation or conquest of states—are regularly multiethnic and multilingual. State bureaucrats are not selected mainly on the basis of kinship, as in chiefdoms, but are professionals selected at least partly on the basis of training and ability. In later states, including most today, the leadership often became nonhereditary, and many states abandoned the entire system of formal hereditary classes carried over from chiefdoms.

OVER THE PAST 13,000 years the predominant trend in human society has been the replacement of smaller, less complex units by larger, more complex ones. Obviously, that is no more than an average long-term trend, with innumerable shifts in either direction: 1,000 amalgamations for 999 reversals. We know from our daily newspaper that large units (for instance, the former USSR, Yugoslavia, and Czechoslovakia) can disintegrate into smaller units, as did Alexander of Macedon's empire over 2,000 years ago. More complex units don't always conquer less complex ones but may succumb to them, as when the Roman and Chinese Empires were overrun by "barbarian" and Mongol chiefdoms, respectively. But the long-term trend has still been toward large, complex societies, culminating in states.

Obviously, too, part of the reason for states' triumphs over simpler entities when the two collide is that states usually enjoy an advantage of weaponry and other technology, and a large numerical advantage in population. But there are also two other potential advantages inherent in chiefdoms and states. First, a centralized decision maker has the advantage at concentrating troops and resources. Second, the official religions and patriotic fervor of many states make their troops willing to fight suicidally.

The latter willingness is one so strongly programmed into us citizens of modern states, by our schools and churches and governments, that we forget what a radical break it marks with previous human history. Every state has its slogan urging its citizens to be prepared to die if necessary for the state: Britain's "For King and Country," Spain's "Por Dios y España," and so on. Similar sentiments motivated 16th-century Aztec warriors: "There is nothing like death in war, nothing like the flowery death so precious to Him [the Aztec national god Huitzilopochtli] who gives life: far off I see it, my heart yearns for it!"

Such sentiments are unthinkable in bands and tribes. In all the accounts that my New Guinea friends have given me of their former tribal wars, there has been not a single hint of tribal patriotism, of a suicidal charge, or of any other military conduct carrying an accepted risk of being killed. Instead, raids are initiated by ambush or by superior force, so as to minimize at all costs the risk that one might die for one's village. But that attitude severely limits the military options of tribes, compared with state societies. Naturally, what makes patriotic and religious fanatics such dangerous opponents is not the deaths of the fanatics themselves, but their willingness to accept the deaths of a fraction of their number in order to annihilate or crush their infidel enemy. Fanaticism in war, of the type that drove recorded Christian and Islamic conquests, was probably unknown on Earth until chiefdoms and especially states emerged within the last 6,000 years.

How DID SMALL, noncentralized, kin-based societies evolve into large centralized ones in which most members are not closely related to each other? Having reviewed the stages in this transformation from bands to states, we now ask what impelled societies thus to transform themselves.

At many moments in history, states have arisen independently—or, as cultural anthropologists say, "pristinely," that is, in the absence of any preexisting surrounding states. Pristine state origins took place at least once, possibly many times, on each of the continents except Australia and North America. Prehistoric states included those of Mesopotamia, North China, the Nile and Indus Valleys, Mesoamerica, the Andes, and West Africa. Native states in contact with European states have arisen from chiefdoms repeatedly in the last three centuries in Madagascar, Hawaii, Tahiti, and many parts of Africa. Chiefdoms have arisen pristinely even more often, in all of the same regions and in North America's Southeast and Pacific Northwest, the Amazon, Polynesia, and sub-Saharan Africa. All these origins of complex societies give us a rich database for understanding their development.

Of the many theories addressing the problem of state origins, the simplest denies that there is any problem to solve. Aristotle considered states the natural condition of human society, requiring no explanation. His error was understandable, because all the societies with which he would have been acquainted—Greek societies of the fourth century B.C.—were states. However, we now know that, as of A.D. 1492, much of the world was instead organized into chiefdoms, tribes, or bands. State formation does demand an explanation.

The next theory is the most familiar one. The French philosopher Jean-Jacques Rousseau speculated that states are formed by a social contract, a rational decision reached when people calculated their self-interest, came to the agreement that they would be better off in a state than in simpler societies, and voluntarily did away with their simpler societies. But observation and historical records have failed to uncover a single case of a state's being formed in that ethereal atmosphere of dispassionate farsightedness. Smaller units do not voluntarily abandon their sovereignty and merge into larger units. They do so only by conquest, or under external duress.

A third theory, still popular with some historians and economists, sets out from the undoubted fact that, in both Mesopotamia and North China and Mexico, large-scale irrigation systems began to be constructed around the time that states started to emerge. The theory also notes that any big, complex system for irrigation or hydraulic management requires a centralized bureaucracy to construct and maintain it. The theory then turns an observed rough correlation in time into a postulated chain of cause and effect. Supposedly, Mesopotamians and North Chinese and Mexicans foresaw the advantages that a large-scale irrigation system would bring them, even though there was at the time no such system within thousands of miles (or anywhere on Earth) to illustrate for them those advantages. Those farsighted people chose to merge their inefficient little chiefdoms into a larger state capable of blessing them with large-scale irrigation.

However, this "hydraulic theory" of state formation is subject to the same objections leveled against social contract theories in general. More specifically, it addresses only the final stage in the evolution of complex societies. It says nothing about what drove the progression from bands to tribes to chiefdoms during all the millennia before the prospect of large-scale irrigation loomed up on the horizon. When historical or archaeological dates are examined in detail, they fail to support the view of irrigation as the driving force for state formation. In Mesopotamia, North China, Mexico, and Madagascar, small-scale irrigation systems already existed before the rise of states. Construction of large-scale irrigation systems did not accompany the emergence of states but came only significantly later in each of those areas. In most of the states formed over the Maya area of

Mesoamerica and the Andes, irrigation systems always remained small-scale ones that local communities could build and maintain themselves. Thus, even in those areas where complex systems of hydraulic management did emerge, they were a secondary consequence of states that must have formed for other reasons.

What seems to me to point to a fundamentally correct view of state formation is an undoubted fact of much wider validity than the correlation between irrigation and the formation of some states—namely, that the size of the regional population is the strongest single predictor of societal complexity. As we have seen, bands number a few dozen individuals, tribes a few hundred, chiefdoms a few thousand to a few tens of thousands, and states generally over about 50,000. In addition to that coarse correlation between regional population size and type of society (band, tribe, and so on), there is a finer trend, within each of those categories, between population and societal complexity: for instance, that chiefdoms with large populations prove to be the most centralized, stratified, and complex ones.

These correlations suggest strongly that regional population size or population density or population pressure has *something* to do with the formation of complex societies. But the correlations do not tell us precisely how population variables function in a chain of cause and effect whose outcome is a complex society. To trace out that chain, let us now remind ourselves how large dense populations themselves arise. Then we can examine why a large but simple society could not maintain itself. With that as background, we shall finally return to the question of how a simpler society actually becomes more complex as the regional population increases.

W e h a v e s e e n that large or dense populations arise only under conditions of food production, or at least under exceptionally productive conditions for hunting-gathering. Some productive hunter-gatherer societies reached the organizational level of chiefdoms, but none reached the level of states: all states nourish their citizens by food production. These considerations, along with the just mentioned correlation between regional population size and societal complexity, have led to a protracted chicken-or-egg debate about the causal relations between food production, population variables, and societal complexity. Is it intensive food production that is the cause, triggering population growth and somehow leading to a complex society? Or are large populations and complex societies instead the cause, somehow leading to intensification of food production?

Posing the question in that either-or form misses the point. Intensified food production and societal complexity stimulate each other, by autocatalysis. That is, population growth leads to societal complexity, by mechanisms that we shall discuss, while societal complexity in turn leads to intensified food production and thereby to population growth. Complex centralized societies are uniquely capable of organizing public works (including irrigation systems), long-distance trade (including the importation of metals to make better agricultural tools), and activities of different groups of economic specialists (such as feeding herders with farmers' cereal, and transferring the herders' livestock to farmers for use as plow animals). All of these capabilities of centralized societies have fostered intensified food production and hence population growth throughout history.

In addition, food production contributes in at least three ways to specific features of complex societies. First, it involves seasonally pulsed inputs of labor. When the harvest has been stored, the farmers' labor becomes available for a centralized political authority to harness—in order to build public works advertising state power (such as the Egyptian pyramids), or to build public works that could feed more mouths (such as Polynesian Hawaii's irrigation systems or fishponds), or to undertake wars of conquest to form larger political entities.

Second, food production may be organized so as to generate stored food surpluses, which permit economic specialization and social stratification. The surpluses can be used to feed all tiers of a complex society: the chiefs, bureaucrats, and other members of the elite; the scribes, craftspeople, and other non-food-producing specialists; and the farmers themselves, during times that they are drafted to construct public works.

Finally, food production permits or requires people to adopt sedentary living, which is a prerequisite for accumulating substantial possessions, developing elaborate technology and crafts, and constructing public works. The importance of fixed residence to a complex society explains why missionaries and governments, whenever they make first contact with previously uncontacted nomadic tribes or bands in New Guinea or the Amazon, universally have two immediate goals. One goal, of course, is the obvious one of "pacifying" the nomads: that is, dissuading them from killing missionaries, bureaucrats, or each other. The other goal is to induce the nomads to settle in villages, so that the missionaries and bureaucrats can find the nomads, bring them services such as medical care and schools, and proselytize and control them.

THUS, FOOD PRODUCTION, which increases population size, also acts in many ways to make features of complex societies *possible*. But that doesn't prove that food production and large populations make complex societies *inevitable*. How can we account for the empirical observation that band or tribal organization just does not work for societies of hundreds of thousands of people, and that all existing large societies have complex centralized organization? We can cite at least four obvious reasons.

One reason is the problem of conflict between unrelated strangers. That problem grows astronomically as the number of people making up the society increases. Relationships within a band of 20 people involve only 190 two-person interactions (20 people times 19 divided by 2), but a band of 2,000 would have 1,999,000 dyads. Each of those dyads represents a potential time bomb that could explode in a murderous argument. Each murder in band and tribal societies usually leads to an attempted revenge killing, starting one more unending cycle of murder and countermurder that destabilizes the society.

In a band, where everyone is closely related to everyone else, people related simultaneously to both quarreling parties step in to mediate quarrels. In a tribe, where many people are still close relatives and everyone at least knows everybody else by name, mutual relatives and mutual friends mediate the quarrel. But once the threshold of "several hundred," below which everyone can know everyone else, has been crossed, increasing numbers of dyads become pairs of unrelated strangers. When strangers fight, few people present will be friends or relatives of both combatants, with self-interest in stopping the fight. Instead, many onlookers will be friends or relatives of only one combatant and will side with that person, escalating the two-person fight into a general brawl. Hence a large society that continues to leave conflict resolution to all of its members is guaranteed to blow up. That factor alone would explain why societies of thousands can exist only if they develop centralized authority to monopolize force and resolve conflicts.

A second reason is the growing impossibility of communal decision making with increasing population size. Decision making by the entire adult population is still possible in New Guinea villages small enough that news and information quickly spread to everyone, that everyone can hear everyone else in a meeting of the whole village, and that everyone who wants to speak at the meeting has the opportunity to do so. But all those prerequisites for communal decision making become unattainable in much larger communities. Even now, in these days of microphones and loud-speakers, we all know that a group meeting is no way to resolve issues for a group of thousands of people. Hence a large society must be structured and centralized if it is to reach decisions effectively.

A third reason involves economic considerations. Any society requires means to transfer goods between its members. One individual may happen to acquire more of some essential commodity on one day and less on another. Because individuals have different talents, one individual consistently tends to wind up with an excess of some essentials and a deficit of others. In small societies with few pairs of members, the resulting necessary transfers of goods can be arranged directly between pairs of individuals or families, by reciprocal exchanges. But the same mathematics that makes direct pairwise conflict resolution inefficient in large societies makes direct pairwise economic transfers also inefficient. Large societies can function economically only if they have a redistributive economy in addition to a reciprocal economy. Goods in excess of an individual's needs must be transferred from the individual to a centralized authority, which then redistributes the goods to individuals with deficits.

A final consideration mandating complex organization for large societies has to do with population densities. Large societies of food producers have not only more members but also higher population densities than do small bands of hunter-gatherers. Each band of a few dozen hunters occupies a large territory, within which they can acquire most of the resources essential to them. They can obtain their remaining necessities by trading with neighboring bands during intervals between band warfare. As population density increases, the territory of that band-sized population of a few dozen would shrink to a small area, with more and more of life's necessities having to be obtained outside the area. For instance, one couldn't just divide Holland's 16,000 square miles and 16,000,000 people into 800,000 individual territories, each encompassing 13 acres and serving as home to an autonomous band of 20 people who remained self-sufficient confined within their 13 acres, occasionally taking advantage of a temporary truce to come to the borders of their tiny territory in order to exchange some trade items and brides with the next band. Such spatial realities require that densely populated regions support large and complexly organized societies.

Considerations of conflict resolution, decision making, economics, and space thus converge in requiring large societies to be centralized. But centralization of power inevitably opens the door—for those who hold the power, are privy to information, make the decisions, and redistribute the goods—to exploit the resulting opportunities to reward themselves and their relatives. To anyone familiar with any modern grouping of people, that's obvious. As early societies developed, those acquiring centralized power gradually established themselves as an elite, perhaps originating as one of several formerly equal-ranked village clans that became "more equal" than the others.

THOSE ARE THE reasons why large societies cannot function with band organization and instead are complex kleptocracies. But we are still left with the question of how small, simple societies actually evolve or amalgamate into large, complex ones. Amalgamation, centralized conflict resolution, decision making, economic redistribution, and kleptocratic religion don't just develop automatically through a Rousseauesque social contract. What drives the amalgamation?

In part, the answer depends upon evolutionary reasoning. I said at the outset of this chapter that societies classified in the same category are not all identical to each other, because humans and human groups are infinitely diverse. For example, among bands and tribes, the big-men of some are inevitably more charismatic, powerful, and skilled in reaching decisions than the big-men of others. Among large tribes, those with stronger big-men and hence greater centralization tend to have an advantage over those with less centralization. Tribes that resolve conflicts as poorly as did the Fayu tend to blow apart again into bands, while ill-governed chiefdoms blow apart into smaller chiefdoms or tribes. Societies with effective conflict resolution, sound decision making, and harmonious economic redistribution can develop better technology, concentrate their military power, seize larger and more productive territories, and crush autonomous smaller societies one by one.

Thus, competition between societies at one level of complexity tends to

Plate 17. An Oyana man from tropical northern South America. Plates 17–20 depict Native South Americans.

Plate 18. A Yanomamo girl from tropical northern South America.

Plate 19. A Fuegian man from the southern tip of South America.

Plate 20. A Quechua man from the Andean highlands of South America.

Plate 21. A man from western Europe (Spain). Plates 21–24 illustrate speakers of Indo-European languages, from the western half of Eurasia.

Plate 22. Another western European: former president Charles de Gaulle of France.

Plate 23. Above: two Scandinavian women (Swedish actress Ingrid Bergman and her daughter). Below: an Armenian man, from western Asia.

Plate 24. Afghan soldiers, from central Asia.

Plate 25. A Khoisan woman from the Kalahari Desert of Botswana, southern Africa.

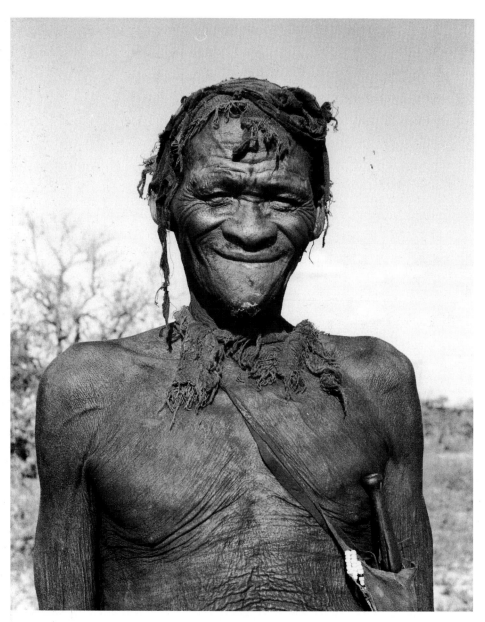

Plate 26. A Khoisan man from the Kalahari Desert of Botswana, south-ern Africa.

Plate 27. A pygmy girl from the Ituri forest of equatorial Africa.

Plate 28 A group of pygmies from the Ituri forest of equatorial Africa.

Plate 29. An East African speaker of a Nilo-Saharan language: a Nuer man from the Sudan.

Plate 30. An East African speaker of an Afro-Asiatic language: Ethiopia's Haile Gebreselassie, winning the men's 10,000-meter race at the 1996 Olympic Games, just ahead of Kenya's Paul Tergat.

Plate 31. An East African speaker of a non-Bantu Niger-Congo language: a Zande woman of the Sudan.

Plate 32. A speaker of a Bantu Niger-Congo language: President Nelson Mandela of South Africa.

lead to societies on the next level of complexity *if* conditions permit. Tribes conquer or combine with tribes to reach the size of chiefdoms, which conquer or combine with other chiefdoms to reach the size of states, which conquer or combine with other states to become empires. More generally, large units potentially enjoy an advantage over individual small units *if*— and that's a big "if"—the large units can solve the problems that come with their larger size, such as perennial threats from upstart claimants to leadership, commoner resentment of kleptocracy, and increased problems associated with economic integration.

The amalgamation of smaller units into larger ones has often been documented historically or archaeologically. Contrary to Rousseau, such amalgamations never occur by a process of unthreatened little societies freely deciding to merge, in order to promote the happiness of their citizens. Leaders of little societies, as of big ones, are jealous of their independence and prerogatives. Amalgamation occurs instead in either of two ways: by merger under the threat of external force, or by actual conquest. Innumerable examples are available to illustrate each mode of amalgamation.

Merger under the threat of external force is well illustrated by the formation of the Cherokee Indian confederation in the U.S. Southeast. The Cherokees were originally divided into 30 or 40 independent chiefdoms, each consisting of a village of about 400 people. Increasing white settlement led to conflicts between Cherokees and whites. When individual Cherokees robbed or assaulted white settlers and traders, the whites were unable to discriminate among the different Cherokee chiefdoms and retaliated indiscriminately against any Cherokees, either by military action or by cutting off trade. In response, the Cherokee chiefdoms gradually found themselves compelled to join into a single confederacy in the course of the 18th century. Initially, the larger chiefdoms in 1730 chose an overall leader, a chief named Moytoy, who was succeeded in 1741 by his son. The first task of these leaders was to punish individual Cherokees who attacked whites, and to deal with the white government. Around 1758 the Cherokees regularized their decision making with an annual council modeled on previous village councils and meeting at one village (Echota), which thereby became a de facto "capital." Eventually, the Cherokees became literate (as we saw in Chapter 12) and adopted a written constitution.

The Cherokee confederacy was thus formed not by conquest but by the amalgamation of previously jealous smaller entities, which merged only when threatened with destruction by powerful external forces. In much the same way, in an example of state formation described in every American history textbook, the white American colonies themselves, one of which (Georgia) had precipitated the formation of the Cherokee state, were impelled to form a nation of their own when threatened with the powerful external force of the British monarchy. The American colonies were initially as jealous of their autonomy as the Cherokee chiefdoms, and their first attempt at amalgamation under the Articles of Confederation (1781) proved unworkable because it reserved too much autonomy to the ex-colonies. Only further threats, notably Shays's Rebellion of 1786 and the unsolved burden of war debt, overcame the ex-colonies' extreme reluctance to sacrifice autonomy and pushed them into adopting our current strong federal constitution in 1787. The 19th-century unification of Germany's jealous principalities proved equally difficult. Three early attempts (the Frankfurt Parliament of 1848, the restored German Confederation of 1850, and the North German Confederation of 1866) failed before the external threat of France's declaration of war in 1870 finally led to the princelets' surrendering much of their power to a central imperial German government in 1871.

The other mode of formation of complex societies, besides merger under threat of external force, is merger by conquest. A well-documented example is the origin of the Zulu state, in southeastern Africa. When first observed by white settlers, the Zulus were divided into dozens of little chiefdoms. During the late 1700s, as population pressure rose, fighting between the chiefdoms became increasingly intense. Among all those chiefdoms, the ubiquitous problem of devising centralized power structures was solved most successfully by a chief called Dingiswayo, who gained ascendancy of the Mtetwa chiefdom by killing a rival around 1807. Dingiswayo developed a superior centralized military organization by drafting young men from all villages and grouping them into regiments by age rather than by their village. He also developed superior centralized political organization by abstaining from slaughter as he conquered other chiefdoms, leaving the conquered chief's family intact, and limiting himself to replacing the conquered chief himself with a relative willing to cooperate with Dingiswayo. He developed superior centralized conflict resolution by expanding the adjudication of quarrels. In that way Dingiswayo was able to conquer and begin the integration of 30 other Zulu chiefdoms. His successors strengthened the resulting embryonic Zulu state by expanding its judicial system, policing, and ceremonies.

This Zulu example of a state formed by conquest can be multiplied almost indefinitely. Native states whose formation from chiefdoms happened to be witnessed by Europeans in the 18th and 19th centuries include the Polynesian Hawaiian state, the Polynesian Tahitian state, the Merina state of Madagascar, Lesotho and Swazi and other southern African states besides that of the Zulus, the Ashanti state of West Africa, and the Ankole and Buganda states of Uganda. The Aztec and Inca Empires were formed by 15th-century conquests, before Europeans arrived, but we know much about their formation from Indian oral histories transcribed by early Spanish settlers. The formation of the Roman state and the expansion of the Macedonian Empire under Alexander were described in detail by contemporary classical authors.

All these examples illustrate that wars, or threats of war, have played a key role in most, if not all, amalgamations of societies. But wars, even between mere bands, have been a constant fact of human history. Why is it, then, that they evidently began causing amalgamations of societies only within the past 13,000 years? We had already concluded that the formation of complex societies is somehow linked to population pressure, so we should now seek a link between population pressure and the outcome of war. Why should wars tend to cause amalgamations of societies when populations are dense but not when they are sparse? The answer is that the fate of defeated peoples depends on population density, with three possible outcomes:

Where population densities are very low, as is usual in regions occupied by hunter-gatherer bands, survivors of a defeated group need only move farther away from their enemies. That tends to be the result of wars between nomadic bands in New Guinea and the Amazon.

Where population densities are moderate, as in regions occupied by food-producing tribes, no large vacant areas remain to which survivors of a defeated band can flee. But tribal societies without intensive food production have no employment for slaves and do not produce large enough food surpluses to be able to yield much tribute. Hence the victors have no use for survivors of a defeated tribe, unless to take the women in marriage. The defeated men are killed, and their territory may be occupied by the victors.

Where population densities are high, as in regions occupied by states or chiefdoms, the defeated still have nowhere to flee, but the victors now have two options for exploiting them while leaving them alive. Because chiefdoms and state societies have economic specialization, the defeated can be used as slaves, as commonly happened in biblical times. Alternatively, because many such societies have intensive food production systems capable of yielding large surpluses, the victors can leave the defeated in place but deprive them of political autonomy, make them pay regular tribute in food or goods, and amalgamate their society into the victorious state or chiefdom. This has been the usual outcome of battles associated with the founding of states or empires throughout recorded history. For example, the Spanish conquistadores wished to exact tribute from Mexico's defeated native populations, so they were very interested in the Aztec Empire's tribute lists. It turned out that the tribute received by the Aztecs each year from subject peoples had included 7,000 tons of corn, 4,000 tons of beans, 4,000 tons of grain amaranth, 2,000,000 cotton cloaks, and huge quantities of cacao beans, war costumes, shields, feather headdresses, and amber.

Thus, food production, and competition and diffusion between societies, led as ultimate causes, via chains of causation that differed in detail but that all involved large dense populations and sedentary living, to the proximate agents of conquest: germs, writing, technology, and centralized political organization. Because those ultimate causes developed differently on different continents, so did those agents of conquest. Hence those agents tended to arise in association with each other, but the association was not strict: for example, an empire arose without writing among the Incas, and writing with few epidemic diseases among the Aztecs. Dingiswayo's Zulus illustrate that each of those agents contributed somewhat independently to history's pattern. Among the dozens of Zulu chiefdoms, the Mtetwa chiefdom enjoyed no advantage whatsoever of technology, writing, or germs over the other chiefdoms, which it nevertheless succeeded in defeating. Its advantage lay solely in the spheres of government and ideology. The resulting Zulu state was thereby enabled to conquer a fraction of a continent for nearly a century.

PART FOUR

AROUND THE WORLD IN FIVE CHAPTERS

CHAPTER 15

YALI'S PEOPLE

W HEN MY WIFE, MARIE, AND I WERE VACATIONING IN
Australia one summer, we decided to visit a site with well-
preserved Aboriginal rock paintings in the desert near the town of Menindee. While I knew of the Australian desert's reputation for dryness and
summer heat, I had already spent long periods working under hot, dry
conditions in the Californian desert and New Guinea savanna, so I considered myself experienced enough to deal with the minor challenges we
would face as tourists in Australia. Carrying plenty of drinking water,
Marie and I set off at noon on a hike of a few miles to the paintings.

The trail from the ranger station led uphill, under a cloudless sky,
through open terrain offering no shade whatsoever. The hot, dry air that
we were breathing reminded me of how it had felt to breathe while sitting
in a Finnish sauna. By the time we reached the cliff site with the paintings,
we had finished our water. We had also lost our interest in art, so we
pushed on uphill, breathing slowly and regularly. Presently I noticed a bird
that was unmistakably a species of babbler, but it seemed enormous compared with any known babbler species. At that point, I realized that I was
experiencing heat hallucinations for the first time in my life. Marie and I
decided that we had better head straight back.

Both of us stopped talking. As we walked, we concentrated on listening to our breathing, calculating the distance to the next landmark, and estimating the remaining time. My mouth and tongue were now dry, and Marie's face was red. When we at last reached the air-conditioned ranger station, we sagged into chairs next to the water cooler, drank down the cooler's last half-gallon of water, and asked the ranger for another bottle. Sitting there exhausted, both physically and emotionally, I reflected that the Aborigines who had made those paintings had somehow spent their entire lives in that desert without air-conditioned retreats, managing to find food as well as water.

To white Australians, Menindee is famous as the base camp for two whites who had suffered worse from the desert's dry heat over a century earlier: the Irish policeman Robert Burke and the English astronomer William Wills, ill-fated leaders of the first European expedition to cross Australia from south to north. Setting out with six camels packing food enough for three months, Burke and Wills ran out of provisions while in the desert north of Menindee. Three successive times, they encountered and were rescued by well-fed Aborigines whose home was that desert, and who plied the explorers with fish, fern cakes, and roasted fat rats. But then Burke foolishly shot his pistol at one of the Aborigines, whereupon the whole group fled. Despite their big advantage over the Aborigines in possessing guns with which to hunt, Burke and Wills starved, collapsed, and died within a month after the Aborigines' departure.

My wife's and my experience at Menindee, and the fate of Burke and Wills, made vivid for me the difficulties of building a human society in Australia. Australia stands out from all the other continents: the differences between Eurasia, Africa, North America, and South America fade into insignificance compared with the differences between Australia and any of those other landmasses. Australia is by far the driest, smallest, flattest, most infertile, climatically most unpredictable, and biologically most impoverished continent. It was the last continent to be occupied by Europeans. Until then, it had supported the most distinctive human societies, and the least numerous human population, of any continent.

Australia thus provides a crucial test of theories about intercontinental differences in societies. It had the most distinctive environment, and also the most distinctive societies. Did the former cause the latter? If so, how? Australia is the logical continent with which to begin our around-the-world tour, applying the lessons of Parts 2 and 3 to understanding the differing histories of all the continents.

MOST LAYPEOPLE WOULD describe as the most salient feature of Native Australian societies their seeming "backwardness." Australia is the sole continent where, in modern times, all native peoples still lived without any of the hallmarks of so-called civilization—without farming, herding, metal, bows and arrows, substantial buildings, settled villages, writing, chiefdoms, or states. Instead, Australian Aborigines were nomadic or seminomadic hunter-gatherers, organized into bands, living in temporary shelters or huts, and still dependent on stone tools. During the last 13,000 years less cultural change has accumulated in Australia than in any other continent. The prevalent European view of Native Australians was already typified by the words of an early French explorer, who wrote, "They are the most miserable people of the world, and the human beings who approach closest to brute beasts."

Yet, as of 40,000 years ago, Native Australian societies enjoyed a big head start over societies of Europe and the other continents. Native Australians developed some of the earliest known stone tools with ground edges, the earliest hafted stone tools (that is, stone ax heads mounted on handles), and by far the earliest watercraft, in the world. Some of the oldest known painting on rock surfaces comes from Australia. Anatomically modern humans may have settled Australia before they settled western Europe. Why, despite that head start, did Europeans end up conquering Australia, rather than vice versa?

Within that question lies another. During the Pleistocene Ice Ages, when much ocean water was sequestered in continental ice sheets and sea level dropped far below its present stand, the shallow Arafura Sea now separating Australia from New Guinea was low, dry land. With the melting of ice sheets between around 12,000 and 8,000 years ago, sea level rose, that low land became flooded, and the former continent of Greater Australia became sundered into the two hemi-continents of Australia and New Guinea (Figure 15.1 on page 299).

The human societies of those two formerly joined landmasses were in modern times very different from each other. In contrast to everything that I just said about Native Australians, most New Guineans, such as Yali's people, were farmers and swineherds. They lived in settled villages and were organized politically into tribes rather than bands. All New Guineans had bows and arrows, and many used pottery. New Guineans tended to have much more substantial dwellings, more seaworthy boats, and more numerous and more varied utensils than did Australians. As a consequence of being food producers instead of hunter-gatherers, New Guineans lived at much higher average population densities than Australians: New Guinea has only one-tenth of Australia's area but supported a native population several times that of Australia's.

Why did the human societies of the larger landmass derived from Pleistocene Greater Australia remain so "backward" in their development, while the societies of the smaller landmass "advanced" much more rapidly? Why didn't all those New Guinea innovations spread to Australia, which is separated from New Guinea by only 90 miles of sea at Torres Strait? From the perspective of cultural anthropology, the geographic distance between Australia and New Guinea is even less than 90 miles, because Torres Strait is sprinkled with islands inhabited by farmers using bows and arrows and culturally resembling New Guineans. The largest Torres Strait island lies only 10 miles from Australia. Islanders carried on a lively trade with Native Australians as well as with New Guineans. How could two such different cultural universes maintain themselves across a calm strait only 10 miles wide and routinely traversed by canoes?

Compared with Native Australians, New Guineans rate as culturally "advanced." But most other modern people consider even New Guineans "backward." Until Europeans began to colonize New Guinea in the late 19th century, all New Guineans were nonliterate, dependent on stone tools, and politically not yet organized into states or (with few exceptions) chiefdoms. Granted that New Guineans had "progressed" beyond Native Australians, why had they not yet "progressed" as far as many Eurasians, Africans, and Native Americans? Thus, Yali's people and their Australian cousins pose a puzzle inside a puzzle.

When asked to account for the cultural "backwardness" of Aboriginal Australian society, many white Australians have a simple answer: supposed deficiencies of the Aborigines themselves. In facial structure and skin color, Aborigines certainly look different from Europeans, leading some late-19th century authors to consider them a missing link between apes and humans. How else can one account for the fact that white English colonists created a literate, food-producing, industrial democracy, within

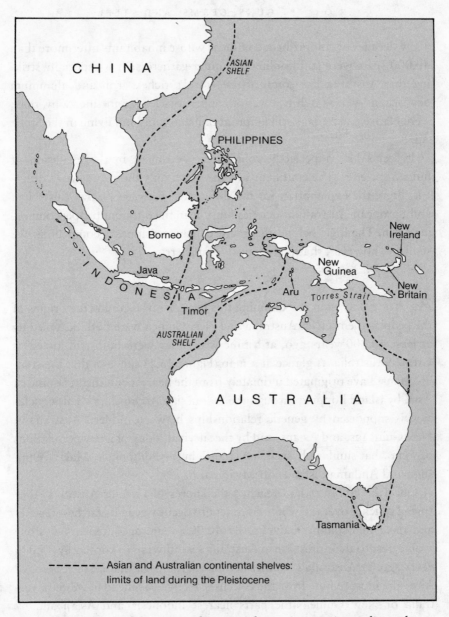

- - - - - Asian and Australian continental shelves:
limits of land during the Pleistocene

Figure 15.1. Map of the region from Southeast Asia to Australia and New Guinea. Solid lines denote the present coastline; the dashed lines are the coastline during Pleistocene times when sea level dropped to below its present stand—that is, the edge of the Asian and Greater Australian shelves. At that time, New Guinea and Australia were joined in an expanded Greater Australia, while Borneo, Java, Sumatra, and Taiwan were part of the Asian mainland.

a few decades of colonizing a continent whose inhabitants after more than 40,000 years were still nonliterate hunter-gatherers? It is especially striking that Australia has some of the world's richest iron and aluminum deposits, as well as rich reserves of copper, tin, lead, and zinc. Why, then, were Native Australians still ignorant of metal tools and living in the Stone Age?

It seems like a perfectly controlled experiment in the evolution of human societies. The continent was the same; only the people were different. Ergo, the explanation for the differences between Native Australian and European-Australian societies must lie in the different people composing them. The logic behind this racist conclusion appears compelling. We shall see, however, that it contains a simple error.

As THE FIRST step in examining this logic, let us examine the origins of the peoples themselves. Australia and New Guinea were both occupied by at least 40,000 years ago, at a time when they were both still joined as Greater Australia. A glance at a map (Figure 15.1) suggests that the colonists must have originated ultimately from the nearest continent, Southeast Asia, by island hopping through the Indonesian Archipelago. This conclusion is supported by genetic relationships between modern Australians, New Guineans, and Asians, and by the survival today of a few populations of somewhat similar physical appearance in the Philippines, Malay Peninsula, and Andaman Islands off Myanmar.

Once the colonists had reached the shores of Greater Australia, they spread quickly over the whole continent to occupy even its farthest reaches and most inhospitable habitats. By 40,000 years ago, fossils and stone tools attest to their presence in Australia's southwestern corner; by 35,000 years ago, in Australia's southeastern corner and Tasmania, the corner of Australia most remote from the colonists' likely beachhead in western Australia or New Guinea (the parts nearest Indonesia and Asia); and by 30,000 years ago, in the cold New Guinea highlands. All of those areas could have been reached overland from a western beachhead. However, the colonization of both the Bismarck and the Solomon Archipelagoes northeast of New Guinea, by 35,000 years ago, required further overwater crossings of dozens of miles. The occupation could have been even more rapid than that apparent spread of dates from 40,000 to 30,000 years ago, since the various dates hardly differ within the experimental error of the radiocarbon method.

At the Pleistocene times when Australia and New Guinea were initially occupied, the Asian continent extended eastward to incorporate the modern islands of Borneo, Java, and Bali, nearly 1,000 miles nearer to Australia and New Guinea than Southeast Asia's present margin. However, at least eight channels up to 50 miles wide still remained to be crossed in getting from Borneo or Bali to Pleistocene Greater Australia. Forty thousand years ago, those crossings may have been achieved by bamboo rafts, low-tech but seaworthy watercraft still in use in coastal South China today. The crossings must nevertheless have been difficult, because after that initial landfall by 40,000 years ago the archaeological record provides no compelling evidence of further human arrivals in Greater Australia from Asia for tens of thousands of years. Not until within the last few thousand years do we encounter the next firm evidence, in the form of the appearance of Asian-derived pigs in New Guinea and Asian-derived dogs in Australia.

Thus, the human societies of Australia and New Guinea developed in substantial isolation from the Asian societies that founded them. That isolation is reflected in languages spoken today. After all those millennia of isolation, neither modern Aboriginal Australian languages nor the major group of modern New Guinea languages (the so-called Papuan languages) exhibit any clear relationships with any modern Asian languages.

The isolation is also reflected in genes and physical anthropology. Genetic studies suggest that Aboriginal Australians and New Guinea highlanders are somewhat more similar to modern Asians than to peoples of other continents, but the relationship is not a close one. In skeletons and physical appearance, Aboriginal Australians and New Guineans are also distinct from most Southeast Asian populations, as becomes obvious if one compares photos of Australians or New Guineans with those of Indonesians or Chinese. Part of the reason for all these differences is that the initial Asian colonists of Greater Australia have had a long time in which to diverge from their stay-at-home Asian cousins, with only limited genetic exchanges during most of that time. But probably a more important reason is that the original Southeast Asian stock from which the colonists of Greater Australia were derived has by now been largely replaced by other Asians expanding out of China.

Aboriginal Australians and New Guineans have also diverged genetically, physically, and linguistically from each other. For instance, among
the major (genetically determined) human blood groups, groups B of the
so-called ABO system and S of the MNS system occur in New Guinea as
well as in most of the rest of the world, but both are virtually absent in
Australia. The tightly coiled hair of most New Guineans contrasts with
the straight or wavy hair of most Australians. Australian languages and
New Guinea's Papuan languages are unrelated not only to Asian languages
but also to each other, except for some spread of vocabulary in both directions across Torres Strait.

All that divergence of Australians and New Guineans from each other
reflects lengthy isolation in very different environments. Since the rise of
the Arafura Sea finally separated Australia and New Guinea from each
other around 10,000 years ago, gene exchange has been limited to tenuous
contact via the chain of Torres Strait islands. That has allowed the populations of the two hemi-continents to adapt to their own environments.
While the savannas and mangroves of coastal southern New Guinea are
fairly similar to those of northern Australia, other habitats of the hemi-
continents differ in almost all major respects.

Here are some of the differences. New Guinea lies nearly on the equator, while Australia extends far into the temperate zones, reaching almost
40 degrees south of the equator. New Guinea is mountainous and
extremely rugged, rising to 16,500 feet and with glaciers capping the highest peaks, while Australia is mostly low and flat—94 percent of its area
lies below 2,000 feet of elevation. New Guinea is one of the wettest areas
on Earth, Australia one of the driest. Most of New Guinea receives over
100 inches of rain annually, and much of the highlands receives over 200
inches, while most of Australia receives less than 20 inches. New Guinea's
equatorial climate varies only modestly from season to season and year to
year, but Australia's climate is highly seasonal and varies from year to year
far more than that of any other continent. As a result, New Guinea is laced
with permanent large rivers, while Australia's permanently flowing rivers
are confined in most years to eastern Australia, and even Australia's largest
river system (the Murray-Darling) has ceased flowing for months during
droughts. Most of New Guinea's land area is clothed in dense rain forest,
while most of Australia's supports only desert and open dry woodland.

New Guinea is covered with young fertile soil, as a consequence of volcanic activity, glaciers repeatedly advancing and retreating and scouring

the highlands, and mountain streams carrying huge quantities of silt to the lowlands. In contrast, Australia has by far the oldest, most infertile, most nutrient-leached soils of any continent, because of Australia's little volcanic activity and its lack of high mountains and glaciers. Despite having only one-tenth of Australia's area, New Guinea is home to approximately as many mammal and bird species as is Australia—a result of New Guinea's equatorial location, much higher rainfall, much greater range of elevations, and greater fertility. All of those environmental differences influenced the two hemi-continents' very disparate cultural histories, which we shall now consider.

THE EARLIEST AND most intensive food production, and the densest populations, of Greater Australia arose in the highland valleys of New Guinea at altitudes between 4,000 and 9,000 feet above sea level. Archaeological excavations uncovered complex systems of drainage ditches dating back to 9,000 years ago and becoming extensive by 6,000 years ago, as well as terraces serving to retain soil moisture in drier areas. The ditch systems were similar to those still used today in the highlands to drain swampy areas for use as gardens. By around 5,000 years ago, pollen analyses testify to widespread deforestation of highland valleys, suggesting forest clearance for agriculture.

Today, the staple crops of highland agriculture are the recently introduced sweet potato, along with taro, bananas, yams, sugarcane, edible grass stems, and several leafy vegetables. Because taro, bananas, and yams are native to Southeast Asia, an undoubted site of plant domestication, it used to be assumed that New Guinea highland crops other than sweet potatoes arrived from Asia. However, it was eventually realized that the wild ancestors of sugarcane, the leafy vegetables, and the edible grass stems are New Guinea species, that the particular types of bananas grown in New Guinea have New Guinea rather than Asian wild ancestors, and that taro and some yams are native to New Guinea as well as to Asia. If New Guinea agriculture had really had Asian origins, one might have expected to find highland crops derived unequivocally from Asia, but there are none. For those reasons it is now generally acknowledged that agriculture arose indigenously in the New Guinea highlands by domestication of New Guinea wild plant species.

New Guinea thus joins the Fertile Crescent, China, and a few other regions as one of the world's centers of independent origins of plant domestication. No remains of the crops actually being grown in the highlands 6,000 years ago have been preserved in archaeological sites. However, that is not surprising, because modern highland staple crops are plant species that do not leave archaeologically visible residues except under exceptional conditions. Hence it seems likely that some of them were also the founding crops of highland agriculture, especially as the ancient drainage systems preserved are so similar to the modern drainage systems used for growing taro.

The three unequivocally foreign elements in New Guinea highland food production as seen by the first European explorers were chickens, pigs, and sweet potatoes. Chickens and pigs were domesticated in Southeast Asia and introduced around 3,600 years ago to New Guinea and most other Pacific islands by Austronesians, a people of ultimately South Chinese origin whom we shall discuss in Chapter 17. (Pigs may have arrived earlier.) As for the sweet potato, native to South America, it apparently reached New Guinea only within the last few centuries, following its introduction to the Philippines by Spaniards. Once established in New Guinea, the sweet potato overtook taro as the highland's leading crop, because of its shorter time required to reach maturity, higher yields per acre, and greater tolerance of poor soil conditions.

The development of New Guinea highland agriculture must have triggered a big population explosion thousands of years ago, because the highlands could have supported only very low population densities of hunter-gatherers after New Guinea's original megafauna of giant marsupials had been exterminated. The arrival of the sweet potato triggered a further explosion in recent centuries. When Europeans first flew over the highlands in the 1930s, they were astonished to see below them a landscape similar to Holland's. Broad valleys were completely deforested and dotted with villages, and drained and fenced fields for intensive food production covered entire valley floors. That landscape testifies to the population densities achieved in the highlands by farmers with stone tools.

Steep terrain, persistent cloud cover, malaria, and risk of drought at lower elevations confine New Guinea highland agriculture to elevations above about 4,000 feet. In effect, the New Guinea highlands are an island of dense farming populations thrust up into the sky and surrounded below by a sea of clouds. Lowland New Guineans on the seacoast and rivers are villagers depending heavily on fish, while those on dry ground away from the coast and rivers subsist at low densities by slash-and-burn agriculture based on bananas and yams, supplemented by hunting and gathering. In contrast, lowland New Guinea swamp dwellers live as nomadic hunter-gatherers dependent on the starchy pith of wild sago palms, which are very productive and yield three times more calories per hour of work than does gardening. New Guinea swamps thus provide a clear instance of an environment where people remained hunter-gatherers because farming could not compete with the hunting-gathering lifestyle.

The sago eaters persisting in lowland swamps exemplify the nomadic hunter-gatherer band organization that must formerly have characterized all New Guineans. For all the reasons that we discussed in Chapters 13 and 14, the farmers and the fishing peoples were the ones to develop more-complex technology, societies, and political organization. They live in permanent villages and tribal societies, often led by a big-man. Some of them construct large, elaborately decorated, ceremonial houses. Their great art, in the form of wooden statues and masks, is prized in museums around the world.

NEW GUINEA THUS became the part of Greater Australia with the most-advanced technology, social and political organization, and art. However, from an urban American or European perspective, New Guinea still rates as "primitive" rather than "advanced." Why did New Guineans continue to use stone tools instead of developing metal tools, remain non-literate, and fail to organize themselves into chiefdoms and states? It turns out that New Guinea had several biological and geographic strikes against it.

First, although indigenous food production did arise in the New Guinea highlands, we saw in Chapter 8 that it yielded little protein. The dietary staples were low-protein root crops, and production of the sole domesticated animal species (pigs and chickens) was too low to contribute much to people's protein budgets. Since neither pigs nor chickens can be harnessed to pull carts, highlanders remained without sources of power other than human muscle power, and also failed to evolve epidemic diseases to repel the eventual European invaders.

A second restriction on the size of highland populations was the limited available area: the New Guinea highlands have only a few broad valleys, notably the Wahgi and Baliem Valleys, capable of supporting dense populations. Still a third limitation was the reality that the mid-montane zone between 4,000 and 9,000 feet was the sole altitudinal zone in New Guinea suitable for intensive food production. There was no food production at all in New Guinea alpine habitats above 9,000 feet, little on the hillslopes between 4,000 and 1,000 feet, and only low-density slash-and-burn agriculture in the lowlands. Thus, large-scale economic exchanges of food, between communities at different altitudes specializing in different types of food production, never developed in New Guinea. Such exchanges in the Andes, Alps, and Himalayas not only increased population densities in those areas, by providing people at all altitudes with a more balanced diet, but also promoted regional economic and political integration.

For all these reasons, the population of traditional New Guinea never exceeded 1,000,000 until European colonial governments brought Western medicine and the end of intertribal warfare. Of the approximately nine world centers of agricultural origins that we discussed in Chapter 5, New Guinea remained the one with by far the smallest population. With a mere 1,000,000 people, New Guinea could not develop the technology, writing, and political systems that arose among populations of tens of millions in China, the Fertile Crescent, the Andes, and Mesoamerica.

New Guinea's population is not only small in aggregate, but also fragmented into thousands of micropopulations by the rugged terrain: swamps in much of the lowlands, steep-sided ridges and narrow canyons alternating with each other in the highlands, and dense jungle swathing both the lowlands and the highlands. When I am engaged in biological exploration in New Guinea, with teams of New Guineans as field assistants, I consider excellent progress to be three miles per day even if we are traveling over existing trails. Most highlanders in traditional New Guinea never went more than 10 miles from home in the course of their lives.

Those difficulties of terrain, combined with the state of intermittent warfare that characterized relations between New Guinea bands or villages, account for traditional New Guinea's linguistic, cultural, and political fragmentation. New Guinea has by far the highest concentration of languages in the world: 1,000 out of the world's 6,000 languages, crammed into an area only slightly larger than that of Texas, and divided into dozens of language families and isolated languages as different from each other as English is from Chinese. Nearly half of all New Guinea languages have fewer than 500 speakers, and even the largest language groups (still with a mere 100,000 speakers) were politically fragmented into hundreds of villages, fighting as fiercely with each other as with speakers of other languages. Each of those microsocieties alone was far too small to support chiefs and craft specialists, or to develop metallurgy and writing.

Besides a small and fragmented population, the other limitation on development in New Guinea was geographic isolation, restricting the inflow of technology and ideas from elsewhere. New Guinea's three neighbors were all separated from New Guinea by water gaps, and until a few thousand years ago they were all even less advanced than New Guinea (especially the New Guinea highlands) in technology and food production. Of those three neighbors, Aboriginal Australians remained hunter-gatherers with almost nothing to offer New Guineans that New Guineans did not already possess. New Guinea's second neighbor was the much smaller islands of the Bismarck and the Solomon Archipelagoes to the east. That left, as New Guinea's third neighbor, the islands of eastern Indonesia. But that area, too, remained a cultural backwater occupied by hunter-gatherers for most of its history. There is no item that can be identified as having reached New Guinea via Indonesia, after the initial colonization of New Guinea over 40,000 years ago, until the time of the Austronesian expansion around 1600 B.C.

With that expansion, Indonesia became occupied by food producers of Asian origins, with domestic animals, with agriculture and technology at least as complex as New Guinea's, and with navigational skills that served as a much more efficient conduit from Asia to New Guinea. Austronesians settled on islands west and north and east of New Guinea, and in the far west and on the north and southeast coasts of New Guinea itself. Austronesians introduced pottery, chickens, and probably dogs and pigs to New Guinea. (Early archaeological surveys claimed pig bones in the New Guinea highlands by 4000 B.C., but those claims have not been confirmed.) For at least the last thousand years, trade connected New Guinea to the technologically much more advanced societies of Java and China. In return for exporting bird of paradise plumes and spices, New Guineans received Southeast Asian goods, including even such luxury items as Dong Son bronze drums and Chinese porcelain.

With time, the Austronesian expansion would surely have had more impact on New Guinea. Western New Guinea would eventually have been incorporated politically into the sultanates of eastern Indonesia, and metal tools might have spread through eastern Indonesia to New Guinea. But— that hadn't happened by A.D. 1511, the year the Portuguese arrived in the

Moluccas and truncated Indonesia's separate train of developments. When Europeans reached New Guinea soon thereafter, its inhabitants were still living in bands or in fiercely independent little villages, and still using stone tools.

WHILE THE NEW Guinea hemi-continent of Greater Australia thus developed both animal husbandry and agriculture, the Australian hemi-continent developed neither. During the Ice Ages Australia had supported even more big marsupials than New Guinea, including diprotodonts (the marsupial equivalent of cows and rhinoceroses), giant kangaroos, and giant wombats. But all those marsupial candidates for animal husbandry disappeared in the wave of extinctions (or exterminations) that accompanied human colonization of Australia. That left Australia, like New Guinea, with no domesticable native mammals. The sole foreign domesticated mammal adopted in Australia was the dog, which arrived from Asia (presumably in Austronesian canoes) around 1500 B.C. and established itself in the wild in Australia to become the dingo. Native Australians kept captive dingos as companions, watchdogs, and even as living blankets, giving rise to the expression "five-dog night" to mean a very cold night. But they did not use dingos / dogs for food, as did Polynesians, or for cooperative hunting of wild animals, as did New Guineans.

Agriculture was another nonstarter in Australia, which is not only the driest continent but also the one with the most infertile soils. In addition, Australia is unique in that the overwhelming influence on climate over most of the continent is an irregular nonannual cycle, the ENSO (acronym for El Niño Southern Oscillation), rather than the regular annual cycle of the seasons so familiar in most other parts of the world. Unpredictable severe droughts last for years, punctuated by equally unpredictable torrential rains and floods. Even today, with Eurasian crops and with trucks and railroads to transport produce, food production in Australia remains a risky business. Herds build up in good years, only to be killed off by drought. Any incipient farmers in Aboriginal Australia would have faced similar cycles in their own populations. If in good years they had settled in villages, grown crops, and produced babies, those large populations would have starved and died off in drought years, when the land could support far fewer people.

The other major obstacle to the development of food production in

Australia was the paucity of domesticable wild plants. Even modern European plant geneticists have failed to develop any crop except macadamia nuts from Australia's native wild flora. The list of the world's potential prize cereals—the 56 wild grass species with the heaviest grains—includes only two Australian species, both of which rank near the bottom of the list (grain weight only 13 milligrams, compared with a whopping 40 milligrams for the heaviest grains elsewhere in the world). That's not to say that Australia had no potential crops at all, or that Aboriginal Australians would never have developed indigenous food production. Some plants, such as certain species of yams, taro, and arrowroot, are cultivated in southern New Guinea but also grow wild in northern Australia and were gathered by Aborigines there. As we shall see, Aborigines in the climatically most favorable areas of Australia were evolving in a direction that might have eventuated in food production. But any food production that did arise indigenously in Australia would have been limited by the lack of domesticable animals, the poverty of domesticable plants, and the difficult soils and climate.

Nomadism, the hunter-gatherer lifestyle, and minimal investment in shelter and possessions were sensible adaptations to Australia's ENSO-driven resource unpredictability. When local conditions deteriorated, Aborigines simply moved to an area where conditions were temporarily better. Rather than depending on just a few crops that could fail, they minimized risk by developing an economy based on a great variety of wild foods, not all of which were likely to fail simultaneously. Instead of having fluctuating populations that periodically outran their resources and starved, they maintained smaller populations that enjoyed an abundance of food in good years and a sufficiency in bad years.

The Aboriginal Australian substitute for food production has been termed "firestick farming." The Aborigines modified and managed the surrounding landscape in ways that increased its production of edible plants and animals, without resorting to cultivation. In particular, they intentionally burned much of the landscape periodically. That served several purposes: the fires drove out animals that could be killed and eaten immediately; fires converted dense thickets into open parkland in which people could travel more easily; the parkland was also an ideal habitat for kangaroos, Australia's prime game animal; and the fires stimulated the growth both of new grass on which kangaroos fed and of fern roots on which Aborigines themselves fed.

We think of Australian Aborigines as desert people, but most of them were not. Instead, their population densities varied with rainfall (because it controls the production of terrestrial wild plant and animal foods) and with abundance of aquatic foods in the sea, rivers, and lakes. The highest population densities of Aborigines were in Australia's wettest and most productive regions: the Murray-Darling river system of the Southeast, the eastern and northern coasts, and the southwestern corner. Those areas also came to support the densest populations of European settlers in modern Australia. The reason we think of Aborigines as desert people is simply that Europeans killed or drove them out of the most desirable areas, leaving the last intact Aboriginal populations only in areas that Europeans didn't want.

Within the last 5,000 years, some of those productive regions witnessed an intensification of Aboriginal food-gathering methods, and a buildup of Aboriginal population density. Techniques were developed in eastern Australia for rendering abundant and starchy, but extremely poisonous, cycad seeds edible, by leaching out or fermenting the poison. The previously unexploited highlands of southeastern Australia began to be visited regularly during the summer, by Aborigines feasting not only on cycad nuts and yams but also on huge hibernating aggregations of a migratory moth called the bogong moth, which tastes like a roasted chestnut when grilled. Another type of intensified food-gathering activity that developed was the freshwater eel fisheries of the Murray-Darling river system, where water levels in marshes fluctuate with seasonal rains. Native Australians constructed elaborate systems of canals up to a mile and a half long, in order to enable eels to extend their range from one marsh to another. Eels were caught by equally elaborate weirs, traps set in dead-end side canals, and stone walls across canals with a net placed in an opening of the wall. Traps at different levels in the marsh came into operation as the water level rose and fell. While the initial construction of those "fish farms" must have involved a lot of work, they then fed many people. Nineteenth-century European observers found villages of a dozen Aboriginal houses at the eel farms, and there are archaeological remains of villages of up to 146 stone houses, implying at least seasonally resident populations of hundreds of people.

Still another development in eastern and northern Australia was the harvesting of seeds of a wild millet, belonging to the same genus as the broomcorn millet that was a staple of early Chinese agriculture. The millet was reaped with stone knives, piled into haystacks, and threshed to obtain the seeds, which were then stored in skin bags or wooden dishes and finally ground with millstones. Several of the tools used in this process, such as the stone reaping knives and grindstones, were similar to the tools independently invented in the Fertile Crescent for processing seeds of other wild grasses. Of all the food-acquiring methods of Aboriginal Australians, millet harvesting is perhaps the one most likely to have evolved eventually into crop production.

Along with intensified food gathering in the last 5,000 years came new types of tools. Small stone blades and points provided more length of sharp edge per pound of tool than the large stone tools they replaced. Hatchets with ground stone edges, once present only locally in Australia, became widespread. Shell fishhooks appeared within the last thousand years.

WHY DID AUSTRALIA not develop metal tools, writing, and politically complex societies? A major reason is that Aborigines remained hunter-gatherers, whereas, as we saw in Chapters 12–14, those developments arose elsewhere only in populous and economically specialized societies of food producers. In addition, Australia's aridity, infertility, and climatic unpredictability limited its hunter-gatherer population to only a few hundred thousand people. Compared with the tens of millions of people in ancient China or Mesoamerica, that meant that Australia had far fewer potential inventors, and far fewer societies to experiment with adopting innovations. Nor were its several hundred thousand people organized into closely interacting societies. Aboriginal Australia instead consisted of a sea of very sparsely populated desert separating several more productive ecological "islands," each of them holding only a fraction of the continent's population and with interactions attenuated by the intervening distance. Even within the relatively moist and productive eastern side of the continent, exchanges between societies were limited by the 1,900 miles from Queensland's tropical rain forests in the northeast to Victoria's temperate rain forests in the southeast, a geographic and ecological distance as great as that from Los Angeles to Alaska.

Some apparent regional or continentwide regressions of technology in Australia may stem from the isolation and relatively few inhabitants of its population centers. The boomerang, that quintessential Australian weapon, was abandoned in the Cape York Peninsula of northeastern Australia. When encountered by Europeans, the Aborigines of southwestern Australia did not eat shellfish. The function of the small stone points that appear in Australian archaeological sites around 5,000 years ago remains uncertain: while an easy explanation is that they may have been used as spearpoints and barbs, they are suspiciously similar to the stone points and barbs used on arrows elsewhere in the world. If they really were so used, the mystery of bows and arrows being present in modern New Guinea but absent in Australia might be compounded: perhaps bows and arrows actually were adopted for a while, then abandoned, across the Australian continent. All these examples remind us of the abandonment of guns in Japan, of bows and arrows and pottery in most of Polynesia, and of other technologies in other isolated societies (Chapter 13).

The most extreme losses of technology in the Australian region took place on the island of Tasmania, 130 miles off the coast of southeastern Australia. At Pleistocene times of low sea level, the shallow Bass Strait now separating Tasmania from Australia was dry land, and the people occupying Tasmania were part of the human population distributed continuously over an expanded Australian continent. When the strait was at last flooded around 10,000 years ago, Tasmanians and mainland Australians became cut off from each other because neither group possessed watercraft capable of negotiating Bass Strait. Thereafter, Tasmania's population of 4,000 hunter-gatherers remained out of contact with all other humans on Earth, living in an isolation otherwise known only from science fiction novels.

When finally encountered by Europeans in A.D. 1642, the Tasmanians had the simplest material culture of any people in the modern world. Like mainland Aborigines, they were hunter-gatherers without metal tools. But they also lacked many technologies and artifacts widespread on the mainland, including barbed spears, bone tools of any type, boomerangs, ground or polished stone tools, hafted stone tools, hooks, nets, pronged spears, traps, and the practices of catching and eating fish, sewing, and starting a fire. Some of these technologies may have arrived or been invented in mainland Australia only after Tasmania became isolated, in which case we can conclude that the tiny Tasmanian population did not independently invent these technologies for itself. Others of these technologies were brought to Tasmania when it was still part of the Australian mainland, and were subsequently lost in Tasmania's cultural isolation. For example, the Tasmanian archaeological record documents the disappearance of fishing, and of awls, needles, and other bone tools, around 1500 B.C. On at least three smaller islands (Flinders, Kangaroo, and King) that were isolated from Australia or Tasmania by rising sea levels around 10,000 years ago, human populations that would initially have numbered around 200 to 400 died out completely.

Tasmania and those three smaller islands thus illustrate in extreme form a conclusion of broad potential significance for world history. Human populations of only a few hundred people were unable to survive indefinitely in complete isolation. A population of 4,000 was able to survive for 10,000 years, but with significant cultural losses and significant failures to invent, leaving it with a uniquely simplified material culture. Mainland Australia's 300,000 hunter-gatherers were more numerous and less isolated than the Tasmanians but still constituted the smallest and most isolated human population of any of the continents. The documented instances of technological regression on the Australian mainland, and the example of Tasmania, suggest that the limited repertoire of Native Australians compared with that of peoples of other continents may stem in part from the effects of isolation and population size on the development and maintenance of technology—like those effects on Tasmania, but less extreme. By implication, the same effects may have contributed to differences in technology between the largest continent (Eurasia) and the next smaller ones (Africa, North America, and South America).

WHY DIDN'T MORE-ADVANCED technology reach Australia from its neighbors, Indonesia and New Guinea? As regards Indonesia, it was separated from northwestern Australia by water and was very different from it ecologically. In addition, Indonesia itself was a cultural and technological backwater until a few thousand years ago. There is no evidence of any new technology or introduction reaching Australia from Indonesia, after Australia's initial colonization 40,000 years ago, until the dingo appeared around 1500 B.C.

The dingo reached Australia at the peak of the Austronesian expansion from South China through Indonesia. Austronesians succeeded in settling all the islands of Indonesia, including the two closest to Australia—Timor and Tanimbar (only 275 and 205 miles from modern Australia, respectively). Since Austronesians covered far greater sea distances in the course of their expansion across the Pacific, we would have to assume that they repeatedly reached Australia, even if we did not have the evidence of the dingo to prove it. In historical times northwestern Australia was visited each year by sailing canoes from the Macassar district on the Indonesian island of Sulawesi (Celebes), until the Australian government stopped the visits in 1907. Archaeological evidence traces the visits back until around A.D. 1000, and they may well have been going on earlier. The main purpose of the visits was to obtain sea cucumbers (also known as bêche-de-mer or trepang), starfish relatives exported from Macassar to China as a reputed aphrodisiac and prized ingredient of soups.

Naturally, the trade that developed during the Macassans' annual visits left many legacies in northwestern Australia. The Macassans planted tamarind trees at their coastal campsites and sired children by Aboriginal women. Cloth, metal tools, pottery, and glass were brought as trade goods, though Aborigines never learned to manufacture those items themselves. Aborigines did acquire from the Macassans some loan words, some ceremonies, and the practices of using dugout sailing canoes and smoking tobacco in pipes.

But none of these influences altered the basic character of Australian society. More important than what happened as a result of the Macassan visits is what did not happen. The Macassans did *not* settle in Australia—undoubtedly because the area of northwestern Australia facing Indonesia is much too dry for Macassan agriculture. Had Indonesia faced the tropical rain forests and savannas of northeastern Australia, the Macassans could have settled, but there is no evidence that they ever traveled that far. Since the Macassans thus came only in small numbers and for temporary visits and never penetrated inland, just a few groups of Australians on a small stretch of coast were exposed to them. Even those few Australians got to see only a fraction of Macassan culture and technology, rather than a full Macassan society with rice fields, pigs, villages, and workshops. Because the Australians remained nomadic hunter-gatherers, they acquired only those few Macassan products and practices compatible with their lifestyle. Dugout sailing canoes and pipes, yes; forges and pigs, no.

Apparently much more astonishing than Australians' resistance to Indonesian influence is their resistance to New Guinea influence. Across the narrow ribbon of water known as Torres Strait, New Guinea farmers who spoke New Guinea languages and had pigs, pottery, and bows and arrows faced Australian hunter-gatherers who spoke Australian languages and lacked pigs, pottery, and bows and arrows. Furthermore, the strait is not an open-water barrier but is dotted with a chain of islands, of which the largest (Muralug Island) lies only 10 miles from the Australian coast. There were regular trading visits between Australia and the islands, and between the islands and New Guinea. Many Aboriginal women came as wives to Muralug Island, where they saw gardens and bows and arrows. How was it that those New Guinea traits did not get transmitted to Australia?

This cultural barrier at Torres Strait is astonishing only because we may mislead ourselves into picturing a full-fledged New Guinea society with intensive agriculture and pigs 10 miles off the Australian coast. In reality, Cape York Aborigines never saw a mainland New Guinean. Instead, there was trade between New Guinea and the islands nearest New Guinea, then between those islands and Mabuiag Island halfway down the strait, then between Mabuiag Island and Badu Island farther down the strait, then between Badu Island and Muralug Island, and finally between Muralug and Cape York.

New Guinea society became attenuated along that island chain. Pigs were rare or absent on the islands. Lowland South New Guineans along Torres Strait practiced not the intensive agriculture of the New Guinea highlands but a slash-and-burn agriculture with heavy reliance on seafoods, hunting, and gathering. The importance of even those slash-and-burn practices decreased from southern New Guinea toward Australia along the island chain. Muralug Island itself, the island nearest Australia, was dry, marginal for agriculture, and supported only a small human population, which subsisted mainly on seafood, wild yams, and mangrove fruits.

The interface between New Guinea and Australia across Torres Strait was thus reminiscent of the children's game of telephone, in which children sit in a circle, one child whispers a word into the ear of the second child, who whispers what she thinks she has just heard to the third child, and the word finally whispered by the last child back to the first child bears no resemblance to the initial word. In the same way, trade along the Torres Strait islands was a telephone game that finally presented Cape York Aborigines with something very different from New Guinea society. In addition, we should not imagine that relations between Muralug Islanders and Cape York Aborigines were an uninterrupted love feast at which Aborigines eagerly sopped up culture from island teachers. Trade instead alternated with war for the purposes of head-hunting and capturing women to become wives.

Despite the dilution of New Guinea culture by distance and war, some New Guinea influence did manage to reach Australia. Intermarriage carried New Guinea physical features, such as coiled rather than straight hair, down the Cape York Peninsula. Four Cape York languages had phonemes unusual for Australia, possibly because of the influence of New Guinea languages. The most important transmissions were of New Guinea shell fishhooks, which spread far into Australia, and of New Guinea outrigger canoes, which spread down the Cape York Peninsula. New Guinea drums, ceremonial masks, funeral posts, and pipes were also adopted on Cape York. But Cape York Aborigines did not adopt agriculture, in part because what they saw of it on Muralug Island was so watered-down. They did not adopt pigs, of which there were few or none on the islands, and which they would in any case have been unable to feed without agriculture. Nor did they adopt bows and arrows, remaining instead with their spears and spear-throwers.

Australia is big, and so is New Guinea. But contact between those two big landmasses was restricted to those few small groups of Torres Strait islanders with a highly attenuated New Guinea culture, interacting with those few small groups of Cape York Aborigines. The latter groups' decisions, for whatever reason, to use spears rather than bows and arrows, and not to adopt certain other features of the diluted New Guinea culture they saw, blocked transmission of those New Guinea cultural traits to all the rest of Australia. As a result, no New Guinea trait except shell fishhooks spread far into Australia. If the hundreds of thousands of farmers in the cool New Guinea highlands had been in close contact with the Aborigines in the cool highlands of southeastern Australia, a massive transfer of intensive food production and New Guinea culture to Australia might have followed. But the New Guinea highlands are separated from the Australian highlands by 2,000 miles of ecologically very different landscape. The New Guinea highlands might as well have been the mountains of the moon, as far as Australians' chances of observing and adopting New Guinea highland practices were concerned.

In short, the persistence of Stone Age nomadic hunter-gatherers in Australia, trading with Stone Age New Guinea farmers and Iron Age Indonesian farmers, at first seems to suggest singular obstinacy on the part of Native Australians. On closer examination, it merely proves to reflect the ubiquitous role of geography in the transmission of human culture and technology.

IT REMAINS FOR us to consider the encounters of New Guinea's and Australia's Stone Age societies with Iron Age Europeans. A Portuguese navigator "discovered" New Guinea in 1526, Holland claimed the western half in 1828, and Britain and Germany divided the eastern half in 1884. The first Europeans settled on the coast, and it took them a long time to penetrate into the interior, but by 1960 European governments had established political control over most New Guineans.

The reasons that Europeans colonized New Guinea, rather than vice versa, are obvious. Europeans were the ones who had the oceangoing ships and compasses to travel to New Guinea; the writing systems and printing presses to produce maps, descriptive accounts, and administrative paperwork useful in establishing control over New Guinea; the political institutions to organize the ships, soldiers, and administration; and the guns to shoot New Guineans who resisted with bow and arrow and clubs. Yet the number of European settlers was always very small, and today New Guinea is still populated largely by New Guineans. That contrasts sharply with the situation in Australia, the Americas, and South Africa, where European settlement was numerous and lasting and replaced the original native population over large areas. Why was New Guinea different?

A major factor was the one that defeated all European attempts to settle the New Guinea lowlands until the 1880s: malaria and other tropical diseases, none of them an acute epidemic crowd infection as discussed in Chapter 11. The most ambitious of those failed lowland settlement plans, organized by the French marquis de Rays around 1880 on the nearby island of New Ireland, ended with 930 out of the 1,000 colonists dead within three years. Even with modern medical treatments available today, many of my American and European friends in New Guinea have been forced to leave because of malaria, hepatitis, or other diseases, while my own health legacy of New Guinea has been a year of malaria and a year of dysentery.

As Europeans were being felled by New Guinea lowland germs, why were Eurasian germs not simultaneously felling New Guineans? Some New Guineans did become infected, but not on the massive scale that killed off most of the native peoples of Australia and the Americas. One lucky break for New Guineans was that there were no permanent European settlements in New Guinea until the 1880s, by which time public health discoveries had made progress in bringing smallpox and other infectious diseases of European populations under control. In addition, the Austronesian expansion had already been bringing a stream of Indonesian settlers and traders to New Guinea for 3,500 years. Since Asian mainland infectious diseases were well established in Indonesia, New Guineans thereby gained long exposure and built up much more resistance to Eurasian germs than did Aboriginal Australians.

The sole part of New Guinea where Europeans do not suffer from severe health problems is the highlands, above the altitudinal ceiling for malaria. But the highlands, already occupied by dense populations of New Guineans, were not reached by Europeans until the 1930s. By then, the Australian and Dutch colonial governments were no longer willing to open up lands for white settlement by killing native people in large numbers or driving them off their lands, as had happened during earlier centuries of European colonialism.

The remaining obstacle to European would-be settlers was that European crops, livestock, and subsistence methods do poorly everywhere in the New Guinea environment and climate. While introduced tropical American crops such as squash, corn, and tomatoes are now grown in small quantities, and tea and coffee plantations have been established in the highlands of Papua New Guinea, staple European crops, like wheat, barley, and peas, have never taken hold. Introduced cattle and goats, kept in small numbers, suffer from tropical diseases, just as do European people themselves. Food production in New Guinea is still dominated by the crops and agricultural methods that New Guineans perfected over the course of thousands of years.

All those problems of disease, rugged terrain, and subsistence contributed to Europeans' leaving eastern New Guinea (now the independent nation of Papua New Guinea) occupied and governed by New Guineans, who nevertheless use English as their official language, write with the alphabet, live under democratic governmental institutions modeled on those of England, and use guns manufactured overseas. The outcome was different in western New Guinea, which Indonesia took over from Holland in 1963 and renamed Irian Jaya province. The province is now governed by Indonesians, for Indonesians. Its rural population is still overwhelmingly New Guinean, but its urban population is Indonesian, as a result of government policy aimed at encouraging Indonesian immigration. Indonesians, with their long history of exposure to malaria and other tropical diseases shared with New Guineans, have not faced as potent a germ barrier as have Europeans. They are also better prepared than Europeans for subsisting in New Guinea, because Indonesian agriculture already included bananas, sweet potatoes, and some other staple crops of New Guinea agriculture. The ongoing changes in Irian Jaya represent the continuation, backed by a centralized government's full resources, of the Austronesian expansion that began to reach New Guinea 3,500 years ago. Indonesians *are* modern Austronesians.

EUROPEANS COLONIZED AUSTRALIA, rather than Native Australians colonizing Europe, for the same reasons that we have just seen in the case of New Guinea. However, the fates of New Guineans and of Aboriginal Australians were very different. Today, Australia is populated and governed by 20 million non-Aborigines, most of them of European descent, plus increasing numbers of Asians arriving since Australia abandoned its previous White Australia immigration policy in 1973. The Aboriginal population declined by 80 percent, from around 300,000 at the time of European settlement to a minimum of 60,000 in 1921. Aborigines today form an underclass of Australian society. Many of them live on mission stations or government reserves, or else work for whites as herdsmen on cattle stations. Why did Aborigines fare so much worse than New Guineans?

The basic reason is Australia's suitability (in some areas) for European food production and settlement, combined with the role of European guns, germs, and steel in clearing Aborigines out of the way. While I already stressed the difficulties posed by Australia's climate and soils, its most productive or fertile areas can nevertheless support European farming. Agriculture in the Australian temperate zone is now dominated by the Eurasian temperate-zone staple crops of wheat (Australia's leading crop), barley, oats, apples, and grapes, along with sorghum and cotton of African Sahel origins and potatoes of Andean origins. In tropical areas of northeastern Australia (Queensland) beyond the optimal range of Fertile Crescent crops, European farmers introduced sugarcane of New Guinea origins, bananas and citrus fruit of tropical Southeast Asian origins, and peanuts of tropical South American origins. As for livestock, Eurasian sheep made it possible to extend food production to arid areas of Australia unsuitable for agriculture, and Eurasian cattle joined crops in moister areas.

Thus, the development of food production in Australia had to await the arrival of non-native crops and animals domesticated in climatically similar parts of the world too remote for their domesticates to reach Australia until brought by transoceanic shipping. Unlike New Guinea, most of Australia lacked diseases serious enough to keep out Europeans. Only in tropical northern Australia did malaria and other tropical diseases force Europeans to abandon their 19th-century attempts at settlement, which succeeded only with the development of 20th-century medicine.

Australian Aborigines, of course, stood in the way of European food production, especially because what was potentially the most productive farmland and dairy country initially supported Australia's densest populations of Aboriginal hunter-gatherers. European settlement reduced the number of Aborigines by two means. One involved shooting them, an option that Europeans considered more acceptable in the 19th and late 18th centuries than when they entered the New Guinea highlands in the 1930s. The last large-scale massacre, of 31 Aborigines, occurred at Alice Springs in 1928. The other means involved European-introduced germs to which Aborigines had had no opportunity to acquire immunity or to evolve genetic resistance. Within a year of the first European settlers' arrival at Sydney, in 1788, corpses of Aborigines who had died in epidemics became a common sight. The principal recorded killers were smallpox, influenza, measles, typhoid, typhus, chicken pox, whooping cough, tuberculosis, and syphilis.

In these two ways, independent Aboriginal societies were eliminated in all areas suitable for European food production. The only societies that survived more or less intact were those in areas of northern and western Australia useless to Europeans. Within one century of European colonization, 40,000 years of Aboriginal traditions had been mostly swept away.

WE CAN NOW return to the problem that I posed near the beginning of this chapter. How, except by postulating deficiencies in the Aborigines themselves, can one account for the fact that white English colonists apparently created a literate, food-producing, industrial democracy, within a few decades of colonizing a continent whose inhabitants after more than 40,000 years were still nonliterate nomadic hunter-gatherers? Doesn't that constitute a perfectly controlled experiment in the evolution of human societies, forcing us to a simple racist conclusion?

The resolution of this problem is simple. White English colonists did not create a literate, food-producing, industrial democracy in Australia. Instead, they imported all of the elements from outside Australia: the livestock, all of the crops (except macadamia nuts), the metallurgical knowledge, the steam engines, the guns, the alphabet, the political institutions, even the germs. All these were the end products of 10,000 years of development in Eurasian environments. By an accident of geography, the colonists who landed at Sydney in 1788 inherited those elements. Europeans have never learned to survive in Australia or New Guinea without their inherited Eurasian technology. Robert Burke and William Wills were smart enough to write, but not smart enough to survive in Australian desert regions where Aborigines were living.

The people who did create a society in Australia were Aboriginal Australians. Of course, the society that they created was not a literate, food-producing, industrial democracy. The reasons follow straightforwardly from features of the Australian environment.

CHAPTER 16

How China Became Chinese

I MMIGRATION, AFFIRMATIVE ACTION, MULTILINGUALISM, ethnic diversity—my state of California was among the pioneers of these controversial policies and is now pioneering a backlash against them. A glance into the classrooms of the Los Angeles public school system, where my sons are being educated, fleshes out the abstract debates with the faces of children. Those children represent over 80 languages spoken in the home, with English-speaking whites in the minority. Every single one of my sons' playmates has at least one parent or grandparent who was born outside the United States; that's true of three of my own sons' four grandparents. But immigration is merely restoring the diversity that America held for thousands of years. Before European settlement, the mainland United States was home to hundreds of Native American tribes and languages and came under control of a single government only within the last hundred years.

In these respects the United States is a thoroughly "normal" country. All but one of the world's six most populous nations are melting pots that achieved political unification recently, and that still support hundreds of languages and ethnic groups. For example, Russia, once a small Slavic state centered on Moscow, did not even begin its expansion beyond the Ural Mountains until A.D. 1582. From then until the 19th century, Russia proceeded to swallow up dozens of non-Slavic peoples, many of which retain their original language and cultural identity. Just as American history is the story of how our continent's expanse became American, Russia's history is the story of how Russia became Russian. India, Indonesia, and Brazil are also recent political creations (or re-creations, in the case of India), home to about 850, 670, and 210 languages, respectively.

The great exception to this rule of the recent melting pot is the world's most populous nation, China. Today, China appears politically, culturally, and linguistically monolithic, at least to laypeople. It was already unified politically in 221 B.C. and has remained so for most of the centuries since then. From the beginnings of literacy in China, it has had only a single writing system, whereas modern Europe uses dozens of modified alphabets. Of China's 1.2 billion people, over 800 million speak Mandarin, the language with by far the largest number of native speakers in the world. Some 300 million others speak seven other languages as similar to Mandarin, and to each other, as Spanish is to Italian. Thus, not only is China not a melting pot, but it seems absurd to ask how China became Chinese. China has *been* Chinese, almost from the beginnings of its recorded history.

We take this seeming unity of China so much for granted that we forget how astonishing it is. One reason why we should not have expected such unity is genetic. While a coarse racial classification of world peoples lumps all Chinese people as so-called Mongoloids, that category conceals much more variation than the differences between Swedes, Italians, and Irish within Europe. In particular, North and South Chinese are genetically and physically rather different: North Chinese are most similar to Tibetans and Nepalese, while South Chinese are similar to Vietnamese and Filipinos. My North and South Chinese friends can often distinguish each other at a glance by physical appearance: the North Chinese tend to be taller, heavier, paler, with more pointed noses, and with smaller eyes that appear more "slanted" (because of what is termed their epicanthic fold).

North and South China differ in environment and climate as well: the north is drier and colder; the south, wetter and hotter. Genetic differences arising in those differing environments imply a long history of moderate isolation between peoples of North and South China. How did those peoples nevertheless end up with the same or very similar languages and cultures?

China's apparent linguistic near-unity is also puzzling in view of the linguistic disunity of other long-settled parts of the world. For instance, we saw in the last chapter that New Guinea, with less than one-tenth of China's area and with only about 40,000 years of human history, has a thousand languages, including dozens of language groups whose differences are far greater than those among the eight main Chinese languages. Western Europe has evolved or acquired about 40 languages just in the 6,000–8,000 years since the arrival of Indo-European languages, including languages as different as English, Finnish, and Russian. Yet fossils attest to human presence in China for over half a million years. What happened to the tens of thousands of distinct languages that must have arisen in China over that long time span?

These paradoxes hint that China too was once diverse, as all other populous nations still are. China differs only by having been unified much earlier. Its "Sinification" involved the drastic homogenization of a huge region in an ancient melting pot, the repopulation of tropical Southeast Asia, and the exertion of a massive influence on Japan, Korea, and possibly even India. Hence the history of China offers the key to the history of all of East Asia. This chapter will tell the story of how China did become Chinese.

A CONVENIENT STARTING point is a detailed linguistic map of China (see Figure 16.1). A glance at it is an eye-opener to all of us accustomed to thinking of China as monolithic. It turns out that, in addition to China's eight "big" languages—Mandarin and its seven close relatives (often referred to collectively simply as "Chinese"), with between 11 million and 800 million speakers each—China also has over 130 "little" languages, many of them with just a few thousand speakers. All these languages, "big" and "little," fall into four language families, which differ greatly in the compactness of their distributions.

At the one extreme, Mandarin and its relatives, which constitute the Chinese subfamily of the Sino-Tibetan language family, are distributed continuously from North to South China. One could walk through China, from Manchuria in the north to the Gulf of Tonkin in the south, while remaining entirely within land occupied by native speakers of Mandarin and its relatives. The other three families have fragmented distributions, being spoken by "islands" of people surrounded by a "sea" of speakers of Chinese and other language families.

Especially fragmented is the distribution of the Miao-Yao (alias Hmong-Mien) family, which consists of 6 million speakers divided among about five languages, bearing the colorful names of Red Miao, White Miao (alias Striped Miao), Black Miao, Green Miao (alias Blue Miao), and Yao. Miao-Yao speakers live in dozens of small enclaves, all surrounded by speakers of other language families and scattered over an area of half a million square miles, extending from South China to Thailand. More than 100,000 Miao-speaking refugees from Vietnam have carried this language family to the United States, where they are better known under the alternative name of Hmong.

Another fragmented language group is the Austroasiatic family, whose most widely spoken languages are Vietnamese and Cambodian. The 60 million Austroasiatic speakers are scattered from Vietnam in the east to the Malay Peninsula in the south and to northern India in the west. The fourth and last of China's language families is the Tai-Kadai family (including Thai and Lao), whose 50 million speakers are distributed from South China southward into Peninsular Thailand and west to Myanmar (Figure 16.1).

Naturally, Miao-Yao speakers did not acquire their current fragmented distribution as a result of ancient helicopter flights that dropped them here and there over the Asian landscape. Instead, one might guess that they once had a more nearly continuous distribution, which became fragmented as speakers of other language families expanded or induced Miao-Yao speakers to abandon their tongues. In fact, much of that process of linguistic fragmentation occurred within the past 2,500 years and is well documented historically. The ancestors of modern speakers of Thai, Lao, and Burmese all moved south from South China and adjacent areas to their present locations within historical times, successively inundating the settled descendants of previous migrations. Speakers of Chinese languages were especially vigorous in replacing and linguistically converting other ethnic groups, whom Chinese speakers looked down upon as primitive and inferior. The recorded history of China's Zhou Dynasty, from 1100 to 221 B.C., describes the conquest and absorption of most of China's non-Chinese-speaking population by Chinese-speaking states.

We can use several types of reasoning to try to reconstruct the linguistic map of East Asia as of several thousand years ago. First, we can reverse the historically known linguistic expansions of recent millennia. Second, we can reason that modern areas with just a single language or related

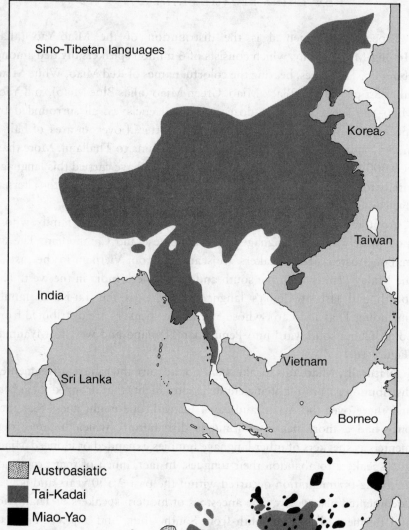

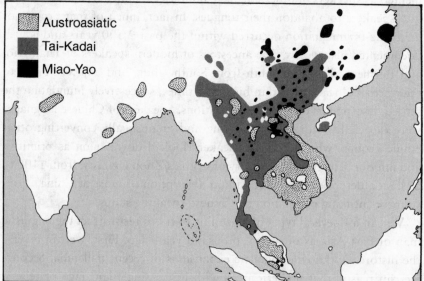

Figure 16.1. The four language families of China and Southeast Asia.

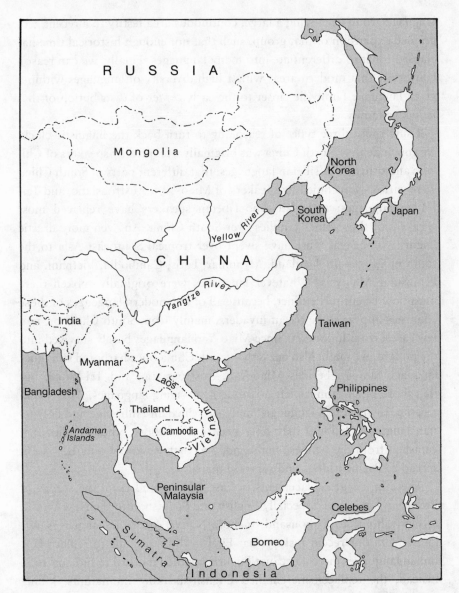

Figure 16.2. Modern political borders in East and Southeast Asia, for use in interpreting the distributions of language families shown in Figure 16.1.

language group occupying a large, continuous area testify to a recent geographic expansion of that group, such that not enough historical time has elapsed for it to differentiate into many languages. Finally, we can reason conversely that modern areas with a high diversity of languages within a given language family lie closer to the early center of distribution of that language family.

Using those three types of reasoning to turn back the linguistic clock, we conclude that North China was originally occupied by speakers of Chinese and other Sino-Tibetan languages; that different parts of South China were variously occupied by speakers of Miao-Yao, Austroasiatic, and Tai-Kadai languages; and that Sino-Tibetan speakers have replaced most speakers of those other families over South China. An even more drastic linguistic upheaval must have swept over tropical Southeast Asia to the south of China—in Thailand, Myanmar, Laos, Cambodia, Vietnam, and Peninsular Malaysia. Whatever languages were originally spoken there must now be entirely extinct, because all of the modern languages of those countries appear to be recent invaders, mainly from South China or, in a few cases, from Indonesia. Since Miao-Yao languages barely survived into the present, we might also guess that South China once harbored still other language families besides Miao-Yao, Austroasiatic, and Tai-Kadai, but that those other families left no modern surviving languages. As we shall see, the Austronesian language family (to which all Philippine and Polynesian languages belong) may have been one of those other families that vanished from the Chinese mainland, and that we know only because it spread to Pacific islands and survived there.

These language replacements in East Asia remind us of the spread of European languages, especially English and Spanish, into the New World, formerly home to a thousand or more Native American languages. We know from our recent history that English did not come to replace U.S. Indian languages merely because English sounded musical to Indians' ears. Instead, the replacement entailed English-speaking immigrants' killing most Indians by war, murder, and introduced diseases, and the surviving Indians' being pressured into adopting English, the new majority language. The immediate causes of that language replacement were the advantages in technology and political organization, stemming ultimately from the advantage of an early rise of food production, that invading Europeans held over Native Americans. Essentially the same processes accounted for the replacement of Aboriginal Australian languages by English, and of subequatorial Africa's original Pygmy and Khoisan languages by Bantu languages.

Hence East Asia's linguistic upheavals raise a corresponding question: what enabled Sino-Tibetan speakers to spread from North China to South China, and speakers of Austroasiatic and the other original South China language families to spread south into tropical Southeast Asia? Here, we must turn to archaeology for evidence of the technological, political, and agricultural advantages that some Asians evidently gained over other Asians.

As EVERYWHERE ELSE in the world, the archaeological record in East Asia for most of human history reveals only the debris of hunter-gatherers using unpolished stone tools and lacking pottery. The first East Asian evidence for something different comes from China, where crop remains, bones of domestic animals, pottery, and polished (Neolithic) stone tools appear by around 7500 B.C. That date is within a thousand years of the beginning of the Neolithic Age and food production in the Fertile Crescent. But because the previous millennium in China is poorly known archaeologically, one cannot decide at present whether the origins of Chinese food production were contemporaneous with those in the Fertile Crescent, slightly earlier, or slightly later. At the least, we can say that China was one of the world's first centers of plant and animal domestication.

China may actually have encompassed two or more independent centers of origins of food production. I already mentioned the ecological differences between China's cool, dry north and warm, wet south. At a given latitude, there are also ecological distinctions between the coastal lowlands and the interior uplands. Different wild plants are native to these disparate environments and would thus have been variously available to incipient farmers in various parts of China. In fact, the earliest identified crops were two drought-resistant species of millet in North China, but rice in South China, suggesting the possibility of separate northern and southern centers of plant domestication.

Chinese sites with the earliest evidence of crops also contained bones of domestic pigs, dogs, and chickens. These domestic animals and crops were gradually joined by China's many other domesticates. Among the animals, water buffalo were most important (for pulling plows), while silkworms, ducks, and geese were others. Familiar later Chinese crops include soy-beans, hemp, citrus fruit, tea, apricots, peaches, and pears. In addition, just as Eurasia's east–west axis permitted many of these Chinese animals and crops to spread westward in ancient times, West Asian domesticates also spread eastward to China and became important there. Especially sig-nificant western contributions to ancient China's economy have been wheat and barley, cows and horses, and (to a lesser extent) sheep and goats.

As elsewhere in the world, in China food production gradually led to the other hallmarks of "civilization" discussed in Chapters 11–14. A superb Chinese tradition of bronze metallurgy had its origins in the third millennium B.C. and eventually resulted in China's developing by far the earliest cast-iron production in the world, around 500 B.C. The following 1,500 years saw the outpouring of Chinese technological inventions, men-tioned in Chapter 13, that included paper, the compass, the wheelbarrow, and gunpowder. Fortified towns emerged in the third millennium B.C., with cemeteries whose great variation between unadorned and luxuriously furnished graves bespeaks emerging class differences. Stratified societies whose rulers could mobilize large labor forces of commoners are also attested by huge urban defensive walls, big palaces, and eventually the Grand Canal (the world's longest canal, over 1,000 miles long), linking North and South China. Writing is preserved from the second millennium B.C. but probably arose earlier. Our archaeological knowledge of China's emerging cities and states then becomes supplemented by written accounts of China's first dynasties, going back to the Xia Dynasty, which arose around 2000 B.C.

As for food production's more sinister by-product of infectious diseases, we cannot specify where within the Old World most major diseases of Old World origin arose. However, European writings from Roman and medieval times clearly describe the arrival of bubonic plague and possibly smallpox from the east, so these germs could be of Chinese or East Asian origin. Influenza (derived from pigs) is even more likely to have arisen in China, since pigs were domesticated so early and became so important there.

China's size and ecological diversity spawned many separate local cul-tures, distinguishable archaeologically by their differing styles of pottery and artifacts. In the fourth millennium B.C. those local cultures expanded geographically and began to interact, compete with each other, and coalesce. Just as exchanges of domesticates between ecologically diverse regions enriched Chinese food production, exchanges between culturally diverse regions enriched Chinese culture and technology, and fierce competition between warring chiefdoms drove the formation of ever larger and more centralized states (Chapter 14).

While China's north–south gradient retarded crop diffusion, the gradient was less of a barrier there than in the Americas or Africa, because China's north–south distances were smaller; and because China's is transected neither by desert, as is Africa and northern Mexico, nor by a narrow isthmus, as is Central America. Instead, China's long east–west rivers (the Yellow River in the north, the Yangtze River in the south) facilitated diffusion of crops and technology between the coast and inland, while its broad east–west expanse and relatively gentle terrain, which eventually permitted those two river systems to be joined by canals, facilitated north–south exchanges. All these geographic factors contributed to the early cultural and political unification of China, whereas western Europe, with a similar area but a more rugged terrain and no such unifying rivers, has resisted cultural and political unification to this day.

Some developments spread from south to north in China, especially iron smelting and rice cultivation. But the predominant direction of spread was from north to south. That trend is clearest for writing: in contrast to western Eurasia, which produced a plethora of early writing systems, such as Sumerian cuneiform, Egyptian hieroglyphics, Hittite, Minoan, and the Semitic alphabet, China developed just a single well-attested writing system. It was perfected in North China, spread and preempted or replaced any other nascent system, and evolved into the writing still used in China today. Other major features of North Chinese societies that spread southward were bronze technology, Sino-Tibetan languages, and state formation. All three of China's first three dynasties, the Xia and Shang and Zhou Dynasties, arose in North China in the second millennium B.C.

Preserved writings of the first millennium B.C. show that ethnic Chinese already tended then (as many still do today) to feel culturally superior to non-Chinese "barbarians," while North Chinese tended to regard even South Chinese as barbarians. For example, a late Zhou Dynasty writer of the first millennium B.C. described China's other peoples as follows: "The people of those five regions—the Middle states and the Rong, Yi, and other wild tribes around them—had all their several natures, which they could not be made to alter. The tribes on the east were called Yi. They had their hair unbound, and tattooed their bodies. Some of them ate their food without its being cooked by fire." The Zhou author went on to describe wild tribes to the south, west, and north as indulging in equally barbaric practices, such as turning their feet inward, tattooing their foreheads, wearing skins, living in caves, not eating cereals, and, of course, eating their food raw.

States organized by or modeled on that Zhou Dynasty of North China spread to South China during the first millennium B.C., culminating in China's political unification under the Qin Dynasty in 221 B.C. Its cultural unification accelerated during that same period, as literate "civilized" Chinese states absorbed, or were copied by, the illiterate "barbarians." Some of that cultural unification was ferocious: for instance, the first Qin emperor condemned all previously written historical books as worthless and ordered them burned, much to the detriment of our understanding of early Chinese history and writing. Those and other draconian measures must have contributed to the spread of North China's Sino-Tibetan languages over most of China, and to reducing the Miao-Yao and other language families to their present fragmented distributions.

Within East Asia, China's head start in food production, technology, writing, and state formation had the consequence that Chinese innovations also contributed heavily to developments in neighboring regions. For instance, until the fourth millennium B.C. most of tropical Southeast Asia was still occupied by hunter-gatherers making pebble and flake stone tools belonging to what is termed the Hoabinhian tradition, named after the site of Hoa Binh, in Vietnam. Thereafter, Chinese-derived crops, Neolithic technology, village living, and pottery similar to that of South China spread into tropical Southeast Asia, probably accompanied by South China's language families. The historical southward expansions of Burmese, Laotians, and Thais from South China completed the Sinification of tropical Southeast Asia. All those modern peoples are recent offshoots of their South Chinese cousins.

So overwhelming was this Chinese steamroller that the former peoples of tropical Southeast Asia have left behind few traces in the region's modern populations. Just three relict groups of hunter-gatherers—the Semang Negritos of the Malay Peninsula, the Andaman Islanders, and the Veddoid Negritos of Sri Lanka—remain to suggest that tropical Southeast Asia's former inhabitants may have been dark-skinned and curly-haired, like modern New Guineans and unlike the light-skinned, straight-haired South

Chinese and the modern tropical Southeast Asians who are their offshoots. Those relict Negritos of Southeast Asia may be the last survivors of the source population from which New Guinea was colonized. The Semang Negritos persisted as hunter-gatherers trading with neighboring farmers but adopted an Austroasiatic language from those farmers—much as, we shall see, Philippine Negrito and African Pygmy hunter-gatherers adopted languages from their farmer trading partners. Only on the remote Andaman Islands do languages unrelated to the South Chinese language families persist—the last linguistic survivors of what must have been hundreds of now extinct aboriginal Southeast Asian languages.

Even Korea and Japan were heavily influenced by China, although their geographic isolation from it ensured that they did not lose their languages or physical and genetic distinctness, as did tropical Southeast Asia. Korea and Japan adopted rice from China in the second millennium B.C., bronze metallurgy by the first millennium B.C., and writing in the first millennium A.D. China also transmitted West Asian wheat and barley to Korea and Japan.

In thus describing China's seminal role in East Asian civilization, we should not exaggerate. It is not the case that all cultural advances in East Asia stemmed from China and that Koreans, Japanese, and tropical Southeast Asians were noninventive barbarians who contributed nothing. The ancient Japanese developed some of the oldest pottery in the world and settled as hunter-gatherers in villages subsisting on Japan's rich seafood resources, long before the arrival of food production. Some crops were probably domesticated first or independently in Japan, Korea, and tropical Southeast Asia.

But China's role was nonetheless disproportionate. For example, the prestige value of Chinese culture is still so great in Japan and Korea that Japan has no thought of discarding its Chinese-derived writing system despite its drawbacks for representing Japanese speech, while Korea is only now replacing its clumsy Chinese-derived writing with its wonderful indigenous han'gŭl alphabet. That persistence of Chinese writing in Japan and Korea is a vivid 20th-century legacy of plant and animal domestication in China nearly 10,000 years ago. Thanks to the achievements of East Asia's first farmers, China became Chinese, and peoples from Thailand to (as we shall see in the next chapter) Easter Island became their cousins.

CHAPTER 17

SPEEDBOAT TO POLYNESIA

P ACIFIC ISLAND HISTORY IS ENCAPSULATED FOR ME IN AN
incident that happened when three Indonesian friends and I walked
into a store in Jayapura, the capital of Indonesian New Guinea. My
friends' names were Achmad, Wiwor, and Sauakari, and the store was
run by a merchant named Ping Wah. Achmad, an Indonesian government
officer, was acting as the boss, because he and I were organizing an ecological survey for the government and had hired Wiwor and Sauakari as local
assistants. But Achmad had never before been in a New Guinea mountain
forest and had no idea what supplies to buy. The results were comical.

At the moment that my friends entered the store, Ping Wah was reading
a Chinese newspaper. When he saw Wiwor and Sauakari, he kept reading
it but then shoved it out of sight under the counter as soon as he noticed
Achmad. Achmad picked up an ax head, causing Wiwor and Sauakari to
laugh, because he was holding it upside down. Wiwor and Sauakari
showed him how to hold it correctly and to test it. Achmad and Sauakari
then looked at Wiwor's bare feet, with toes splayed wide from a lifetime
of not wearing shoes. Sauakari picked out the widest available shoes and
held them against Wiwor's feet, but the shoes were still too narrow, sending Achmad and Sauakari and Ping Wah into peals of laughter. Achmad
picked up a plastic comb with which to comb out his straight, coarse black

hair. Glancing at Wiwor's tough, tightly coiled hair, he handed the comb to Wiwor. It immediately stuck in Wiwor's hair, then broke as soon as Wiwor pulled on the comb. Everyone laughed, including Wiwor. Wiwor responded by reminding Achmad that he should buy lots of rice, because there would be no food to buy in New Guinea mountain villages except sweet potatoes, which would upset Achmad's stomach—more hilarity.

Despite all the laughter, I could sense the underlying tensions. Achmad was Javan, Ping Wah Chinese, Wiwor a New Guinea highlander, and Sauakari a New Guinea lowlander from the north coast. Javans dominate the Indonesian government, which annexed western New Guinea in the 1960s and used bombs and machine guns to crush New Guinean opposition. Achmad later decided to stay in town and to let me do the forest survey alone with Wiwor and Sauakari. He explained his decision to me by pointing to his straight, coarse hair, so unlike that of New Guineans, and saying that New Guineans would kill anyone with hair like his if they found him far from army backup.

Ping Wah had put away his newspaper because importation of Chinese writing is nominally illegal in Indonesian New Guinea. In much of Indonesia the merchants are Chinese immigrants. Latent mutual fear between the economically dominant Chinese and politically dominant Javans erupted in 1966 in a bloody revolution, when Javans slaughtered hundreds of thousands of Chinese. As New Guineans, Wiwor and Sauakari shared most New Guineans' resentment of Javan dictatorship, but they also scorned each other's groups. Highlanders dismiss lowlanders as effete sago eaters, while lowlanders dismiss highlanders as primitive big-heads, referring both to their massive coiled hair and to their reputation for arrogance. Within a few days of my setting up an isolated forest camp with Wiwor and Sauakari, they came close to fighting each other with axes.

Tensions among the groups that Achmad, Wiwor, Sauakari, and Ping Wah represent dominate the politics of Indonesia, the world's fourth-most-populous nation. These modern tensions have roots going back thousands of years. When we think of major overseas population movements, we tend to focus on those since Columbus's discovery of the Americas, and on the resulting replacements of non-Europeans by Europeans within historic times. But there were also big overseas movements long before Columbus, and prehistoric replacements of non-European peoples by other non-European peoples. Wiwor, Achmad, and Sauakari represent three prehistorical waves of people that moved overseas from the Asian mainland into the

Pacific. Wiwor's highlanders are probably descended from an early wave that had colonized New Guinea from Asia by 40,000 years ago. Achmad's ancestors arrived in Java ultimately from the South China coast, around 4,000 years ago, completing the replacement there of people related to Wiwor's ancestors. Sauakari's ancestors reached New Guinea around 3,600 years ago, as part of that same wave from the South China coast, while Ping Wah's ancestors still occupy China.

The population movement that brought Achmad's and Sauakari's ancestors to Java and New Guinea, respectively, termed the Austronesian expansion, was among the biggest population movements of the last 6,000 years. One prong of it became the Polynesians, who populated the most remote islands of the Pacific and were the greatest seafarers among Neolithic peoples. Austronesian languages are spoken today as native languages over more than half of the globe's span, from Madagascar to Easter Island. In this book on human population movements since the end of the Ice Ages, the Austronesian expansion occupies a central place, as one of the most important phenomena to be explained. Why did Austronesian people, stemming ultimately from mainland China, colonize Java and the rest of Indonesia and replace the original inhabitants there, instead of Indonesians colonizing China and replacing the Chinese? Having occupied all of Indonesia, why were the Austronesians then unable to occupy more than a narrow coastal strip of the New Guinea lowlands, and why were they completely unable to displace Wiwor's people from the New Guinea highlands? How did the descendants of Chinese emigrants become transformed into Polynesians?

TODAY, THE POPULATION of Java, most other Indonesian islands (except the easternmost ones), and the Philippines is rather homogeneous. In appearance and genes those islands' inhabitants are similar to South Chinese, and even more similar to tropical Southeast Asians, especially those of the Malay Peninsula. Their languages are equally homogeneous: while 374 languages are spoken in the Philippines and western and central Indonesia, all of them are closely related and fall within the same sub-subfamily (Western Malayo-Polynesian) of the Austronesian language family. Austronesian languages reached the Asian mainland on the Malay Peninsula and in small pockets in Vietnam and Cambodia, near the westernmost Indonesian islands of Sumatra and Borneo, but they occur nowhere else on the mainland (Figure 17.1). Some Austronesian words

Distribution of Austronesian languages

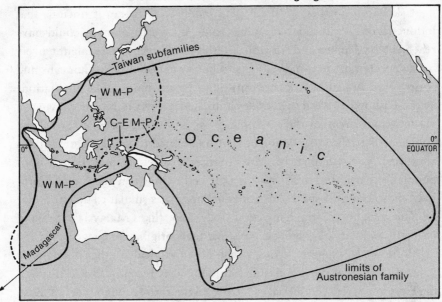

Figure 17.1. The Austronesian language family consists of four subfamilies, three of them confined to Taiwan and one (Malayo-Polynesian) widespread. The latter subfamily in turn consists of two sub-subfamilies, Western Malayo-Polynesian (= W M-P) and Central-Eastern Malayo-Polynesian (= C-E M-P). The latter sub-subfamily in turn consists of four sub-sub-subfamilies, the very widespread Oceanic one to the east and three others to the west in a much smaller area comprising Halmahera, nearby islands of eastern Indonesia, and the west end of New Guinea.

borrowed into English include "taboo" and "tattoo" (from a Polynesian language), "boondocks" (from the Tagalog language of the Philippines), and "amok," "batik," and "orangutan" (from Malay).

That genetic and linguistic uniformity of Indonesia and the Philippines is initially as surprising as is the predominant linguistic uniformity of China. The famous Java *Homo erectus* fossils prove that humans have occupied at least western Indonesia for a million years. That should have given ample time for humans to evolve genetic and linguistic diversity and tropical adaptations, such as dark skins like those of many other tropical peoples—but instead Indonesians and Filipinos have light skins.

It is also surprising that Indonesians and Filipinos are so similar to tropical Southeast Asians and South Chinese in other physical features besides light skins and in their genes. A glance at a map makes it obvious that Indonesia offered the only possible route by which humans could have reached New Guinea and Australia 40,000 years ago, so one might naively have expected modern Indonesians to be like modern New Guineans and Australians. In reality, there are only a few New Guinean–like populations in the Philippine / western Indonesia area, notably the Negritos living in mountainous areas of the Philippines. As is also true of the three New Guinean–like relict populations that I mentioned in speaking of tropical Southeast Asia (Chapter 16), the Philippine Negritos could be relicts of populations ancestral to Wiwor's people before they reached New Guinea. Even those Negritos speak Austronesian languages similar to those of their Filipino neighbors, implying that they too (like Malaysia's Semang Negritos and Africa's Pygmies) have lost their original language.

All these facts suggest strongly that either tropical Southeast Asians or South Chinese speaking Austronesian languages recently spread through the Philippines and Indonesia, replacing all the former inhabitants of those islands except the Philippine Negritos, and replacing all the original island languages. That event evidently took place too recently for the colonists to evolve dark skins, distinct language families, or genetic distinctiveness or diversity. Their languages are of course much more *numerous* than the eight dominant Chinese languages of mainland China, but are no more *diverse.* The proliferation of many similar languages in the Philippines and Indonesia merely reflects the fact that the islands never underwent a political and cultural unification, as did China.

Details of language distributions provide valuable clues to the route of this hypothesized Austronesian expansion. The whole Austronesian language family consists of 959 languages, divided among four subfamilies. But one of those subfamilies, termed Malayo-Polynesian, comprises 945 of those 959 languages and covers almost the entire geographic range of the Austronesian family. Before the recent overseas expansion of Europeans speaking Indo-European languages, Austronesian was the most widespread language family in the world. That suggests that the Malayo-Polynesian subfamily differentiated recently out of the Austronesian family and spread far from the Austronesian homeland, giving rise to many local languages, all of which are still closely related because there has been too little time to develop large linguistic differences. For the location of that Austronesian homeland, we should therefore look not to Malayo-

Polynesian but to the other three Austronesian subfamilies, which differ considerably more from each other and from Malayo-Polynesian than the sub-subfamilies of Malayo-Polynesian differ among each other.

It turns out that those three other subfamilies have coincident distributions, all of them tiny compared with the distribution of Malayo-Polynesian. They are confined to aborigines of the island of Taiwan, lying only 90 miles from the South China mainland. Taiwan's aborigines had the island largely to themselves until mainland Chinese began settling in large numbers within the last thousand years. Still more mainlanders arrived after 1945, especially after the Chinese Communists defeated the Chinese Nationalists in 1949, so that aborigines now constitute only 2 percent of Taiwan's population. The concentration of three out of the four Austronesian subfamilies on Taiwan suggests that, within the present Austronesian realm, Taiwan is the homeland where Austronesian languages have been spoken for the most millennia and have consequently had the longest time in which to diverge. All other Austronesian languages, from those on Madagascar to those on Easter Island, would then stem from a population expansion out of Taiwan.

WE CAN NOW turn to archaeological evidence. While the debris of ancient village sites does not include fossilized words along with bones and pottery, it does reveal movements of people and cultural artifacts that could be associated with languages. Like the rest of the world, most of the present Austronesian realm—Taiwan, the Philippines, Indonesia, and many Pacific islands—was originally occupied by hunter-gatherers lacking pottery, polished stone tools, domestic animals, and crops. (The sole exceptions to this generalization are the remote islands of Madagascar, eastern Melanesia, Polynesia, and Micronesia, which were never reached by hunter-gatherers and remained empty of humans until the Austronesian expansion.) The first archaeological signs of something different within the Austronesian realm come from—Taiwan. Beginning around the fourth millennium B.C., polished stone tools and a distinctive decorated pottery style (so-called Ta-p'en-k'eng pottery) derived from earlier South China mainland pottery appeared on Taiwan and on the opposite coast of the South China mainland. Remains of rice and millet at later Taiwanese sites provide evidence of agriculture.

Ta-p'en-k'eng sites of Taiwan and the South China coast are full of fish bones and mollusk shells, as well as of stone net sinkers and adzes suitable for hollowing out a wooden canoe. Evidently, those first Neolithic occupants of Taiwan had watercraft adequate for deep-sea fishing and for regular sea traffic across Taiwan Strait, separating that island from the China coast. Thus, Taiwan Strait may have served as the training ground where mainland Chinese developed the open-water maritime skills that would permit them to expand over the Pacific.

One specific type of artifact linking Taiwan's Ta-p'en-k'eng culture to later Pacific island cultures is a bark beater, a stone implement used for pounding the fibrous bark of certain tree species into rope, nets, and clothing. Once Pacific peoples spread beyond the range of wool-yielding domestic animals and fiber plant crops and hence of woven clothing, they became dependent on pounded bark "cloth" for their clothing. Inhabitants of Rennell Island, a traditional Polynesian island that did not become Westernized until the 1930s, told me that Westernization yielded the wonderful side benefit that the island became quiet. No more sounds of bark beaters everywhere, pounding out bark cloth from dawn until after dusk every day!

Within a millennium or so after the Ta-p'en-k'eng culture reached Taiwan, archaeological evidence shows that cultures obviously derived from it spread farther and farther from Taiwan to fill up the modern Austronesian realm (Figure 17.2). The evidence includes ground stone tools, pottery, bones of domestic pigs, and crop remains. For example, the decorated Ta-p'en-k'eng pottery on Taiwan gave way to undecorated plain or red pottery, which has also been found at sites in the Philippines and on the Indonesian islands of Celebes and Timor. This cultural "package" of pottery, stone tools, and domesticates appeared around 3000 B.C. in the Philippines, around 2500 B.C. on the Indonesian islands of Celebes and North Borneo and Timor, around 2000 B.C. on Java and Sumatra, and around 1600 B.C. in the New Guinea region. There, as we shall see, the expansion assumed a speedboat pace, as bearers of the cultural package raced eastward into the previously uninhabited Pacific Ocean beyond the Solomon Archipelago. The last phases of the expansion, during the millennium after A.D. 1, resulted in the colonization of every Polynesian and Micronesian island capable of supporting humans. Astonishingly, it also swept westward across the Indian Ocean to the east coast of Africa, resulting in the colonization of the island of Madagascar.

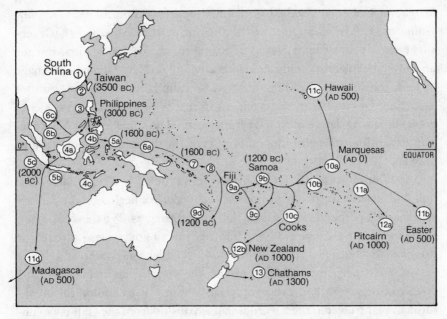

Figure 17.2. The paths of the Austronesian expansion, with approximate dates when each region was reached. 4a = Borneo, 4b = Celebes, 4c = Timor (around 2500 B.C.). 5a = Halmahera (around 1600 B.C.). 5b = Java, 5c = Sumatra (around 2000 B.C.). 6a = Bismarck Archipelago (around 1600 B.C.). 6b = Malay Peninsula, 6c = Vietnam (around 1000 B.C.). 7 = Solomon Archipelago (around 1600 B.C.). 8 = Santa Cruz, 9c = Tonga, 9d = New Caledonia (around 1200 B.C.). 10b = Society Islands, 10c = Cook Islands, 11a = Tuamotu Archipelago (around A.D. 1).

At least until the expansion reached coastal New Guinea, travel between islands was probably by double-outrigger sailing canoes, which are still widespread throughout Indonesia today. That boat design represented a major advance over the simple dugout canoes prevalent among traditional peoples living on inland waterways throughout the world. A dugout canoe is just what its name implies: a solid tree trunk "dug out" (that is, hollowed out), and its ends shaped, by an adze. Since the canoe is as round-bottomed as the trunk from which it was carved, the least imbalance in weight distribution tips the canoe toward the overweighted side.

Whenever I've been paddled in dugouts up New Guinea rivers by New Guineans, I have spent much of the trip in terror: it seemed that every slight movement of mine risked capsizing the canoe and spilling out me and my binoculars to commune with crocodiles. New Guineans manage to look secure while paddling dugouts on calm lakes and rivers, but not even New Guineans can use a dugout in seas with modest waves. Hence some stabilizing device must have been essential not only for the Austronesian expansion through Indonesia but even for the initial colonization of Taiwan.

The solution was to lash two smaller logs ("outriggers") parallel to the hull and several feet from it, one on each side, connected to the hull by poles lashed perpendicular to the hull and outriggers. Whenever the hull starts to tip toward one side, the buoyancy of the outrigger on that side prevents the outrigger from being pushed under the water and hence makes it virtually impossible to capsize the vessel. The invention of the double-outrigger sailing canoe may have been the technological break-through that triggered the Austronesian expansion from the Chinese mainland.

TWO STRIKING COINCIDENCES between archaeological and linguistic evidence support the inference that the people bringing a Neolithic culture to Taiwan, the Philippines, and Indonesia thousands of years ago spoke Austronesian languages and were ancestral to the Austronesian speakers still inhabiting those islands today. First, both types of evidence point unequivocally to the colonization of Taiwan as the first stage of the expansion from the South China coast, and to the colonization of the Philippines and Indonesia from Taiwan as the next stage. If the expansion had proceeded from tropical Southeast Asia's Malay Peninsula to the nearest Indonesian island of Sumatra, then to other Indonesian islands, and finally to the Philippines and Taiwan, we would find the deepest divisions (reflecting the greatest time depth) of the Austronesian language family among the modern languages of the Malay Peninsula and Sumatra, and the languages of Taiwan and the Philippines would have differentiated only recently within a single subfamily. Instead, the deepest divisions are in Taiwan, and the languages of the Malay Peninsula and Sumatra fall together in the same sub-sub-subfamily: a recent branch of the Western Malayo-Polynesian sub-subfamily, which is in turn a fairly recent branch of the Malayo-Polynesian subfamily. Those details of linguistic relationships agree perfectly with the archaeological evidence that the colonization of the Malay Peninsula was recent, and followed rather than preceded the colonization of Taiwan, the Philippines, and Indonesia.

The other coincidence between archaeological and linguistic evidence concerns the cultural baggage that ancient Austronesians used. Archaeology provides us with direct evidence of culture in the form of pottery, pig and fish bones, and so on. One might initially wonder how a linguist, studying only modern languages whose unwritten ancestral forms remain unknown, could ever figure out whether Austronesians living on Taiwan 6,000 years ago had pigs. The solution is to reconstruct the vocabularies of vanished ancient languages (so-called protolanguages) by comparing vocabularies of modern languages derived from them.

For instance, the words meaning "sheep" in many languages of the Indo-European language family, distributed from Ireland to India, are quite similar: "avis," "avis," "ovis," "oveja," "ovtsa," "owis," and "oi" in Lithuanian, Sanskrit, Latin, Spanish, Russian, Greek, and Irish, respectively. (The English "sheep" is obviously from a different root, but English retains the original root in the word "ewe.") Comparison of the sound shifts that the various modern Indo-European languages have undergone during their histories suggests that the original form was "owis" in the ancestral Indo-European language spoken around 6,000 years ago. That unwritten ancestral language is termed Proto-Indo-European.

Evidently, Proto-Indo-Europeans 6,000 years ago had sheep, in agreement with archaeological evidence. Nearly 2,000 other words of their vocabulary can similarly be reconstructed, including words for "goat," "horse," "wheel," "brother," and "eye." But no Proto-Indo-European word can be reconstructed for "gun," which uses different roots in different modern Indo-European languages: "gun" in English, "fusil" in French, "ruzhyo" in Russian, and so on. That shouldn't surprise us: people 6,000 years ago couldn't possibly have had a word for guns, which were invented only within the past 1,000 years. Since there was thus no inherited shared root meaning "gun," each Indo-European language had to invent or borrow its own word when guns were finally invented.

Proceeding in the same way, we can compare modern Taiwanese, Philippine, Indonesian, and Polynesian languages to reconstruct a Proto-Austronesian language spoken in the distant past. To no one's surprise, that reconstructed Proto-Austronesian language had words with meanings such as "two," "bird," "ear," and "head louse": of course, Proto-Austronesians could count to 2, knew of birds, and had ears and lice. More interestingly, the reconstructed language had words for "pig," "dog," and "rice," which must therefore have been part of Proto-Austronesian culture. The reconstructed language is full of words indicating a maritime economy, such as "outrigger canoe," "sail," "giant clam," "octopus," "fish trap," and "sea turtle." This linguistic evidence regarding the culture of Proto-Austronesians, wherever and whenever they lived, agrees well with the archaeological evidence regarding the pottery-making, sea-oriented, food-producing people living on Taiwan around 6,000 years ago.

The same procedure can be applied to reconstruct Proto-Malayo-Polynesian, the ancestral language spoken by Austronesians *after* emigrating from Taiwan. Proto-Malayo-Polynesian contains words for many tropical crops like taro, breadfruit, bananas, yams, and coconuts, for which no word can be reconstructed in Proto-Austronesian. Thus, the linguistic evidence suggests that many tropical crops were added to the Austronesian repertoire after the emigration from Taiwan. This conclusion agrees with archaeological evidence: as colonizing farmers spread southward from Taiwan (lying about 23 degrees north of the equator) toward the equatorial tropics, they came to depend increasingly on tropical root and tree crops, which they proceeded to carry with them out into the tropical Pacific.

How could those Austronesian-speaking farmers from South China via Taiwan replace the original hunter-gatherer population of the Philippines and western Indonesia so completely that little genetic and no linguistic evidence of that original population survived? The reasons resemble the reasons why Europeans replaced or exterminated Native Australians within the last two centuries, and why South Chinese replaced the original tropical Southeast Asians earlier: the farmers' much denser populations, superior tools and weapons, more developed watercraft and maritime skills, and epidemic diseases to which the farmers but not the hunter-gatherers had some resistance. On the Asian mainland Austronesian-speaking farmers were able similarly to replace some of the former hunter-gatherers of the Malay Peninsula, because Austronesians colonized the peninsula from the south and east (from the Indonesian islands of Sumatra and Borneo) around the same time that Austroasiatic-speaking farmers were colonizing the peninsula from the north (from Thailand). Other Austronesians managed to establish themselves in parts of southern Vietnam and Cambodia to become the ancestors of the modern Chamic minority of those countries.

However, Austronesian farmers could spread no farther into the Southeast Asian mainland, because Austroasiatic and Tai-Kadai farmers had already replaced the former hunter-gatherers there, and because Austronesian farmers had no advantage over Austroasiatic and Tai-Kadai farmers. Although we infer that Austronesian speakers originated from coastal South China, Austronesian languages today are not spoken anywhere in mainland China, possibly because they were among the hundreds of former Chinese languages eliminated by the southward expansion of Sino-Tibetan speakers. But the language families closest to Austronesian are thought to be Tai-Kadai, Austroasiatic, and Miao-Yao. Thus, while Austronesian languages in China may not have survived the onslaught of Chinese dynasties, some of their sister and cousin languages did.

WE HAVE NOW followed the initial stages of the Austronesian expansion for 2,500 miles from the South China coast, through Taiwan and the Philippines, to western and central Indonesia. In the course of that expansion, Austronesians came to occupy all habitable areas of those islands, from the seacoast to the interior, and from the lowlands to the mountains. By 1500 B.C. their familiar archaeological hallmarks, including pig bones and plain red-slipped pottery, show that they had reached the eastern Indonesian island of Halmahera, less than 200 miles from the western end of the big mountainous island of New Guinea. Did they proceed to overrun that island, just as they had already overrun the big mountainous islands of Celebes, Borneo, Java, and Sumatra?

They did not, as a glance at the faces of most modern New Guineans makes obvious, and as detailed studies of New Guinean genes confirm. My friend Wiwor and all other New Guinea highlanders differ obviously from Indonesians, Filipinos, and South Chinese in their dark skins, tightly coiled hair, and face shapes. Most lowlanders from New Guinea's interior and south coast resemble the highlanders except that they tend to be taller. Geneticists have failed to find characteristic Austronesian gene markers in blood samples from New Guinea highlanders.

But peoples of New Guinea's north and east coasts, and of the Bismarck and Solomon Archipelagoes north and east of New Guinea, present a more complex picture. In appearance, they are variably intermediate between highlanders like Wiwor and Indonesians like Achmad, though on the average considerably closer to Wiwor. For instance, my friend Sauakari from the north coast has wavy hair intermediate between Achmad's straight hair and Wiwor's coiled hair, and skin somewhat paler than Wiwor's, though considerably darker than Achmad's. Genetically, the Bismarck and Solomon islanders and north coastal New Guineans are about 15 percent Austronesian and 85 percent like New Guinea highlanders. Hence Austronesians evidently reached the New Guinea region but failed completely to penetrate the island's interior and were genetically diluted by New Guinea's previous residents on the north coast and islands.

Modern languages tell essentially the same story but add detail. In Chapter 15 I explained that most New Guinea languages, termed Papuan languages, are unrelated to any language families elsewhere in the world. Without exception, every language spoken in the New Guinea mountains, the whole of southwestern and south-central lowland New Guinea, including the coast, and the interior of northern New Guinea is a Papuan language. But Austronesian languages are spoken in a narrow strip immediately on the north and southeast coasts. Most languages of the Bismarck and Solomon islands are Austronesian: Papuan languages are spoken only in isolated pockets on a few islands.

Austronesian languages spoken in the Bismarcks and Solomons and north coastal New Guinea are related, as a separate sub-sub-subfamily termed Oceanic, to the sub-sub-subfamily of languages spoken on Halmahera and the west end of New Guinea. That linguistic relationship confirms, as one would expect from a map, that Austronesian speakers of the New Guinea region arrived by way of Halmahera. Details of Austronesian and Papuan languages and their distributions in North New Guinea testify to long contact between the Austronesian invaders and the Papuan-speaking residents. Both the Austronesian and the Papuan languages of the region show massive influences of each other's vocabularies and grammars, making it difficult to decide whether certain languages are basically Austronesian languages influenced by Papuan ones or the reverse. As one travels from village to village along the north coast or its fringing islands, one passes from a village with an Austronesian language to a village with a Papuan language and then to another Austronesian-speaking village, without any genetic discontinuity at the linguistic boundaries.

All this suggests that descendants of Austronesian invaders and of original New Guineans have been trading, intermarrying, and acquiring each other's genes and languages for several thousand years on the North New Guinea coast and its islands. That long contact transferred Austronesian languages more effectively than Austronesian genes, with the result that most Bismarck and Solomon islanders now speak Austronesian languages, even though their appearance and most of their genes are still Papuan. But neither the genes nor the languages of the Austronesians penetrated New Guinea's interior. The outcome of their invasion of New Guinea was thus very different from the outcome of their invasion of Borneo, Celebes, and other big Indonesian islands, where their steamroller eliminated almost all traces of the previous inhabitants' genes and languages. To understand what happened in New Guinea, let us now turn to the evidence from archaeology.

AROUND 1600 B.C., almost simultaneously with their appearance on Halmahera, the familiar archaeological hallmarks of the Austronesian expansion—pigs, chickens, dogs, red-slipped pottery, and adzes of ground stone and of giant clamshells—appear in the New Guinea region. But two features distinguish the Austronesians' arrival there from their earlier arrival in the Philippines and Indonesia.

The first feature consists of pottery designs, which are aesthetic features of no economic significance but which do let archaeologists immediately recognize an early Austronesian site. Whereas most early Austronesian pottery in the Philippines and Indonesia was undecorated, pottery in the New Guinea region was finely decorated with geometric designs arranged in horizontal bands. In other respects the pottery preserved the red slip and the vessel forms characteristic of earlier Austronesian pottery in Indonesia. Evidently, Austronesian settlers in the New Guinea region got the idea of "tattooing" their pots, perhaps inspired by geometric designs that they had already been using on their bark cloth and body tattoos. This style is termed Lapita pottery, after an archaeological site named Lapita, where it was described.

The much more significant distinguishing feature of early Austronesian sites in the New Guinea region is their distribution. In contrast to those in the Philippines and Indonesia, where even the earliest known Austronesian sites are on big islands like Luzon and Borneo and Celebes, sites with Lapita pottery in the New Guinea region are virtually confined to small islets fringing remote larger islands. To date, Lapita pottery has been found at only one site (Aitape) on the north coast of New Guinea itself, and at a couple of sites in the Solomons. Most Lapita sites of the New Guinea region are in the Bismarcks, on islets off the coast of the larger Bismarck islands, occasionally on the coasts of the larger islands themselves. Since (as we shall see) the makers of Lapita pottery were capable of sailing thousands of miles, their failure to transfer their villages a few miles to the large Bismarck islands, or a few dozen miles to New Guinea, was certainly not due to inability to get there.

The basis of Lapita subsistence can be reconstructed from the garbage excavated by archaeologists at Lapita sites. Lapita people depended heavily on seafood, including fish, porpoises, sea turtles, sharks, and shellfish. They had pigs, chickens, and dogs and ate the nuts of many trees (including coconuts). While they probably also ate the usual Austronesian root crops, such as taro and yams, evidence of those crops is hard to obtain, because hard nut shells are much more likely than soft roots to persist for thousands of years in garbage heaps.

Naturally, it is impossible to prove directly that the people who made Lapita pots spoke an Austronesian language. However, two facts make this inference virtually certain. First, except for the decorations on the pots, the pots themselves and their associated cultural paraphernalia are similar to the cultural remains found at Indonesian and Philippine sites ancestral to modern Austronesian-speaking societies. Second, Lapita pottery also appears on remote Pacific islands with no previous human inhabitants, with no evidence of a major second wave of settlement subsequent to that bringing Lapita pots, and where the modern inhabitants speak an Austronesian language (more of this below). Hence Lapita pottery may be safely assumed to mark Austronesians' arrival in the New Guinea region.

What were those Austronesian pot makers doing on islets adjacent to bigger islands? They were probably living in the same way as modern pot makers lived until recently on islets in the New Guinea region. In 1972 I visited such a village on Malai Islet, in the Siassi island group, off the medium-sized island of Umboi, off the larger Bismarck island of New Britain. When I stepped ashore on Malai in search of birds, knowing nothing about the people there, I was astonished by the sight that greeted me.

Instead of the usual small village of low huts, surrounded by large gardens sufficient to feed the village, and with a few canoes drawn up on the beach, most of the area of Malai was occupied by two-story wooden houses side by side, leaving no ground available for gardens—the New Guinea equivalent of downtown Manhattan. On the beach were rows of big canoes. It turned out that Malai islanders, besides being fishermen, were also specialized potters, carvers, and traders, who lived by making beautifully decorated pots and wooden bowls, transporting them in their canoes to larger islands and exchanging their wares for pigs, dogs, vegetables, and other necessities. Even the timber for Malai canoes was obtained by trade from villagers on nearby Umboi Island, since Malai does not have trees big enough to be fashioned into canoes.

In the days before European shipping, trade between islands in the New Guinea region was monopolized by such specialized groups of canoe-building potters, skilled in sailing without navigational instruments, and living on offshore islets or occasionally in mainland coastal villages. By the time I reached Malai in 1972, those indigenous trade networks had collapsed or contracted, partly because of competition from European motor vessels and aluminum pots, partly because the Australian colonial government forbade long-distance canoe voyaging after some accidents in which traders were drowned. I would guess that the Lapita potters were the inter-island traders of the New Guinea region in the centuries after 1600 B.C.

The spread of Austronesian languages to the north coast of New Guinea itself, and over even the largest Bismarck and Solomon islands, must have occurred mostly after Lapita times, since Lapita sites themselves were concentrated on Bismarck islets. Not until around A.D. 1 did pottery derived from the Lapita style appear on the south side of New Guinea's southeast peninsula. When Europeans began exploring New Guinea in the late 19th century, all the remainder of New Guinea's south coast still supported populations only of Papuan-language speakers, even though Austronesian-speaking populations were established not only on the southeastern peninsula but also on the Aru and Kei Islands (lying 70–80 miles off western New Guinea's south coast). Austronesians thus had thousands of years in which to colonize New Guinea's interior and its southern coast from nearby bases, but they never did so. Even their colonization of North New Guinea's coastal fringe was more linguistic than genetic: all northern coastal peoples remained predominantly New Guineans in their genes. At most, some of them merely adopted Austronesian languages, possibly in order to communicate with the long-distance traders who linked societies.

THUS, THE OUTCOME of the Austronesian expansion in the New Guinea region was opposite to that in Indonesia and the Philippines. In the latter region the indigenous population disappeared—presumably driven off, killed, infected, or assimilated by the invaders. In the former region the indigenous population mostly kept the invaders out. The invaders (the Austronesians) were the same in both cases, and the indigenous populations may also have been genetically similar to each other, if the original Indonesian population supplanted by Austronesians really was related to New Guineans, as I suggested earlier. Why the opposite outcomes?

The answer becomes obvious when one considers the differing cultural circumstances of Indonesia's and New Guinea's indigenous populations. Before Austronesians arrived, most of Indonesia was thinly occupied by hunter-gatherers lacking even polished stone tools. In contrast, food production had already been established for thousands of years in the New Guinea highlands, and probably in the New Guinea lowlands and in the Bismarcks and Solomons as well. The New Guinea highlands supported some of the densest populations of Stone Age people anywhere in the modern world.

Austronesians enjoyed few advantages in competing with those established New Guinean populations. Some of the crops on which Austronesians subsisted, such as taro, yams, and bananas, had probably already been independently domesticated in New Guinea before Austronesians arrived. The New Guineans readily integrated Austronesian chickens, dogs, and especially pigs into their food-producing economies. New Guineans already had polished stone tools. They were at least as resistant to tropical diseases as were Austronesians, because they carried the same five types of genetic protections against malaria as did Austronesians, and some or all of those genes evolved independently in New Guinea. New Guineans were already accomplished seafarers, although not as accomplished as the makers of Lapita pottery. Tens of thousands of years before the arrival of Austronesians, New Guineans had colonized the Bismarck and Solomon Archipelagoes, and a trade in obsidian (a volcanic stone suitable for making sharp tools) was thriving in the Bismarcks at least 18,000 years before the Austronesians arrived. New Guineans even seem to have expanded recently westward against the Austronesian tide, into eastern Indonesia, where languages spoken on the islands of North Halmahera and of Timor are typical Papuan languages related to some languages of western New Guinea.

In short, the variable outcomes of the Austronesian expansion strikingly illustrate the role of food production in human population movements. Austronesian food-producers migrated into two regions (New Guinea and Indonesia) occupied by resident peoples who were probably related to each other. The residents of Indonesia were still hunter-gatherers, while the residents of New Guinea were already food producers and had developed many of the concomitants of food production (dense populations, disease resistance, more advanced technology, and so on). As a result, while the Austronesian expansion swept away the original Indonesians, it failed to make much headway in the New Guinea region, just as it also failed to make headway against Austroasiatic and Tai-Kadai food producers in tropical Southeast Asia.

We have now traced the Austronesian expansion through Indonesia and up to the shores of New Guinea and tropical Southeast Asia. In Chapter 19 we shall trace it across the Indian Ocean to Madagascar, while in Chapter 15 we saw that ecological difficulties kept Austronesians from establishing themselves in northern and western Australia. The expansion's remaining thrust began when the Lapita potters sailed far eastward into the Pacific beyond the Solomons, into an island realm that no other humans had reached previously. Around 1200 B.C. Lapita potsherds, the familiar triumvirate of pigs and chickens and dogs, and the usual other archaeological hallmarks of Austronesians appeared on the Pacific archipelagoes of Fiji, Samoa, and Tonga, over a thousand miles east of the Solomons. Early in the Christian era, most of those same hallmarks (with the notable exception of pottery) appeared on the islands of eastern Polynesia, including the Societies and Marquesas. Further long overwater canoe voyages brought settlers north to Hawaii, east to Pitcairn and Easter Islands, and southwest to New Zealand. The native inhabitants of most of those islands today are the Polynesians, who thus are the direct descendants of the Lapita potters. They speak Austronesian languages closely related to those of the New Guinea region, and their main crops are the Austronesian package that included taro, yams, bananas, coconuts, and breadfruit.

With the occupation of the Chatham Islands off New Zealand around

A.D. 1400, barely a century before European "explorers" entered the Pacific, the task of exploring the Pacific was finally completed by Asians. Their tradition of exploration, lasting tens of thousands of years, had begun when Wiwor's ancestors spread through Indonesia to New Guinea and Australia. It ended only when it had run out of targets and almost every habitable Pacific island had been occupied.

To anyone interested in world history, human societies of East Asia and the Pacific are instructive, because they provide so many examples of how environment molds history. Depending on their geographic homeland, East Asian and Pacific peoples differed in their access to domesticable wild plant and animal species and in their connectedness to other peoples. Again and again, people with access to the prerequisites for food production, and with a location favoring diffusion of technology from elsewhere, replaced peoples lacking these advantages. Again and again, when a single wave of colonists spread out over diverse environments, their descendants developed in separate ways, depending on those environmental differences.

For instance, we have seen that South Chinese developed indigenous food production and technology, received writing and still more technology and political structures from North China, and went on to colonize tropical Southeast Asia and Taiwan, largely replacing the former inhabitants of those areas. Within Southeast Asia, among the descendants or relatives of those food-producing South Chinese colonists, the Yumbri in the mountain rain forests of northeastern Thailand and Laos reverted to living as hunter-gatherers, while the Yumbri's close relatives the Vietnamese (speaking a language in the same sub-subfamily of Austroasiatic as the Yumbri language) remained food producers in the rich Red Delta and established a vast metal-based empire. Similarly, among Austronesian emigrant farmers from Taiwan and Indonesia, the Punan in the rain forests of Borneo were forced to turn back to the hunter-gatherer lifestyle, while their relatives living on Java's rich volcanic soils remained food producers, founded a kingdom under the influence of India, adopted writing, and built the great Buddhist monument at Borobudur. The Austronesians who went on to colonize Polynesia became isolated from East Asian metallurgy and writing and hence remained without writing or metal. As we saw in Chapter 2, though, Polynesian political and social organization and economies underwent great diversification in different environments. Within a millennium, East Polynesian colonists had reverted to hunting-gathering on the Chathams while building a protostate with intensive food production on Hawaii.

When Europeans at last arrived, their technological and other advantages enabled them to establish temporary colonial domination over most of tropical Southeast Asia and the Pacific islands. However, indigenous germs and food producers prevented Europeans from settling most of this region in significant numbers. Within this area, only New Zealand, New Caledonia, and Hawaii—the largest and most remote islands, lying farthest from the equator and hence in the most nearly temperate (Europe-like) climates—now support large European populations. Thus, unlike Australia and the Americas, East Asia and most Pacific islands remain occupied by East Asian and Pacific peoples.

CHAPTER 18

HEMISPHERES COLLIDING

T HE LARGEST POPULATION REPLACEMENT OF THE LAST 13,000 years has been the one resulting from the recent collision between Old World and New World societies. Its most dramatic and decisive moment, as we saw in Chapter 3, occurred when Pizarro's tiny army of Spaniards captured the Inca emperor Atahuallpa, absolute ruler of the largest, richest, most populous, and administratively and technologically most advanced Native American state. Atahuallpa's capture symbolizes the European conquest of the Americas, because the same mix of proximate factors that caused it was also responsible for European conquests of other Native American societies. Let us now return to that collision of hemispheres, applying what we have learned since Chapter 3. The basic question to be answered is: why did Europeans reach and conquer the lands of Native Americans, instead of vice versa? Our starting point will be a comparison of Eurasian and Native American societies as of A.D. 1492, the year of Columbus's "discovery" of the Americas.

O UR COMPARISON BEGINS with food production, a major determinant of local population size and societal complexity—hence an ultimate factor behind the conquest. The most glaring difference between American and Eurasian food production involved big domestic mammal species. In Chapter 9 we encountered Eurasia's 13 species, which became its chief source of animal protein (meat and milk), wool, and hides, its main mode of land transport of people and goods, its indispensable vehicles of warfare, and (by drawing plows and providing manure) a big enhancer of crop production. Until waterwheels and windmills began to replace Eurasia's mammals in medieval times, they were also the major source of its "industrial" power beyond human muscle power—for example, for turning grindstones and operating water lifts. In contrast, the Americas had only one species of big domestic mammal, the llama / alpaca, confined to a small area of the Andes and the adjacent Peruvian coast. While it was used for meat, wool, hides, and goods transport, it never yielded milk for human consumption, never bore a rider, never pulled a cart or a plow, and never served as a power source or vehicle of warfare.

That's an enormous set of differences between Eurasian and Native American societies—due largely to the Late Pleistocene extinction (extermination?) of most of North and South America's former big wild mammal species. If it had not been for those extinctions, modern history might have taken a different course. When Cortés and his bedraggled adventurers landed on the Mexican coast in 1519, they might have been driven into the sea by thousands of Aztec cavalry mounted on domesticated native American horses. Instead of the Aztecs' dying of smallpox, the Spaniards might have been wiped out by American germs transmitted by disease-resistant Aztecs. American civilizations resting on animal power might have been sending their own conquistadores to ravage Europe. But those hypothetical outcomes were foreclosed by mammal extinctions thousands of years earlier.

Those extinctions left Eurasia with many more wild candidates for domestication than the Americas offered. Most candidates disqualify themselves as potential domesticates for any of half a dozen reasons. Hence Eurasia ended up with its 13 species of big domestic mammals and the Americas with just its one very local species. Both hemispheres also had domesticated species of birds and small mammals—the turkey, guinea pig, and Muscovy duck very locally and the dog more widely in the Americas; chickens, geese, ducks, cats, dogs, rabbits, honeybees, silkworms, and some others in Eurasia. But the significance of all those species of small domestic animals was trivial compared with that of the big ones.

Eurasia and the Americas also differed with respect to plant food production, though the disparity here was less marked than for animal food production. In 1492 agriculture was widespread in Eurasia. Among the few Eurasian hunter-gatherers lacking both crops and domestic animals were the Ainu of northern Japan, Siberian societies without reindeer, and small hunter-gatherer groups scattered through the forests of India and tropical Southeast Asia and trading with neighboring farmers. Some other Eurasian societies, notably the Central Asian pastoralists and the reindeer-herding Lapps and Samoyeds of the Arctic, had domestic animals but little or no agriculture. Virtually all other Eurasian societies engaged in agriculture as well as in herding animals.

Agriculture was also widespread in the Americas, but hunter-gatherers occupied a larger fraction of the Americas' area than of Eurasia's. Those regions of the Americas without food production included all of northern North America and southern South America, the Canadian Great Plains, and all of western North America except for small areas of the U.S. Southwest that supported irrigation agriculture. It is striking that the areas of Native America without food production included what today, after Europeans' arrival, are some of the most productive farmlands and pastures of both North and South America: the Pacific states of the United States, Canada's wheat belt, the pampas of Argentina, and the Mediterranean zone of Chile. The former absence of food production in these lands was due entirely to their local paucity of domesticable wild animals and plants, and to geographic and ecological barriers that prevented the crops and the few domestic animal species of other parts of the Americas from arriving. Those lands became productive not only for European settlers but also, in some cases, for Native Americans, as soon as Europeans introduced suitable domestic animals and crops. For instance, Native American societies became renowned for their mastery of horses, and in some cases of cattle and sheepherding, in parts of the Great Plains, the western United States, and the Argentine pampas. Those mounted plains warriors and Navajo sheepherders and weavers now figure prominently in white Americans' image of American Indians, but the basis for that image was created only after 1492. These examples demonstrate that the sole missing ingredients required to sustain food production in large areas of the Americas were domestic animals and crops themselves.

In those parts of the Americas that did support Native American agriculture, it was constrained by five major disadvantages vis-à-vis Eurasian agriculture: widespread dependence on protein-poor corn, instead of

Eurasia's diverse and protein-rich cereals; hand planting of individual seeds, instead of broadcast sowing; tilling by hand instead of plowing by animals, which enables one person to cultivate a much larger area, and which also permits cultivation of some fertile but tough soils and sods that are difficult to till by hand (such as those of the North American Great Plains); lack of animal manuring to increase soil fertility; and just human muscle power, instead of animal power, for agricultural tasks such as threshing, grinding, and irrigation. These differences suggest that Eurasian agriculture as of 1492 may have yielded on the average more calories and protein per person-hour of labor than Native American agriculture did.

SUCH DIFFERENCES IN food production constituted a major ultimate cause of the disparities between Eurasian and Native American societies. Among the resulting proximate factors behind the conquest, the most important included differences in germs, technology, political organization, and writing. Of these, the one linked most directly to the differences in food production was germs. The infectious diseases that regularly visited crowded Eurasian societies, and to which many Eurasians consequently developed immune or genetic resistance, included all of history's most lethal killers: smallpox, measles, influenza, plague, tuberculosis, typhus, cholera, malaria, and others. Against that grim list, the sole crowd infectious diseases that can be attributed with certainty to pre-Columbian Native American societies were nonsyphilitic treponemas. (As I explained in Chapter 11, it remains uncertain whether syphilis arose in Eurasia or in the Americas, and the claim that human tuberculosis was present in the Americas before Columbus is in my opinion unproven.)

This continental difference in harmful germs resulted paradoxically from the difference in useful livestock. Most of the microbes responsible for the infectious diseases of crowded human societies evolved from very similar ancestral microbes causing infectious diseases of the domestic animals with which food producers began coming into daily close contact around 10,000 years ago. Eurasia harbored many domestic animal species and hence developed many such microbes, while the Americas had very few of each. Other reasons why Native American societies evolved so few lethal microbes were that villages, which provide ideal breeding grounds for epidemic diseases, arose thousands of years later in the Americas than in Eurasia; and that the three regions of the New World supporting urban societies (the Andes, Mesoamerica, and the U.S. Southeast) were never connected by fast, high-volume trade on the scale that brought plague, influenza, and possibly smallpox to Europe from Asia. As a result, even malaria and yellow fever, the infectious diseases that eventually became major obstacles to European colonization of the American tropics, and that posed the biggest barrier to the construction of the Panama Canal, are not American diseases at all but are caused by microbes of Old World tropical origin, introduced to the Americas by Europeans.

Rivaling germs as proximate factors behind Europe's conquest of the Americas were the differences in all aspects of technology. These differences stemmed ultimately from Eurasia's much longer history of densely populated, economically specialized, politically centralized, interacting and competing societies dependent on food production. Five areas of technology may be singled out:

First, metals—initially copper, then bronze, and finally iron—were used for tools in all complex Eurasian societies as of 1492. In contrast, although copper, silver, gold, and alloys were used for ornaments in the Andes and some other parts of the Americas, stone and wood and bone were still the principal materials for tools in all Native American societies, which made only limited local use of copper tools.

Second, military technology was far more potent in Eurasia than in the Americas. European weapons were steel swords, lances, and daggers, supplemented by small firearms and artillery, while body armor and helmets were also made of solid steel or else of chain mail. In place of steel, Native Americans used clubs and axes of stone or wood (occasionally copper in the Andes), slings, bows and arrows, and quilted armor, constituting much less effective protection and weaponry. In addition, Native American armies had no animals to oppose to horses, whose value for assaults and fast transport gave Europeans an overwhelming advantage until some Native American societies themselves adopted them.

Third, Eurasian societies enjoyed a huge advantage in their sources of power to operate machines. The earliest advance over human muscle power was the use of animals—cattle, horses, and donkeys—to pull plows and to turn wheels for grinding grain, raising water, and irrigating or draining fields. Waterwheels appeared in Roman times and then proliferated, along with tidal mills and windmills, in the Middle Ages. Coupled to systems of geared wheels, those engines harnessing water and wind power were used not only to grind grain and move water but also to serve myriad manufacturing purposes, including crushing sugar, driving blast furnace bellows, grinding ores, making paper, polishing stone, pressing oil, producing salt, producing textiles, and sawing wood. It is conventional to define the Industrial Revolution arbitrarily as beginning with the harnessing of steam power in 18th-century England, but in fact an industrial revolution based on water and wind power had begun already in medieval times in many parts of Europe. As of 1492, all of those operations to which animal, water, and wind power were being applied in Eurasia were still being carried out by human muscle power in the Americas.

Long before the wheel began to be used in power conversion in Eurasia, it had become the basis of most Eurasian land transport—not only for animal-drawn vehicles but also for human-powered wheelbarrows, which enabled one or more people, still using just human muscle power, to transport much greater weights than they could have otherwise. Wheels were also adopted in Eurasian pottery making and in clocks. None of those uses of the wheel was adopted in the Americas, where wheels are attested only in Mexican ceramic toys.

The remaining area of technology to be mentioned is sea transport. Many Eurasian societies developed large sailing ships, some of them capable of sailing against the wind and crossing the ocean, equipped with sextants, magnetic compasses, sternpost rudders, and cannons. In capacity, speed, maneuverability, and seaworthiness, those Eurasian ships were far superior to the rafts that carried out trade between the New World's most advanced societies, those of the Andes and Mesoamerica. Those rafts sailed with the wind along the Pacific coast. Pizarro's ship easily ran down and captured such a raft on his first voyage toward Peru.

In ADDITION TO their germs and technology, Eurasian and Native American societies differed in their political organization. By late medieval or Renaissance times, most of Eurasia had come under the rule of organized states. Among these, the Habsburg, Ottoman, and Chinese states, the Mogul state of India, and the Mongol state at its peak in the 13th century started out as large polyglot amalgamations formed by the conquest of other states. For that reason they are generally referred to as empires. Many Eurasian states and empires had official religions that contributed to state cohesion, being invoked to legitimize the political leadership and to sanction wars against other peoples. Tribal and band societies in Eurasia were largely confined to the Arctic reindeer herders, the Siberian hunter-gatherers, and the hunter-gatherer enclaves in the Indian subcontinent and tropical Southeast Asia.

The Americas had two empires, those of the Aztecs and Incas, which resembled their Eurasian counterparts in size, population, polyglot make-up, official religions, and origins in the conquest of smaller states. In the Americas those were the sole two political units capable of mobilizing resources for public works or war on the scale of many Eurasian states, whereas seven European states (Spain, Portugal, England, France, Holland, Sweden, and Denmark) had the resources to acquire American colonies between 1492 and 1666. The Americas also held many chiefdoms (some of them virtually small states) in tropical South America, Meso-america beyond Aztec rule, and the U.S. Southeast. The rest of the Americas was organized only at the tribal or band level.

The last proximate factor to be discussed is writing. Most Eurasian states had literate bureaucracies, and in some a significant fraction of the populace other than bureaucrats was also literate. Writing empowered European societies by facilitating political administration and economic exchanges, motivating and guiding exploration and conquest, and making available a range of information and human experience extending into remote places and times. In contrast, use of writing in the Americas was confined to the elite in a small area of Mesoamerica. The Inca Empire employed an accounting system and mnemonic device based on knots (termed quipu), but it could not have approached writing as a vehicle for transmitting detailed information.

THUS, EURASIAN SOCIETIES in the time of Columbus enjoyed big advantages over Native American societies in food production, germs, technology (including weapons), political organization, and writing. These were the main factors tipping the outcome of the post-Columbian colli-sions. But those differences as of A.D. 1492 represent just one snapshot of historical trajectories that had extended over at least 13,000 years in the Americas, and over a much longer time in Eurasia. For the Americas, in particular, the 1492 snapshot captures the end of the independent trajec-tory of Native Americans. Let us now trace out the earlier stages of those trajectories.

Table 18.1 summarizes approximate dates of the appearance of key developments in the main "homelands" of each hemisphere (the Fertile Crescent and China in Eurasia, the Andes and Amazonia and Mesoamerica in the Americas). It also includes the trajectory for the minor New World homeland of the eastern United States, and that for England, which is not a homeland at all but is listed to illustrate how rapidly developments spread from the Fertile Crescent.

This table is sure to horrify any knowledgeable scholar, because it reduces exceedingly complex histories to a few seemingly precise dates. In reality, all of those dates are merely attempts to label arbitrary points along a continuum. For example, more significant than the date of the first metal tool found by some archaeologist is the time when a significant fraction of all tools was made of metal, but how common must metal tools be to rate as "widespread"? Dates for the appearance of the same development may differ among different parts of the same homeland. For instance, within the Andean region pottery appears about 1,300 years earlier in coastal Ecuador (3100 B.C.) than in Peru (1800 B.C.). Some dates, such as those for the rise of chiefdoms, are more difficult to infer from the archaeological record than are dates of artifacts like pottery or metal tools. Some of the dates in Table 18.1 are very uncertain, especially those for the onset of American food production. Nevertheless, as long as one understands that the table is a simplification, it is useful for comparing continental histories.

The table suggests that food production began to provide a large fraction of human diets around 5,000 years earlier in the Eurasian homelands than in those of the Americas. A caveat must be mentioned immediately: while there is no doubt about the antiquity of food production in Eurasia, there is controversy about its onset in the Americas. In particular, archaeologists often cite considerably older claimed dates for domesticated plants at Coxcatlán Cave in Mexico, at Guitarrero Cave in Peru, and at some other American sites than the dates given in the table. Those claims are now being reevaluated for several reasons: recent direct radiocarbon dating of crop remains themselves has in some cases been yielding younger dates; the older dates previously reported were based instead on charcoal thought to be contemporaneous with the plant remains, but possibly not so; and the status of some of the older plant remains as crops or just as collected wild plants is uncertain. Still, even if plant domestication did begin earlier in the Americas than the dates shown in Table 18.1, agricul-

TABLE 18.1 **Historical Trajectories of Eurasia and the Americas**

Approximate Date of Adoption	Eurasia		
	Fertile Crescent	China	England
Plant domestication	8500 B.C.	by 7500 B.C.	3500 B.C.
Animal domestication	8000 B.C.	by 7500 B.C.	3500 B.C.
Pottery	7000 B.C.	by 7500 B.C.	3500 B.C.
Villages	9000 B.C.	by 7500 B.C.	3000 B.C.
Chiefdoms	5500 B.C.	4000 B.C.	2500 B.C.
Widespread metal tools or artifacts (copper and/or bronze)	4000 B.C.	2000 B.C.	2000 B.C.
States	3700 B.C.	2000 B.C.	500 A.D.
Writing	3200 B.C.	by 1300 B.C.	A.D. 43
Widespread iron tools	900 B.C.	500 B.C.	650 B.C.

This table gives approximate dates of widespread adoption of significant developments in three Eurasian and four Native American areas. Dates for animal domestication neglect dogs, which were domesticated earlier than food-producing animals in both Eurasia and

ture surely did not provide the basis for most human calorie intake and sedentary existence in American homelands until much later than in Eurasian homelands.

As we saw in Chapters 5 and 10, only a few relatively small areas of each hemisphere acted as a "homeland" where food production first arose and from which it then spread. Those homelands were the Fertile Crescent and China in Eurasia, and the Andes and Amazonia, Mesoamerica, and the eastern United States in the Americas. The rate of spread of key developments is especially well understood for Europe, thanks to the many archaeologists at work there. As Table 18.1 summarizes for England, once food production and village living had arrived from the Fertile Crescent after a long lag (5,000 years), the subsequent lag for England's adoption of chiefdoms, states, writing, and especially metal tools was much shorter: 2,000 years for the first widespread metal tools of copper and bronze, and only 250 years for widespread iron tools. Evidently, it was much easier for one society of already sedentary farmers to "borrow" metallurgy from

	Native America		
Andes	Amazonia	Mesoamerica	Eastern U.S.
by 3000 B.C.	3000 B.C.	by 3000 B.C.	2500 B.C.
3500 B.C.	?	500 B.C.	—
3100–1800 B.C.	6000 B.C.	1500 B.C.	2500 B.C.
3100–1800 B.C.	6000 B.C.	1500 B.C.	500 B.C.
by 1500 B.C.	A.D. 1	1500 B.C.	200 B.C.
A.D. 1000	—	—	—
A.D. 1	—	300 B.C.	—
—	—	600 B.C.	—
—	—	—	—

the Americas. Chiefdoms are inferred from archaeological evidence, such as ranked burials, architecture, and settlement patterns. The table greatly simplifies a complex mass of historical facts: see the text for some of the many important caveats.

another such society than for nomadic hunter-gatherers to "borrow" food production from sedentary farmers (or to be replaced by the farmers).

WHY WERE THE trajectories of all key developments shifted to later dates in the Americas than in Eurasia? Four groups of reasons suggest themselves: the later start, more limited suite of wild animals and plants available for domestication, greater barriers to diffusion, and possibly smaller or more isolated areas of dense human populations in the Americas than in Eurasia.

As for Eurasia's head start, humans have occupied Eurasia for about a million years, far longer than they have lived in the Americas. According to the archaeological evidence discussed in Chapter 1, humans entered the Americas at Alaska only around 12,000 B.C., spread south of the Canadian ice sheets as Clovis hunters a few centuries before 11,000 B.C., and reached the southern tip of South America by 10,000 B.C. Even if the disputed claims of older human occupation sites in the Americas prove valid, those postulated pre-Clovis inhabitants remained for unknown reasons very sparsely distributed and did not launch a Pleistocene proliferation of hunter-gatherer societies with expanding populations, technology, and art as in the Old World. Food production was already arising in the Fertile Crescent only 1,500 years after the time when Clovis-derived hunter-gatherers were just reaching southern South America.

Several possible consequences of that Eurasian head start deserve consideration. First, could it have taken a long time after 11,000 B.C. for the Americas to fill up with people? When one works out the likely numbers involved, one finds that this effect would make only a trivial contribution to the Americas' 5,000-year lag in food-producing villages. The calculations given in Chapter 1 tell us that even if a mere 100 pioneering Native Americans had crossed the Canadian border into the lower United States and increased at a rate of only 1 percent per year, they would have saturated the Americas with hunter-gatherers within 1,000 years. Spreading south at a mere one mile per month, those pioneers would have reached the southern tip of South America only 700 years after crossing the Canadian border. Those postulated rates of spread and of population increase are very low compared with actual known rates for peoples occupying previously uninhabited or sparsely inhabited lands. Hence the Americas were probably fully occupied by hunter-gatherers within a few centuries of the arrival of the first colonists.

Second, could a large part of the 5,000-year lag have represented the time that the first Americans required to become familiar with the new local plant species, animal species, and rock sources that they encountered? If we can again reason by analogy with New Guinean and Polynesian hunter-gatherers and farmers occupying previously unfamiliar environments—such as Maori colonists of New Zealand or Tudawhe colonists of New Guinea's Karimui Basin—the colonists probably discovered the best rock sources and learned to distinguish useful from poisonous wild plants and animals in much less than a century.

Third, what about Eurasians' head start in developing locally appropriate technology? The early farmers of the Fertile Crescent and China were heirs to the technology that behaviorially modern *Homo sapiens* had been developing to exploit local resources in those areas for tens of thousands of years. For instance, the stone sickles, underground storage pits, and other technology that hunter-gatherers of the Fertile Crescent had been evolving to utilize wild cereals were available to the first cereal farmers of the Fertile Crescent. In contrast, the first settlers of the Americas arrived in Alaska with equipment appropriate to the Siberian Arctic tundra. They had to invent for themselves the equipment suitable to each new habitat they encountered. That technology lag may have contributed significantly to the delay in Native American developments.

An even more obvious factor behind the delay was the wild animals and plants available for domestication. As I discussed in Chapter 6, when hunter-gatherers adopt food production, it is not because they foresee the potential benefits awaiting their remote descendants but because incipient food production begins to offer advantages over the hunter-gatherer lifestyle. Early food production was less competitive with hunting-gathering in the Americas than in the Fertile Crescent or China, partly owing to the Americas' virtual lack of domesticable wild mammals. Hence early American farmers remained dependent on wild animals for animal protein and necessarily remained part-time hunter-gatherers, whereas in both the Fertile Crescent and China animal domestication followed plant domestication very closely in time to create a food producing package that quickly won out over hunting-gathering. In addition, Eurasian domestic animals made Eurasian agriculture itself more competitive by providing fertilizer, and eventually by drawing plows.

Features of American wild plants also contributed to the lesser competitiveness of Native American food production. That conclusion is clearest for the eastern United States, where less than a dozen crops were domesticated, including small-seeded grains but no large-seeded grains, pulses, fiber crops, or cultivated fruit or nut trees. It is also clear for Mesoamerica's staple grain of corn, which spread to become a dominant crop elsewhere in the Americas as well. Whereas the Fertile Crescent's wild wheat and barley evolved into crops with minimal changes and within a few centuries, wild teosinte may have required several thousand years to evolve into corn, having to undergo drastic changes in its reproductive biology and energy allocation to seed production, loss of the seed's rock-hard casings, and an enormous increase in cob size.

As a result, even if one accepts the recently postulated later dates for the onset of Native American plant domestication, about 1,500 or 2,000 years would have elapsed between that onset (about 3000–2500 B.C.) and widespread year-round villages (1800–500 B.C.) in Mesoamerica, the inland Andes, and the eastern United States. Native American farming served for a long time just as a small supplement to food acquisition by hunting-gathering, and supported only a sparse population. If one accepts the traditional, earlier dates for the onset of American plant domestication, then 5,000 years instead of 1,500 or 2,000 years elapsed before food production supported villages. In contrast, villages were closely associated in time with the rise of food production in much of Eurasia. (The hunter-gatherer lifestyle itself was sufficiently productive to support villages even before the adoption of agriculture in parts of both hemispheres, such as Japan and the Fertile Crescent in the Old World, and coastal Ecuador and Amazonia in the New World.) The limitations imposed by locally available domesticates in the New World are well illustrated by the transformations of Native American societies themselves when other crops or animals arrived, whether from elsewhere in the Americas or from Eurasia. Examples include the effects of corn's arrival in the eastern United States and Amazonia, the llama's adoption in the northern Andes after its domestication to the south, and the horse's appearance in many parts of North and South America.

In addition to Eurasia's head start and wild animal and plant species, developments in Eurasia were also accelerated by the easier diffusion of animals, plants, ideas, technology, and people in Eurasia than in the Americas, as a result of several sets of geographic and ecological factors. Eurasia's east–west major axis, unlike the Americas' north–south major axis, permitted diffusion without change in latitude and associated environmental variables. In contrast to Eurasia's consistent east–west breadth, the New World was constricted over the whole length of Central America and especially at Panama. Not least, the Americas were more fragmented by areas unsuitable for food production or for dense human populations. These ecological barriers included the rain forests of the Panamanian isthmus separating Mesoamerican societies from Andean and Amazonian societies; the deserts of northern Mexico separating Mesoamerica from U.S. southwestern and southeastern societies; dry areas of Texas separating the U.S. Southwest from the Southeast; and the deserts and high mountains fencing off U.S. Pacific coast areas that would otherwise have been suitable for food production. As a result, there was no diffusion of domestic animals, writing, or political entities, and limited or slow diffusion of crops and technology, between the New World centers of Mesoamerica, the eastern United States, and the Andes and Amazonia.

Some specific consequences of these barriers within the Americas deserve mention. Food production never diffused from the U.S. Southwest and Mississippi Valley to the modern American breadbaskets of California and Oregon, where Native American societies remained hunter-gatherers merely because they lacked appropriate domesticates. The llama, guinea pig, and potato of the Andean highlands never reached the Mexican highlands, so Mesoamerica and North America remained without domestic mammals except for dogs. Conversely, the domestic sunflower of the eastern United States never reached Mesoamerica, and the domestic turkey of Mesoamerica never made it to South America or the eastern United States. Mesoamerican corn and beans took 3,000 and 4,000 years, respectively, to cover the 700 miles from Mexico's farmlands to the eastern U.S. farmlands. After corn's arrival in the eastern United States, seven centuries more passed before the development of a corn variety productive in North American climates triggered the Mississippian emergence. Corn, beans, and squash may have taken several thousand years to spread from Mesoamerica to the U.S. Southwest. While Fertile Crescent crops spread west and east sufficiently fast to preempt independent domestication of the same species or else domestication of closely related species elsewhere, the barriers within the Americas gave rise to many such parallel domestications of crops.

As striking as these effects of barriers on crop and livestock diffusion are the effects on other features of human societies. Alphabets of ultimately eastern Mediterranean origin spread throughout all complex societies of Eurasia, from England to Indonesia, except for areas of East Asia where derivatives of the Chinese writing system took hold. In contrast, the New World's sole writing systems, those of Mesoamerica, never spread to the complex Andean and eastern U.S. societies that might have adopted them. The wheels invented in Mesoamerica as parts of toys never met the llamas domesticated in the Andes, to generate wheeled transport for the New World. From east to west in the Old World, the Macedonian Empire and the Roman Empire both spanned 3,000 miles, the Mongol Empire 6,000 miles. But the empires and states of Mesoamerica had no political relations with, and apparently never even heard of, the chiefdoms of the eastern United States 700 miles to the north or the empires and states of the Andes 1,200 miles to the south.

The greater geographic fragmentation of the Americas compared with Eurasia is also reflected in distributions of languages. Linguists agree in grouping all but a few Eurasian languages into about a dozen language families, each consisting of up to several hundred related languages. For example, the Indo-European language family, which includes English as well as French, Russian, Greek, and Hindi, comprises about 144 languages. Quite a few of those families occupy large contiguous areas—in the case of Indo-European, the area encompassing most of Europe east through much of western Asia to India. Linguistic, historical, and archaeological evidence combines to make clear that each of these large, contiguous distributions stems from a historical expansion of an ancestral language, followed by subsequent local linguistic differentiation to form a family of related languages (Table 18.2). Most such expansions appear to be attributable to the advantages that speakers of the ancestral language, belonging to food-producing societies, held over hunter-gatherers. We already discussed such historical expansions in Chapters 16 and 17 for the Sino-Tibetan, Austronesian, and other East Asian language families. Among major expansions of the last millennium are those that carried Indo-European languages from Europe to the Americas and Australia, the Russian language from eastern Europe across Siberia, and Turkish (a language of the Altaic family) from Central Asia westward to Turkey.

With the exception of the Eskimo-Aleut language family of the American Arctic and the Na-Dene language family of Alaska, northwestern Canada, and the U.S. Southwest, the Americas lack examples of large-scale language expansions widely accepted by linguists. Most linguists specializing in Native American languages do not discern large, clear-cut groupings other than Eskimo-Aleut and Na-Dene. At most, they consider the evidence sufficient only to group other Native American languages (variously estimated to number from 600 to 2,000) into a hundred or more language groups or isolated languages. A controversial minority view is that of the linguist Joseph Greenberg, who groups all Native American languages other than Eskimo-Aleut and Na-Dene languages into a single large family, termed Amerind, with about a dozen subfamilies.

Some of Greenberg's subfamilies, and some groupings recognized by more-traditional linguists, may turn out to be legacies of New World population expansions driven in part by food production. These legacies may include the Uto-Aztecan languages of Mesoamerica and the western United States, the Oto-Manguean languages of Mesoamerica, the Natchez-Muskogean languages of the U.S. Southeast, and the Arawak languages of the West Indies. But the difficulties that linguists have in agreeing

TABLE 18.2 **Language Expansions in the Old World**

Inferred Date	Language Family or Language	Expansion	Ultimate Driving Force
6000 or 4000 B.C.	Indo-European	Ukraine or Anatolia →Europe, C. Asia, India	food production or horse-based pastoralism
6000 B.C.–2000 B.C.	Elamo-Dravidian	Iran →India	food production
4000 B.C.–present	Sino-Tibetan	Tibetan Plateau, N. China → S. China, tropical S.E. Asia	food production
3000 B.C.–1000 B.C.	Austronesian	S. China →Indonesia, Pacific islands	food production
3000 B.C.–A.D. 1000	Bantu	Nigeria and Cameroon →S. Africa	food production
3000 B.C.–A.D. 1	Austroasiatic	S. China →tropical S.E. Asia, India	food production
1000 B.C.–A.D. 1500	Tai-Kadai, Miao-Yao	S. China →tropical S.E. Asia	food production
A.D. 892	Hungarian	Ural Mts. → Hungary	horse-based pastoralism
A.D. 1000–A.D. 1300	Altaic (Mongol, Turkish)	Asian steppes →Europe, Turkey, China, India	horse-based pastoralism
A.D. 1480–A.D. 1638	Russian	European Russia →Asiatic Siberia	food production

on groupings of Native American languages reflect the difficulties that complex Native American societies themselves faced in expanding within the New World. Had any food-producing Native American peoples succeeded in spreading far with their crops and livestock and rapidly replacing hunter-gatherers over a large area, they would have left legacies of easily recognized language families, as in Eurasia, and the relationships of Native American languages would not be so controversial.

Thus, we have identified three sets of ultimate factors that tipped the advantage to European invaders of the Americas: Eurasia's long head start on human settlement; its more effective food production, resulting from greater availability of domesticable wild plants and especially of animals; and its less formidable geographic and ecological barriers to intracontinental diffusion. A fourth, more speculative ultimate factor is suggested by some puzzling non-inventions in the Americas: the non-inventions of writing and wheels in complex Andean societies, despite a time depth of those societies approximately equal to that of complex Mesoamerican societies that did make those inventions; and wheels' confinement to toys and their eventual disappearance in Mesoamerica, where they could presumably have been useful in human-powered wheelbarrows, as in China. These puzzles remind one of equally puzzling non-inventions, or else disappearances of inventions, in small isolated societies, including Aboriginal Tasmania, Aboriginal Australia, Japan, Polynesian islands, and the American Arctic. Of course, the Americas in aggregate are anything but small: their combined area is fully 76 percent that of Eurasia, and their human population as of A.D. 1492 was probably also a large fraction of Eurasia's. But the Americas, as we have seen, are broken up into "islands" of societies with tenuous connections to each other. Perhaps the histories of Native American wheels and writing exemplify the principles illustrated in a more extreme form by true island societies.

AFTER AT LEAST 13,000 years of separate developments, advanced American and Eurasian societies finally collided within the last thousand years. Until then, the sole contacts between human societies of the Old and the New Worlds had involved the hunter-gatherers on opposite sides of the Bering Strait.

There were no Native American attempts to colonize Eurasia, except at the Bering Strait, where a small population of Inuit (Eskimos) derived from

Alaska established itself across the strait on the opposite Siberian coast. The first documented Eurasian attempt to colonize the Americas was by the Norse at Arctic and sub-Arctic latitudes (Figure 18.1). Norse from Norway colonized Iceland in A.D. 874, then Norse from Iceland colonized Greenland in A.D. 986, and finally Norse from Greenland repeatedly visited the northeastern coast of North America between about A.D. 1000 and 1350. The sole Norse archaeological site discovered in the Americas is on Newfoundland, possibly the region described as Vinland in Norse sagas, but these also mention landings evidently farther north, on the coasts of Labrador and Baffin Island.

Iceland's climate permitted herding and extremely limited agriculture, and its area was sufficient to support a Norse-derived population that has persisted to this day. But most of Greenland is covered by an ice cap, and even the two most favorable coastal fjords were marginal for Norse food production. The Greenland Norse population never exceeded a few thousand. It remained dependent on imports of food and iron from Norway, and of timber from the Labrador coast. Unlike Easter Island and other

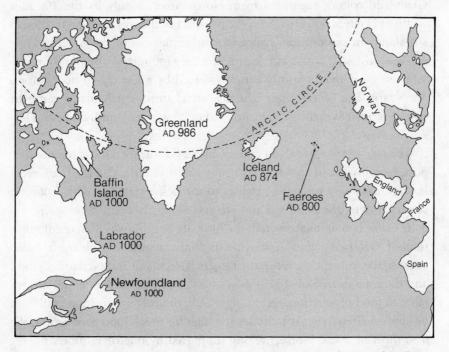

Figure 18.1. The Norse expansion from Norway across the North Atlantic, with dates or approximate dates when each area was reached.

remote Polynesian islands, Greenland could not support a self-sufficient food-producing society, though it did support self-sufficient Inuit hunter-gatherer populations before, during, and after the Norse occupation period. The populations of Iceland and Norway themselves were too small and too poor for them to continue their support of the Greenland Norse population.

In the Little Ice Age that began in the 13th century, the cooling of the North Atlantic made food production in Greenland, and Norse voyaging to Greenland from Norway or Iceland, even more marginal than before. The Greenlanders' last known contact with Europeans came in 1410 with an Icelandic ship that arrived after being blown off course. When Europeans finally began again to visit Greenland in 1577, its Norse colony no longer existed, having evidently disappeared without any record during the 15th century.

But the coast of North America lay effectively beyond the reach of ships sailing directly from Norway itself, given Norse ship technology of the period A.D. 986–1410. The Norse visits were instead launched from the Greenland colony, separated from North America only by the 200-mile width of Davis Strait. However, the prospect of that tiny marginal colony's sustaining an exploration, conquest, and settlement of the Americas was nil. Even the sole Norse site located on Newfoundland apparently represents no more than a winter camp occupied by a few dozen people for a few years. The Norse sagas describe attacks on their Vinland camp by people termed Skraelings, evidently either Newfoundland Indians or Dorset Eskimos.

The fate of the Greenland colony, medieval Europe's most remote outpost, remains one of archaeology's romantic mysteries. Did the last Greenland Norse starve to death, attempt to sail off, intermarry with Eskimos, or succumb to disease or Eskimo arrows? While those questions of proximate cause remain unanswered, the ultimate reasons why Norse colonization of Greenland and America failed are abundantly clear. It failed because the source (Norway), the targets (Greenland and Newfoundland), and the time (A.D. 984–1410) guaranteed that Europe's potential advantages of food production, technology, and political organization could not be applied effectively. At latitudes too high for much food production, the iron tools of a few Norse, weakly supported by one of Europe's poorer states, were no match for the stone, bone, and wooden tools of Eskimo and Indian hunter-gatherers, the world's greatest masters of Arctic survival skills.

THE SECOND EURASIAN attempt to colonize the Americas succeeded because it involved a source, target, latitude, and time that allowed Europe's potential advantages to be exerted effectively. Spain, unlike Norway, was rich and populous enough to support exploration and subsidize colonies. Spanish landfalls in the Americas were at subtropical latitudes highly suitable for food production, based at first mostly on Native American crops but also on Eurasian domestic animals, especially cattle and horses. Spain's transatlantic colonial enterprise began in 1492, at the end of a century of rapid development of European oceangoing ship technology, which by then incorporated advances in navigation, sails, and ship design developed by Old World societies (Islam, India, China, and Indonesia) in the Indian Ocean. As a result, ships built and manned in Spain itself were able to sail to the West Indies; there was nothing equivalent to the Greenland bottleneck that had throttled Norse colonization. Spain's New World colonies were soon joined by those of half a dozen other European states.

The first European settlements in the Americas, beginning with the one founded by Columbus in 1492, were in the West Indies. The island Indians, whose estimated population at the time of their "discovery" exceeded a million, were rapidly exterminated on most islands by disease, dispossession, enslavement, warfare, and casual murder. Around 1508 the first colony was founded on the American mainland, at the Isthmus of Panama. Conquest of the two large mainland empires, those of the Aztecs and Incas, followed in 1519–1520 and 1532–1533, respectively. In both conquests European-transmitted epidemics (probably smallpox) made major contributions, by killing the emperors themselves, as well as a large fraction of the population. The overwhelming military superiority of even tiny numbers of mounted Spaniards, together with their political skills at exploiting divisions within the native population, did the rest. European conquest of the remaining native states of Central America and northern South America followed during the 16th and 17th centuries.

As for the most advanced native societies of North America, those of the U.S. Southeast and the Mississippi River system, their destruction was accomplished largely by germs alone, introduced by early European explorers and advancing ahead of them. As Europeans spread throughout the Americas, many other native societies, such as the Mandans of the Great Plains and the Sadlermiut Eskimos of the Arctic, were also wiped out by disease, without need for military action. Populous native societies not thereby eliminated were destroyed in the same way the Aztecs and Incas had been—by full-scale wars, increasingly waged by professional European soldiers and their native allies. Those soldiers were backed by the political organizations initially of the European mother countries, then of the European colonial governments in the New World, and finally of the independent neo-European states that succeeded the colonial governments.

Smaller native societies were destroyed more casually, by small-scale raids and murders carried out by private citizens. For instance, California's native hunter-gatherers initially numbered about 200,000 in aggregate, but they were splintered among a hundred tribelets, none of which required a war to be defeated. Most of those tribelets were killed off or dispossessed during or soon after the California gold rush of 1848–52, when large numbers of immigrants flooded the state. As one example, the Yahi tribelet of northern California, numbering about 2,000 and lacking firearms, was destroyed in four raids by armed white settlers: a dawn raid on a Yahi village carried out by 17 settlers on August 6, 1865; a massacre of Yahis surprised in a ravine in 1866; a massacre of 33 Yahis tracked to a cave around 1867; and a final massacre of about 30 Yahis trapped in another cave by 4 cowboys around 1868. Many Amazonian Indian groups were similarly eliminated by private settlers during the rubber boom of the late 19th and early 20th centuries. The final stages of the conquest are being played out in the present decade, as the Yanomamo and other Amazonian Indian societies that remain independent are succumbing to disease, being murdered by miners, or being brought under control by missionaries or government agencies.

The end result has been the elimination of populous Native American societies from most temperate areas suitable for European food production and physiology. In North America those that survived as sizable intact communities now live mostly on reservations or other lands considered undesirable for European food production and mining, such as the Arctic and arid areas of the U.S. West. Native Americans in many tropical areas have been replaced by immigrants from the Old World tropics (especially black Africans, along with Asian Indians and Javanese in Suriname).

In parts of Central America and the Andes, the Native Americans were originally so numerous that, even after epidemics and wars, much of the population today remains Native American or mixed. That is especially true at high altitudes in the Andes, where genetically European women have physiological difficulties even in reproducing, and where native Andean crops still offer the most suitable basis for food production. However, even where Native Americans do survive, there has been extensive replacement of their culture and languages with those of the Old World. Of the hundreds of Native American languages originally spoken in North America, all except 187 are no longer spoken at all, and 149 of these last 187 are moribund in the sense that they are being spoken only by old people and no longer learned by children. Of the approximately 40 New World nations, all now have an Indo-European language or creole as the official language. Even in the countries with the largest surviving Native American populations, such as Peru, Bolivia, Mexico, and Guatemala, a glance at photographs of political and business leaders shows that they are disproportionately Europeans, while several Caribbean nations have black African leaders and Guyana has had Asian Indian leaders.

The original Native American population has been reduced by a debated large percentage: estimates for North America range up to 95 percent. But the total human population of the Americas is now approximately ten times what it was in 1492, because of arrivals of Old World peoples (Europeans, Africans, and Asians). The Americas' population now consists of a mixture of peoples originating from all continents except Australia. That demographic shift of the last 500 years—the most massive shift on any continent except Australia—has its ultimate roots in developments between about 11,000 B.C. and A.D. 1.

CHAPTER 19

HOW AFRICA BECAME
BLACK

N O MATTER HOW MUCH ONE HAS READ ABOUT AFRICA beforehand, one's first impressions from actually being there are overwhelming. On the streets of Windhoek, capital of newly independent Namibia, I saw black Herero people, black Ovambos, whites, and Namas, different again from both blacks and whites. They were no longer mere pictures in a textbook, but living humans in front of me. Outside Windhoek, the last of the formerly widespread Kalahari Bushmen were struggling for survival. But what most surprised me in Namibia was a street sign: one of downtown Windhoek's main roads was called Goering Street!

Surely, I thought, no country could be so dominated by unrepentant Nazis as to name a street after the notorious Nazi *Reichskommissar* and founder of the Luftwaffe, Hermann Goering! No, it turned out that the street instead commemorated Hermann's father, Heinrich Goering, founding *Reichskommissar* of the former German colony of South-West Africa, which became Namibia. But Heinrich was also a problematic figure, for his legacy included one of the most vicious attacks by European colonists on Africans, Germany's 1904 war of extermination against the Hereros. Today, while events in neighboring South Africa command more of the world's attention, Namibia as well is struggling to deal with its colonial past and establish a multiracial society. Namibia illustrated for me how inseparable Africa's past is from its present.

Most Americans and many Europeans equate native Africans with blacks, white Africans with recent intruders, and African racial history with the story of European colonialism and slave trading. There is an obvious reason why we focus on those particular facts: blacks are the sole native Africans familiar to most Americans, because they were brought in large numbers as slaves to the United States. But very different peoples may have occupied much of modern black Africa until as recently as a few thousand years ago, and so-called African blacks themselves are heterogeneous. Even before the arrival of white colonialists, Africa already harbored not just blacks but (as we shall see) five of the world's six major divisions of humanity, and three of them are confined as natives to Africa. One-quarter of the world's languages are spoken only in Africa. No other continent approaches this human diversity.

Africa's diverse peoples resulted from its diverse geography and its long prehistory. Africa is the only continent to extend from the northern to the southern temperate zone, while also encompassing some of the world's driest deserts, largest tropical rain forests, and highest equatorial mountains. Humans have lived in Africa far longer than anywhere else: our remote ancestors originated there around 7 million years ago, and anatomically modern *Homo sapiens* may have arisen there since then. The long interactions between Africa's many peoples generated its fascinating prehistory, including two of the most dramatic population movements of the past 5,000 years—the Bantu expansion and the Indonesian colonization of Madagascar. All of those past interactions continue to have heavy consequences, because the details of who arrived where before whom are shaping Africa today.

How *did* those five divisions of humanity get to be where they are now in Africa? Why were blacks the ones who came to be so widespread, rather than the four other groups whose existence Americans tend to forget? How can we ever hope to wrest the answers to those questions from Africa's preliterate past, lacking the written evidence that teaches us about the spread of the Roman Empire? African prehistory is a puzzle on a grand scale, still only partly solved. As it turns out, the story has some little-appreciated but striking parallels with the American prehistory that we encountered in the preceding chapter.

THE FIVE MAJOR human groups to which Africa was already home by A.D. 1000 are those loosely referred to by laypeople as blacks, whites, African Pygmies, Khoisan, and Asians. Figure 19.1 depicts their distributions, while the portraits following page 288 will remind you of their striking differences in skin color, hair form and color, and facial features. Blacks were formerly confined to Africa, Pygmies and Khoisan still live only there, while many more whites and Asians live outside Africa than in it. These five groups constitute or represent all the major divisions of humanity except for Aboriginal Australians and their relatives.

Many readers may already be protesting: don't stereotype people by classifying them into arbitrary "races"! Yes, I acknowledge that each of these so-called major groups is very diverse. To lump people as different as Zulus, Somalis, and Ibos under the single heading of "blacks" ignores the differences between them. We ignore equally big differences when we lump Africa's Egyptians and Berbers with each other and with Europe's Swedes under the single heading of "whites." In addition, the divisions between blacks, whites, and the other major groups are arbitrary, because each such group shades into others: all human groups on Earth have mated with humans of every other group that they encountered. Nevertheless, as we'll see, recognizing these major groups is still so useful for understanding history that I'll use the group names as shorthand, without repeating the above caveats in every sentence.

Of the five African groups, representatives of many populations of blacks and whites are familiar to Americans and Europeans and need no physical description. Blacks occupied the largest area of Africa even as of A.D. 1400: the southern Sahara and most of sub-Saharan Africa (see Figure 19.1). While American blacks of African descent originated mainly from Africa's west coastal zone, similar peoples traditionally occupied East Africa as well, north to the Sudan and south to the southeast coast of South Africa itself. Whites, ranging from Egyptians and Libyans to Moroccans, occupied Africa's north coastal zone and the northern Sahara. Those North Africans would hardly be confused with blue-eyed blond-haired Swedes, but most laypeople would still call them "whites" because they have lighter skin and straighter hair than peoples to the south termed "blacks." Most of Africa's blacks and whites depended on farming or herding, or both, for their living.

In contrast, the next two groups, the Pygmies and Khoisan, include

Peoples of Africa (as of AD 1400)

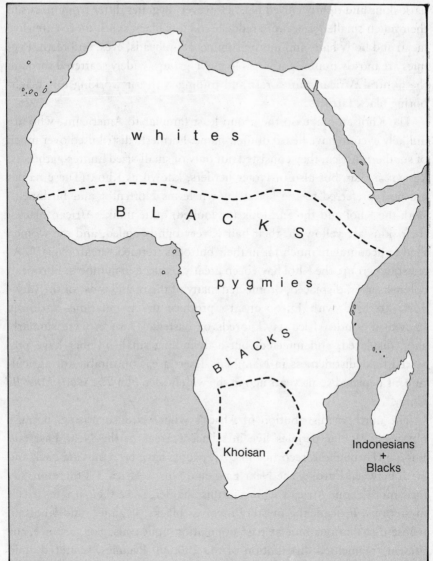

Figure 19.1. See the text for caveats about describing distributions of African peoples in terms of these familiar but problematical groupings.

hunter-gatherers without crops or livestock. Like blacks, Pygmies have dark skins and tightly curled hair. However, Pygmies differ from blacks in their much smaller size, more reddish and less black skins, more extensive facial and body hair, and more prominent foreheads, eyes, and teeth. Pygmies are mostly hunter-gatherers living in groups widely scattered through the Central African rain forest and trading with (or working for) neighboring black farmers.

The Khoisan make up the group least familiar to Americans, who are unlikely even to have heard of their name. Formerly distributed over much of southern Africa, they consisted not only of small-sized hunter-gatherers, known as San, but also of larger herders, known as Khoi. (These names are now preferred to the better-known terms Hottentot and Bushmen.) Both the Khoi and the San look (or looked) quite unlike African blacks: their skins are yellowish, their hair is very tightly coiled, and the women tend to accumulate much fat in their buttocks (termed "steatopygia"). As a distinct group, the Khoi have been greatly reduced in numbers: European colonists shot, displaced, or infected many of them, and most of the survivors interbred with Europeans to produce the populations variously known in South Africa as Coloreds or Basters. The San were similarly shot, displaced, and infected, but a dwindling small number have preserved their distinctness in Namibian desert areas unsuitable for agriculture, as depicted some years ago in the widely seen film *The Gods Must Be Crazy.*

The northern distribution of Africa's whites is unsurprising, because physically similar peoples live in adjacent areas of the Near East and Europe. Throughout recorded history, people have been moving back and forth between Europe, the Near East, and North Africa. I'll therefore say little more about Africa's whites in this chapter, since their origins aren't mysterious. Instead, the mystery involves blacks, Pygmies, and Khoisan, whose distributions hint at past population upheavals. For instance, the present fragmented distribution of the 200,000 Pygmies, scattered amid 120 million blacks, suggests that Pygmy hunters were formerly widespread through the equatorial forests until displaced and isolated by the arrival of black farmers. The Khoisan area of southern Africa is surprisingly small for a people so distinct in anatomy and language. Could the Khoisan, too, have been originally more widespread until their more northerly populations were somehow eliminated?

I've saved the biggest anomaly for last. The large island of Madagascar lies only 250 miles off the East African coast, much closer to Africa than to any other continent, and separated by the whole expanse of the Indian Ocean from Asia and Australia. Madagascar's people prove to be a mixture of two elements. Not surprisingly, one element is African blacks, but the other consists of people instantly recognizable, from their appearance, as tropical Southeast Asians. Specifically, the language spoken by all the people of Madagascar—Asians, blacks, and mixed—is Austronesian and very similar to the Ma'anyan language spoken on the Indonesian island of Borneo, over 4,000 miles across the open Indian Ocean from Madagascar. No other people remotely resembling Borneans live within thousands of miles of Madagascar.

These Austronesians, with their Austronesian language and modified Austronesian culture, were already established on Madagascar by the time it was first visited by Europeans, in 1500. This strikes me as the single most astonishing fact of human geography for the entire world. It's as if Columbus, on reaching Cuba, had found it occupied by blue-eyed, blond-haired Scandinavians speaking a language close to Swedish, even though the nearby North American continent was inhabited by Native Americans speaking Amerindian languages. How on earth could prehistoric people of Borneo, presumably voyaging in boats without maps or compasses, end up in Madagascar?

THE CASE OF Madagascar tells us that peoples' languages, as well as their physical appearance, can yield important clues to their origins. Just by looking at the people of Madagascar, we'd have known that some of them came from tropical Southeast Asia, but we wouldn't have known from which area of tropical Southeast Asia, and we'd never have guessed Borneo. What else can we learn from African languages that we didn't already know from African faces?

The mind-boggling complexities of Africa's 1,500 languages were clarified by Stanford University's great linguist Joseph Greenberg, who recognized that all those languages fall into just five families (see Figure 19.2 for their distribution). Readers accustomed to thinking of linguistics as dull and technical may be surprised to learn what fascinating contributions Figure 19.2 makes to our understanding of African history.

If we begin by comparing Figure 19.2 with Figure 19.1, we'll see a rough correspondence between language families and anatomically

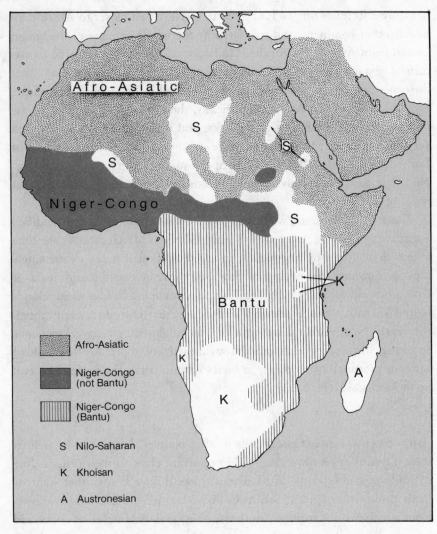

Figure 19.2. Language families of Africa.

defined human groups: languages of a given language family tend to be spoken by distinct people. In particular, Afroasiatic speakers mostly prove to be people who would be classified as whites or blacks, Nilo-Saharan and Niger-Congo speakers prove to be blacks, Khoisan speakers Khoisan, and Austronesian speakers Indonesian. This suggests that languages have tended to evolve along with the people who speak them.

Concealed at the top of Figure 19.2 is our first surprise, a big shock for Eurocentric believers in the superiority of so-called Western civilization. We're taught that Western civilization originated in the Near East, was brought to brilliant heights in Europe by the Greeks and Romans, and produced three of the world's great religions: Christianity, Judaism, and Islam. Those religions arose among peoples speaking three closely related languages, termed Semitic languages: Aramaic (the language of Christ and the Apostles), Hebrew, and Arabic, respectively. We instinctively associate Semitic peoples with the Near East.

However, Greenberg determined that Semitic languages really form only one of six or more branches of a much larger language family, Afroasiatic, all of whose other branches (and other 222 surviving languages) are confined to Africa. Even the Semitic subfamily itself is mainly African, 12 of its 19 surviving languages being confined to Ethiopia. This suggests that Afroasiatic languages arose in Africa, and that only one branch of them spread to the Near East. Hence it may have been Africa that gave birth to the languages spoken by the authors of the Old and New Testaments and the Koran, the moral pillars of Western civilization.

The next surprise in Figure 19.2 is a seeming detail on which I didn't comment when I just told you that distinct peoples tend to have distinct languages. Among Africa's five groups of people—blacks, whites, Pygmies, Khoisan, and Indonesians—only the Pygmies lack any distinct languages: each band of Pygmies speaks the same language as the neighboring group of black farmers. However, if one compares a given language as spoken by Pygmies with the same language as spoken by blacks, the Pygmy version seems to contain some unique words with distinctive sounds.

Originally, of course, people as distinctive as the Pygmies, living in a place as distinctive as the equatorial African rain forest, were surely isolated enough to develop their own language family. However, today those languages are gone, and we already saw from Figure 19.1 that the Pygmies' modern distribution is highly fragmented. Thus, distributional and linguistic clues combine to suggest that the Pygmy homeland was engulfed by invading black farmers, whose languages the remaining Pygmies adopted, leaving only traces of their original languages in some words and sounds. We saw previously that much the same is true of the Malaysian Negritos (Semang) and Philippine Negritos, who adopted Austroasiatic and Austronesian languages, respectively, from the farmers who came to surround them.

The fragmented distribution of Nilo-Saharan languages in Figure 19.2 similarly implies that many speakers of those languages have been engulfed by speakers of Afroasiatic or Niger-Congo languages. But the distribution of Khoisan languages testifies to an even more dramatic engulfing. Those languages are famously unique in the whole world in their use of clicks as consonants. (If you've been puzzled by the name !Kung Bushman, the exclamation mark is not an expression of premature astonishment; it's just how linguists denote a click.) All existing Khoisan languages are confined to southern Africa, with two exceptions. Those exceptions are two very distinctive, click-laden Khoisan languages named Hadza and Sandawe, stranded in Tanzania more than 1,000 miles from the nearest Khoisan languages of southern Africa.

In addition, Xhosa and a few other Niger-Congo languages of southern Africa are full of clicks. Even more unexpectedly, clicks or Khoisan words also appear in two Afroasiatic languages spoken by blacks in Kenya, stranded still farther from present Khoisan peoples than are the Hadza and Sandawe peoples of Tanzania. All this suggests that Khoisan languages and peoples formerly extended far north of their present southern African distribution, until they too, like the Pygmies, were engulfed by the blacks, leaving only linguistic legacies of their former presence. That's a unique contribution of the linguistic evidence, something we could hardly have guessed just from physical studies of living people.

I have saved the most remarkable contribution of linguistics for last. If you look again at Figure 19.2, you'll see that the Niger-Congo language family is distributed all over West Africa and most of subequatorial Africa, apparently giving no clue as to where within that enormous range the family originated. However, Greenberg recognized that all Niger-Congo languages of subequatorial Africa belong to a single language subgroup termed Bantu. That subgroup accounts for nearly half of the 1,032 Niger-Congo languages and for more than half (nearly 200 million) of the Niger-Congo speakers. But all those 500 Bantu languages are so similar to each other that they have been facetiously described as 500 dialects of a single language.

Collectively, the Bantu languages constitute only a single, low-order subfamily of the Niger-Congo language family. Most of the 176 other subfamilies are crammed into West Africa, a small fraction of the entire Niger-Congo range. In particular, the most distinctive Bantu languages, and the non-Bantu Niger-Congo languages most closely related to Bantu languages, are packed into a tiny area of Cameroon and adjacent eastern Nigeria.

Evidently, the Niger-Congo language family arose in West Africa; the Bantu branch of it arose at the east end of that range, in Cameroon and Nigeria; and the Bantu then spread out of that homeland over most of subequatorial Africa. That spread must have begun long ago enough that the ancestral Bantu language had time to split into 500 daughter languages, but nevertheless recently enough that all those daughter languages are still very similar to each other. Since all other Niger-Congo speakers, as well as the Bantu, are blacks, we couldn't have inferred who migrated in which direction just from the evidence of physical anthropology.

To make this type of linguistic reasoning clear, let me give you a familiar example: the geographic origins of the English language. Today, by far the largest number of people whose first language is English live in North America, with others scattered over the globe in Britain, Australia, and other countries. Each of those countries has its own dialects of English. If we knew nothing else about language distributions and history, we might have guessed that the English language arose in North America and was carried overseas to Britain and Australia by colonists.

But all those English dialects form only one low-order subgroup of the Germanic language family. All the other subgroups—the various Scandinavian, German, and Dutch languages—are crammed into northwestern Europe. In particular, Frisian, the other Germanic language most closely related to English, is confined to a tiny coastal area of Holland and western Germany. Hence a linguist would immediately deduce correctly that the English language arose in coastal northwestern Europe and spread around the world from there. In fact, we know from recorded history that English really was carried from there to England by invading Anglo-Saxons in the fifth and sixth centuries A.D.

Essentially the same line of reasoning tells us that the nearly 200 million Bantu people, now flung over much of the map of Africa, arose from Cameroon and Nigeria. Along with the North African origins of Semites and the origins of Madagascar's Asians, that's another conclusion that we couldn't have reached without linguistic evidence.

We had already deduced, from Khoisan language distributions and the lack of distinct Pygmy languages, that Pygmies and Khoisan peoples had formerly ranged more widely, until they were engulfed by blacks. (I'm using "engulfing" as a neutral all-embracing word, regardless of whether the process involved conquest, expulsion, interbreeding, killing, or epidemics.) We've now seen, from Niger-Congo language distributions, that the blacks who did the engulfing were the Bantu. The physical and linguistic evidence considered so far has let us infer these prehistoric engulfings, but it still hasn't solved their mysteries for us. Only the further evidence that I'll now present can help us answer two more questions: What advantages enabled the Bantu to displace the Pygmies and Khoisan? When did the Bantu reach the former Pygmy and Khoisan homelands?

To APPROACH THE question about the Bantu's advantages, let's examine the remaining type of evidence from the living present—the evidence derived from domesticated plants and animals. As we saw in previous chapters, that evidence is important because food production led to high population densities, germs, technology, political organization, and other ingredients of power. Peoples who, by accident of their geographic location, inherited or developed food production thereby became able to engulf geographically less endowed people.

When Europeans reached sub-Saharan Africa in the 1400s, Africans were growing five sets of crops (Figure 19.3), each of them laden with significance for African history. The first set was grown only in North Africa, extending to the highlands of Ethiopia. North Africa enjoys a Mediterranean climate, characterized by rainfall concentrated in the winter months. (Southern California also experiences a Mediterranean climate, explaining why my basement and that of millions of other southern Californians often gets flooded in the winter but infallibly dries out in the summer.) The Fertile Crescent, where agriculture arose, enjoys that same Mediterranean pattern of winter rains.

Hence North Africa's original crops all prove to be ones adapted to germinating and growing with winter rains, and known from archaeological evidence to have been first domesticated in the Fertile Crescent beginning around 10,000 years ago. Those Fertile Crescent crops spread into climatically similar adjacent areas of North Africa and laid the foundations for the rise of ancient Egyptian civilization. They include such familiar crops as wheat, barley, peas, beans, and grapes. These are familiar to us precisely because they also spread into climatically similar adjacent areas of Europe, thence to America and Australia, and became some of the staple crops of temperate-zone agriculture around the world.

Origins of African crops, with examples

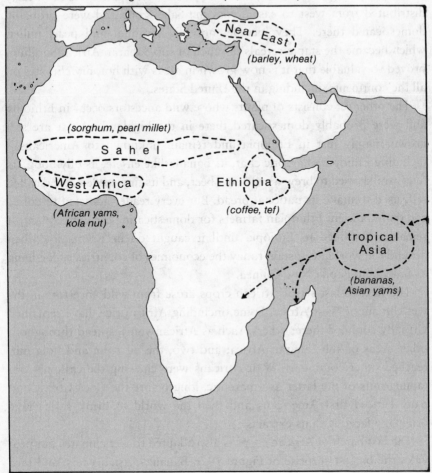

Figure 19.3. The areas of origin of crops grown traditionally in Africa (that is, before the arrival of crops carried by colonizing Europeans), with examples of two crops from each area.

As one travels south in Africa across the Saharan desert and reencounters rain in the Sahel zone just south of the desert, one notices that Sahel rains fall in the summer rather than in the winter. Even if Fertile Crescent crops adapted to winter rain could somehow have crossed the Sahara, they would have been difficult to grow in the summer-rain Sahel zone. Instead, we find two sets of African crops whose wild ancestors occur just south of the Sahara, and which are adapted to summer rains and less seasonal variation in day length. One set consists of plants whose ancestors are widely distributed from west to east across the Sahel zone and were probably domesticated there. They include, notably, sorghum and pearl millet, which became the staple cereals of much of sub-Saharan Africa. Sorghum proved so valuable that it is now grown in areas with hot, dry climates on all the continents, including in the United States.

The other set consists of plants whose wild ancestors occur in Ethiopia and were probably domesticated there in the highlands. Most are still grown mainly just in Ethiopia and remain unknown to Americans—including Ethiopia's narcotic chat, its banana-like ensete, its oily noog, its finger millet used to brew its national beer, and its tiny-seeded cereal called teff, used to make its national bread. But every reader addicted to coffee can thank ancient Ethiopian farmers for domesticating the coffee plant. It remained confined to Ethiopia until it caught on in Arabia and then around the world, to sustain today the economies of countries as far-flung as Brazil and Papua New Guinea.

The next-to-last set of African crops arose from wild ancestors in the wet climate of West Africa. Some, including African rice, have remained virtually confined there; others, such as African yams, spread throughout other areas of sub-Saharan Africa; and two, the oil palm and kola nut, reached other continents. West Africans were chewing the caffeine-containing nuts of the latter as a narcotic, long before the Coca-Cola Company enticed first Americans and then the world to drink a beverage originally laced with its extracts.

The last batch of African crops is also adapted to wet climates but provides the biggest surprise of Figure 19.3. Bananas, Asian yams, and taro were already widespread in sub-Saharan Africa in the 1400s, and Asian rice was established on the coast of East Africa. But those crops originated in tropical Southeast Asia. Their presence in Africa would astonish us, if the presence of Indonesian people on Madagascar had not already alerted us to Africa's prehistoric Asian connection. Did Austronesians sailing from Borneo land on the East African coast, bestow their crops on grateful African farmers, pick up African fishermen, and sail off into the sunrise to colonize Madagascar, leaving no other Austronesian traces in Africa?

The remaining surprise is that all of Africa's indigenous crops—those of the Sahel, Ethiopia, and West Africa—originated north of the equator. Not a single African crop originated south of it. This already gives us a hint why speakers of Niger-Congo languages, stemming from north of the equator, were able to displace Africa's equatorial Pygmies and subequatorial Khoisan people. The failure of the Khoisan and Pygmies to develop agriculture was due not to any inadequacy of theirs as farmers but merely to the accident that southern Africa's wild plants were mostly unsuitable for domestication. Neither Bantu nor white farmers, heirs to thousands of years of farming experience, were subsequently able to develop southern African native plants into food crops.

Africa's domesticated animal species can be summarized much more quickly than its plants, because there are so few of them. The sole animal that we know for sure was domesticated in Africa, because its wild ancestor is confined there, is a turkeylike bird called the guinea fowl. Wild ancestors of domestic cattle, donkeys, pigs, dogs, and house cats were native to North Africa but also to Southwest Asia, so we can't yet be certain where they were first domesticated, although the earliest dates currently known for domestic donkeys and house cats favor Egypt. Recent evidence suggests that cattle may have been domesticated independently in North Africa, Southwest Asia, and India, and that all three of those stocks have contributed to modern African cattle breeds. Otherwise, all the remainder of Africa's domestic mammals must have been domesticated elsewhere and introduced as domesticates to Africa, because their wild ancestors occur only in Eurasia. Africa's sheep and goats were domesticated in Southwest Asia, its chickens in Southeast Asia, its horses in southern Russia, and its camels probably in Arabia.

The most unexpected feature of this list of African domestic animals is again a negative one. The list includes not a single one of the big wild mammal species for which Africa is famous and which it possesses in such abundance—its zebras and wildebeests, its rhinos and hippos, its giraffes and buffalo. As we'll see, that reality was as fraught with consequences for African history as was the absence of native domestic plants in subequatorial Africa.

This quick tour through Africa's food staples suffices to show that some of them traveled a long way from their points of origin, both inside and outside Africa. In Africa as elsewhere in the world, some peoples were much "luckier" than others, in the suites of domesticable wild plant and animal species that they inherited from their environment. By analogy with the engulfing of Aboriginal Australian hunter-gatherers by British colonists fed on wheat and cattle, we have to suspect that some of the "lucky" Africans parlayed their advantage into engulfing their African neighbors. Now, at last, let's turn to the archaeological record to find out who engulfed whom when.

WHAT CAN ARCHAEOLOGY can tell us about actual dates and places for the rise of farming and herding in Africa? Any reader steeped in the history of Western civilization would be forgiven for assuming that African food production began in ancient Egypt's Nile Valley, land of the pharaohs and pyramids. After all, Egypt by 3000 B.C. was undoubtedly the site of Africa's most complex society, and one of the world's earliest centers of writing. In fact, though, possibly the earliest archaeological evidence for food production in Africa comes instead from the Sahara.

Today, of course, much of the Sahara is so dry that it cannot support even grass. But between about 9000 and 4000 B.C. the Sahara was more humid, held numerous lakes, and teemed with game. In that period, Saharans began to tend cattle and make pottery, then to keep sheep and goats, and they may also have been starting to domesticate sorghum and millet. Saharan pastoralism precedes the earliest known date (5200 B.C.) for the arrival of food production in Egypt, in the form of a full package of Southwest Asian winter crops and livestock. Food production also arose in West Africa and Ethiopia, and by around 2500 B.C. cattle herders had already crossed the modern border from Ethiopia into northern Kenya.

While those conclusions rest on archaeological evidence, there is also an independent method for dating the arrival of domestic plants and animals: by comparing the words for them in modern languages. Comparisons of terms for plants in southern Nigerian languages of the Niger-Congo family show that the words fall into three groups. First are cases in which the word for a particular crop is very similar in all those southern Nigerian languages. Those crops prove to be ones like West African yams, oil palm, and kola nut—plants that were already believed on botanical and other evidence to be native to West Africa and first domesticated there. Since those are the oldest West African crops, all modern southern Nigerian languages inherited the same original set of words for them.

Next come crops whose names are consistent only among the languages falling within a small subgroup of those southern Nigerian languages. Those crops turn out to be ones believed to be of Indonesian origin, such as bananas and Asian yams. Evidently, those crops reached southern Nigeria only after languages began to break up into subgroups, so each subgroup coined or received different names for the new plants, which the modern languages of only that particular subgroup inherited. Last come crop names that aren't consistent within language groups at all, but instead follow trade routes. These prove to be New World crops like corn and peanuts, which we know were introduced into Africa after the beginnings of transatlantic ship traffic (A.D. 1492) and diffused since then along trade routes, often bearing their Portuguese or other foreign names.

Thus, even if we possessed no botanical or archaeological evidence whatsoever, we would still be able to deduce from the linguistic evidence alone that native West African crops were domesticated first, that Indonesian crops arrived next, and that finally the European introductions came in. The UCLA historian Christopher Ehret has applied this linguistic approach to determining the sequence in which domestic plants and animals became utilized by the people of each African language family. By a method termed glottochronology, based on calculations of how rapidly words tend to change over historical time, comparative linguistics can even yield estimated dates for domestications or crop arrivals.

Putting together direct archaeological evidence of crops with the more indirect linguistic evidence, we deduce that the people who were domesticating sorghum and millet in the Sahara thousands of years ago spoke languages ancestral to modern Nilo-Saharan languages. Similarly, the people who first domesticated wet-country crops of West Africa spoke languages ancestral to the modern Niger-Congo languages. Finally, speakers of ancestral Afroasiatic languages may have been involved in domesticating the crops native to Ethiopia, and they certainly introduced Fertile Crescent crops to North Africa.

Thus, the evidence derived from plant names in modern African languages permits us to glimpse the existence of three languages being spoken in Africa thousands of years ago: ancestral Nilo-Saharan, ancestral Niger-Congo, and ancestral Afroasiatic. In addition, we can glimpse the existence of ancestral Khoisan from other linguistic evidence, though not that of crop names (because ancestral Khoisan people domesticated no crops). Now surely, since Africa harbors 1,500 languages today, it is big enough to have harbored more than four ancestral languages thousands of years ago. But all those other languages must have disappeared—either because the people speaking them survived but lost their original language, like the

Pygmies, or because the people themselves disappeared.

The survival of modern Africa's four native language families (that is, the four other than the recently arrived Austronesian language of Madagascar) isn't due to the intrinsic superiority of those languages as vehicles for communication. Instead, it must be attributed to a historical accident: ancestral speakers of Nilo-Saharan, Niger-Congo, and Afroasiatic happened to be living at the right place and time to acquire domestic plants and animals, which let them multiply and either replace other peoples or impose their language. The few modern Khoisan speakers survived mainly because of their isolation in areas of southern Africa unsuitable for Bantu farming.

BEFORE WE TRACE Khoisan survival beyond the Bantu tide, let's see what archaeology tells us about Africa's other great prehistoric population movement—the Austronesian colonization of Madagascar. Archaeologists exploring Madagascar have now proved that Austronesians had arrived at least by A.D. 800, possibly as early as A.D. 300. There the Austronesians encountered (and proceeded to exterminate) a strange world of living animals as distinctive as if they had come from another planet, because those animals had evolved on Madagascar during its long isolation. They included giant elephant birds, primitive primates called lemurs as big as gorillas, and pygmy hippos. Archaeological excavations of the earliest human settlements on Madagascar yield remains of iron tools, livestock, and crops, so the colonists were not just a small canoeload of fishermen blown off course; they formed a full-fledged expedition. How did that prehistoric 4,000-mile expedition come about?

One hint is in an ancient book of sailors' directions, the *Periplus of the Erythrean Sea,* written by an anonymous merchant living in Egypt around A.D. 100. The merchant describes an already thriving sea trade connecting India and Egypt with the coast of East Africa. With the spread of Islam after A.D. 800, Indian Ocean trade becomes well documented archaeologically by copious quantities of Mideastern (and occasionally even Chinese!) products such as pottery, glass, and porcelain in East African coastal settlements. The traders waited for favorable winds to let them cross the Indian Ocean directly between East Africa and India. When the Portuguese navigator Vasco da Gama became the first European to sail around the southern cape of Africa and reached the Kenya coast in 1498, he encountered

Swahili trading settlements and picked up a pilot who guided him on that direct route to India.

But there was an equally vigorous sea trade from India eastward, between India and Indonesia. Perhaps the Austronesian colonists of Madagascar reached India from Indonesia by that eastern trade route and then fell in with the westward trade route to East Africa, where they joined with Africans and discovered Madagascar. That union of Austronesians and East Africans lives on today in Madagascar's basically Austronesian language, which contains loan words from coastal Kenyan Bantu languages. But there are no corresponding Austronesian loan words in Kenyan languages, and other traces of Austronesians are very thin on the ground in East Africa: mainly just Africa's possible legacy of Indonesian musical instruments (xylophones and zithers) and, of course, the Austronesian crops that became so important in African agriculture. Hence one wonders whether Austronesians, instead of taking the easier route to Madagascar via India and East Africa, somehow (incredibly) sailed straight across the Indian Ocean, discovered Madagascar, and only later got plugged into East African trade routes. Thus, some mystery remains about Africa's most surprising fact of human geography.

WHAT CAN ARCHAEOLOGY tell us about the other great population movement in recent African prehistory—the Bantu expansion? We saw from the twin evidence of modern peoples and their languages that sub-Saharan Africa was not always a black continent, as we think of it today. Instead, this evidence suggested that Pygmies had once been widespread in the rain forest of Central Africa, while Khoisan peoples had been widespread in drier parts of subequatorial Africa. Can archaeology test those assumptions?

In the case of the Pygmies, the answer is "not yet," merely because archaeologists have yet to discover ancient human skeletons from the Central African forests. For the Khoisan, the answer is "yes." In Zambia, to the north of the modern Khoisan range, archaeologists have found skulls of people possibly resembling the modern Khoisan, as well as stone tools resembling those that Khoisan peoples were still making in southern Africa at the time Europeans arrived.

As for how the Bantu came to replace those northern Khoisan, archaeological and linguistic evidence suggest that the expansion of ancestral

Bantu farmers from West Africa's inland savanna south into its wetter coastal forest may have begun as early as 3000 B.C. (Figure 19.4). Words still widespread in all Bantu languages show that, already then, the Bantu had cattle and wet-climate crops such as yams, but that they lacked metal and were still engaged in much fishing, hunting, and gathering. They even lost their cattle to disease borne by tsetse flies in the forest. As they spread into the Congo Basin's equatorial forest zone, cleared gardens, and increased in numbers, they began to engulf the Pygmy hunter-gatherers and compress them into the forest itself.

By soon after 1000 B.C. the Bantu had emerged from the eastern side of the forest into the more open country of East Africa's Rift Valley and Great Lakes. Here they encountered a melting pot of Afroasiatic and Nilo-Saharan farmers and herders growing millet and sorghum and raising live-stock in drier areas, along with Khoisan hunter-gatherers. Thanks to their wet-climate crops inherited from their West African homeland, the Bantu were able to farm in wet areas of East Africa unsuitable for all those previous occupants. By the last centuries B.C. the advancing Bantu had reached the East African coast.

In East Africa the Bantu began to acquire millet and sorghum (along with the Nilo-Saharan names for those crops), and to reacquire cattle, from their Nilo-Saharan and Afroasiatic neighbors. They also acquired iron, which had just begun to be smelted in Africa's Sahel zone. The origins of ironworking in sub-Saharan Africa soon after 1000 B.C. are still unclear. That early date is suspiciously close to dates for the arrival of Near Eastern ironworking techniques in Carthage, on the North African coast. Hence historians often assume that knowledge of metallurgy reached sub-Saharan Africa from the north. On the other hand, copper smelting had been going on in the West African Sahara and Sahel since at least 2000 B.C. That could have been the precursor to an independent African discovery of iron metallurgy. Strengthening that hypothesis, the iron-smelting techniques of smiths in sub-Saharan Africa were so different from those of the Mediterranean as to suggest independent development: African smiths discovered how to produce high temperatures in their village furnaces and manufacture steel over 2,000 years before the Bessemer furnaces of 19th-century Europe and America.

With the addition of iron tools to their wet-climate crops, the Bantu had finally put together a military-industrial package that was unstoppable in the subequatorial Africa of the time. In East Africa they still had to

The Bantu expansion: 3000 BC to AD 500

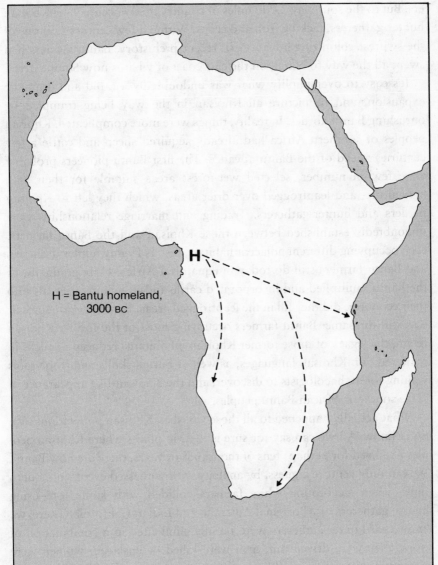

Figure 19.4. Approximate paths of the expansion that carried people speaking Bantu languages, originating from a homeland (designated H) in the northwest corner of the current Bantu area, over eastern and southern Africa between 3000 B.C. and A.D. 500.

compete against numerous Nilo-Saharan and Afroasiatic Iron Age farmers. But to the south lay 2,000 miles of country thinly occupied by Khoisan
hunter-gatherers, lacking iron and crops. Within a few centuries, in one of
the swiftest colonizing advances of recent prehistory, Bantu farmers had
swept all the way to Natal, on the east coast of what is now South Africa.

It's easy to oversimplify what was undoubtedly a rapid and dramatic
expansion, and to picture all Khoisan in the way being trampled by
onrushing Bantu hordes. In reality, things were more complicated. Khoisan
peoples of southern Africa had already acquired sheep and cattle a few
centuries ahead of the Bantu advance. The first Bantu pioneers probably
were few in number, selected wet-forest areas suitable for their yam
agriculture, and leapfrogged over drier areas, which they left to Khoisan
herders and hunter-gatherers. Trading and marriage relationships were
undoubtedly established between those Khoisan and the Bantu farmers,
each occupying different adjacent habitats, just as Pygmy hunter-gatherers
and Bantu farmers still do today in equatorial Africa. Only gradually, as
the Bantu multiplied and incorporated cattle and dry-climate cereals into
their economy, did they fill in the leapfrogged areas. But the eventual result
was still the same: Bantu farmers occupying most of the former Khoisan
realm; the legacy of those former Khoisan inhabitants reduced to clicks in
scattered non-Khoisan languages, as well as buried skulls and stone tools
waiting for archaeologists to discover; and the Khoisan-like appearance of
some southern African Bantu peoples.

What actually happened to all those vanished Khoisan populations? We
don't know. All we can say for sure is that, in places where Khoisan peoples had lived for perhaps tens of thousands of years, there are now Bantu.
We can only venture a guess, by analogy with witnessed events in modern
times when steel-toting white farmers collided with stone tool–using
hunter-gatherers of Aboriginal Australia and Indian California. There, we
know that hunter-gatherers were rapidly eliminated in a combination of
ways: they were driven out, men were killed or enslaved, women were
appropriated as wives, and both sexes became infected with epidemics of
the farmers' diseases. An example of such a disease in Africa is malaria,
which is borne by mosquitoes that breed around farmers' villages, and to
which the invading Bantu had already developed genetic resistance but
Khoisan hunter-gatherers probably had not.

However, Figure 19.1, of recent African human distributions, reminds
us that the Bantu did not overrun all the Khoisan, who did survive in

southern African areas unsuitable for Bantu agriculture. The southernmost Bantu people, the Xhosa, stopped at the Fish River on South Africa's south coast, 500 miles east of Cape Town. It's not that the Cape of Good Hope itself is too dry for agriculture: it is, after all, the breadbasket of modern South Africa. Instead, the Cape has a Mediterranean climate of winter rains, in which the Bantu summer-rain crops do not grow. By 1652, the year the Dutch arrived at Cape Town with their winter-rain crops of Near Eastern origin, the Xhosa had still not spread beyond the Fish River.

That seeming detail of plant geography had enormous implications for politics today. One consequence was that, once South African whites had quickly killed or infected or driven off the Cape's Khoisan population, whites could claim correctly that they had occupied the Cape before the Bantu and thus had prior rights to it. That claim needn't be taken seriously, since the prior rights of the Cape Khoisan didn't inhibit whites from dispossessing them. The much heavier consequence was that the Dutch settlers in 1652 had to contend only with a sparse population of Khoisan herders, not with a dense population of steel-equipped Bantu farmers. When whites finally spread east to encounter the Xhosa at the Fish River in 1702, a period of desperate fighting began. Even though Europeans by then could supply troops from their secure base at the Cape, it took nine wars and 175 years for their armies, advancing at an average rate of less than one mile per year, to subdue the Xhosa. How could whites have succeeded in establishing themselves at the Cape at all, if those first few arriving Dutch ships had faced such fierce resistance?

Thus, the problems of modern South Africa stem at least in part from a geographic accident. The homeland of the Cape Khoisan happened to contain few wild plants suitable for domestication; the Bantu happened to inherit summer-rain crops from their ancestors of 5,000 years ago; and Europeans happened to inherit winter-rain crops from their ancestors of nearly 10,000 years ago. Just as the sign "Goering Street" in the capital of newly independent Namibia reminded me, Africa's past has stamped itself deeply on Africa's present.

THAT'S HOW THE Bantu were able to engulf the Khoisan, instead of vice versa. Now let's turn to the remaining question in our puzzle of African prehistory: why Europeans were the ones to colonize sub-Saharan Africa. That it was not the other way around is especially surprising, because

Africa was the sole cradle of human evolution for millions of years, as well as perhaps the homeland of anatomically modern *Homo sapiens*. To these advantages of Africa's enormous head start were added those of highly diverse climates and habitats and of the world's highest human diversity. An extraterrestrial visiting Earth 10,000 years ago might have been forgiven for predicting that Europe would end up as a set of vassal states of a sub-Saharan African empire.

The proximate reasons behind the outcome of Africa's collision with Europe are clear. Just as in their encounter with Native Americans, Europeans entering Africa enjoyed the triple advantage of guns and other technology, widespread literacy, and the political organization necessary to sustain expensive programs of exploration and conquest. Those advantages manifested themselves almost as soon as the collisions started: barely four years after Vasco da Gama first reached the East African coast, in 1498, he returned with a fleet bristling with cannons to compel the surrender of East Africa's most important port, Kilwa, which controlled the Zimbabwe gold trade. But why did Europeans develop those three advantages before sub-Saharan Africans could?

As we have discussed, all three arose historically from the development of food production. But food production was delayed in sub-Saharan Africa (compared with Eurasia) by Africa's paucity of domesticable native animal and plant species, its much smaller area suitable for indigenous food production, and its north–south axis, which retarded the spread of food production and inventions. Let's examine how those factors operated.

First, as regards domestic animals, we've already seen that those of sub-Saharan Africa came from Eurasia, with the possible exception of a few from North Africa. As a result, domestic animals did not reach sub-Saharan Africa until thousands of years after they began to be utilized by emerging Eurasian civilizations. That's initially surprising, because we think of Africa as *the* continent of big wild mammals. But we saw in Chapter 9 that a wild animal, to be domesticated, must be sufficiently docile, submissive to humans, cheap to feed, and immune to diseases and must grow rapidly and breed well in captivity. Eurasia's native cows, sheep, goats, horses, and pigs were among the world's few large wild animal species to pass all those tests. Their African equivalents—such as the African buffalo, zebra, bush pig, rhino, and hippopotamus—have never been domesticated, not even in modern times.

It's true, of course, that some large African animals have occasionally been *tamed*. Hannibal enlisted tamed African elephants in his unsuccessful war against Rome, and ancient Egyptians may have tamed giraffes and other species. But none of those tamed animals was actually domesticated—that is, selectively bred in captivity and genetically modified so as to become more useful to humans. Had Africa's rhinos and hippos been domesticated and ridden, they would not only have fed armies but also have provided an unstoppable cavalry to cut through the ranks of European horsemen. Rhino-mounted Bantu shock troops could have overthrown the Roman Empire. It never happened.

A second factor is a corresponding, though less extreme, disparity between sub-Saharan Africa and Eurasia in domesticable plants. The Sahel, Ethiopia, and West Africa did yield indigenous crops, but many fewer varieties than grew in Eurasia. Because of the limited variety of wild starting material suitable for plant domestication, even Africa's earliest agriculture may have begun several thousand years later than that of the Fertile Crescent.

Thus, as far as plant and animal domestication was concerned, the head start and high diversity lay with Eurasia, not with Africa. A third factor is that Africa's area is only about half that of Eurasia. Furthermore, only about one-third of its area falls within the sub-Saharan zone north of the equator that was occupied by farmers and herders before 1000 B.C. Today, the total population of Africa is less than 700 million, compared with 4 billion for Eurasia. But, all other things being equal, more land and more people mean more competing societies and inventions, hence a faster pace of development.

The remaining factor behind Africa's slower rate of post-Pleistocene development compared with Eurasia's is the different orientation of the main axes of these continents. Like that of the Americas, Africa's major axis is north–south, whereas Eurasia's is east–west (Figure 10.1). As one moves along a north–south axis, one traverses zones differing greatly in climate, habitat, rainfall, day length, and diseases of crops and livestock. Hence crops and animals domesticated or acquired in one part of Africa had great difficulty in moving to other parts. In contrast, crops and animals moved easily between Eurasian societies thousands of miles apart but at the same latitude and sharing similar climates and day lengths.

The slow passage or complete halt of crops and livestock along Africa's north–south axis had important consequences. For example, the Mediterranean crops that became Egypt's staples require winter rains and seasonal variation in day length for their germination. Those crops were unable to spread south of the Sudan, beyond which they encountered summer rains and little or no seasonal variation in daylight. Egypt's wheat and barley never reached the Mediterranean climate at the Cape of Good Hope until European colonists brought them in 1652, and the Khoisan never developed agriculture. Similarly, the Sahel crops adapted to summer rain and to little or no seasonal variation in day length were brought by the Bantu into southern Africa but could not grow at the Cape itself, thereby halting the advance of Bantu agriculture. Bananas and other tropical Asian crops for which Africa's climate is eminently suitable, and which today are among the most productive staples of tropical African agriculture, were unable to reach Africa by land routes. They apparently did not arrive until the first millennium A.D., long after their domestication in Asia, because they had to wait for large-scale boat traffic across the Indian Ocean.

Africa's north–south axis also seriously impeded the spread of livestock. Equatorial Africa's tsetse flies, carrying trypanosomes to which native African wild mammals are resistant, proved devastating to introduced Eurasian and North African species of livestock. The cows that the Bantu acquired from the tsetse-free Sahel zone failed to survive the Bantu expansion through the equatorial forest. Although horses had already reached Egypt around 1800 B.C. and transformed North African warfare soon thereafter, they did not cross the Sahara to drive the rise of cavalry-mounted West African kingdoms until the first millennium A.D., and they never spread south through the tsetse fly zone. While cattle, sheep, and goats had already reached the northern edge of the Serengeti in the third millennium B.C., it took more than 2,000 years beyond that for livestock to cross the Serengeti and reach southern Africa.

Similarly slow in spreading down Africa's north–south axis was human technology. Pottery, recorded in the Sudan and Sahara around 8000 B.C., did not reach the Cape until around A.D. 1. Although writing developed in Egypt by 3000 B.C. and spread in an alphabetized form to the Nubian kingdom of Meroë, and although alphabetic writing reached Ethiopia (possibly from Arabia), writing did not arise independently in the rest of Africa, where it was instead brought in from the outside by Arabs and Europeans.

In short, Europe's colonization of Africa had nothing to do with differences between European and African peoples themselves, as white racists assume. Rather, it was due to accidents of geography and biogeography—in particular, to the continents' different areas, axes, and suites of wild plant and animal species. That is, the different historical trajectories of Africa and Europe stem ultimately from differences in real estate.

THE FUTURE OF
HUMAN HISTORY
AS A SCIENCE

YALI'S QUESTION WENT TO THE HEART OF THE CURRENT human condition, and of post-Pleistocene human history. Now that we have completed this brief tour over the continents, how shall we answer Yali?

I would say to Yali: the striking differences between the long-term histories of peoples of the different continents have been due not to innate differences in the peoples themselves but to differences in their environments. I expect that if the populations of Aboriginal Australia and Eurasia could have been interchanged during the Late Pleistocene, the original Aboriginal Australians would now be the ones occupying most of the Americas and Australia, as well as Eurasia, while the original Aboriginal Eurasians would be the ones now reduced to downtrodden population fragments in Australia. One might at first be inclined to dismiss this assertion as meaningless, because the experiment is imaginary and my claim about its outcome cannot be verified. But historians are nevertheless able to evaluate related hypotheses by retrospective tests. For instance, one can examine what did happen when European farmers were transplanted to Greenland or the U.S. Great Plains, and when farmers stemming ultimately from China emigrated to the Chatham Islands, the rain forests of Borneo, or the volcanic soils of Java or Hawaii. These tests confirm that the same ancestral peoples either ended up extinct, or returned to living as hunter-gatherers, or went on to build complex states, depending on their environments. Similarly, Aboriginal Australian hunter-gatherers, variously transplanted to Flinders Island, Tasmania, or southeastern Australia, ended up extinct, or as hunter-gatherers with the modern world's simplest technology, or as canal builders intensively managing a productive fishery, depending on their environments.

Of course, the continents differ in innumerable environmental features affecting trajectories of human societies. But a mere laundry list of every possible difference does not constitute an answer to Yali's question. Just four sets of differences appear to me to be the most important ones.

The first set consists of continental differences in the wild plant and animal species available as starting materials for domestication. That's because food production was critical for the accumulation of food surpluses that could feed non-food-producing specialists, and for the buildup of large populations enjoying a military advantage through mere numbers even before they had developed any technological or political advantage. For both of those reasons, all developments of economically complex, socially stratified, politically centralized societies beyond the level of small nascent chiefdoms were based on food production.

But most wild animal and plant species have proved unsuitable for domestication: food production has been based on relatively few species of livestock and crops. It turns out that the number of wild candidate species for domestication varied greatly among the continents, because of differences in continental areas and also (in the case of big mammals) in Late Pleistocene extinctions. These extinctions were much more severe in Australia and the Americas than in Eurasia or Africa. As a result, Africa ended up biologically somewhat less well endowed than the much larger Eurasia, the Americas still less so, and Australia even less so, as did Yali's New Guinea (with one-seventieth of Eurasia's area and with all of its original big mammals extinct in the Late Pleistocene).

On each continent, animal and plant domestication was concentrated in a few especially favorable homelands accounting for only a small fraction of the continent's total area. In the case of technological innovations and political institutions as well, most societies acquire much more from other societies than they invent themselves. Thus, diffusion and migration within a continent contribute importantly to the development of its societies, which tend in the long run to share each other's developments (insofar as environments permit) because of the processes illustrated in such simple form by Maori New Zealand's Musket Wars. That is, societies initially lacking an advantage either acquire it from societies possessing it or (if they fail to do so) are replaced by those other societies.

Hence a second set of factors consists of those affecting rates of diffusion and migration, which differed greatly among continents. They were most rapid in Eurasia, because of its east-west major axis and its relatively modest ecological and geographical barriers. The reasoning is straightforward for movements of crops and livestock, which depend strongly on climate and hence on latitude. But similar reasoning also applies to the diffusion of technological innovations, insofar as they are best suited without modification to specific environments. Diffusion was slower in Africa and especially in the Americas, because of those continents' north–south major axes and geographic and ecological barriers. It was also difficult in traditional New Guinea, where rugged terrain and the long backbone of high mountains prevented any significant progress toward political and linguistic unification.

Related to these factors affecting diffusion *within* continents is a third set of factors influencing diffusion *between* continents, which may also help build up a local pool of domesticates and technology. Ease of intercontinental diffusion has varied, because some continents are more isolated than others. Within the last 6,000 years it has been easiest from Eurasia to sub-Saharan Africa, supplying most of Africa's species of livestock. But interhemispheric diffusion made no contribution to Native America's complex societies, isolated from Eurasia at low latitudes by broad oceans, and at high latitudes by geography and by a climate suitable just for hunting-gathering. To Aboriginal Australia, isolated from Eurasia by the water barriers of the Indonesian Archipelago, Eurasia's sole proven contribution was the dingo.

The fourth and last set of factors consists of continental differences in area or total population size. A larger area or population means more potential inventors, more competing societies, more innovations available to adopt—and more pressure to adopt and retain innovations, because societies failing to do so will tend to be eliminated by competing societies. That fate befell African pygmies and many other hunter-gatherer populations displaced by farmers. Conversely, it also befell the stubborn, conservative Greenland Norse farmers, replaced by Eskimo hunter-gatherers whose subsistence methods and technology were far superior to those of the Norse under Greenland conditions. Among the world's landmasses, area and the number of competing societies were largest for Eurasia, much smaller for Australia and New Guinea and especially for Tasmania. The Americas, despite their large aggregate area, were fragmented by geography and ecology and functioned effectively as several poorly connected smaller continents.

Those four sets of factors constitute big environmental differences that can be quantified objectively and that are not subject to dispute. While one can contest my subjective impression that New Guineans are on the average smarter than Eurasians, one cannot deny that New Guinea has a much smaller area and far fewer big animal species than Eurasia. But mention of these environmental differences invites among historians the label "geographic determinism," which raises hackles. The label seems to have unpleasant connotations, such as that human creativity counts for nothing, or that we humans are passive robots helplessly programmed by climate, fauna, and flora. Of course these fears are misplaced. Without human inventiveness, all of us today would still be cutting our meat with stone tools and eating it raw, like our ancestors of a million years ago. All human societies contain inventive people. It's just that some environments provide more starting materials, and more favorable conditions for utilizing inventions, than do other environments.

THESE ANSWERS TO Yali's question are longer and more complicated than Yali himself would have wanted. Historians, however, may find them too brief and oversimplified. Compressing 13,000 years of history on all continents into a 400-page book works out to an average of about one page per continent per 150 years, making brevity and simplification inevitable. Yet the compression brings a compensating benefit: long-term comparisons of regions yield insights that cannot be won from short-term studies of single societies.

Naturally, a host of issues raised by Yali's question remain unresolved. At present, we can put forward some partial answers plus a research agenda for the future, rather than a fully developed theory. The challenge now is to develop human history as a science, on a par with acknowledged historical sciences such as astronomy, geology, and evolutionary biology. Hence it seems appropriate to conclude this book by looking to the future of the discipline of history, and by outlining some of the unresolved issues.

The most straightforward extension of this book will be to quantify further, and thus to establish more convincingly the role of, intercontinental differences in the four sets of factors that appear to be most important. To illustrate differences in starting materials for domestication, I provided numbers for each continent's total of large wild terrestrial mammalian herbivores and omnivores (Table 9.2) and of large-seeded cereals (Table 8.1). One extension would be to assemble corresponding numbers for large-seeded legumes (pulses), such as beans, peas, and vetches. In addition, I mentioned factors disqualifying big mammalian candidates for domestication, but I did not tabulate how many candidates are disqualified by each factor on each continent. It would be interesting to do so, especially for Africa, where a higher percentage of candidates is disqualified than in Eurasia: which disqualifying factors are most important in Africa, and what has selected for their high frequency in African mammals? Quantitative data should also be assembled to test my preliminary calculations suggesting differing rates of diffusion along the major axes of Eurasia, the Americas, and Africa.

A SECOND EXTENSION will be to smaller geographic scales and shorter time scales than those of this book. For instance, the following obvious question has probably occurred to readers already: why, within Eurasia, were European societies, rather than those of the Fertile Crescent or China or India, the ones that colonized America and Australia, took the lead in technology, and became politically and economically dominant in the modern world? A historian who had lived at any time between 8500 B.C. and A.D. 1450, and who had tried then to predict future historical trajectories, would surely have labeled Europe's eventual dominance as the least likely outcome, because Europe was the most backward of those three Old World regions for most of those 10,000 years. From 8500 B.C. until the rise of Greece and then Italy after 500 B.C., almost all major innovations in western Eurasia—animal domestication, plant domestication, writing, metallurgy, wheels, states, and so on—arose in or near the Fertile Crescent. Until the proliferation of water mills after about A.D. 900, Europe west or north of the Alps contributed nothing of significance to Old World technology or civilization; it was instead a recipient of developments from the eastern Mediterranean, Fertile Crescent, and China. Even from A.D. 1000 to 1450 the flow of science and technology was predominantly into

Europe from the Islamic societies stretching from India to North Africa, rather than vice versa. During those same centuries China led the world in technology, having launched itself on food production nearly as early as the Fertile Crescent did.

Why, then, did the Fertile Crescent and China eventually lose their enormous leads of thousands of years to late-starting Europe? One can, of course, point to proximate factors behind Europe's rise: its development of a merchant class, capitalism, and patent protection for inventions, its failure to develop absolute despots and crushing taxation, and its Greco-Judeo-Christian tradition of critical empirical inquiry. Still, for all such proximate causes one must raise the question of ultimate cause: why did these proximate factors themselves arise in Europe, rather than in China or the Fertile Crescent?

For the Fertile Crescent, the answer is clear. Once it had lost the head start that it had enjoyed thanks to its locally available concentration of domesticable wild plants and animals, the Fertile Crescent possessed no further compelling geographic advantages. The disappearance of that head start can be traced in detail, as the westward shift in powerful empires. After the rise of Fertile Crescent states in the fourth millennium B.C., the center of power initially remained in the Fertile Crescent, rotating between empires such as those of Babylon, the Hittites, Assyria, and Persia. With the Greek conquest of all advanced societies from Greece east to India under Alexander the Great in the late fourth century B.C., power finally made its first shift irrevocably westward. It shifted farther west with Rome's conquest of Greece in the second century B.C., and after the fall of the Roman Empire it eventually moved again, to western and northern Europe.

The major factor behind these shifts becomes obvious as soon as one compares the modern Fertile Crescent with ancient descriptions of it. Today, the expressions "Fertile Crescent" and "world leader in food production" are absurd. Large areas of the former Fertile Crescent are now desert, semidesert, steppe, or heavily eroded or salinized terrain unsuited for agriculture. Today's ephemeral wealth of some of the region's nations, based on the single nonrenewable resource of oil, conceals the region's long-standing fundamental poverty and difficulty in feeding itself.

In ancient times, however, much of the Fertile Crescent and eastern Mediterranean region, including Greece, was covered with forest. The region's transformation from fertile woodland to eroded scrub or desert has been elucidated by paleobotanists and archaeologists. Its woodlands were cleared for agriculture, or cut to obtain construction timber, or burned as firewood or for manufacturing plaster. Because of low rainfall and hence low primary productivity (proportional to rainfall), regrowth of vegetation could not keep pace with its destruction, especially in the presence of overgrazing by abundant goats. With the tree and grass cover removed, erosion proceeded and valleys silted up, while irrigation agriculture in the low-rainfall environment led to salt accumulation. These processes, which began in the Neolithic era, continued into modern times. For instance, the last forests near the ancient Nabataean capital of Petra, in modern Jordan, were felled by the Ottoman Turks during construction of the Hejaz railroad just before World War I.

Thus, Fertile Crescent and eastern Mediterranean societies had the misfortune to arise in an ecologically fragile environment. They committed ecological suicide by destroying their own resource base. Power shifted westward as each eastern Mediterranean society in turn undermined itself, beginning with the oldest societies, those in the east (the Fertile Crescent). Northern and western Europe has been spared this fate, not because its inhabitants have been wiser but because they have had the good luck to live in a more robust environment with higher rainfall, in which vegetation regrows quickly. Much of northern and western Europe is still able to support productive intensive agriculture today, 7,000 years after the arrival of food production. In effect, Europe received its crops, livestock, technology, and writing systems from the Fertile Crescent, which then gradually eliminated itself as a major center of power and innovation.

That is how the Fertile Crescent lost its huge early lead over Europe. Why did China also lose its lead? Its falling behind is initially surprising, because China enjoyed undoubted advantages: a rise of food production nearly as early as in the Fertile Crescent; ecological diversity from North to South China and from the coast to the high mountains of the Tibetan plateau, giving rise to a diverse set of crops, animals, and technology; a large and productive expanse, nourishing the largest regional human population in the world; and an environment less dry or ecologically fragile than the Fertile Crescent's, allowing China still to support productive intensive agriculture after nearly 10,000 years, though its environmental problems are increasing today and are more serious than western Europe's.

These advantages and head start enabled medieval China to lead the world in technology. The long list of its major technological firsts includes cast iron, the compass, gunpowder, paper, printing, and many others mentioned earlier. It also led the world in political power, navigation, and control of the seas. In the early 15th century it sent treasure fleets, each consisting of hundreds of ships up to 400 feet long and with total crews of up to 28,000, across the Indian Ocean as far as the east coast of Africa, decades before Columbus's three puny ships crossed the narrow Atlantic Ocean to the Americas' east coast. Why didn't Chinese ships proceed around Africa's southern cape westward and colonize Europe, before Vasco da Gama's own three puny ships rounded the Cape of Good Hope eastward and launched Europe's colonization of East Asia? Why didn't Chinese ships cross the Pacific to colonize the Americas' west coast? Why, in brief, did China lose its technological lead to the formerly so backward Europe?

The end of China's treasure fleets gives us a clue. Seven of those fleets sailed from China between A.D. 1405 and 1433. They were then suspended as a result of a typical aberration of local politics that could happen anywhere in the world: a power struggle between two factions at the Chinese court (the eunuchs and their opponents). The former faction had been identified with sending and captaining the fleets. Hence when the latter faction gained the upper hand in a power struggle, it stopped sending fleets, eventually dismantled the shipyards, and forbade oceangoing shipping. The episode is reminiscent of the legislation that strangled development of public electric lighting in London in the 1880s, the isolationism of the United States between the First and Second World Wars, and any number of backward steps in any number of countries, all motivated by local political issues. But in China there was a difference, because the entire region was politically unified. One decision stopped fleets over the whole of China. That one temporary decision became irreversible, because no shipyards remained to turn out ships that would prove the folly of that temporary decision, and to serve as a focus for rebuilding other shipyards.

Now contrast those events in China with what happened when fleets of exploration began to sail from politically fragmented Europe. Christopher Columbus, an Italian by birth, switched his allegiance to the duke of Anjou in France, then to the king of Portugal. When the latter refused his request for ships in which to explore westward, Columbus turned to the duke of Medina-Sedonia, who also refused, then to the count of Medina-Celi, who did likewise, and finally to the king and queen of Spain, who denied Columbus's first request but eventually granted his renewed appeal. Had

Europe been united under any one of the first three rulers, its colonization of the Americas might have been stillborn.

In fact, precisely because Europe was fragmented, Columbus succeeded on his fifth try in persuading one of Europe's hundreds of princes to sponsor him. Once Spain had thus launched the European colonization of America, other European states saw the wealth flowing into Spain, and six more joined in colonizing America. The story was the same with Europe's cannon, electric lighting, printing, small firearms, and innumerable other innovations: each was at first neglected or opposed in some parts of Europe for idiosyncratic reasons, but once adopted in one area, it eventually spread to the rest of Europe.

These consequences of Europe's disunity stand in sharp contrast to those of China's unity. From time to time the Chinese court decided to halt other activities besides overseas navigation: it abandoned development of an elaborate water-driven spinning machine, stepped back from the verge of an industrial revolution in the 14th century, demolished or virtually abolished mechanical clocks after leading the world in clock construction, and retreated from mechanical devices and technology in general after the late 15th century. Those potentially harmful effects of unity have flared up again in modern China, notably during the madness of the Cultural Revolution in the 1960s and 1970s, when a decision by one or a few leaders closed the whole country's school systems for five years.

China's frequent unity and Europe's perpetual disunity both have a long history. The most productive areas of modern China were politically joined for the first time in 221 B.C. and have remained so for most of the time since then. China has had only a single writing system from the beginnings of literacy, a single dominant language for a long time, and substantial cultural unity for two thousand years. In contrast, Europe has never come remotely close to political unification: it was still splintered into 1,000 independent statelets in the 14th century, into 500 statelets in A.D. 1500, got down to a minimum of 25 states in the 1980s, and is now up again to nearly 40 at the moment that I write this sentence. Europe still has 45 languages, each with its own modified alphabet, and even greater cultural diversity. The disagreements that continue today to frustrate even modest attempts at European unification through the European Economic Community (EEC) are symptomatic of Europe's ingrained commitment to disunity.

Hence the real problem in understanding China's loss of political and technological preeminence to Europe is to understand China's chronic unity and Europe's chronic disunity. The answer is again suggested by maps (see page 415). Europe has a highly indented coastline, with five large peninsulas that approach islands in their isolation, and all of which evolved independent languages, ethnic groups, and governments: Greece, Italy, Iberia, Denmark, and Norway / Sweden. China's coastline is much smoother, and only the nearby Korean Peninsula attained separate importance. Europe has two islands (Britain and Ireland) sufficiently big to assert their political independence and to maintain their own languages and ethnicities, and one of them (Britain) big and close enough to become a major independent European power. But even China's two largest islands, Taiwan and Hainan, have each less than half the area of Ireland; neither was a major independent power until Taiwan's emergence in recent decades; and Japan's geographic isolation kept it until recently much more isolated politically from the Asian mainland than Britain has been from mainland Europe. Europe is carved up into independent linguistic, ethnic, and political units by high mountains (the Alps, Pyrenees, Carpathians, and Norwegian border mountains), while China's mountains east of the Tibetan plateau are much less formidable barriers. China's heartland is bound together from east to west by two long navigable river systems in rich alluvial valleys (the Yangtze and Yellow Rivers), and it is joined from north to south by relatively easy connections between these two river systems (eventually linked by canals). As a result, China very early became dominated by two huge geographic core areas of high productivity, themselves only weakly separated from each other and eventually fused into a single core. Europe's two biggest rivers, the Rhine and Danube, are smaller and connect much less of Europe. Unlike China, Europe has many scattered small core areas, none big enough to dominate the others for long, and each the center of chronically independent states.

Once China was finally unified, in 221 B.C., no other independent state ever had a chance of arising and persisting for long in China. Although periods of disunity returned several times after 221 B.C., they always ended in reunification. But the unification of Europe has resisted the efforts of such determined conquerors as Charlemagne, Napoleon, and Hitler; even the Roman Empire at its peak never controlled more than half of Europe's area.

Thus, geographic connectedness and only modest internal barriers gave China an initial advantage. North China, South China, the coast, and the

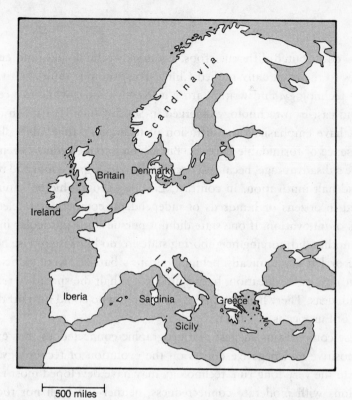

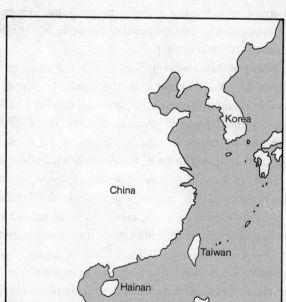

Comparison of the coastlines of China and of Europe, drawn to the same scale. Note that Europe's is much more indented and includes more large peninsulas and two large islands.

interior contributed different crops, livestock, technologies, and cultural features to the eventually unified China. For example, millet cultivation, bronze technology, and writing arose in North China, while rice cultivation and cast-iron technology emerged in South China. For much of this book I have emphasized the diffusion of technology that takes place in the absence of formidable barriers. But China's connectedness eventually became a disadvantage, because a decision by one despot could and repeatedly did halt innovation. In contrast, Europe's geographic balkanization resulted in dozens or hundreds of independent, competing statelets and centers of innovation. If one state did not pursue some particular innovation, another did, forcing neighboring states to do likewise or else be conquered or left economically behind. Europe's barriers were sufficient to prevent political unification, but insufficient to halt the spread of technology and ideas. There has never been one despot who could turn off the tap for all of Europe, as of China.

These comparisons suggest that geographic connectedness has exerted both positive and negative effects on the evolution of technology. As a result, in the very long run, technology may have developed most rapidly in regions with moderate connectedness, neither too high nor too low. Technology's course over the last 1,000 years in China, Europe, and possibly the Indian subcontinent exemplifies those net effects of high, moderate, and low connectedness, respectively.

Naturally, additional factors contributed to history's diverse courses in different parts of Eurasia. For instance, the Fertile Crescent, China, and Europe differed in their exposure to the perennial threat of barbarian invasions by horse-mounted pastoral nomads of Central Asia. One of those nomad groups (the Mongols) eventually destroyed the ancient irrigation systems of Iran and Iraq, but none of the Asian nomads ever succeeded in establishing themselves in the forests of western Europe beyond the Hungarian plains. Environmental factors also include the Fertile Crescent's geographically intermediate location, controlling the trade routes linking China and India to Europe, and China's more remote location from Eurasia's other advanced civilizations, making China a gigantic virtual island within a continent. China's relative isolation is especially relevant to its adoption and then rejection of technologies, so reminiscent of the rejections on Tasmania and other islands (Chapters 13 and 15). But this brief discussion may at least indicate the relevance of environmental factors to smaller-scale and shorter-term patterns of history, as well as to history's broadest pattern.

The histories of the Fertile Crescent and China also hold a salutary lesson for the modern world: circumstances change, and past primacy is no guarantee of future primacy. One might even wonder whether the geographical reasoning employed throughout this book has at last become wholly irrelevant in the modern world, now that ideas diffuse everywhere instantly on the Internet and cargo is routinely airfreighted overnight between continents. It might seem that entirely new rules apply to competition between the world's peoples, and that as a result new powers are emerging—such as Taiwan, Korea, Malaysia, and especially Japan.

On reflection, though, we see that the supposedly new rules are just variations on the old ones. Yes, the transistor, invented at Bell Labs in the eastern United States in 1947, leapt 8,000 miles to launch an electronics industry in Japan—but it did not make the shorter leap to found new industries in Zaire or Paraguay. The nations rising to new power are still ones that were incorporated thousands of years ago into the old centers of dominance based on food production, or that have been repopulated by peoples from those centers. Unlike Zaire or Paraguay, Japan and the other new powers were able to exploit the transistor quickly because their populations already had a long history of literacy, metal machinery, and centralized government. The world's two earliest centers of food production, the Fertile Crescent and China, still dominate the modern world, either through their immediate successor states (modern China), or through states situated in neighboring regions influenced early by those two centers (Japan, Korea, Malaysia, and Europe), or through states repopulated or ruled by their overseas emigrants (the United States, Australia, Brazil). Prospects for world dominance of sub-Saharan Africans, Aboriginal Australians, and Native Americans remain dim. The hand of history's course at 8000 B.C. lies heavily on us.

AMONG OTHER FACTORS relevant to answering Yali's question, cultural factors and influences of individual people loom large. To take the former first, human cultural traits vary greatly around the world. Some of that cultural variation is no doubt a product of environmental variation, and I have discussed many examples in this book. But an important question concerns the possible significance of local cultural factors unrelated to the environment. A minor cultural feature may arise for trivial, temporary local reasons, become fixed, and then predispose a society toward more important cultural choices, as is suggested by applications of chaos theory to other fields of science. Such cultural processes are among history's wild cards that would tend to make history unpredictable.

As one example, I mentioned in Chapter 13 the QWERTY keyboard for typewriters. It was adopted initially, out of many competing keyboard designs, for trivial specific reasons involving early typewriter construction in America in the 1860s, typewriter salesmanship, a decision in 1882 by a certain Ms. Longley who founded the Shorthand and Typewriter Institute in Cincinnati, and the success of Ms. Longley's star typing pupil Frank McGurrin, who thrashed Ms. Longley's non-QWERTY competitor Louis Taub in a widely publicized typing contest in 1888. The decision could have gone to another keyboard at any of numerous stages between the 1860s and the 1880s; nothing about the American environment favored the QWERTY keyboard over its rivals. Once the decision had been made, though, the QWERTY keyboard became so entrenched that it was also adopted for computer keyboard design a century later. Equally trivial specific reasons, now lost in the remote past, may have lain behind the Sumerian adoption of a counting system based on 12 instead of 10 (leading to our modern 60-minute hour, 24-hour day, 12-month year, and 360-degree circle), in contrast to the widespread Mesoamerican counting system based on 20 (leading to its calendar using two concurrent cycles of 260 named days and a 365-day year).

Those details of typewriter, clock, and calendar design have not affected the competitive success of the societies adopting them. But it is easy to imagine how they could have. For example, if the QWERTY keyboard of the United States had not been adopted elsewhere in the world as well—say, if Japan or Europe had adopted the much more efficient Dvorak keyboard—that trivial decision in the 19th century might have had big consequences for the competitive position of 20th-century American technology.

Similarly, a study of Chinese children suggested that they learn to write more quickly when taught an alphabetic transcription of Chinese sounds (termed pinyin) than when taught traditional Chinese writing, with its thousands of signs. It has been suggested that the latter arose because of their convenience for distinguishing the large numbers of Chinese words possessing differing meanings but the same sounds (homophones). If so, the abundance of homophones in the Chinese language may have had a large impact on the role of literacy in Chinese society, yet it seems unlikely that there was anything in the Chinese environment selecting for a language rich in homophones. Did a linguistic or cultural factor account for the otherwise puzzling failure of complex Andean civilizations to develop writing? Was there anything about India's environment predisposing toward rigid socioeconomic castes, with grave consequences for the development of technology in India? Was there anything about the Chinese environment predisposing toward Confucian philosophy and cultural conservatism, which may also have profoundly affected history? Why was proselytizing religion (Christianity and Islam) a driving force for colonization and conquest among Europeans and West Asians but not among Chinese?

These examples illustrate the broad range of questions concerning cultural idiosyncrasies, unrelated to environment and initially of little significance, that might evolve into influential and long-lasting cultural features. Their significance constitutes an important unanswered question. It can best be approached by concentrating attention on historical patterns that remain puzzling after the effects of major environmental factors have been taken into account.

WHAT ABOUT THE effects of idiosyncratic individual people? A familiar modern example is the narrow failure, on July 20, 1944, of the assassination attempt against Hitler and of a simultaneous uprising in Berlin. Both had been planned by Germans who were convinced that the war could not be won and who wanted to seek peace then, at a time when the eastern front between the German and Russian armies still lay mostly within Russia's borders. Hitler was wounded by a time bomb in a briefcase placed under a conference table; he might have been killed if the case had been placed slightly closer to the chair where he was sitting. It is likely that the modern map of Eastern Europe and the Cold War's course would have been significantly different if Hitler had indeed been killed and if World War II had ended then.

Less well known but even more fateful was a traffic accident in the summer of 1930, over two years before Hitler's seizure of power in Germany, when a car in which he was riding in the "death seat" (right front passenger seat) collided with a heavy trailer truck. The truck braked just in time to avoid running over Hitler's car and crushing him. Because of the degree to which Hitler's psychopathology determined Nazi policy and success, the form of an eventual World War II would probably have been quite different if the truck driver had braked one second later.

One can think of other individuals whose idiosyncrasies apparently influenced history as did Hitler's: Alexander the Great, Augustus, Buddha, Christ, Lenin, Martin Luther, the Inca emperor Pachacuti, Mohammed, William the Conqueror, and the Zulu king Shaka, to name a few. To what extent did each really change events, as opposed to "just" happening to be the right person in the right place at the right time? At the one extreme is the view of the historian Thomas Carlyle: "Universal history, the history of what man [sic] has accomplished in this world, is at bottom the History of the Great Men who have worked here." At the opposite extreme is the view of the Prussian statesman Otto von Bismarck, who unlike Carlyle had long firsthand experience of politics' inner workings: "The statesman's task is to hear God's footsteps marching through history, and to try to catch on to His coattails as He marches past."

Like cultural idiosyncrasies, individual idiosyncrasies throw wild cards into the course of history. They may make history inexplicable in terms of environmental forces, or indeed of any generalizable causes. For the purposes of this book, however, they are scarcely relevant, because even the most ardent proponent of the Great Man theory would find it difficult to interpret history's broadest pattern in terms of a few Great Men. Perhaps Alexander the Great did nudge the course of western Eurasia's already literate, food-producing, iron-equipped states, but he had nothing to do with the fact that western Eurasia already supported literate, food-producing, iron-equipped states at a time when Australia still supported only nonliterate hunter-gatherer tribes lacking metal tools. Nevertheless, it remains an open question how wide and lasting the effects of idiosyncratic individuals on history really are.

THE DISCIPLINE OF history is generally not considered to be a science, but something closer to the humanities. At best, history is classified among the social sciences, of which it rates as the least scientific. While the field of government is often termed "political science" and the Nobel Prize in economics refers to "economic science," history departments rarely if ever label themselves "Department of Historical Science." Most historians do not think of themselves as scientists and receive little training in acknowledged sciences and their methodologies. The sense that history is nothing more than a mass of details is captured in numerous aphorisms: "History is just one damn fact after another," "History is more or less bunk," "There is no law of history any more than of a kaleidoscope," and so on.

One cannot deny that it is more difficult to extract general principles from studying history than from studying planetary orbits. However, the difficulties seem to me not fatal. Similar ones apply to other historical subjects whose place among the natural sciences is nevertheless secure, including astronomy, climatology, ecology, evolutionary biology, geology, and paleontology. People's image of science is unfortunately often based on physics and a few other fields with similar methodologies. Scientists in those fields tend to be ignorantly disdainful of fields to which those methodologies are inappropriate and which must therefore seek other methodologies—such as my own research areas of ecology and evolutionary biology. But recall that the word "science" means "knowledge" (from the Latin *scire,* "to know," and *scientia,* "knowledge"), to be obtained by whatever methods are most appropriate to the particular field. Hence I have much empathy with students of human history for the difficulties they face.

Historical sciences in the broad sense (including astronomy and the like) share many features that set them apart from nonhistorical sciences such as physics, chemistry, and molecular biology. I would single out four: methodology, causation, prediction, and complexity.

In physics the chief method for gaining knowledge is the laboratory experiment, by which one manipulates the parameter whose effect is in question, executes parallel control experiments with that parameter held constant, holds other parameters constant throughout, replicates both the experimental manipulation and the control experiment, and obtains quantitative data. This strategy, which also works well in chemistry and molecular biology, is so identified with science in the minds of many people that experimentation is often held to be the essence of the scientific method. But laboratory experimentation can obviously play little or no role in many of the historical sciences. One cannot interrupt galaxy formation, start and stop hurricanes and ice ages, experimentally exterminate grizzly bears in a few national parks, or rerun the course of dinosaur evolution. Instead, one must gain knowledge in these historical sciences by other means, such as observation, comparison, and so-called natural experiments (to which I shall return in a moment).

Historical sciences are concerned with chains of proximate and ultimate causes. In most of physics and chemistry the concepts of "ultimate cause," "purpose," and "function" are meaningless, yet they are essential to understanding living systems in general and human activities in particular. For instance, an evolutionary biologist studying Arctic hares whose fur color turns from brown in summer to white in winter is not satisfied with identifying the mundane proximate causes of fur color in terms of the fur pigments' molecular structures and biosynthetic pathways. The more important questions involve function (camouflage against predators?) and ultimate cause (natural selection starting with an ancestral hare population with seasonally unchanging fur color?). Similarly, a European historian is not satisfied with describing the condition of Europe in both 1815 and 1918 as having just achieved peace after a costly pan-European war. Understanding the contrasting chains of events leading up to the two peace treaties is essential to understanding why an even more costly pan-European war broke out again within a few decades of 1918 but not of 1815. But chemists do not assign a purpose or function to a collision of two gas molecules, nor do they seek an ultimate cause for the collision.

Still another difference between historical and nonhistorical sciences involves prediction. In chemistry and physics the acid test of one's understanding of a system is whether one can successfully predict its future behavior. Again, physicists tend to look down on evolutionary biology and history, because those fields appear to fail this test. In historical sciences, one can provide a posteriori explanations (e.g., why an asteroid impact on Earth 66 million years ago may have driven dinosaurs but not many other species to extinction), but a priori predictions are more difficult (we would be uncertain which species would be driven to extinction if we did not have the actual past event to guide us). However, historians and historical scientists do make and test predictions about what future discoveries of data will show us about past events.

The properties of historical systems that complicate attempts at prediction can be described in several alternative ways. One can point out that human societies and dinosaurs are extremely complex, being characterized by an enormous number of independent variables that feed back on each other. As a result, small changes at a lower level of organization can lead to emergent changes at a higher level. A typical example is the effect of that one truck driver's braking response, in Hitler's nearly fatal traffic accident of 1930, on the lives of a hundred million people who were killed or wounded in World War II. Although most biologists agree that biological systems are in the end wholly determined by their physical properties and obey the laws of quantum mechanics, the systems' complexity means, for practical purposes, that that deterministic causation does not translate into predictability. Knowledge of quantum mechanics does not help one understand why introduced placental predators have exterminated so many Australian marsupial species, or why the Allied Powers rather than the Central Powers won World War I.

Each glacier, nebula, hurricane, human society, and biological species, and even each individual and cell of a sexually reproducing species, is unique, because it is influenced by so many variables and made up of so many variable parts. In contrast, for any of the physicist's elementary particles and isotopes and of the chemist's molecules, all individuals of the entity are identical to each other. Hence physicists and chemists can formulate universal deterministic laws at the macroscopic level, but biologists and historians can formulate only statistical trends. With a very high probability of being correct, I can predict that, of the next 1,000 babies born at the University of California Medical Center, where I work, not fewer than 480 or more than 520 will be boys. But I had no means of knowing in advance that my own two children would be boys. Similarly, historians note that tribal societies may have been more likely to develop into chiefdoms if the local population was sufficiently large and dense and if there was potential for surplus food production than if that was not the case. But each such local population has its own unique features, with the result that chiefdoms did emerge in the highlands of Mexico, Guatemala, Peru, and Madagascar, but not in those of New Guinea or Guadalcanal.

Still another way of describing the complexity and unpredictability of historical systems, despite their ultimate determinacy, is to note that long chains of causation may separate final effects from ultimate causes lying outside the domain of that field of science. For example, the dinosaurs may have been exterminated by the impact of an asteroid whose orbit was completely determined by the laws of classical mechanics. But if there had been any paleontologists living 67 million years ago, they could not have predicted the dinosaurs' imminent demise, because asteroids belong to a field of science otherwise remote from dinosaur biology. Similarly, the Lit-

tle Ice Age of A.D. 1300–1500 contributed to the extinction of the Greenland Norse, but no historian, and probably not even a modern cli-
matologist, could have predicted the Little Ice Age.

THUS, THE DIFFICULTIES historians face in establishing cause-and-
effect relations in the history of human societies are broadly similar to
the difficulties facing astronomers, climatologists, ecologists, evolutionary
biologists, geologists, and paleontologists. To varying degrees, each of
these fields is plagued by the impossibility of performing replicated, controlled experimental interventions, the complexity arising from enormous
numbers of variables, the resulting uniqueness of each system, the conse-
quent impossibility of formulating universal laws, and the difficulties of
predicting emergent properties and future behavior. Prediction in history,
as in other historical sciences, is most feasible on large spatial scales and
over long times, when the unique features of millions of small-scale brief
events become averaged out. Just as I could predict the sex ratio of the
next 1,000 newborns but not the sexes of my own two children, the historian can recognize factors that made inevitable the broad outcome of the
collision between American and Eurasian societies after 13,000 years of
separate developments, but not the outcome of the 1960 U.S. presidential
election. The details of which candidate said what during a single televised
debate in October 1960 could have given the electoral victory to Nixon
instead of to Kennedy, but no details of who said what could have blocked
the European conquest of Native Americans.

How can students of human history profit from the experience of scientists in other historical sciences? A methodology that has proved useful
involves the comparative method and so-called natural experiments. While
neither astronomers studying galaxy formation nor human historians can
manipulate their systems in controlled laboratory experiments, they both
can take advantage of natural experiments, by comparing systems differing in the presence or absence (or in the strong or weak effect) of some
putative causative factor. For example, epidemiologists, forbidden to feed
large amounts of salt to people experimentally, have still been able to identify effects of high salt intake by comparing groups of humans who already
differ greatly in their salt intake; and cultural anthropologists, unable to
provide human groups experimentally with varying resource abundances
for many centuries, still study long-term effects of resource abundance on

human societies by comparing recent Polynesian populations living on islands differing naturally in resource abundance. The student of human history can draw on many more natural experiments than just comparisons among the five inhabited continents. Comparisons can also utilize large islands that have developed complex societies in a considerable degree of isolation (such as Japan, Madagascar, Native American Hispaniola, New Guinea, Hawaii, and many others), as well as societies on hundreds of smaller islands and regional societies within each of the continents.

Natural experiments in any field, whether in ecology or human history, are inherently open to potential methodological criticisms. Those include confounding effects of natural variation in additional variables besides the one of interest, as well as problems in inferring chains of causation from observed correlations between variables. Such methodological problems have been discussed in great detail for some of the historical sciences. In particular, epidemiology, the science of drawing inferences about human diseases by comparing groups of people (often by retrospective historical studies), has for a long time successfully employed formalized procedures for dealing with problems similar to those facing historians of human societies. Ecologists have also devoted much attention to the problems of natural experiments, a methodology to which they must resort in many cases where direct experimental interventions to manipulate relevant ecological variables would be immoral, illegal, or impossible. Evolutionary biologists have recently been developing ever more sophisticated methods for drawing conclusions from comparisons of different plants and animals of known evolutionary histories.

In short, I acknowledge that it is much more difficult to understand human history than to understand problems in fields of science where history is unimportant and where fewer individual variables operate. Nevertheless, successful methodologies for analyzing historical problems have been worked out in several fields. As a result, the histories of dinosaurs, nebulas, and glaciers are generally acknowledged to belong to fields of science rather than to the humanities. But introspection gives us far more insight into the ways of other humans than into those of dinosaurs. I am thus optimistic that historical studies of human societies can be pursued as scientifically as studies of dinosaurs—and with profit to our own society today, by teaching us what shaped the modern world, and what might shape our future.

ACKNOWLEDGMENTS

I T IS A PLEASURE FOR ME TO ACKNOWLEDGE THE CONTRIBU-
tions of many people to this book. My teachers at Roxbury Latin
School introduced me to the fascination of history. My great debt to my
many New Guinea friends will be obvious from the frequency with which
I cite their experiences. I owe an equally great debt (and absolution from
responsibility for my errors) to my many scientist friends and professional
colleagues, who patiently explained the subtleties of their subjects and
read my drafts. In particular, Peter Bellwood, Kent Flannery, Patrick
Kirch, and my wife, Marie Cohen, read the whole manuscript, and Charles
Heiser, Jr., David Keightley, Bruce Smith, Richard Yarnell, and Daniel
Zohary each read several chapters. Earlier versions of several of the chapters appeared as articles in *Discover* magazine and in *Natural History*
magazine. The National Geographic Society, World Wildlife Fund, and
University of California at Los Angeles supported my fieldwork on Pacific
islands. I have been fortunate to have John Brockman and Katinka Matson
as my agents, Lori Iversen and Lori Rosen as my research assistants and
secretaries, Ellen Modecki as my illustrator, and as my editors Donald
Lamm at W. W. Norton, Neil Belton and Will Sulkin at Jonathan Cape,
Willi Köhler at Fischer, Marc Zabludoff and Mark Wheeler and Polly
Shulman at *Discover*, and Ellen Goldensohn and Alan Ternes at *Natural
History*.

FURTHER READINGS

THESE SUGGESTIONS ARE FOR THOSE INTERESTED IN READing further. Hence, in addition to key books and papers, I have favored references that provide comprehensive listings of the earlier literature. A journal title (in italics) is followed by the volume number, followed after a colon by the first and last page numbers, and then the year of publication in parentheses.

Prologue

Among references relevant to most chapters of this book is an enormous compendium of human gene frequencies entitled *The History and Geography of Human Genes*, by L. Luca Cavalli-Sforza, Paolo Menozzi, and Alberto Piazza (Princeton: Princeton University Press, 1994). This remarkable book approximates a history of everything about everybody, because the authors begin their accounts of each continent with a convenient summary of the continent's geography, ecology, and environment, followed by the prehistory, history, languages, physical anthropology, and culture of its peoples. L. Luca Cavalli-Sforza and Francisco Cavalli-Sforza, *The Great Human Diasporas* (Reading, Mass.: Addison-Wesley, 1995), covers similar material but is written for the general reader rather than for specialists.

Another convenient source is a series of five volumes entitled *The Illus-trated History of Humankind*, ed. Göran Burenhult (San Francisco: Har-perCollins, 1993–94). The five individual volumes in this series are enti-tled, respectively, *The First Humans, People of the Stone Age, Old World Civilizations, New World and Pacific Civilizations,* and *Traditional Peo-ples Today.*

Several series of volumes published by Cambridge University Press (Cambridge, England, various dates) provide histories of particular regions or eras. One series consists of books entitled *The Cambridge His-tory of [X],* where X is variously Africa, Early Inner Asia, China, India, Iran, Islam, Japan, Latin America, Poland, and Southeast Asia. Another series is *The Cambridge Encyclopedia of [X],* where X is variously Africa, China, Japan, Latin America and the Caribbean, Russia and the former Soviet Union, Australia, the Middle East and North Africa, and India, Pakistan, and adjacent countries. Still other series include *The Cambridge Ancient History, The Cambridge Medieval History, The Cambridge Mod-ern History, The Cambridge Economic History of Europe,* and *The Cam-bridge Economic History of India.*

Three encyclopedic accounts of the world's languages are Barbara Grimes, *Ethnologue: Languages of the World,* 13th ed. (Dallas: Summer Institute of Linguistics, 1996), Merritt Ruhlen, *A Guide to the World's Languages,* (Stanford: Stanford University Press, 1987), and C. F. Voegelin and F. M. Voegelin, *Classification and Index of the World's Languages* (New York: Elsevier, 1977).

Among large-scale comparative histories, Arnold Toynbee, *A Study of History,* 12 vols. (London: Oxford University Press, 1934–54), stands out. An excellent history of Eurasian civilization, especially western Eurasian civilization, is William McNeill, *The Rise of the West* (Chicago: University of Chicago Press, 1991). The same author's *A World History* (New York: Oxford University Press, 1979), despite its title, also maintains a focus on western Eurasian civilization, as does V. Gordon Childe, *What Happened in History,* rev. ed. (Baltimore: Penguin Books, 1954). Another compara-tive history with a focus on western Eurasia, C. D. Darlington, *The Evolu-tion of Man and Society* (New York: Simon and Schuster, 1969), is by a biologist who recognizes some of the same links between continental his-tory and domestication that I discuss. Two books by Alfred Crosby are distinguished studies of the European overseas expansion with emphasis on its accompanying plants, animals, and germs: *The Columbian Exchange: Biological Consequences of 1492* (Westport, Conn.: Greenwood, 1972) and *Ecological Imperialism: The Biological Expansion of Europe, 900–1900* (Cambridge: Cambridge University Press, 1986). Marvin Harris, *Cannibals and Kings: The Origins of Cultures* (New York: Vintage Books, 1978), and Marshall Sahlins and Elman Service, eds., *Evolution and Culture* (Ann Arbor: University of Michigan Press, 1960), are comparative histories from the perspective of cultural anthropologists. Ellen Semple, *Influences of Geographic Environment* (New York: Holt, 1911), is an example of earlier efforts to study geographic influences on human societies. Other important historical studies are listed under further readings for the Epilogue. My book *The Third Chimpanzee* (New York: HarperCollins, 1992), especially its chapter 14, on the comparative histories of Eurasia and the Americas, provided the starting point for my thinking about the present book.

The best-known or most notorious recent entrant into the debate about group differences in intelligence is Richard Herrnstein and Charles Murray, *The Bell Curve: Intelligence and Class Structure in American Life* (New York: Free Press, 1994).

Chapter 1

Excellent books about early human evolution include Richard Klein, *The Human Career* (Chicago: University of Chicago Press, 1989), Roger Lewin, *Bones of Contention* (New York: Simon and Schuster, 1989), Paul Mellars and Chris Stringer, eds., *The Human Revolution: Behavioural and Biological Perspectives on the Origins of Modern Humans* (Edinburgh: Edinburgh University Press, 1989), Richard Leakey and Roger Lewin, *Origins Reconsidered* (New York: Doubleday, 1992), D. Tab Rasmussen, ed., *The Origin and Evolution of Humans and Humanness* (Boston: Jones and Bartlett, 1993), Matthew Nitecki and Doris Nitecki, eds., *Origins of Anatomically Modern Humans* (New York: Plenum, 1994), and Chris Stringer and Robin McKie, *African Exodus* (London: Jonathan Cape, 1996). Three popular books dealing specifically with the Neanderthals are Christopher Stringer and Clive Gamble, *In Search of the Neanderthals* (New York:

Thames and Hudson, 1993), Erik Trinkaus and Pat Shipman, *The Neandertals* (New York: Knopf, 1993), and Ian Tattersall, *The Last Neanderthal* (New York: Macmillan, 1995).

Genetic evidence of human origins is the subject of the two books by L. Luca Cavalli-Sforza et al. already cited under the Prologue, and of chapter 1 of my book *The Third Chimpanzee*. Two technical papers with recent advances in the genetic evidence are J. L. Mountain and L. L. Cavalli-Sforza, "Inference of human evolution through cladistic analysis of nuclear DNA restriction polymorphism," *Proceedings of the National Academy of Sciences* 91:6515–19 (1994), and D. B. Goldstein et al., "Genetic absolute dating based on microsatellites and the origin of modern humans," ibid. 92:6723–27 (1995).

References to the human colonization of Australia, New Guinea, and the Bismarck and Solomon Archipelagoes, and to extinctions of large animals there, are listed under further readings for Chapter 15. In particular, Tim Flannery, *The Future Eaters* (New York: Braziller, 1995), discusses those subjects in clear, understandable terms and explains the problems with claims of very recent survival of extinct big Australian mammals.

The standard text on Late Pleistocene and Recent extinctions of large animals is Paul Martin and Richard Klein, eds., *Quaternary Extinctions* (Tucson: University of Arizona Press, 1984). More recent updates are Richard Klein, "The impact of early people on the environment: The case of large mammal extinctions," pp. 13–34 in J. E. Jacobsen and J. Firor, *Human Impact on the Environment* (Boulder, Colo.: Westview Press, 1992), and Anthony Stuart, "Mammalian extinctions in the Late Pleistocene of Northern Eurasia and North America," *Biological Reviews* 66:453–62 (1991). David Steadman summarizes recent evidence that extinction waves accompanied human settlement of Pacific islands in his paper "Prehistoric extinctions of Pacific island birds: Biodiversity meets zooarchaeology," *Science* 267:1123–31 (1995).

Popular accounts of the settlement of the Americas, the accompanying extinctions of large mammals, and the resulting controversies are Brian Fagan, *The Great Journey: The Peopling of Ancient America* (New York: Thames and Hudson, 1987), and chapter 18 of my book *The Third Chimpanzee*, both of which provide many other references. Ronald Carlisle, ed., *Americans before Columbus: Ice-Age Origins* (Pittsburgh: University of Pittsburgh, 1988), includes a chapter by J. M. Adovasio and his colleagues on pre-Clovis evidence at the Meadowcroft site. Papers by C. Vance

Haynes, Jr., an expert on the Clovis horizon and reported pre-Clovis sites, include "Contributions of radiocarbon dating to the geochronology of the peopling of the New World," pp. 354–74 in R. E. Taylor, A. Long, and R. S. Kra, eds., *Radiocarbon after Four Decades* (New York: Springer, 1992), and "Clovis-Folson geochronology and climate change," pp. 219–36 in Olga Soffer and N. D. Praslov, eds., *From Kostenki to Clovis: Upper Paleolithic Paleo-Indian Adaptations* (New York: Plenum, 1993). Pre-Clovis claims for the Pedra Furada site are argued by N. Guidon and G. Delibrias, "Carbon-14 dates point to man in the Americas 32,000 years ago," *Nature* 321:769–71 (1986), and David Meltzer et al., "On a Pleistocene human occupation at Pedra Furada, Brazil," *Antiquity* 68:695–714 (1994). Other publications relevant to the pre-Clovis debate include T. D. Dillehay et al., "Earliest hunters and gatherers of South America," *Journal of World Prehistory* 6:145–204 (1992), T. D. Dillehay, *Monte Verde: A Late Pleistocene Site in Chile* (Washington, D.C.; Smithsonian Institution Press, 1989), T. D. Dillehay and D. J. Meltzer, eds., *The First Americans: Search and Research* (Boca Raton: CRC Press, 1991), Thomas Lynch "Glacial-age man in South America?—a critical review," *American Antiquity* 55:12–36 (1990), John Hoffecker et al., "The colonization of Beringia and the peopling of the New World," *Science* 259:46–53 (1993), and A. C. Roosevelt et al., "Paleoindian cave dwellers in the Amazon: The peopling of the Americas," *Science* 272:373–84 (1996).

Chapter 2

Two outstanding books explicitly concerned with cultural differences among Polynesian islands are Patrick Kirch, *The Evolution of the Polynesian Chiefdoms* (Cambridge: Cambridge University Press, 1984), and the same author's *The Wet and the Dry* (Chicago: University of Chicago Press, 1994). Much of Peter Bellwood's *The Polynesians,* rev. ed. (London: Thames and Hudson, 1987), also deals with this problem. Notable books dealing with specific Polynesian islands include Michael King, *Moriori* (Auckland: Penguin, 1989), on the Chatham Islands, Patrick Kirch, *Feathered Gods and Fishhooks* (Honolulu: University of Hawaii Press, 1985), on Hawaii, Patrick Kirch and Marshall Sahlins, *Anahulu* (Chicago: University of Chicago Press, 1992), also on Hawaii, Jo Anne Van Tilburg, *Easter Island* (Washington, D.C.: Smithsonian Institution Press, 1994), and Paul Bahn and John Flenley, *Easter Island, Earth Island* (London: Thames and Hudson, 1992).

Chapter 3

My account of Pizarro's capture of Atahuallpa combines the eyewitness accounts by Francisco Pizarro's brothers Hernando Pizarro and Pedro Pizarro and by Pizarro's companions Miguel de Estete, Cristóbal de Mena, Ruiz de Arce, and Francisco de Xerez. The accounts by Hernando Pizarro, Miguel de Estete, and Francisco de Xerez have been translated by Clements Markham, *Reports on the Discovery of Peru,* Hakluyt Society, 1st ser., vol. 47 (New York, 1872); Pedro Pizarro's account, by Philip Means, *Relation of the Discovery and Conquest of the Kingdoms of Peru* (New York: Cortés Society, 1921); and Cristóbal de Mena's account, by Joseph Sinclair, *The Conquest of Peru, as Recorded by a Member of the Pizarro Expedition* (New York, 1929). The account by Ruiz de Arce was reprinted in *Boletín de la Real Academia de Historia* (Madrid) 102:327–84 (1933). John Hemming's excellent *The Conquest of the Incas* (San Diego: Harcourt Brace Jovanovich, 1970) gives a full account of the capture and indeed of the whole conquest, with an extensive bibliography. A 19th-century account of the conquest, William H. Prescott's *History of the Conquest of Peru* (New York, 1847), is still highly readable and ranks among the classics of historical writing. Corresponding modern and classic 19th-century accounts of the Spanish conquest of the Aztecs are, respectively, Hugh Thomas, *Conquest: Montezuma, Cortés, and the Fall of Old Mexico* (New York: Simon and Schuster, 1993), and William Prescott, *History of the Conquest of Mexico* (New York, 1843). Contemporary eyewitness accounts of the conquest of the Aztecs were written by Cortés himself (reprinted as Hernando Cortés, *Five Letters of Cortés to the Emperor* [New York: Norton, 1969]) and by many of Cortés's companions (reprinted in Patricia de Fuentes, ed., *The Conquistadors* [Norman: University of Oklahoma Press, 1993]).

Chapters 4–10

References for these seven chapters on food production will be combined, since many of the references apply to more than one of them.

Five important sources, all of them excellent and fact-filled, address the question how food production evolved from the hunter-gatherer lifestyle: Kent Flannery, "The origins of agriculture," *Annual Reviews of Anthropology* 2:271–310 (1973); Jack Harlan, *Crops and Man,* 2nd ed. (Madison, Wis.: American Society of Agronomy, 1992); Richard MacNeish, *The Origins of Agriculture and Settled Life* (Norman: University of Oklahoma Press, 1992); David Rindos, *The Origins of Agriculture: An Evolutionary Perspective* (San Diego: Academic Press, 1984); and Bruce Smith, *The Emergence of Agriculture* (New York: Scientific American Library, 1995). Notable older references about food production in general include two multi-author volumes: Peter Ucko and G. W. Dimbleby, eds., *The Domestication and Exploitation of Plants and Animals* (Chicago: Aldine, 1969), and Charles Reed, ed., *Origins of Agriculture* (The Hague: Mouton, 1977). Carl Sauer, *Agricultural Origins and Dispersals* (New York: American Geographical Society, 1952), is a classic early comparison of Old World and New World food production, while Erich Isaac, *Geography of Domestication* (Englewood Cliffs, N. J.: Prentice-Hall, 1970), addresses the questions of where, when, and how regarding plant and animal domestication.

Among references specifically about plant domestication, Daniel Zohary and Maria Hopf, *Domestication of Plants in the Old World,* 2nd ed. (Oxford: Oxford University Press, 1993), stands out. It provides the most detailed account of plant domestication available for any part of the world. For each significant crop grown in western Eurasia, the book summarizes archaeological and genetic evidence about its domestication and subsequent spread.

Among important multi-author books on plant domestication are C. Wesley Cowan and Patty Jo Watson, eds., *The Origins of Agriculture* (Washington, D.C.: Smithsonian Institution Press, 1992), David Harris and Gordon Hillman, eds., *Foraging and Farming: The Evolution of Plant Exploitation* (London: Unwin Hyman, 1989), and C. Barigozzi, ed., *The Origin and Domestication of Cultivated Plants* (Amsterdam: Elsevier, 1986). Two engaging popular accounts of plant domestication by Charles Heiser, Jr., are *Seed to Civilization: The Story of Food,* 3rd ed. (Cambridge: Harvard University Press, 1990), and *Of Plants and People* (Norman: University of Oklahoma Press, 1985). J. Smartt and N. W. Simmonds, ed., *Evolution of Crop Plants,* 2nd ed. (London: Longman, 1995), is the standard reference volume summarizing information about all of the world's major crops and many minor ones. Three excellent papers describe the changes that evolve automatically in wild plants under human cultivation: Mark Blumler and Roger Byrne, "The ecological genetics of domestication and the origins of agriculture," *Current Anthropology* 32:23–54 (1991); Charles Heiser, Jr., "Aspects of unconscious selection and the evolution of domesticated plants," *Euphytica* 37:77–81 (1988); and Daniel Zohary, "Modes of evolution in plants under domestication," in W. F. Grant, ed., *Plant Biosystematics* (Montreal: Academic Press, 1984). Mark Blumler, "Independent inventionism and recent genetic evidence on plant domestication," *Economic Botany* 46:98–111 (1992), evaluates the evidence for multiple domestications of the same wild plant species, as opposed to single origins followed by spread.

Among writings of general interest in connection with animal domestication, the standard encyclopedic reference work to the world's wild mammals is Ronald Nowak, ed., *Walker's Mammals of the World,* 5th ed. (Baltimore: Johns Hopkins University Press, 1991). Juliet Clutton-Brock, *Domesticated Animals from Early Times* (London: British Museum [Natural History], 1981), gives an excellent summary of all important domesticated mammals. I. L. Mason, ed., *Evolution of Domesticated Animals* (London: Longman, 1984), is a multi-author volume discussing each significant domesticated animal individually. Simon Davis, *The Archaeology of Animals* (New Haven: Yale University Press, 1987), provides an excellent account of what can be learned from mammal bones in archaeological sites. Juliet Clutton-Brock, ed., *The Walking Larder* (London: Unwin-Hyman, 1989), presents 31 papers about how humans have domesticated, herded, hunted, and been hunted by animals around the world. A comprehensive book in German about domesticated animals is Wolf Herre and Manfred Röhrs, *Haustiere zoologisch gesehen* (Stuttgart: Fischer, 1990). Stephen Budiansky, *The Covenant of the Wild* (New York: William Morrow, 1992), is a popular account of how animal domestication evolved automatically from relationships between humans and animals. An important paper on how domestic animals became used for plowing, transport, wool, and milk is Andrew Sherratt, "Plough and pastoralism: Aspects of the secondary products revolution," pp. 261–305 in Ian Hodder et al., eds., *Pattern of the Past* (Cambridge: Cambridge University Press, 1981).

Accounts of food production in particular areas of the world include a deliciously detailed mini-encyclopedia of Roman agricultural practices, Pliny, *Natural History,* vols. 17–19 (Latin text side-by-side with English translation in the Loeb Classical Library edition [Cambridge: Harvard University Press, 1961]); Albert Ammerman and L. L. Cavalli-Sforza, *The Neolithic Transition and the Genetics of Populations in Europe* (Princeton: Princeton University Press, 1984), analyzing the spread of food production from the Fertile Crescent westward across Europe; Graeme Barker, *Prehistoric Farming in Europe* (Cambridge: Cambridge University Press, 1985), and Alasdair Whittle, *Neolithic Europe: A Survey* (Cambridge: Cambridge University Press, 1985), for Europe; Donald Henry, *From Foraging to Agriculture: The Levant at the End of the Ice Age* (Philadelphia: University of Pennsylvania Press, 1989), for the lands bordering the eastern shore of the Mediterranean; and D. E. Yen, "Domestication: Lessons from New Guinea," pp. 558–69 in Andrew Pawley, ed., *Man and a Half* (Auckland: Polynesian Society, 1991), for New Guinea. Edward Schafer, *The Golden Peaches of Samarkand* (Berkeley: University of California Press, 1963), describes the animals, plants, and other things imported into China during the T'ang dynasty.

The following are accounts of plant domestication and crops in specific parts of the world. For Europe and the Fertile Crescent: Willem van Zeist et al., eds., *Progress in Old World Palaeoethnobotany* (Rotterdam: Balkema, 1991), and Jane Renfrew, *Paleoethnobotany* (London: Methuen, 1973). For the Harappan civilization of the Indus Valley, and for the Indian subcontinent in general: Steven Weber, *Plants and Harappan Subsistence* (New Delhi: American Institute of Indian Studies, 1991). For New World crops: Charles Heiser, Jr., "New perspectives on the origin and evolution of New World domesticated plants: Summary," *Economic Botany* 44(3 suppl.):111–16 (1990), and the same author's "Origins of some cultivated New World plants," *Annual Reviews of Ecology and Systematics* 10:309–26 (1979). For a Mexican site that may document the transition from hunting-gathering to early agriculture in Mesoamerica: Kent Flannery, ed., *Guilá Naquitz* (New York: Academic Press, 1986). For an account of crops grown in the Andes during Inca times, and their potential uses today: National Research Council, *Lost Crops of the Incas* (Washington, D.C.: National Academy Press, 1989). For plant domestication in the eastern and / or southwestern United States: Bruce Smith "Origins of agriculture in eastern North America," *Science* 246:1566–71 (1989); William Keegan, ed., *Emergent Horticultural Economies of the Eastern Woodlands* (Carbondale: Southern Illinois University, 1987); Richard Ford, ed., *Prehistoric Food Production in North America* (Ann Arbor: University of

Michigan Museum of Anthropology, 1985); and R. G. Matson, *The Origins of Southwestern Agriculture* (Tucson: University of Arizona Press, 1991). Bruce Smith, "The origins of agriculture in the Americas," *Evolutionary Anthropology* 3:174–84 (1995), discusses the revisionist view, based on accelerator mass spectrometry dating of very small plant samples, that the origins of agriculture in the Americas were much more recent than previously believed.

The following are accounts of animal domestication and livestock in specific parts of the world. For central and eastern Europe: S. Bökönyi, *History of Domestic Mammals in Central and Eastern Europe* (Budapest: Akadémiai Kiadó, 1974). For Africa: Andrew Smith, *Pastoralism in Africa* (London: Hurst, 1992). For the Andes: Elizabeth Wing, "Domestication of Andean mammals," pp. 246–64 in F. Vuilleumier and M. Monasterio, eds., *High Altitude Tropical Biogeography* (Oxford: Oxford University Press, 1986).

References on specific important crops include the following. Thomas Sodestrom et al., eds., *Grass Systematics and Evolution* (Washington, D.C.: Smithsonian Institution Press, 1987), is a comprehensive multi-author account of grasses, the plant group that gave rise to our cereals, now the world's most important crops. Hugh Iltis, "From teosinte to maize: The catastrophic sexual transmutation," *Science* 222:886–94 (1983), gives an account of the drastic changes in reproductive biology involved in the evolution of corn from teosinte, its wild ancestor. Yan Wenming, "China's earliest rice agricultural remains," *Indo-Pacific Prehistory Association Bulletin* 10:118–26 (1991), discusses early rice domestication in South China. Two books by Charles Heiser, Jr., are popular accounts of particular crops: *The Sunflower* (Norman: University of Oklahoma Press, 1976) and *The Gourd Book* (Norman: University of Oklahoma Press, 1979).

Many papers or books are devoted to accounts of particular domesticated animal species. R. T. Loftus et al., "Evidence for two independent domestications of cattle," *Proceedings of the National Academy of Sciences U.S.A.* 91:2757–61 (1994), uses evidence from mitochondrial DNA to demonstrate that cattle were domesticated independently in western Eurasia and in the Indian subcontinent. For horses: Juliet Clutton-Brock, *Horse Power* (Cambridge: Harvard University Press, 1992), Richard Meadow and Hans-Peter Uerpmann, eds., *Equids in the Ancient World* (Wiesbaden: Reichert, 1986), Matthew J. Kust, *Man and Horse in History*

(Alexandria, Va.: Plutarch Press, 1983), and Robin Law, *The Horse in West African History* (Oxford: Oxford University Press, 1980). For pigs: Colin Groves, *Ancestors for the Pigs: Taxonomy and Phylogeny of the Genus* Sus (Technical Bulletin no. 3, Department of Prehistory, Research School of Pacific Studies, Australian National University [1981]). For llamas: Kent Flannery, Joyce Marcus, and Robert Reynolds, *The Flocks of the Wamani* (San Diego: Academic Press, 1989). For dogs: Stanley Olsen, *Origins of the Domestic Dog* (Tucson: University of Arizona Press, 1985). John Varner and Jeannette Varner, *Dogs of the Conquest* (Norman: University of Oklahoma Press, 1983), describes the Spaniards' use of dogs as military weapons to kill Indians during the Spanish conquests of the Americas. Clive Spinnage, *The Natural History of Antelopes* (New York: Facts on File, 1986), gives an account of the biology of antelopes, and hence a starting point for trying to understand why none of these seemingly obvious candidates for domestication was actually domesticated. Derek Goodwin, *Domestic Birds* (London: Museum Press, 1965), summarizes the bird species that have been domesticated, and R. A. Donkin, *The Muscovy Duck* Cairina moschata domestica (Rotterdam: Balkema, 1989), discusses one of the sole two bird species domesticated in the New World.

Finally, the complexities of calibrating radiocarbon dates are discussed by G. W. Pearson, "How to cope with calibration," *Antiquity* 61:98–103 (1987), R. E. Taylor, eds., *Radiocarbon after Four Decades: An Interdisciplinary Perspective* (New York: Springer, 1992), M. Stuiver et al., "Calibration," *Radiocarbon* 35:1–244 (1993), S. Bowman "Using radiocarbon: An update," *Antiquity* 68:838–43 (1994), and R. E. Taylor, M. Stuiver, and C. Vance Haynes, Jr., "Calibration of the Late Pleistocene radiocarbon time scale: Clovis and Folsom age estimates," *Antiquity* vol. 70 (1996).

Chapter 11

For a gripping account of the impact of disease on a human population, nothing can match Thucydides' account of the plague of Athens, in book 2 of his *Peloponnesian War* (available in many translations).

Three classic accounts of disease in history are Hans Zinsser, *Rats, Lice, and History* (Boston: Little, Brown, 1935), Geddes Smith, *A Plague on Us* (New York: Commonwealth Fund, 1941), and William McNeill, *Plagues and Peoples* (Garden City, N.Y.: Doubleday, 1976). The last book, written by a distinguished historian rather than by a physician, has been especially influential in bringing historians to recognize the impacts of disease, as have been the two books by Alfred Crosby listed under the further readings for the Prologue.

Friedrich Vogel and Arno Motulsky, *Human Genetics,* 2nd ed. (Berlin: Springer, 1986), the standard textbook on human genetics, is a convenient reference for natural selection of human populations by disease, and for the development of genetic resistance against specific diseases. Roy Anderson and Robert May, *Infectious Diseases of Humans* (Oxford: Oxford University Press, 1992), is a clear mathematical treatment of disease dynamics, transmission, and epidemiology. MacFarlane Burnet, *Natural History of Infectious Disease* (Cambridge: Cambridge University Press, 1953), is a classic by a distinguished medical researcher, while Arno Karlen, *Man and Microbes* (New York: Putnam, 1995), is a recent popular account.

Books and articles specifically concerned with the evolution of human infectious diseases include Aidan Cockburn, *Infectious Diseases: Their Evolution and Eradication* (Springfield, Ill.: Thomas, 1967); the same author's "Where did our infectious diseases come from?" pp. 103–13 in *Health and Disease in Tribal Societies,* CIBA Foundation Symposium, no. 49 (Amsterdam: Elsevier, 1977); George Williams and Randolph Nesse, "The dawn of Darwinian medicine," *Quarterly Reviews of Biology* 66:1–62 (1991); and Paul Ewald, *Evolution of Infectious Disease* (New York: Oxford University Press, 1994).

Francis Black, "Infectious diseases in primitive societies," *Science* 187:515–18 (1975), discusses the differences between endemic and acute diseases in their impact on, and maintenance in, small isolated societies. Frank Fenner, "Myxoma virus and *Oryctolagus cuniculus:* Two colonizing species," pp. 485–501 in H. G. Baker and G. L. Stebbins, eds., *Genetics of Colonizing Species* (New York: Academic Press, 1965), describes the spread and evolution of Myxoma virus among Australian rabbits. Peter Panum, *Observations Made during the Epidemic of Measles on the Faroe Islands in the Year 1846* (New York: American Public Health Association, 1940), illustrates how the arrival of an acute epidemic disease in an isolated nonresistant population quickly kills or immunizes the whole population. Francis Black, "Measles endemicity in insular populations: Critical community size and its evolutionary implication," *Journal of Theoretical*

Biology 11:207–11 (1966), uses such measles epidemics to calculate the minimum size of population required to maintain measles. Andrew Dobson, "The population biology of parasite-induced changes in host behavior," *Quarterly Reviews of Biology* 63:139–65 (1988), discusses how parasites enhance their own transmission by changing the behavior of their host. Aidan Cockburn and Eve Cockburn, eds., *Mummies, Diseases, and Ancient Cultures* (Cambridge: Cambridge University Press, 1983), illustrates what can be learned from mummies about past impacts of diseases.

As for accounts of disease impacts on previously unexposed populations, Henry Dobyns, *Their Number Became Thinned* (Knoxville: University of Tennessee Press, 1983), marshals evidence for the view that European-introduced diseases killed up to 95 percent of all Native Americans. Subsequent books or articles arguing that controversial thesis include John Verano and Douglas Ubelaker, eds., *Disease and Demography in the Americas* (Washington, D.C.: Smithsonian Institution Press, 1992); Ann Ramenofsky, *Vectors of Death* (Albuquerque: University of New Mexico Press, 1987); Russell Thornton, *American Indian Holocaust and Survival* (Norman: University of Oklahoma Press, 1987); and Dean Snow, "Microchronology and demographic evidence relating to the size of the pre-Columbian North American Indian population," *Science* 268:1601–4 (1995). Two accounts of depopulation caused by European-introduced diseases among Hawaii's Polynesian population are David Stannard, *Before the Horror: The Population of Hawaii on the Eve of Western Contact* (Honolulu: University of Hawaii Press, 1989), and O. A. Bushnell, *The Gifts of Civilization: Germs and Genocide in Hawaii* (Honolulu: University of Hawaii Press, 1993). The near-extermination of the Sadlermiut Eskimos by a dysentery epidemic in the winter of 1902–3 is described by Susan Rowley, "The Sadlermiut: Mysterious or misunderstood?" pp. 361–84 in David Morrison and Jean-Luc Pilon, eds., *Threads of Arctic Prehistory* (Hull: Canadian Museum of Civilization, 1994). The reverse phenomenon, of European deaths due to diseases encountered overseas, is discussed by Philip Curtin, *Death by Migration: Europe's Encounter with the Tropical World in the 19th Century* (Cambridge: Cambridge University Press, 1989).

Among accounts of specific diseases, Stephen Morse, ed., *Emerging Viruses* (New York: Oxford University Press, 1993), contains many valuable chapters on "new" viral diseases of humans; so does Mary Wilson et al., eds., *Disease in Evolution*, Annals of the New York Academy of Sciences, vol. 740 (New York, 1995). References for other diseases include the following. For bubonic plague: Colin McEvedy, "Bubonic plague," *Scientific American* 258(2):118–23 (1988). For cholera: Norman Longmate, *King Cholera* (London: Hamish Hamilton, 1966). For influenza: Edwin Kilbourne, *Influenza* (New York: Plenum, 1987), and Robert Webster et al., "Evolution and ecology of influenza A viruses," *Microbiological Reviews* 56:152–79 (1992). For Lyme disease: Alan Barbour and Durland Fish, "The biological and social phenomenon of Lyme disease," *Science* 260:1610–16 (1993), and Allan Steere, "Lyme disease: A growing threat to urban populations," *Proceedings of the National Academy of Sciences* 91:2378–83 (1994).

For the evolutionary relationships of human malarial parasites: Thomas McCutchan et al., "Evolutionary relatedness of *Plasmodium* species as determined by the structure of DNA," *Science* 225:808–11 (1984), and A. P. Waters et al., "*Plasmodium falciparum* appears to have arisen as a result of lateral transfer between avian and human hosts," *Proceedings of the National Academy of Sciences* 88:3140–44 (1991). For the evolutionary relationships of measles virus: E. Norrby et al., "Is rinderpest virus the archevirus of the *Morbillivirus* genus?" *Intervirology* 23:228–32 (1985), and Keith Murray et al., "A morbillivirus that caused fatal disease in horses and humans," *Science* 268:94–97 (1995). For pertussis, also known as whooping cough: R. Gross et al., "Genetics of pertussis toxin," *Molecular Microbiology* 3:119–24 (1989). For smallpox: Donald Hopkins, *Princes and Peasants: Smallpox in History* (Chicago: University of Chicago Press, 1983); F. Vogel and M. R. Chakravartti, "ABO blood groups and smallpox in a rural population of West Bengal and Bihar (India)," *Human Genetics* 3:166–80 (1966); and my article "A pox upon our genes," *Natural History* 99(2):26–30 (1990). For monkeypox, a disease related to smallpox: Zdeněk Ježek and Frank Fenner, *Human Monkeypox* (Basel: Karger, 1988). For syphilis: Claude Quétel, *History of Syphilis* (Baltimore: Johns Hopkins University Press, 1990). For tuberculosis: Guy Youmans, *Tuberculosis* (Philadelphia: Saunders, 1979). For the claim that human tuberculosis was present in Native Americans before Columbus's arrival: in favor, Wilmar Salo et al., "Identification of *Mycobacterium tuberculosis* DNA in a pre-Columbian Peruvian mummy," *Proceedings of the National Academy of Sciences* 91:2091–94 (1994); opposed, William Stead et al., "When did *Mycobacterium tuberculosis* infection first occur in the New World?" *American Journal of Respiratory Critical Care Medicine* 151:1267–68 (1995).

Chapter 12

Books providing general accounts of writing and of particular writing systems include David Diringer, *Writing* (London: Thames and Hudson, 1982), I. J. Gelb, *A Study of Writing,* 2nd ed. (Chicago: University of Chicago Press, 1963), Geoffrey Sampson, *Writing Systems* (Stanford: Stanford University Press, 1985), John DeFrancis, *Visible Speech* (Honolulu: University of Hawaii Press, 1989), Wayne Senner, ed., *The Origins of Writing* (Lincoln: University of Nebraska Press, 1991), and J. T. Hooker, ed., *Reading the Past* (London: British Museum Press, 1990). A comprehensive account of significant writing systems, with plates depicting texts in each system, is David Diringer, *The Alphabet,* 3rd ed., 2 vols. (London: Hutchinson, 1968). Jack Goody, *The Domestication of the Savage Mind* (Cambridge: Cambridge University Press, 1977), and Robert Logan, *The Alphabet Effect* (New York: Morrow, 1986), discuss the impact of literacy in general and of the alphabet in particular. Uses of early writing are discussed by Nicholas Postgate et al., "The evidence for early writing: Utilitarian or ceremonial?" *Antiquity* 69:459–80 (1995).

Exciting accounts of decipherments of previously illegible scripts are given by Maurice Pope, *The Story of Decipherment* (London: Thames and Hudson, 1975), Michael Coe, *Breaking the Maya Code* (New York: Thames and Hudson, 1992), John Chadwick, *The Decipherment of Linear B* (Cambridge: Cambridge University Press, 1992), Yves Duhoux, Thomas Palaima, and John Bennet, eds., *Problems in Decipherment* (Louvain-la-Neuve: Peeters, 1989), and John Justeson and Terrence Kaufman, "A decipherment of epi-Olmec hieroglyphic writing," *Science* 259:1703–11 (1993).

Denise Schmandt-Besserat's two-volume *Before Writing* (Austin: University of Texas Press, 1992) presents her controversial reconstruction of the origins of Sumerian writing from clay tokens over the course of nearly 5,000 years. Hans Nissen et al., eds., *Archaic Bookkeeping* (Chicago: University of Chicago Press, 1994), describes Mesopotamian tablets that represent the earliest stages of cuneiform itself. Joseph Naveh, *Early History of the Alphabet* (Leiden: Brill, 1982), traces the emergence of alphabets in the eastern Mediterranean region. The remarkable Ugaritic alphabet is the subject of Gernot Windfuhr, "The cuneiform signs of Ugarit," *Journal of Near Eastern Studies* 29:48–51 (1970). Joyce Marcus, *Mesoamerican Writing Systems: Propaganda, Myth, and History in Four Ancient Civilizations* (Princeton: Princeton University Press, 1992), and Elizabeth Boone and Walter Mignolo, *Writing without Words* (Durham: Duke University Press, 1994), describe the development and uses of Mesoamerican writing systems. William Boltz, *The Origin and Early Development of the Chinese Writing System* (New Haven: American Oriental Society, 1994), and the same author's "Early Chinese writing," *World Archaeology* 17:420–36 (1986), do the same for China. Finally, Janet Klausner, *Sequoyah's Gift* (New York: HarperCollins, 1993), is an account readable by children, but equally interesting to adults, of Sequoyah's development of the Cherokee syllabary.

Chapter 13

The standard detailed history of technology is the eight-volume *A History of Technology*, by Charles Singer et al. (Oxford: Clarendon Press, 1954–84). One-volume histories are Donald Cardwell, *The Fontana History of Technology* (London: Fontana Press, 1994), Arnold Pacey, *Technology in World Civilization* (Cambridge: MIT Press, 1990), and Trevor Williams, *The History of Invention* (New York: Facts on File, 1987). R. A. Buchanan, *The Power of the Machine* (London: Penguin Books, 1994), is a short history of technology focusing on the centuries since A.D. 1700. Joel Mokyr, *The Lever of Riches* (New York: Oxford University Press, 1990), discusses why the rate of development of technology has varied with time and place. George Basalla, *The Evolution of Technology* (Cambridge: Cambridge University Press, 1988), presents an evolutionary view of technological change. Everett Rogers, *Diffusion of Innovations*, 3rd ed. (New York: Free Press, 1983), summarizes modern research on the transfer of innovations, including the QWERTY keyboard. David Holloway, *Stalin and the Bomb* (New Haven: Yale University Press, 1994), dissects the relative contributions of blueprint copying, idea diffusion (by espionage), and independent invention to the Soviet atomic bomb.

Preeminent among regional accounts of technology is the series *Science and Civilization in China,* by Joseph Needham (Cambridge: Cambridge University Press), of which 5 volumes in 16 parts have appeared since 1954, with a dozen more parts on the way. Ahmad al-Hassan and Donald Hill, *Islamic Technology* (Cambridge: Cambridge University Press, 1992), and K. D. White, *Greek and Roman Technology* (London: Thames and Hudson, 1984), summarize technology's history for those cultures.

Two conspicuous examples of somewhat isolated societies adopting and then abandoning technologies potentially useful in competition with other societies involve Japan's abandonment of firearms, after their adoption in A.D. 1543, and China's abandonment of its large oceangoing fleets after A.D. 1433. The former case is described by Noel Perrin, *Giving Up the Gun* (Boston: Hall, 1979), and the latter by Louise Levathes, *When China Ruled the Seas* (New York: Simon and Schuster, 1994). An essay entitled "The disappearance of useful arts," pp. 190–210 in W. H. B. Rivers, *Psychology and Ethnology* (New York: Harcourt, Brace, 1926), gives similar examples among Pacific islanders.

Articles on the history of technology will be found in the quarterly journal *Technology and Culture,* published by the Society for the History of Technology since 1959. John Staudenmaier, *Technology's Storytellers* (Cambridge: MIT Press, 1985), analyzes the papers in its first twenty years.

Specific fields providing material for those interested in the history of technology include electric power, textiles, and metallurgy. Thomas Hughes, *Networks of Power* (Baltimore: Johns Hopkins University Press, 1983), discusses the social, economic, political, and technical factors in the electrification of Western society from 1880 to 1930. Dava Sobel, *Longitude* (New York: Walker, 1995), describes the development of John Harrison's chronometers that solved the problem of determining longitude at sea. E. J. W. Barber, *Prehistoric Textiles* (Princeton: Princeton University Press, 1991), sets out the history of cloth in Eurasia from its beginnings more than 9,000 years ago. Accounts of the history of metallurgy over wide regions or even over the world include Robert Maddin, *The Beginning of the Use of Metals and Alloys* (Cambridge: MIT Press, 1988), Theodore Wertime and James Muhly, eds., *The Coming of the Age of Iron* (New Haven: Yale University Press, 1980), R. D. Penhallurick, *Tin in Antiquity* (London: Institute of Metals, 1986), James Muhly, "Copper and Tin," *Transactions of the Connecticut Academy of Arts and Sciences* 43:155–535 (1973), and Alan Franklin, Jacqueline Olin, and Theodore

Wertime, *The Search for Ancient Tin* (Washington, D.C.: Smithsonian Institution Press, 1978). Accounts of metallurgy for local regions include R. F. Tylecote, *The Early History of Metallurgy in Europe* (London: Longman, 1987), and Donald Wagner, *Iron and Steel in Ancient China* (Leiden: Brill, 1993).

Chapter 14

The fourfold classification of human societies into bands, tribes, chiefdoms, and states owes much to two books by Elman Service: *Primitive Social Organization* (New York: Random House, 1962) and *Origins of the State and Civilization* (New York: Norton, 1975). A related classification of societies, using different terminology, is Morton Fried, *The Evolution of Political Society* (New York: Random House, 1967). Three important review articles on the evolution of states and societies are Kent Flannery, "The cultural evolution of civilizations," *Annual Review of Ecology and Systematics* 3:399–426 (1972), the same author's "Prehistoric social evolution," pp. 1–26 in Carol and Melvin Ember, eds., *Research Frontiers in Anthropology* (Englewood Cliffs: Prentice-Hall, 1995), and Henry Wright, "Recent research on the origin of the state," *Annual Review of Anthropology* 6:379–97 (1977). Robert Carneiro, "A theory of the origin of the state," *Science* 169:733–38 (1970), argues that states arise through warfare under conditions in which land is ecologically limiting. Karl Wittfogel, *Oriental Despotism* (New Haven: Yale University Press, 1957), relates state origins to large-scale irrigation and hydraulic management. Three essays in *On the Evolution of Complex Societies,* by William Sanders, Henry Wright, and Robert Adams (Malibu: Undena, 1984), present differing views of state origins, while Robert Adams, *The Evolution of Urban Society* (Chicago: Aldine, 1966), contrasts state origins in Mesopotamia and Mesoamerica.

Among studies of the evolution of societies in specific parts of the world, sources for Mesopotamia include Robert Adams, *Heartland of Cities* (Chicago: University of Chicago Press, 1981), and J. N. Postgate, *Early Mesopotamia* (London: Routledge, 1992); for Mesoamerica, Richard Blanton et al., *Ancient Mesoamerica* (Cambridge: Cambridge University Press, 1981), and Joyce Marcus and Kent Flannery, *Zapotec Civilization* (London: Thames and Hudson, 1996); for the Andes, Richard

Burger, *Chavin and the Origins of Andean Civilization* (New York, Thames and Hudson, 1992), and Jonathan Haas et al., eds., *The Origins and Development of the Andean State* (Cambridge: Cambridge University Press, 1987); for American chiefdoms, Robert Drennan and Carlos Uribe, eds., *Chiefdoms in the Americas* (Lanham, Md.: University Press of America, 1987); for Polynesian societies, the books cited under Chapter 2; and for the Zulu state, Donald Morris, *The Washing of the Spears* (London: Jonathan Cape, 1966).

Chapter 15

Books covering the prehistory of both Australia and New Guinea include Alan Thorne and Robert Raymond, *Man on the Rim: The Peopling of the Pacific* (North Ryde: Angus and Robertson, 1989), J. Peter White and James O'Connell, *A Prehistory of Australia, New Guinea, and Sahul* (Sydney: Academic Press, 1982), Jim Allen et al., eds., *Sunda and Sahul* (London: Academic Press, 1977), M. A. Smith et al., eds., *Sahul in Review* (Canberra: Australian National University, 1993), and Tim Flannery, *The Future Eaters* (New York: Braziller, 1995). The first and third of these books discuss the prehistory of island Southeast Asia as well. A recent account of the history of Australia itself is Josephine Flood, *Archaeology of the Dreamtime*, rev. ed. (Sydney: Collins, 1989). Some additional key papers on Australian prehistory are Rhys Jones, "The fifth continent: Problems concerning the human colonization of Australia," *Annual Reviews of Anthropology* 8:445–66 (1979), Richard Roberts et al., "Thermoluminescence dating of a 50,000-year-old human occupation site in northern Australia," *Nature* 345:153–56 (1990), and Jim Allen and Simon Holdaway, "The contamination of Pleistocene radiocarbon determinations in Australia," *Antiquity* 69:101–12 (1995). Robert Attenborough and Michael Alpers, eds., *Human Biology in Papua New Guinea* (Oxford: Clarendon Press, 1992), summarizes New Guinea archaeology as well as languages and genetics.

As for the prehistory of Northern Melanesia (the Bismarck and Solomon Archipelagoes, northeast and east of New Guinea), discussion will be found in the above-cited books by Thorne and Raymond, Flannery, and Allen et al. Papers pushing back the dates for the earliest occupation of Northern Melanesia include Stephen Wickler and Matthew Spriggs, "Pleistocene human occupation of the Solomon Islands, Melanesia,"

Antiquity 62:703–6 (1988), Jim Allen et al., "Pleistocene dates for the human occupation of New Ireland, Northern Melanesia," *Nature* 331:707–9 (1988), Jim Allen et al., "Human Pleistocene adaptations in the tropical island Pacific: Recent evidence from New Ireland, a Greater Australian outlier," *Antiquity* 63:548–61 (1989), and Christina Pavlides and Chris Gosden, "35,000-year-old sites in the rainforests of West New Britain, Papua New Guinea," *Antiquity* 68:604–10 (1994). References to the Austronesian expansion around the coast of New Guinea will be found under further readings for Chapter 17.

Two books on the history of Australia after European colonization are Robert Hughes, *The Fatal Shore* (New York: Knopf, 1987), and Michael Cannon, *The Exploration of Australia* (Sydney: Reader's Digest, 1987). Aboriginal Australians themselves are the subject of Richard Broome, *Aboriginal Australians* (Sydney: Allen and Unwin, 1982), and Henry Reynolds, *Frontier* (Sydney: Allen and Unwin, 1987). An incredibly detailed history of New Guinea, from the earliest written records until 1902, is the three-volume work by Arthur Wichmann, *Entdeckungs-geschichte von Neu-Guinea* (Leiden: Brill, 1909–12). A shorter and more readable account is Gavin Souter, *New Guinea: The Last Unknown* (Sydney: Angus and Robertson, 1964). Bob Connolly and Robin Anderson, *First Contact* (New York: Viking, 1987), movingly describes the first encounters of highland New Guineans with Europeans.

For detailed accounts of New Guinea's Papuan (i.e., non-Austronesian) languages, see Stephen Wurm, *Papuan Languages of Oceania* (Tübingen: Gunter Narr, 1982), and William Foley, *The Papuan Languages of New Guinea* (Cambridge: Cambridge University Press, 1986); and of Australian languages, see Stephen Wurm, *Languages of Australia and Tasmania* (The Hague: Mouton, 1972), and R. M. W. Dixon, *The Languages of Australia* (Cambridge: Cambridge University Press, 1980).

An entrance into the literature on plant domestication and origins of food production in New Guinea can be found in Jack Golson, "Bulmer phase II: Early agriculture in the New Guinea highlands," pp. 484–91 in Andrew Pawley, ed., *Man and a Half* (Auckland: Polynesian Society, 1991), and D. E. Yen, "Polynesian cultigens and cultivars: The question of origin," pp. 67–95 in Paul Cox and Sandra Banack, eds., *Islands, Plants, and Polynesians* (Portland: Dioscorides Press, 1991).

Numerous articles and books are devoted to the fascinating problem of why trading visits of Indonesians and of Torres Strait islanders to Australia produced only limited cultural change. C. C. Macknight, "Macassans and Aborigines," *Oceania* 42:283–321 (1972), discusses the Macassan visits, while D. Walker, ed., *Bridge and Barrier: The Natural and Cultural History of Torres Strait* (Canberra: Australian National University, 1972), discusses connections at Torres Strait. Both connections are also discussed in the above-cited books by Flood, White and O'Connell, and Allen et al.

Early eyewitness accounts of the Tasmanians are reprinted in N. J. B. Plomley, *The Baudin Expedition and the Tasmanian Aborigines 1802* (Hobart: Blubber Head Press, 1983), N. J. B. Plomley, *Friendly Mission: The Tasmanian Journals and Papers of George Augustus Robinson, 1829–1834* (Hobart: Tasmanian Historical Research Association, 1966), and Edward Duyker, *The Discovery of Tasmania: Journal Extracts from the Expeditions of Abel Janszoon Tasman and Marc-Joseph Marion Dufresne, 1642 and 1772* (Hobart: St. David's Park Publishing, 1992). Papers debating the effects of isolation on Tasmanian society include Rhys Jones, "The Tasmanian Paradox," pp. 189–284 in R. V. S. Wright, ed., *Stone Tools as Cultural Markers* (Canberra: Australian Institute of Aboriginal Studies, 1977); Rhys Jones, "Why did the Tasmanians stop eating fish?" pp. 11–48 in R. Gould, ed., *Explorations in Ethnoarchaeology* (Albuquerque: University of New Mexico Press, 1978); D. R. Horton, "Tasmanian adaptation," *Mankind* 12:28–34 (1979); I. Walters, "Why did the Tasmanians stop eating fish?: A theoretical consideration," *Artefact* 6:71–77 (1981); and Rhys Jones, "Tasmanian Archaeology," *Annual Reviews of Anthropology* 24:423–46 (1995). Results of Robin Sim's archaeological excavations on Flinders Island are described in her article "Prehistoric human occupation on the King and Furneaux Island regions, Bass Strait," pp. 358–74 in Marjorie Sullivan et al., eds., *Archaeology in the North* (Darwin: North Australia Research Unit, 1994).

Chapters 16 and 17

Relevant readings cited under previous chapters include those on East Asian food production (Chapters 4–10), Chinese writing (Chapter 12), Chinese technology (Chapter 13), and New Guinea and the Bismarcks and Solomons in general (Chapter 15). James Matisoff, "Sino-Tibetan linguistics: Present state and future prospects," *Annual Reviews of Anthropology* 20:469–504 (1991), reviews Sino-Tibetan languages and their wider relationships. Takeru Akazawa and Emoke Szathmáry, eds., *Prehistoric Mongoloid Dispersals* (Oxford: Oxford University Press, 1996), and Dennis Etler, "Recent developments in the study of human biology in China: A review," Human Biology 64:567–85 (1992), discuss evidence of Chinese or East Asian relationships and dispersal. Alan Thorne and Robert Raymond, *Man on the Rim* (North Ryde: Angus and Robertson, 1989), describes the archaeology, history, and culture of Pacific peoples, including East Asians and Pacific islanders. Adrian Hill and Susan Serjeantson, eds., *The Colonization of the Pacific: A Genetic Trail* (Oxford: Clarendon Press, 1989), interprets the genetics of Pacific islanders, Aboriginal Australians, and New Guineans in terms of their inferred colonization routes and histories. Evidence based on tooth structure is interpreted by Christy Turner III, "Late Pleistocene and Holocene population history of East Asia based on dental variation," *American Journal of Physical Anthropology* 73:305–21 (1987), and "Teeth and prehistory in Asia," *Scientific American* 260 (2):88–96 (1989).

Among regional accounts of archaeology, China is covered by Kwang-chih Chang, *The Archaeology of Ancient China*, 4th ed. (New Haven: Yale University Press, 1987), David Keightley, ed., *The Origins of Chinese Civilization* (Berkeley: University of California Press, 1983), and David Keightley, "Archaeology and mentality: The making of China," *Representations* 18:91–128 (1987). Mark Elvin, *The Pattern of the Chinese Past* (Stanford: Stanford University Press, 1973), examines China's history since its political unification. Convenient archaeological accounts of Southeast Asia include Charles Higham, *The Archaeology of Mainland Southeast Asia* (Cambridge: Cambridge University Press, 1989); for Korea, Sarah Nelson, *The Archaeology of Korea* (Cambridge: Cambridge University Press, 1993); for Indonesia, the Philippines, and tropical Southeast Asia, Peter Bellwood, *Prehistory of the Indo-Malaysian Archipelago* (Sydney: Academic Press, 1985); for peninsular Malaysia, Peter Bellwood, "Cultural and biological differentiation in Peninsular Malaysia: The last 10,000 years," *Asian Perspectives* 32:37–60 (1993); for the Indian subcontinent, Bridget and Raymond Allchin, *The Rise of Civilization in India and Pakistan* (Cambridge: Cambridge University Press, 1982); for Island Southeast Asia and the Pacific with special emphasis on Lapita, a series of five articles in *Antiquity* 63:547–626 (1989) and Patrick Kirch, *The Lapita Peoples: Ancestors of the Oceanic World* (London: Basil Blackwell, 1996); and for the Austronesian expansion as a whole, Andrew Pawley and Malcolm Ross, "Austronesian historical linguistics and culture history," *Annual Reviews of Anthropology* 22:425–59 (1993), and Peter Bellwood et al., *The Austronesians: Comparative and Historical Perspectives* (Canberra: Australian National University, 1995).

Geoffrey Irwin, *The Prehistoric Exploration and Colonization of the Pacific* (Cambridge: Cambridge University Press, 1992), is an account of Polynesian voyaging, navigation, and colonization. The dating of the settlement of New Zealand and eastern Polynesia is debated by Atholl Anderson, "The chronology of colonisation in New Zealand," *Antiquity* 65:767–95 (1991), and "Current approaches in East Polynesian colonisation research," *Journal of the Polynesian Society* 104:110–32 (1995), and Patrick Kirch and Joanna Ellison, "Palaeoenvironmental evidence for human colonization of remote Oceanic islands," *Antiquity* 68:310–21 (1994).

Chapter 18

Many relevant further readings for this chapter will be found listed under those for other chapters: under Chapter 3 for the conquests of the Incas and Aztecs, Chapters 4–10 for plant and animal domestication, Chapter 11 for infectious diseases, Chapter 12 for writing, Chapter 13 for technology, Chapter 14 for political institutions, and Chapter 16 for China. Convenient worldwide comparisons of dates for the onset of food production will be found in Bruce Smith, *The Emergence of Agriculture* (New York: Scientific American Library, 1995).

Some discussions of the historical trajectories summarized in Table 18.1, other than references given under previous chapters, are as follows. For England: Timothy Darvill, *Prehistoric Britain* (London: Batsford, 1987). For the Andes: Jonathan Haas et al., *The Origins and Development of the Andean State* (Cambridge: Cambridge University Press, 1987); Michael Moseley, *The Incas and Their Ancestors* (New York: Thames and Hudson, 1992); and Richard Burger, *Chavin and the Origins of Andean Civilization* (New York: Thames and Hudson, 1992). For Amazonia: Anna Roosevelt, *Parmana* (New York: Academic Press, 1980), and Anna Roosevelt et al., "Eighth millennium pottery from a prehistoric shell midden in the Brazilian Amazon," *Science* 254:1621–24 (1991). For Mesoamerica: Michael Coe, *Mexico*, 3rd ed. (New York: Thames and Hudson,

1984), and Michael Coe, *The Maya,* 3rd ed. (New York: Thames and Hudson, 1984). For the eastern United States: Vincas Steponaitis, "Prehistoric archaeology in the southeastern United States, 1970–1985," *Annual Reviews of Anthropology* 15:363–404 (1986); Bruce Smith, "The archaeology of the southeastern United States: From Dalton to de Soto, 10,500–500 B.P.," *Advances in World Archaeology* 5:1–92 (1986); William Keegan, ed., *Emergent Horticultural Economies of the Eastern Woodlands* (Carbondale: Southern Illinois University, 1987); Bruce Smith, "Origins of agriculture in eastern North America," *Science* 246:1566–71 (1989); Bruce Smith, *The Mississippian Emergence* (Washington, D.C.: Smithsonian Institution Press, 1990); and Judith Bense, *Archaeology of the Southeastern United States* (San Diego: Academic Press, 1994). A compact reference on Native Americans of North America is Philip Kopper, *The Smithsonian Book of North American Indians before the Coming of the Europeans* (Washington, D.C.: Smithsonian Institution Press, 1986). Bruce Smith, "The origins of agriculture in the Americas," *Evolutionary Anthropology* 3:174–84 (1995), discusses the controversy over early versus late dates for the onset of New World food production.

Anyone inclined to believe that New World food production and societies were limited by the culture or psychology of Native Americans themselves, rather than by limitations of the wild species available to them for domestication, should consult three accounts of the transformation of Great Plains Indian societies by the arrival of the horse: Frank Row, *The Indian and the Horse* (Norman: University of Oklahoma Press, 1955), John Ewers, *The Blackfeet: Raiders on the Northwestern Plains* (Norman: University of Oklahoma Press, 1958), and Ernest Wallace and E. Adamson Hoebel, *The Comanches: Lords of the South Plains* (Norman: University of Oklahoma Press, 1986).

Among discussions of the spread of language families in relation to the rise of food production, a classic account for Europe is Albert Ammerman and L. L. Cavalli-Sforza, *The Neolithic Transition and the Genetics of Populations in Europe* (Princeton: Princeton University Press, 1984), while Peter Bellwood, "The Austronesian dispersal and the origin of languages," *Scientific American* 265(1):88–93 (1991), does the same for the Austronesian realm. Studies citing examples from around the world are the two books by L. L. Cavalli-Sforza et al. and the book by Merritt Ruhlen cited as further readings for the Prologue. Two books with diametrically opposed interpretations of the Indo-European expansion provide entrances into that controversial literature: Colin Renfrew, *Archaeology and Language: The Puzzle of Indo-European Origins* (Cambridge: Cambridge University Press, 1987), and J. P. Mallory, *In Search of the Indo-Europeans* (London: Thames and Hudson, 1989). Sources on the Russian expansion across Siberia are George Lantzeff and Richard Pierce, *Eastward to Empire* (Montreal: McGill-Queens University Press, 1973), and W. Bruce Lincoln, *The Conquest of a Continent* (New York: Random House, 1994).

As for Native American languages, the majority view that recognizes many separate language families is exemplified by Lyle Campbell and Marianne Mithun, *The Languages of Native America* (Austin: University of Texas, 1979). The opposing view, lumping all Native American languages other than Eskimo-Aleut and Na-Dene languages into the Amerind family, is presented by Joseph Greenberg, *Language in the Americas* (Stanford: Stanford University Press, 1987), and Merritt Ruhlen, *A Guide to the World's Languages,* vol. 1 (Stanford: Stanford University Press, 1987).

Standard accounts of the origin and spread of the wheel for transport in Eurasia are M. A. Littauer and J. H. Crouwel, *Wheeled Vehicles and Ridden Animals in the Ancient Near East* (Leiden: Brill, 1979), and Stuart Piggott, *The Earliest Wheeled Transport* (London: Thames and Hudson, 1983).

Books on the rise and demise of the Norse colonies in Greenland and America include Finn Gad, *The History of Greenland,* vol. 1 (Montreal: McGill-Queens University Press, 1971), G. J. Marcus, *The Conquest of the North Atlantic* (New York: Oxford University Press, 1981), Gwyn Jones, *The Norse Atlantic Saga,* 2nd ed. (New York: Oxford University Press, 1986), and Christopher Morris and D. James Rackham, eds., *Norse and Later Settlement and Subsistence in the North Atlantic* (Glasgow: University of Glasgow, 1992). Two volumes by Samuel Eliot Morison provide masterly accounts of early European voyaging to the New World: *The European Discovery of America: The Northern Voyages,* A.D. *500–1600* (New York: Oxford University Press, 1971) and *The European Discovery of America: The Southern Voyages,* A.D. *1492–1616* (New York: Oxford University Press, 1974). The beginnings of Europe's overseas expansion are treated by Felipe Fernández-Armesto, *Before Columbus: Exploration and Colonization from the Mediterranean to the Atlantic, 1229–1492* (London: Macmillan Education, 1987). Not to be missed is Columbus's own day-by-day account of history's most famous voyage, reprinted as

Oliver Dunn and James Kelley, Jr., *The Diario of Christopher Columbus's First Voyage to America, 1492–1493* (Norman: University of Oklahoma Press, 1989).

As an antidote to this book's mostly dispassionate account of how peoples conquered or slaughtered other peoples, read the classic account of the destruction of the Yahi tribelet of northern California and the emergence of Ishi, its solitary survivor: Theodora Kroeber, *Ishi in Two Worlds* (Berkeley: University of California Press, 1961). The disappearance of native languages in the Americas and elsewhere is the subject of Robert Robins and Eugenius Uhlenbeck, *Endangered Languages* (Providence: Berg, 1991), Joshua Fishman, *Reversing Language Shift* (Clevedon: Multilingual Matters, 1991), and Michael Krauss, "The world's languages in crisis," *Language* 68:4–10 (1992).

Chapter 19

Books on the archaeology, prehistory, and history of the African continent include Roland Oliver and Brian Fagan, *Africa in the Iron Age* (Cambridge: Cambridge University Press, 1975), Roland Oliver and J. D. Fage, *A Short History of Africa,* 5th ed. (Harmondsworth: Penguin, 1975), J. D. Fage, *A History of Africa* (London: Hutchinson, 1978), Roland Oliver, *The African Experience* (London: Weidenfeld and Nicolson, 1991), Thurstan Shaw et al., eds., *The Archaeology of Africa: Food, Metals, and Towns* (New York: Routledge, 1993), and David Phillipson, *African Archaeology,* 2nd ed. (Cambridge: Cambridge University Press, 1993). Correlations between linguistic and archaeological evidence of Africa's past are summarized by Christopher Ehret and Merrick Posnansky, eds., *The Archaeological and Linguistic Reconstruction of African History* (Berkeley: University of California Press, 1982). The role of disease is discussed by Gerald Hartwig and K. David Patterson, eds., *Disease in African History* (Durham: Duke University Press, 1978).

As for food production, many of the listed further readings for Chapters 4–10 discuss Africa. Also of note are Christopher Ehret, "On the antiquity of agriculture in Ethiopia," *Journal of African History* 20:161–77 (1979); J. Desmond Clark and Steven Brandt, eds., *From Hunters to Farmers: The Causes and Consequences of Food Production in Africa* (Berkeley: University of California Press, 1984); Art Hansen and Della McMillan, eds.,

Food in Sub-Saharan Africa (Boulder, Colo.: Rienner, 1986); Fred Wendorf et al., "Saharan exploitation of plants 8,000 years B.P.," *Nature* 359:721–24 (1992); Andrew Smith, *Pastoralism in Africa* (London: Hurst, 1992); and Andrew Smith, "Origin and spread of pastoralism in Africa," *Annual Reviews of Anthropology* 21:125–41 (1992).

For information about Madagascar, two starting points are Robert Dewar and Henry Wright, "The culture history of Madagascar," *Journal of World Prehistory* 7:417–66 (1993), and Pierre Verin, *The History of Civilization in North Madagascar* (Rotterdam: Balkema, 1986). A detailed study of the linguistic evidence about the source for the colonization of Madagascar is Otto Dahl, *Migration from Kalimantan to Madagascar* (Oslo: Norwegian University Press, 1991). Possible musical evidence for Indonesian contact with East Africa is described by A. M. Jones, *Africa and Indonesia: The Evidence of the Xylophone and Other Musical and Cultural Factors* (Leiden: Brill, 1971). Important evidence about the early settlement of Madagascar comes from dated bones of now extinct animals as summarized by Robert Dewar, "Extinctions in Madagascar: The loss of the subfossil fauna," pp. 574–93 in Paul Martin and Richard Klein, eds., *Quaternary Extinctions* (Tucson: University of Arizona Press, 1984). A tantalizing subsequent fossil discovery is reported by R. D. E. MacPhee and David Burney, "Dating of modified femora of extinct dwarf *Hippopotamus* from Southern Madagascar," *Journal of Archaeological Science* 18:695–706 (1991). The onset of human colonization is assessed from paleobotanical evidence by David Burney, "Late Holocene vegetational change in Central Madagascar," *Quaternary Research* 28:130–43 (1987).

Epilogue

Links between environmental degradation and the decline of civilization in Greece are explored by Tjeerd van Andel et al., "Five thousand years of land use and abuse in the southern Argolid," *Hesperia* 55:103–28 (1986), Tjeerd van Andel and Curtis Runnels, *Beyond the Acropolis: A Rural Greek Past* (Stanford: Stanford University Press, 1987), and Curtis Runnels, "Environmental degradation in ancient Greece," *Scientific American* 272(3):72–75 (1995). Patricia Fall et al., "Fossil hyrax middens from the Middle East: A record of paleovegetation and human disturbance," pp. 408–27 in Julio Betancourt et al., eds., *Packrat Middens* (Tucson: University of Arizona Press, 1990), does the same for the decline of Petra, as does Robert Adams, *Heartland of Cities* (Chicago: University of Chicago Press, 1981), for Mesopotamia.

A stimulating interpretation of the differences between the histories of China, India, Islam, and Europe is provided by E. L. Jones, *The European Miracle,* 2nd ed. (Cambridge: Cambridge University Press, 1987). Louise Levathes, *When China Ruled the Seas* (New York: Simon and Schuster, 1994), describes the power struggle that led to the suspension of China's treasure fleets. The further readings for Chapters 16 and 17 provide other references for early Chinese history.

The impact of Central Asian nomadic pastoralists on Eurasia's complex civilizations of settled farmers is discussed by Bennett Bronson, "The role of barbarians in the fall of states," pp. 196–218 in Norman Yoffee and George Cowgill, eds., *The Collapse of Ancient States and Civilizations* (Tucson: University of Arizona Press, 1988).

The possible relevance of chaos theory to history is discussed by Michael Shermer in the paper "Exorcising Laplace's demon: Chaos and antichaos, history and metahistory," *History and Theory* 34:59–83 (1995). Shermer's paper also provides a bibliography for the triumph of the QWERTY keyboard, as does Everett Rogers, *Diffusion of Innovations,* 3rd ed. (New York: Free Press, 1983).

An eyewitness account of the traffic accident that nearly killed Hitler in 1930 will be found in the memoirs of Otto Wagener, a passenger in Hitler's car. Those memoirs have been edited by Henry Turner, Jr., as a book, *Hitler: Memoirs of a Confidant* (New Haven: Yale University Press, 1978). Turner goes on to speculate on what might have happened if Hitler had died in 1930, in his chapter "Hitler's impact on history," in David Wetzel, ed., *German History: Ideas, Institutions, and Individuals* (New York: Praeger, 1996).

The many distinguished books by historians interested in problems of long-term history include Sidney Hook, *The Hero in History* (Boston: Beacon Press, 1943), Patrick Gardiner, ed., *Theories of History* (New York: Free Press, 1959), Fernand Braudel, *Civilization and Capitalism* (New York: Harper and Row, 1979), Fernand Braudel, *On History* (Chicago: University of Chicago Press, 1980), Peter Novick, *That Noble Dream* (Cambridge: Cambridge University Press, 1988), and Henry Hobhouse, *Forces of Change* (London: Sedgewick and Jackson, 1989).

Several writings by the biologist Ernst Mayr discuss the differences between historical and nonhistorical sciences, with particular reference to the contrast between biology and physics, but much of what Mayr says is also applicable to human history. His views will be found in his *Evolution and the Diversity of Life* (Cambridge: Harvard University Press, 1976), chap. 25, and in *Towards a New Philosophy of Biology* (Cambridge: Harvard University Press, 1988), chaps. 1–2.

The methods by which epidemiologists reach cause-and-effect conclusions about human diseases, without resorting to laboratory experiments on people, are discussed in standard epidemiology texts, such as A. M. Lilienfeld and D. E. Lilienfeld, *Foundations of Epidemiology*, 3rd ed. (New York: Oxford University Press, 1994). Uses of natural experiments are considered from the viewpoint of an ecologist in my chapter "Overview: Laboratory experiments, field experiments, and natural experiments," pp. 3–22 in Jared Diamond and Ted Case, eds., *Community Ecology* (New York: Harper and Row; 1986). Paul Harvey and Mark Pagel, *The Comparative Method in Evolutionary Biology* (Oxford: Oxford University Press, 1991), analyzes how to extract conclusions by comparing species.

CREDITS

Plate 14. Dan Hrdy, Anthro-Photo.

Plate 15. Rodman Wanamaker, American Museum of Natural History. Negative 316824.

Plate 16. Marjorie Shostak, Anthro-Photo.

BETWEEN PP. 288 AND 289

Plate 17. Boris Malkin, Anthro-Photo.

Plate 18. Napoleon Chagnon, Anthro-Photo.

Plate 19. Kirschner, American Museum of Natural History. Negative 235230.

Plates 20, 22, 24, 30, and 32. AP/Wide World Photos.

Plate 21. Gladstone, Anthro-Photo.

Plate 23. Above, AP/Wide World Photos. Below, W. B., American Museum of Natural History. Negative 2A13829.

Plate 25. Marjorie Shostak, Anthro-Photo.

Plate 26. Irven DeVore, Anthro-Photo.

Plate 27. Steve Winn, Anthro-Photo.

Plate 28. J.B. Thorpe, American Museum of Natural History. Negative 336181.

Plates 29 and 31. J. F. E. Bloss, Anthro-Photo.

INDEX

Page numbers in *italics* refer to illustrations, maps and tables.

Aboriginal Australians:
    band societies of, 267–68, 297
    in coastal and river areas, 155, 310
    cultural diffusion barriers for, 311,
        313–17, 407
    current underclass status of, 319
    in desert environment, 296, 310
    Eurasian diseases and, 213, 318, 320
    European conquest of, 102, 310, 319,
        320, 389–90
    evolutionary ancestry of, 300–302, 316
    as hunter-gatherers, 102, 113, 155,
        297, 307, 309–11, 314
    languages of, 301, 302, 316, 328
    plant management practices of, 107,
        155, 309, 310
    population size of, 296, 298, 310,
        311, 313, 319
    racist theories on, 298–300, 320–21
    rock paintings of, 295, 297
    technological innovation and, 251–52,
        253, 258, 311–17
    villages constructed by, 155, 310
    watercraft developed by, 297
    weapons used by, 312, 316
    wild foods of, 296, 309–11
accelerator mass spectrometry, 96

acorns, 115, 116, 118, 128–29
Africa, 376–401
    Asian links with, 377, 378, 380–81
    Bantu expansion in, 103, 133, 163,
        386, 393–97, 395, 407
    diffusion barriers in, 237, 238, 262–
        63, 399–400
    diseases in, 197, 204, 208, 213, 396
    domesticated animals in, 98, 162, 162,
        163–64, 175, 186, 389, 406
    early crops of, 126, 126–27, 133,
        386–91, 387
    European conquest of, 187, 397–401
    five population groups in, 377–81, 398
    human evolution in, 36, 38–39, 40,
        50, 377, 398
    languages of, 329, 377, 381–86, 382,
        390–92
    nomadic bands in, 267
    non-animal protein sources in, 125
    North, Eurasian culture related to, 161
    north-south axis of, 186–87, 188, 263,
        399–400
    population levels in, 263, 399
    racial oppression in, 187
    spread of food production in, 98, 133,
        180, 186–87, 188

Africa (*continued*)
  state formation in, 290–91, 292
  technological receptivity of societies in,
    252
Afroasiatic language family, 382, 383,
    384, 391, 392, 394
agave, 125–26, *127*
agriculture, *see* crop cultivation; plants
AIDS, 197, 199, 201, 205, 208
Ainu, 165, 170–71, 356
airplanes, 206, 243, 245, 247
Alexander of Macedon, 281, 291, 410,
    420
almonds, 114, 118, 129
alpacas, 159, *160*, 161, *167*, 178, 213
alphabets, 190, 217, 225–28, 230, 235,
    236, 255, 259, 323, 333, 367,
    400
amaranths, 180, 188
Amazonian cultures, *100, 126–27*, 203,
    266, 267, 374
American colonies, unification of, 290
Americas:
  animal extinctions in, 46–47, 162,
    175, 213, 355, 406
  barriers to cultural diffusion in, 177–
    80, 262, 366–67, 370, 407
  current population level of, 375
  diseases brought to, 204, 210–12,
    357–58
  domestic animals in, 76–77, 142, 158,
    178, 213, 262, 355, 365
  historical trajectory of key develop-
    ments in, 360–70, *363*
  human presence in, 35, 38, 44–50, 67
  modern band societies in, 268
  native peoples of, *see* Native
    Americans
  Norse voyages to, 371–73, *371*
  north-south axis of, 176, 187–88, 190,
    255, 262, 366
  onset of food production in, 96, 98,
    99, *100*, 361–62, *363*, 364–65
  population density of, 263
  population replacement in, 354, 373–
    75
  spread of food production inhibited in,
    177–80, 366–67
  technology diffusion in, 255, 262
Americas, European conquest of, 67–81
  Atahuallpa's capture and, 68–74, 77,
    354
  centralized political structure and, 78,
    374
  horses used in, 76–77

infectious diseases and, 77–78, 197,
    210–11, 355, 373–75
  literacy as factor in, 78–80
  maritime technology for, 78, 373
  progress of, 373–75
  weaponry in, 74–75, 76, 374
amygdalin, 114, 118
Andaman Islanders, 332–33
Andes:
  crops of, 98, 100, 126–27, 178, 185,
    187–88, 213, 367, 375
  survival of Native American population
    in, 375
animal extinctions:
  in Americas, 46–47, 162, 175, 213,
    355, 406
  in Australia/New Guinea, 42–44, 46,
    162–63, 175, 304, 308, 406
  breeding programs for prevention of,
    168
  climatic theory of, 47
  of domestic mammals' ancestors, *160*,
    175
  food production intensified after, 110
  in Polynesia, 60
animals:
  latitude-related climate adaptations of,
    184–85
  taming vs. domestication of, 159,
    165
  territorial behavior of, 173–74
animals, domestic, 157–75
  animal extinctions and, 44, 47, 406
  crop production enhanced by, 88–89,
    98, 128, 330, 357
  earliest, 35, 142, *362–63*
  evolutionary alterations in, 159–61
  human diseases and, *87, 92*, 164,
    195–97, 206–9, *207*, 213–14, 330,
    355, 357
  initial sites for domestication of, 98–
    102, *100*, 141, 142, 329–30, 389
  for land transport, 91, 248
  as military advantage, 76–77, 91, 358
  morphology of wild species vs., 95,
    159–61
  number of potential candidates for, 44,
    132
  as pets, 163, 164–65, *166*, *167*, 196,
    206, 207
  as power source, 355, 358
  regional differences in, 157–75, 355
  as source of fibers, 90, 126, 159, 164,
    170
  wildlife decline as motive for, 110

wild mammals' suitability for, 131–32
see also mammals
anisakiasis, 198
Anna Karenina (Tolstoy), 157, 169, 174
annual plants, 120–21, 136, 139
Antarctica, 44, 266
antelope, 167–68, 172, 173–74
apes, human evolution from, 36, 204
apples, 115, 118, 122, 124–25, 134, 152, 155–56, 185–86
apricots, 122, 185
Arafura Sea, 297, 302
architecture, public, 269, 273, 274, 279
Aristotle, 282–83
arrowroot, 309
Asia:
   China's language families in, 324–29, 326, 327
   expansion to Australia/New Guinea from, 41–42, 51–52, 300–301
   initial human presence in, 37, 40
   prehistoric coastline of, 299, 301
asses, North African, 171
Atahuallpa, 68–74, 75, 77, 78, 79, 80, 86, 211, 354
atoll types, 58
atomic bomb, 225, 242
aurochs, 160, 163, 166
Australia:
   Aboriginals of, *see* Aboriginal Australians
   desert environment in, 295–96, 310
   domesticates imported to, 189, 263, 308, 319–20, 407
   environmental limits on food production in, 178, 308–9
   European conquest of, 297, 319–21, 375
   geological/climatic conditions in, 302, 303, 308, 311, 351
   mineral resources of, 300
   Murray-Darling river system of, 302, 310
   New Guinea's separation from, 297, 298, 299, 302, 316
   population size of, 263, 319
   rabbit eradication efforts in, 209
   sheep raised in, 196
Australia/New Guinea:
   geographic isolation of, 257, 263
   human presence in, 38, 41–44, 49, 51–52, 297, 300–301, 308
   large-animal extinctions in, 42–44, 46, 162–63, 175, 304, 308, 406
   mineral resources of, 241, 300

separation of, 297, 299, 302
stone tools used in, 241
Australopithecus africanus, 36
Austroasiatic language group, 325, 328, 333, 345, 351, 352, 369, 383, 392, 393
Austronesian expansion, 336–53
   crops spread by, 344, 350, 351
   linguistic evidence of, 336–39, 337, 342–45, 346–47, 369, 382, 383
   to Madagascar, 340, 377, 380–81, 388, 392–93
   to New Guinea, 307–8, 318, 319, 336, 345–51
   pottery developments of, 339, 340, 345, 347–50, 351
   routes of, 103, 313–14, 318, 339–40, 341, 342–43, 345, 346, 351–52, 388, 393
   watercraft for, 341–42, 351
automobiles, invention of, 243
axis orientations, 176–91, 177, 255, 262, 263, 330, 366, 399–400
   of Africa, 186–87, 188, 263, 399–400
   of Americas, 176, 187–88, 190, 255, 262, 366
   of Eurasia, 176, 183–86, 330, 366, 399–400
   latitude-related climate conditions and, 183–86, 399–400
   technological diffusion and, 190
Aztec Empire, 360
   Spanish conquest of, 210, 355, 373
   tribute collected by, 292
   warrior religious ideology of, 281

Bali, as part of prehistoric Asia, 301
Bali cattle, 161
Balkans, Fertile Crescent food production spread to, 187
bamboo rafts, 301
bananas, 119, 122, 127, 128, 132, 148, 186, 303, 305, 319, 344, 388, 391, 400
band societies, 203–4, 265–70, 277, 286–88
banteng, 159, 161, 163, 167
Bantu:
   food production spread by, 133, 186–87, 190, 394, 397, 400
   geographic origins of, 385
   iron metallurgy of, 394–96
   languages of, 329, 369, 384–86, 393, 394

Bantu (*continued*)
   subequatorial-African expansion of, 103, 163, 386, 393–97, *395*
bark beaters, 340
barley:
   domestication of, 120, 124, 137
   as founder crop, *126,* 139, 141, 145–46, 182
   nutritive value of, 125, 138, 151
   spread of, 330, 333
Bar-Yosef, Ofer, 145–46
beans, 109, 118, 125, *126, 127,* 151, 179, 180, 188, 367
bears, 165, 170–71
bees, 158
beets, 122
Bering land bridge, 38, 41, 44, 46
berries, 114, 115, 116, 117, 128, 129–30, 152
birds, domesticated, 158, 165, 207, *207,* 389
birth intervals, 89
Bismarck, Otto von, 420
bison, 163, 164, 167, 168
bitter vetch, 141
Black Death (bubonic plague), 196–97, 199, 202, 205, 206, 212, 330, 357, 358
Blackfoot Indians, 85, 86, 389, 398
black pepper, 185
blueberries, 114, 117, 128, 152
blueprint copying:
   new writing systems developed through, 224, 225–28
   technological diffusion by, 256
Blumler, Mark, 139, *140,* 153
bogong moth, 310
bone tools, 39, 90
bonobos, 36, 270
boomerangs, 311–12
Borneo:
   Austronesian influence in, 336, 340, *341,* 344, 348, 381
   hunter-gatherer reversion in, 352
   as part of prehistoric Asia, *299,* 301
Böttger, Johann, 256
bows and arrows, 258, 298, 312, 316, 358
Brahms, Johannes, 267
brain size:
   of domestic vs. wild animals, 159
   human, 36, 38, 40
brain structure, language skills and, 40
breadfruit, 128, 148, 344

Britain, Roman authority withdrawn from, 279
broadcast seeding, 126–28, 357
bronze, 259, 330, 331, 333
bubonic plague (Black Death), 196–97, 199, 202, 205, 206, 212, 330, 357, 358
buffalo:
   African, 163, 171, 389, 398
   see also water buffalo
bureaucrats, 89–90, *269,* 274, 280, 281
burial practices, 38, 39, 330
Burke, Robert, 296, 321

cabbage, 118, 122
Cajamarca, Atahuallpa captured at, 68–74, 77
calibrated radiocarbon dates, 35*n,* 96–97
California, University of, at Davis, 115
camels, 159, *160, 162,* 166, *167,* 389
canal technology, 155, 253, 310, 330, 331
Candia, Pedro de, 70
cannibalism:
   disease transmitted through, 198, 208
   protein deficiency linked to, 149
canoes, 258, 314, 341–42, 351
capitalism, 250
carbon 14/carbon 12 ratios, *95, 96*
   see also radiocarbon dating
Carlyle, Thomas, 420
carnivores, unsuitability of as domesticates, 169
cashews, 128
cassava (manioc), *127,* 128, 132, 178
cassowary, 147, 165
cast-iron production, 253, 330
cats, 158, 173, 207, 389
cattle (cows), 98, 141, 159, *160,* 166, *167,* 169, 186, 206–7, *207, 356,* 389, 390, 400
cavalry, foot soldiers routed by, 76–77
cave paintings, 39–40, 48, *51*
centralized societies:
   in chiefdoms, 273–74, 275–76, 278
   economy controlled by, 279
   information flow limited in, 273, 279
   public order maintained under, 277
   religious support for efforts of, 277–78, 359
   technological advancement under, 251
cereals:
   Australian paucity of, 309
   domestication of, 110, 111, 124, *126, 127*

as founder crops, 141, 142, 145–46
nutritive value of, 125, 128, 132, 138
productive yields from, 136–37
sites for onset of cultivation of, 133,
    388, 394
technologies developed for farming of,
    110–11, 310–11
tropical climates and, 148
Chalcuchima, 79–80
charcoal residues, radiocarbon dating of,
    95–96
Charles V, Holy Roman Emperor, 68, 74
Chatham Islands:
    Austronesian expansion to, 351–52
    hunter-gatherers in, 55, 353
    Maori conquest of Moriori settlements
        on, 53–57
cheetahs, 165, 170
chenopods, 180, 188
Cherokee confederacy, 289–90
Cherokee language, writing system
    developed for, 228–30, 229
cherries, 122, 124–25
chicken pox, 320
chickens, domestication of, 158, 185,
    304, 389
chickpeas, 97, 126, 141
chiefdoms, 268, 269, 273–76, 278, 279–
    80, 282, 290–91, 292, 362–63
chili peppers, 179, 180, 188
Chimbu tribe, 252
chimpanzees, 36, 270
China:
    agricultural techniques developed in,
        124, 186
    Austronesian expansion from, 340, 342
    crops cultivated in, 125–26, 126–27,
        137, 185, 310, 329, 330
    cultural exchanges in, 330–31
    cultural expansion from, 186, 325–28,
        333
    developmental lead lost by, 409–10,
        411–17
    domestic animals of, 158, 185, 329–30
    earliest evidence of human presence in,
        324
    environmental/climatic variety in, 323,
        329, 411
    ethnic attitudes in, 331–32
    genetic diversity in, 323
    geographic connectedness of, 414–16,
        415
    gunpowder developed in, 247, 253,
        330
    innovation vs. conservatism in, 253,
        258, 330, 411–13
    linguistic history of, 323–29, 326, 327,
        332, 338, 345, 369, 413, 418–19
    New Guinea immigrants from, 335
    non-animal protein sources in, 125
    North vs. South, 323, 329, 331–32
    political unity of, 323, 332, 338, 412–
        14, 416
    pottery from, 253, 254, 256
    printing development in, 241, 253,
        259
    as site of food production origins, 98,
        99, 100, 189, 329–30, 411
    writing system of, 217, 218, 219, 224,
        230, 231, 232, 235, 236–37, 259,
        323, 330, 331, 333, 367, 413,
        418–19
China, People's Republic of, population
    of, 279, 323
cholera, 196–97, 199, 200, 202, 206,
    214, 357
cities:
    infectious diseases spread in, 205
    villages vs., 279
citrus fruit, 185
clans, 271
climate:
    animal extinctions and, 43–44, 47
    of Australia vs. New Guinea, 302
    biodiversity linked to, 138–39
    cold, 39, 44, 46, 372–73
    crop diffusion and, 183–86, 189–90
    of drought cycles, 308
    latitude-related features of, 183–86
    Mediterranean, 136, 138–41, 139, 184,
        399–400
    plant habitats expanded by global
        changes in, 110
    seasonal variation in, 302, 308, 387–
        88
    technological innovation vs., 251
Clovis hunters, 45–49, 363–64
coffee cultivation, 185, 252, 388
cold climates, human survival in, 39, 44,
    46, 372–73
Colledge, Susan, 144–45
Columbus, Christopher, 67, 79, 197,
    211, 213, 335, 354, 412–13
communal decision process, 272, 286–
    87
condors, 168
conflict resolution, societal systems for,
    265–66, 268, 271–72, 280, 286

conquest:
  diseases spread by, 77–78, 197, 210–13, 357, 373–74
  literacy as factor in, 78–80, 215–16
  religious justification for, 69, 71–72, 73–74, 90, 266, 278, 281, 282 359, 419
  state amalgamation through, 289, 290–92
  suicidal fighting in support of, 281–82
  tribute gained from, 292
continental differences in cultural development:
  axis orientation, 176, 177, 178, 183–91, 399–400
  diffusion factors in, 406–7
  domestication potential in, 406
  environmental adaptation and, 51–52
  geographical connectedness and, 414–16, 415
  initial settlement dates and, 50–51
  mutability of, 417
  role of idiosyncracy in, 417–20
  total area and population size in, 407–8
Cook, James, 214
Cooke, William, 245
copper metallurgy, 259, 358, 394
corn:
  for animal feed, 169
  cultivation of, 126, 127, 132, 148
  diffusion of, 109, 151, 187, 188, 367, 391
  domestication of, 118, 137, 142, 185
  nutritive value of, 125, 138, 151, 356
  wild ancestors of, 114, 137
Cortés, Hernán, 75, 79, 80, 91, 210, 355
cotton, 90, 119, 125–26, 127, 180, 188
cotton gin, 242, 245
cowpeas, 125, 126
cows (cattle), 98, 141, 159, 160, 166, 167, 169, 186, 206–7, 207, 356, 389, 390, 400
crafts specialists, 272, 274
Cro-Magnons, 39–41
crop cultivation:
  in Africa, 387–91, 387
  in altitude range over short distance, 140–41
  continental diffusion of, 178–91, 356
  in diverse Polynesian environments, 60–61

domestic animals used in, 88–89, 98, 128, 329–30, 357
eight founder crops of, 141
for fibers, 119, 125–26
of former weeds, 125
of fruit and nut trees, 124–25, 128–29, 155–56
latitude-related climate features and, 184
linguistic evidence of, 390–91
by Native Americans vs. Eurasians, 355–57
natural selection and, 116–18, 120, 123
nutritive value and, 125, 128, 149, 356–57
for oils, 119
preemptive domestication and, 178–80
reproductive biology and, 121–22
storage factors and, 124, 136
tools and technologies for, 88–89, 110–11, 126–28, 156, 357
twelve leading species for, 132, 136
Cuban Missile Crisis, 279
cucumber, 127, 185
Cuitláhuac, 77, 210
cult houses, 273
cumin, 185
cuneiform, 217, 218–24, 221, 230, 232, 234, 236–37
Custer, George, 75
cycad nuts, 310
Cyril, Saint, 225
Cyrillic alphabets, 225

Daimler, Gottfried, 243
Darwin, Charles, 123, 130
dates (fruit), 124, 133
dating, radiocarbon, 35n, 47, 95–97
deer, 172, 173–74, 208
desert environment, 295–96
determinatives, 220, 222
Dingiswayo, 290, 292
dingos, 308, 313–14
diphtheria, 212
diseases, infectious:
  domestic animals in spread of, 87, 92, 164, 195–97, 206–9, 207, 213–14, 330, 355, 357
  epidemics of, 202–14, 357–58
  European conquests furthered by, 77–78, 197, 210–13, 357, 373–74
  food production related to development of, 86, 87, 195
  four evolutionary stages of, 207–10

genetic defenses against, 201
germ transmission strategies and, 198–200, 201–2, 209–10
immune defenses against, 200–202, 204, 317–18, 357, 396
population and, 203–6
sexual transmission of, 196, 199
symptoms of bodily responses to, 199–201
of tropical climates, 78, 197, 214, 358
dodo, extinction of, 43
dogs, 141, 152, 158, 161, 164, 166, 167, 169, 170, 173, 213, 308, 389
infectious diseases and, 199, 207, 207
Domestication of Plants in the Old World (Zohary and Hopf), *181*
dominance hierarchy, 173, 174
donkeys, 159, *160, 167,* 171, 389
drought cycles, 308
ducks, 158, *207,* 213
dugout canoes, 314, 341–42
dysentery, 203–4, 317

eagles, 165
Easter Island:
giant statues of, *65*
writing system of, 224, 230–31
eastern United States, Native American groups in:
early crops domesticated by, 98, *100,* 126, *126–27,* 150–51, 179
indigenous biota vs. imported additions cultivated by, 146, 150–53, 155–56
east-west axes, continental diffusion along, 176, *177,* 178, 183–86, 330, 366, 399–400
economy:
centralized control of, 279, 287
of non-food-producers, 268, 272, 279, 285, 292
redistributive, *269,* 275, 277, 287
Edison, Thomas, 241, 243, 244, 245
eel fisheries, 310
eggplants, 118
Egypt, ancient:
food production in, 101, 102, 178, 181–82, 390, 400
hieroglyphs of, 217, 218, *219,* 224, 226–27, 230, 231–33, *233,* 235, 236, 400
Ehret, Christopher, 391
eland, 167–68, 172

electric lighting, 245, 247, 249
elephants, 159, 165, 169, 399
elk (red deer), 167, 168, 172
English Channel, 41
English language, geographic history of, 385
ENSO (El Niño Southern Oscillation), 308, 309
equids, 171
Eskimos:
Arctic survival skills of, 372–73
in band societies, 268
Eurasian colonization and, 370–71
European diseases contracted by, 374
technologies abandoned by, 258
Ethiopia:
crops of, 126, *126–27,* 181, 185, 388, 391
food production begun in, 99, *100,* 101, 390
writing system in, 227, 400
ethnic diversity, political incorporation of, 322–23
ethnobiology, 143–46
Eurasia:
defined, 161
diseases from, 197, 205–6, 212–13
east-west axis of, 176, 183–86, 330, 366, 399–400
European dominance of, 409–17
food production in Americas vs., 354–57
historical trajectory of key developments in, 360–70, *362*
language expansions of, 91, 367–68, *369,* 375
large-animal extinctions in, 44
large-mammal domestication in, 157–75
population density of, 263
as site for technological innovation, 241, 261–64, 358–59
spread of food production in, 178, 180–81, *182,* 189, 191
technological diffusion in, 255, 256, 257, 259, 261–62
Europe:
Cro-Magnon dominance in, 39, 40–41
Eurasia dominated by, 409–17
genetic immunities evolved in, 201
infectious diseases from, 77–78, 197
initial human presence in, 37, 49
language replacements from, 328

Europe (*continued*)
  literate tradition in, 78–80, 359
  maritime technology of, 78, 359
  New World conquered by, 67–81, 197, 354, 355, 373–75
  onset of food production in, *100*, 101, 103, 109
  Pacific conquests of, 353
  political/geographic fragmentation of, 412–16, *415*
  pottery making in, 103
  tropical diseases of colonists from, 197, 214, 317, 358

Fayu bands, 265–66, 267, 269, 288
ferrets, 158, 173
Fertile Crescent (Near East) (Southwestern Asia):
  climate of, 136, 138–39
  crops of, 123–25, *126–27*, 133, 134
  developmental lead lost by, 409–11, 416–17
  diffusion process for food package from, 178, 179–87, *181*, 189–90, 390, 391
  domesticates spread from, 99–100, 101, 102
  elements of food production package in, 141–42
  environmental and biotic advantages for food production onset in, 134–43
  evolution of social organization in, 271, 273
  hunter-gatherer decline in, 142
  mammal domesticates in, 141, 142
  map of, *135*
  natural biodiversity of, 138–41
  pottery from, 254
  sequence of crop development in, 123–25
  as site for food production's origin, 97, 98, 99, *100*, 329
  technological spread from, 182
  topographical variety in, 140–41
fertilizer, 88, 205
fiber production, 90, 119, 125–26, *127*
figs, 124, 133
Fiji Islands:
  European diseases in, 78, 213–14
  guns introduced in, 76
Finnish language, 226
fire:
  early human use of, 38
  for land management, 309
firearms, *see* guns

firestick farming, 309
fish, diseases from, 198
fish farms, 205, 310
fishing skills, 39, 253
Flannery, Tim, 51–52
flax, 90, 119, 120, 121, 125, *127*, 132, 141, 142, 182
food production:
  archaeological evidence of, 94–98
  combination of local flora needed for, 134–56
  continental axis orientations in spread of, 176, 178, 183–91
  defined, 86
  dense population supported through, 88–89, 111–12, 195, 204–5, 284–86
  diffusion of, 176–91
  east-west axis of Eurasian diffusion for, 176, 183–86, 330, 366, 399–400
  evolution of epidemic diseases related to, *86–87*, 195–96, 205, 357
  geographic differences in history of, 93–94, 98–103, *99*, *100*, 406–7
  hunting-gathering competition with, 55, 86, 147, 153–54, 365
  from indigenous biota vs. imported additions, 146–53
  local ethnobiological knowledge in, 144–46
  military advantages and, 86–92
  non-food-producing specialists enabled by, 89–90, 261, 285
  nutrition levels in, 112, 305
  onset of, 93–103, 155–56, 176–77, 262, 303–4, 329–30
  population replacements concurrent with onset of, 101–3, 344–45, 351, 352
  in pre-Columbian America vs. Eurasia, 354–57
  sedentary lifestyle in, 89, 205, 261, 285–86
  state control of, 279
  surplus management for, 89–90, 285
  technological developments linked to onset of, 110–11, 261–62, 263, 358–59, 364–65
  writing development and, 236–37
Foré, 143–44, 208, 270–71
founder domesticates, 100–102, *100*, 141
fruit:
  onset of cultivation of, 133–34
  seed dispersal by, 116–17

seedless mutations of, 119, 122
fur animals, 158

Galton, Francis, 165, 168
Gama, Vasco da, 392–93, 398, 412
gasoline, extraction of, 247
gaur, 159, 161, 163, 167
gazelles, 142, 165, 172
geese, 158
geographic determinism, 408
Germany, unification of, 290
germination, natural inhibitors of, 121
germs, evolution of, 92, 207–10
    see also diseases, infectious
giraffes, 165, 389, 399
glass, 241, 246
glottochronology, 391
goats, 141, 159, 160, 166, 167, 172,
    173, 186, 389, 390, 400
Goering, Heinrich, 376
Goering, Hermann, 376
gonorrhea, 214
goosefoot, 126, 150, 151, 179
gorillas, 36, 168, 169, 270
gourds, 127
government:
    communal decision process used for,
        272, 286–87
    spread of religion linked with, 266–67
grafting, 124, 156
Grand Canyon, 47
grapes, 115, 119, 122, 124, 133, 134,
    152
grasses, 303
    early cultivation of, 125, 126, 145–46
    worldwide survey of, 125, 126, 153
    see also cereals
Great Leap Forward, 39, 40, 41, 52
Greek alphabet, 217, 226, 227, 235,
    236
Greenberg, Joseph, 368, 381, 383, 384
Greenland, Norse settlement in, 371–72,
    373, 407–8
grizzly bears, 165, 170–71
groundnuts, 125, 126
guanaco, 160
guinea fowl, 389
guinea pigs, 158, 159, 178, 187, 213
gunpowder, 225, 247, 253, 330
guns, 76, 241, 249, 255–58, 312, 343
Gutenberg, Johannes, 241, 259–60

Halmahera, 337, 341, 345, 346
han'gul alphabet, 230, 231, 333

Hannibal, 159, 399
harquebuses, 76
Harris, David, 144–45
haus tamburan, 273
Hawaii:
    chiefdoms of, 274–76, 277, 278, 280,
        291
    epidemic disease in, 214
    food production in, 352
    isolation of, 237, 238
    political unification of, 64, 66, 291
hemp, 90, 119, 125–26, 127
Henry, Joseph, 245
hepatitis, 317
herd animals, social characteristics of,
    172–74
herders:
    seasonal movement of, 270
    in sub-Saharan Africa, 98, 102, 113,
        163–64, 396
hereditary social position, 273, 274–75,
    279, 281
hieroglyphs, 217, 218, 219, 224, 226–27,
    230, 231–32, 233, 235
Hillman, Gordon, 144–45
hippopotamus, 171, 389, 398, 399
history, as science, 408, 420–25
Hitler, Adolf, 414, 419–20, 423
Hmong-Mien (Miao-Yao) language
    family, 325, 328, 332, 345, 369
Hobbes, Thomas, 104
Homo erectus, 36–38, 337
Homo habilis, 36
Homo sapiens, 37–38
honeybees, 158
hookworms, 199, 202, 204
Hopewell culture, 152
Hopf, Maria, 181, 181
horses:
    in Africa, 186, 400
    in Americas, 162, 356, 358
    domestication of, 159, 160, 163, 167,
        171, 389
    social dominance in bands of, 172–73
    Eurasian diffusion of, 91, 262
    for long-distance transport, 91
    military use of, 76–77, 91, 164, 358
    motor vehicles vs., 243, 244
Huascar, 77, 211
Huayna Capac, Emperor of Incas, 77,
    211, 212
humans:
    biological evolution of, 36–41
    geographical colonization patterns of,
        36–52

hunter-gatherers:
African herders vs., 102, 113, 163–64
in band societies, 268, 270
in chiefdoms, 274, 284
disease vulnerability of, 203–4
end of, 86, 113
ethnobiological knowledge of, 143–45
farmers reverted to, 55, 109
food producers' conquest and replacement of, 102–3, 112, 113, 344–45, 351, 352
food production in competition with, 112, 147, 153–54, 365
in 1492 Eurasia vs. Americas, 356, 360
landscape management practiced by, 106–7
in modern New Guinea, 147, 305
nutritional status of, 112
population densities of, 45, 56, 88, 89, 204, 205
sedentary societies of, 90, 136, 142, 144
of Southeast Asia, 332–33
hunting skills:
animal extinctions and, 42–44, 47, 175
of protohumans, 39, 43
Huygens, Christiaan, 245
hydraulic management, 283–84

Ice Ages, 35
land bridges during, 38, 41, 297, 299
idea diffusion:
of porcelain technology, 256
writing systems developed through, 224–25, 228–33
immune system, 200–202, 204
Inca Empire:
animals of, 170
disease epidemics and, 77, 373
geographic isolation of, 237, 238, 262
incandescent light bulb, 245
Incas, European conquest of:
Atahuallpa's capture and, 68–74, 77
cavalry vs. foot soldiers in conquest of, 76–77
centralized political organization and, 78, 360
literacy as aid to, 78–80
military equipment of, 74–76
India:
Chinese influence on, 324
crops cultivated in, 126, 126–27
domesticates from, 185
food production spread to, 181, 182, 189

sea trade routes with, 392–93
Indo-European languages, regional expansion of, 91, 324, 368, 369, 375
Indonesia, 324, 368, 369, 375
agricultural crops of, 319, 390–91
Austronesian expansion and, 103, 307–8, 313, 318, 336, 337–38, 342, 343, 347–48, 350, 393
colonization of, 41, 51–52
New Guinean cultural influence from, 307
population of, 335
western New Guinea controlled by, 318–19, 334–36
Industrial Revolution, 123, 359
Indus Valley, food production's development in, 100, 101, 178, 189
influenza, 92, 196–97, 199, 200–201, 202, 207, 212, 214, 320, 330, 357, 358
information, government control of, 268, 279
insects:
diseases transmitted by, 199, 208
domesticated, 158
Irian Jaya, 318–19
iron metallurgy, 259, 330, 331, 394–96, 362–63
irrigation systems, 205, 275, 283–84, 356
Islam, 253, 256
cultural diffusion of, geographic factors in, 257
incendiary weapons in wars of, 247
Iyau, 277

Japan:
Ainu society in, 165, 170–71, 356
Chinese influence on, 324, 333
cultural isolationism in, 257–58
guns abandoned in, 257–58, 312
hunter-gatherer lifestyle in, 109
pottery from, 254, 333
transistor technology acquired by, 248–49, 256
writing systems of, 217, 248, 333
Java:
Asian mainland joined to, 299, 301
Austronesian expansion to, 336, 340, 341
Java man, 36, 337
jewelry, earliest evidence of, 39
jicama, 127

Job's tears, 148
Jordan Valley, plants selected for domestication in, 145–46

Kamehameha I, King of Hawaii, 64
kangaroos, 147, 163, 308, 309
Kennedy, John F., 279
Khoisan peoples:
    Bantu encroachment on, 187, 385–86, 393–97
    genetic background of, 378–80
    as hunter-gatherers vs. herders, 102, 113, 164, 396
    language family of, 329, 382, 384, 385, 391
    no crops domesticated by, 187, 389, 391, 400
    white decimation of, 78, 187, 213, 396, 397
Kingdon, Jonathan, 51–52
Kirikiri, 265
Kislev, Mordechai, 145–46
kleptocracies, four sustaining strategies for, 276–78
knotweed, 126, 150, 151
koalas, 169
kola nuts, 388, 390
konohiki, 274, 280
Korea:
    Chinese influence in, 324, 333
    writing system developed for, 230, 231, 333
Korean hemorrhagic fever, 199
kuru (laughing sickness), 198, 208

labor force:
    diversity of, 62–63
    seasonal shifts in, 285
    technological innovation related to size of, 249–50
Langley, Samuel, 245
languages:
    for address of royalty, 280
    African diversity of, 381–86, 382, 390–92
    anatomical basis for, 40
    ancestral vs. modern, 343–44
    of Australia/New Guinea vs. Asia, 301, 302
    of Austronesian family, 325, 328, 333, 345, 351, 352, 369, 383, 392, 393
    of China and Southeast Asia, 323–29, 326, 327, 332
    click sounds in, 384
    cultural history deduced from, 343–44
    Eurasian movements of, 91, 367–68, 369, 375
    of Native Americans, 328, 367–70, 375
    political connectedness reflected in, 413
    replacements of, 325–29, 332
    writing systems modified for differences in, 216, 225, 226
Lapita pottery, 347–50, 351
Lascaux Cave, 40
Lassa fever, 208
latitude, climate features related to, 183–86
laughing sickness (kuru), 198, 208
leather, 90
leeks, 125
legumes, 124, 125
lentils, 120, 125, 126, 141
leprosy, 204, 205
lettuce, 122, 124, 125
Lévi-Strauss, Claude, 235
Lilienthal, Otto, 245
lima beans, 118, 126, 179, 188
Linearbandkeramik culture, 89
Linear B writing system, 217, 226, 234–35, 240
lions, 169, 171
Liszt, Franz, 267
literacy, see writing systems
llamas, 159, 160, 161, 167, 178, 187, 213, 262, 367
logograms, 217, 234–35, 236
Los Angeles public schools, ethnic diversity in, 322
luxury goods, 269, 274
Lyme disease, 208

macadamia nuts, 128, 309, 321
Macassans, Australian Aboriginal contact with, 314
Madagascar, Austronesian expansion to, 340, 377, 380–81, 388, 392–93
Malai Islet, 348–49
malaria, 196–97, 201, 202, 207, 212, 214, 270
    altitudinal ceiling for, 318
    European susceptibility to, 317, 320, 357, 358
    immunity to, 350, 396
    transmission of, 199, 205
Malayo-Polynesian language group, 336, 337, 338–39, 342–43, 344

Malay Peninsula, Austronesian expansion
to, 336, 337, *341,* 342–43, 344
mammals:
aquatic, 158–59
extinctions of, 46–47, *160,* 175, 213,
355, 406
large species of, 42, 46–47
as milk sources, 88
small, as domesticates, 158, 166
mammals, large domesticated, 157–75
African paucity of, 389, 398–99, 400
aquatic, 158–59
captive breeding suitability of, 169–70
continental diffusion of, 178, 186,
187–88
diet requirements of, 169
domestication dates for, 142, 165–66,
167
fourteen ancient species of, 159, *160–
61,* 161–63, 166, 355
growth rates of, 169
modern efforts at developing, 163,
166–68
rapid acceptance of Eurasian species
of, 163–64
size of, 159
social characteristics of, 172–74
suitability criteria for, 131–32, 157,
166–75, 398–99
temperament as factor in, 170–72
unequal global distribution of candidates for, 141, 161–63, 174–75,
355, 389, 406, 409
Manco, 77
Mandan Indians, 212, 374
Mandarin, 323, 324
Manhattan Project, 242
manioc (cassava), *127,* 128, 132, 178
manure, 88, 355, 357
Maori:
British defeat of, 90
Moriori conquered by, *53–57*
muskets adopted by, 255
New Zealand colonized by, 45, 51
maritime technology:
of Austronesian expansion, 313, 341–
42
Eurasian origins of, 241
of European expansion, 78, 359
marsupials, extinct, 304, 308
Marx, Karl, 276
Matthew, Saint, 175
Maya societies:
barriers to cultural diffusion from, 262

writing system developed by, 217, 222,
235
maygrass, *127,* 150, 151
Meadowcroft rock shelter, 48, 49
measles, 92, 196–97, 203, 204, 206,
207, 212, 213–14, 320, 357
Mediterranean region:
climate typified by, 136, 138–41, *139,*
184, 399–400
earliest evidence of watercraft in, 41
megafauna, extinctions of, 42–44, 46–47,
162, 175, 213, 355
melons, 116, 118, 119, *127,* 182
Mena, Cristobal de, 79
Merina state, 291
Mesoamerica:
barriers to cultural diffusion from,
262, 366–67
diffusion to and from South America
in, 178, 180, 187–88
domestic animals in, 142, 158, 178,
213
early crops of, *100,* 125–26, *126–27,*
179
languages of, 368
non-animal protein sources in, 125
as site of food production's origin, 98,
100
social organization begun in, 273
technological advances in, 248, 370
writing systems developed in, 190,
217, 218, 222–24, *223,* 230, 235,
236–37, 360, 367
metallurgy, 182, *255,* 259, 263, 330,
352, 358, 361, 362–63, *362–63*
Miao-Yao (Hmong-Mien) language
family, 325, 328, 332, 345, *369*
military:
Eurasian technological advantages in,
358
food supplies for, 90
ideology of patriotic suicide in, 281–82
motor transport in, 243
religious motivation of, 69, 71–72, 73–
74, 90, 266, 278, 281, 282, 359
milk production, 88, 159, 182
millets, 125, *126,* 185, 310–11, 329,
388, 390, 394
missionaries, 266, 285–86
mithan, *161*
Mobutu Sese Seko, 276
Mongol Empire, 367
Mongoloids, 323
monkey viruses, 197, 204, 208

monoculture fields, 126–28
Monte Verde site, 48–49
Montezuma, 77, 80
moose, 167, 168
Moriori society, Maori conquest of, 53–57
Morse, Samuel, 245
mosquitoes, 199, 205, 208, 396
moths:
  as food, 310
  natural selection for industrial melanism in, 123
motor vehicles, invention of, 243
Mtetwa chiefdom, 290, 292
mumps, 203, 205, 212
Muralug Island, 315–16
murder, among band and tribal societies, 265–66, 277
Murray-Darling river system, 302, 310
Muscovy ducks, 158, 213
mushrooms, 114, 143–44
muskets, 255
musk ox, 167
mustard seeds, 119, 145
myxo virus, 209, 210

Namibia, colonial history of, 376–77
Native Americans:
  crops cultivated by, 109, 356–57
  cultural diversity of, 322
  disease epidemics among, 77–78, 197, 199, 202, 203–4, 210–12, 357, 373–74
  domestic animals of, 164, 213, 355, 356
  of Eastern U.S., 98, *100*, 126, *126–27*, 146, 150–53, *155–56*, 179
  Eurasian food production vs., 354–57
  European conquest of, 67–81, 85–86, 197, 210–11, 328, 354–75
  geographic/ecological isolation of, 178–80, 237, 238, 357–58, 367, 407
  as hunter-gatherers, 85, 102, 113, 274, 356, 364, 365, 367
  independent inventions of, 248, 255, 367, 369
  innovation vs. tradition among, 252–53
  languages of, 328, 367–70, 375
  of Mississippi Valley, 211, 237
  population levels of, 211, 213, 374–75
  technological disadvantages of, 358–59
  of West Indies, 213, 373
  writing systems of, 217, 218, 222–24, *223*, 228–30, *229*, 235, 238, 360

  see also specific Native American groups
natural selection:
  for disease immunity, 201
  human crop cultivation vs., 116–18, 120, 123, 130
Nature, 48
Navajo, 164, 252–53, 356
Neanderthals, 38, 40–41, 44
Near East, *see* Fertile Crescent
Negritos, 332–33, 338, 383
Newcomen, Thomas, 244–45
New Guinea:
  Australia separated from, 297, 298, 299, 302
  Austronesian expansion to, 307–8, 318, 319, 336, 345–51
  diverse languages of, 301, 302, 324, *337*, 346–47
  domestic animals in, 148, 304, 305, 307, 308, 315
  early crops of, 126, *126–27*, 148
  environmental conditions in, 147, 302–3, 305–6
  European presence in, 298, 307–8, 317–19
  food production in, 147–50, 298, 303–6, 308, 318, 319
  geographic barriers to cultural diffusion in, 306, 307, 407
  giant marsupials exterminated on, 304
  indigenous biota vs. imported additions cultivated in, 146–50
  indigenous fauna of, 303, 147, 148–49
  Indonesian province of, 318–19, 334–36
  initial human presence in, 41–44, 147, 300–301
  intertribal warfare in, 306–7
  onset of food production in, 99, *99*, *100*, 303–4, 305
  political fragmentation in, 306–7
  population density of, 298, 304, 305–6
  Torres Strait population from, 314–16
  see also Australia/New Guinea
New Guineans, modern:
  art of, 305
  band societies of, 265–66, 267, 269–70, 298
  Chinese immigrants as, 335
  diseases of, 204, 208, 317–18
  eastern vs. western, 318–19
  ethnic tensions among, 334–36

New Guineans, modern (*continued*)
ethnobiological expertise of, 143–44,
145, 147, 149
European colonization among, 298
evolutionary ancestry of, 300–302,
333, 335–36, 345–46
highland agriculture vs. lowland
subsistence for, 147–50, 304–5,
315, 335
innovative vs. conservative cultures in,
252
languages of, 270, 301, 302, 306–7
Native Australians vs., 297–98, 302
pets kept by, 165, 167
population distribution in, 304–5, 306
stone tools of, 38, 298
tribal groups of, 143–44, 208, 270–73,
277, 298, 305
New Zealand:
Austronesian expansion to, 351
geological diversity of, 58
Maori ancestors in, 45, 54
mineral resources of, 58, 64, 66
Niger-Congo language family, 382, 384–
86, 389, 390, 391, 392
Nilo-Saharan language family, 382, 384,
391, 392, 394
Ninan Cuyuchi, 77
Norse, North Atlantic expansion efforts
of, 371–73, *371*, 407–8
North Africa, Eurasian culture related to,
161
north-south continental axes, 176, 178,
186–90, 255, 262, 263, 366, 399–
400
nuts, 114, 115, 118, 128–29, 148, 151–
52, 388

oak trees, 115, 118, 128–29, 151–52
oats, 125, 185
oca, *127*, 128
ogham alphabet, 226, 230–31
olives, 115, 119, 124, 133–34
onagers, 171–72
On the Origin of Species (Darwin), 130
oranges, 119, 122
Otto, Nikolaus, 243, 244

Pacific Northwest, hunter-gather
chiefdoms in, 274
papermaking techniques, 253, 256, 259,
330
Papin, Denis, 244
Papuan languages, 301, 302, 346–47

Patagonia, Clovis hunter-gatherer
expansion to, 45
patent law, 244, 250
patriotism, conquest furthered by, 281–82
peaches, 122, 185
peanuts, *126*, 178, 391
pears, 124–25
peas, 95, 115, 117–18, 120, 121, 124,
125, *126*, 141, 182, 183
pecans, 115, 128, 152
peccaries, 157, 163
Pedro Furada, cave paintings at, 48
pertussis (whooping cough), 199, 203,
207, 212
petroleum products, 247
pets, 163, 164–65, 166, 167, 196, 206,
207
Phaistos disk, 239–40, *240*, 245, 253,
259–60
Philippines:
Austronesian expansion to, 103, 337–
38, 343, 347–48, 350
crops brought to, 149
food production's spread from, 178
languages of, 328, 333, 336, 337–38,
342, 343–44, 383
phonemes, 217, 218
phonograph, invention of, 243
pigs:
domestication of, 141, 159, *160*, 163,
166, *167*, 304, 307, 330, 389
human diseases and, 198, 213
pineapples, 122
Pizarro, Francisco, 68–74, 75, 76, 77,
78, 79, 80, 86, 91, 210–11, 354,
359
Pizarro, Hernando, 69, 70, 79–80
Pizarro, Juan, 70
Pizarro, Pedro, 69
plague, bubonic (Black Death), 196–97,
199, 202, 205, 206, 212, 330,
357, 358
plants:
atmospheric carbon absorbed by, 95
dioecious species of, 122
reproductive processes of, 121–22,
137–38
self-fertilization of, 122, 124
plants, domestication of, 114–56
alterations undergone through, 95,
115–23, 136–37, 146
in China, 329–30
defined, 114
earliest known dates for, 35, 99, *100*,
361–62, *362–63*

hermaphroditic selfers and, 137–38
initial sites for, 97, 98–102, *100*, 254,
    303–4, 388, 390
interspecific hybrids, 138
local ethnobiological knowledge
    employed in, 143–46
modern lack of major additions to,
    132–33
natural selection process vs., 116–18,
    120, 123, 130
in New Guinea, 303–4
nutritional yield and, 88, 125, 138,
    142, 149, 151, 356–57
preemptive domestication and, 178–80
prehistoric climate changes and, 110
regional potential for required variety
    of, 134–56, 399, 409
single vs. multiple instances of, 179–
    80, 182–83, 188
size increases in, 117–18
variations in ease of, 123–30, 137
wild mutants in, 120–22, 129, 178–
    79
plants, wild:
almonds, 114, 118
of Australia, 309
berries, 114, 116
bitterness of, 114, 118–19
cereals, 110, 111, 136, 137
domestication potential of, 131–33,
    136–38
food production's onset based on entire
    regional assortment of, 134–56
germination inhibition in, 120–21
grass species, 139, *140*, 153
local ethnobiological knowledge of,
    143–46
number of species of, 132
poisonous, 114, 118–19, 143–44
Plato, 276
Pleistocene Era, end of, 35
plow animals, 88–89, 126, 128, 329,
    357
plums, 122, 124–25, 152
pneumonia, 196
polio, 205
political systems:
centralized, 78, 251, 273–79, 359
ethnic diversity encompassed by, 322–
    23
of Eurasian societies vs. Native
    Americans, 359–60
of Inca Empire, 78, 360
of kleptocracies, 276–78
Polynesian diversity of, 61–64

population density and, 62, 63–64,
    285–86
in sedentary societies, 89–90
Spanish conquests enabled by, 78
spread of religion linked with, 266–67
technological advancement and, 251
units of, 61–62
writing development linked to, 234–37
see also social organization
Polynesian islands:
Austronesian expansion to, 336
chiefdoms in, 273, 274–76, 277, 278,
    280, 291
domestic animals on, 60, 148
human adaptation to diverse environ-
    ments in, 55–66, 352–53
languages of, 328, 337, 343–44
metallurgy and writing absent on, 352
seafaring expertise developed on, 336
spread of food production to, 178,
    186
technologies abandoned on, 258, 312
Polynesian islands, environmental
    variations in:
agricultural development influenced by,
    60–61, 110
in climate, 58
economic specialization and, 62–64
geological types of, 58–59
isolation and, 59, 62, 64
marine resources of, 59
material culture and, 64–65
political organization and, 61–64
in size, 59
subsistence practices and, 59–61
in terrain fragmentation, 59, 62
pomegranates, 124
poppy cultivation, 101, 119, 182, 185
population density:
agricultural productivity vs., 60, 89,
    305–6
bidirectional links of food production
    with, 88–89, 111–12, 195, 204–5,
    284–86
defeated peoples' fates tied to, 291–92
epidemic diseases linked with, 87, 203,
    204–6
labor force diversity and, 62–63
political organization affected by, 62,
    63–64, 285–86
of Polynesian environments, 61–63
for sedentary society vs. nomadic
    peoples, 89
societal complexity related to, 284–88
population growth, 45, 56

population size:
for epidemic diseases, 203–6
social organization and, 266–67, *268*, 271, 273, 279, 284–92
technological development linked to, 257, 261, 262, 263, 370, 407–8
porcelain, 253, 256
potatoes, 118, *127*, 128, 132, 185, 187, sweet, *127*, 128, 132, 149, 150, 153, 178, 303, 304, 319
pottery:
in Africa, 263, 400
of Austronesian expansion, 339, 340, 345, 347–50, 351
from conquering cultures, 103
first appearances of, 254, 261, 333, *362–63*
furnace technology for, 259
Polynesian abandonment of, 258, 312
porcelain, 253, 254, 256
power sources, mechanical, 358–59
preemptive domestication, 178–80, 182–83
priests, 90, 235, 278, 280
printing methods, 240–41, 253, 259–60
protein sources:
animals as, 142, 149
deficiencies in, 148–49
non-animal, 125, 138, 142, 149, 151, 356–57
Proto-Indo-Europeans, 343
protolanguages, 343
public works, 275, 278, 279, 285
pulses, 125, *126*, *127*, 132, 141, 142, 149
Punan, 352
Pygmies, 329, 333, 338, 378–80, 383, 385–86, 389, 392, 393, 396

quince, 185
quinoa, 125, *126*
quipu, 360
Quizo Yupanqui, 76–77
QWERTY keyboards, 248, 249, 418

rabbits, 158, 166, 207, 209
rabies, 199
radiocarbon dating, *35n*, 47, 95–97
radishes, 125
ragweed, 151
rainfall, crop diffusion and, 189, 190
Recent Era, 35
red deer (elk), 167, 168, 172

redistributive economy, *269*, 275, 277, 287
reindeer, 159, *160*, *161*, 172, 173, 356
religion:
conquest justified by, 69, 71–72, 73–74, 90, 266, 278, 281, 282, 359, 419
kleptocracies supported by, *269*, 277–78
spread of government linked with, 266–67
state leaders elevated by, 280
technological innovation and, 250
tribal supernatural beliefs institutionalized as, 277–78
resource supply, technological innovation vs., 251
rhinoceros, 168, 174, 389, 398, 399
rice cultivation, 125, *126*, 132, 138, 148, 151, 329, 331, 333, 388
rinderpest, 206–7
rock paintings, 295, 297
rodents, 158, 205, 208, 209
Roman alphabet, 225, 226, 227, 228, 236
Roman Empire:
food production in, 185–86
geographic range of, 367, 414
root crops, *127*, 128, 132, 148, 149
Rothschild, Lord Walter, 171
Rousseau, Jean-Jacques, 283, 288, 289
rubella, 199, 203
Russia, Imperial, ethnic diversity incorporated in, 322–23
Russian language, 225, 368, *369*
rye, 125

sago palm tree, 147, 270, 305
Sahara, African food production begun in, 390
Sahel zone:
crops of, *126–27*, 137, 186, 387–88, 400
east-west crop diffusion in, 186
metallurgy from, 394
onset of food production in, 98, *100*
salmonella, 198
samurai, 257–58
San people, 78, 380
see also Khoisan peoples
Savage, Charlie, 76
Savery, Thomas, 245–46
schistosomes, 199, 205
science, history as, 408, 420–25

sea transport, *see* maritime technology; watercraft
sedentary societies, 89
  disease transmission in, 205
  population density and, 89
  state control and, 285–86
  technological innovation fostered in, 260–61
seeds:
  broadcast sowing of, 126–28, 357
  of cereals, 122, 136–37
  competitive pressure of farming environment for, 123
  crop cultivation for, 119, 136
  mutant, 120–22
  natural dispersal and germination of, 115–17, 118
  in pods, 120
Sejong, King of Korea, 230
selfers, 137–38
Semang Negritos, 332–33, 338, 383
Semitic languages, 226–27, 383
sense organs, of domestic vs. wild animals, 159
Sepik River, 273
Sequoyah, 228–30, *229*, 232
sesame seeds, 119, 185
sheep, 141, 159, *160*, 164, 165, *167*, 172, 173, 174, 181, 186, 196, 356, 389, 390, 400
Siberia, hunter-gatherers in, 102, 356, 360, 370–71
sickness, earliest evidence of care during, 38
silk production, 158, 256
Sino-Tibetan language family, 324, 328, 329, 331, 332, *369*
skull development, human, 37
slash-and-burn agriculture, 305, 306, 315
slavery, 204, 210, 250–51, *269*, 272, 275, 279–80, 292, 377
sleeping sickness, 199, 201
smallpox, 77, 78, 92, 199, 203
  among Aboriginal Australians, 320
  domestic animals related to, 196–97, 207
  first appearance of, 205, 330
  in Hawaii, 217
  immunity to, 357
  modern control of, 318
  Native Americans killed by, 199, 210, 212, 355, 373
  as Plague of Antoninus, 205
  transmission of, 199, 358

social contract, 283
social organization:
  amalgamation of, 288–92
  in bands, 203–4, 265–70, 277, 286–88
  in chiefdoms, *268, 269,* 273–76, 278, 279–80, 282, 290–91, 292, *362–63*
  conflict resolution methods related to size of, 265–66, 271–72, 286
  disintegration of, 281, 288
  food production linked to, 283–86
  four categories of, 267–81, *268, 269*
  hereditary status in, 273, 274–75, 279, 281
  of Native Americans vs. Eurasians, 359–60
  population size and, 266–67, *268,* 271, 273, 279, 284
  as state, 267–92
  technological innovation vs., 250
  of tribes, *268, 269,* 270–73, 277
  wealth distribution and, 272, 274, 276–78
sorghum, 125, *126,* 132, 133, 186, 388, 390, 394
Soto, Hernando de, 70, 211
South Africa, food production's spread inhibited in, 178
South America:
  crops of, 126
  domestic animals from, 213
  sites of food production's origin in, 98, *100*
Southeast Asia:
  Austronesian expansion from, *see* Austronesian expansion
  Chinese language families in, 325, *326, 327,* 328
  human ancestors in, 36, 301
  prehistoric coastline of, *299,* 301
  repopulation of, 324, 332–33
Southwest Asia, *see* Fertile Crescent
soybeans, 125, *126,* 132
squashes:
  as containers, 150
  domestication of, 109, 119, 122, *127,* 150, 179, 180
  spread of, 151, 180, 188, 367
Stalin, Joseph, 225
state societies, *268, 269,* 278–92
  in Americas vs. Eurasia, 359–60, *362–63*
  archaeological evidence of, 278
  bureaucrats in, *269,* 274, 280, 281

state societies (*continued*)
  conditions for formation of, 282–92
  military advantages of, 281–82, 359
  multiple ethnicities in, 280–81, 322–23
  percentage of globe occupied by, 266, 283
  religion in support of, 280, 359
  suicidal patriotism and, 281–82
steam power, 241, 242, 244–45, 359
steel:
  African manufacture of, 394
  Eurasian development of, 241
  Native Americans conquered with, 74, 76
stone tools:
  of Aboriginal Australians, 297
  archaeological identification of, 47–48
  of Clovis hunters, 45
  earliest use of, 36, 38, 260
  for farming, 304, 311
  in modern societies, 36, 38, 241, 253, 298
  standardization of, 39
  from volcanic stone, 58, 64–65
strawberries, 114, 115, 116, 117, 124, 128, 129–30, 152
street lighting, gas vs. electricity for, 247, 249
sugarcane, *126*, 132, 148, 303
Sumatra, Asian mainland joined to, *299*
Sumerian cuneiform, 217, 218–24, *221*, 230, 232, 234, 236–37
sumpweed, 150, 151
sunflowers, 119, 121, 122, 150, *151*, 188
supernatural beliefs, religious institutionalization of, 277–78
supersonic transport, 247
sushi, 198
sweet potatoes, *127*, 128, 132, 149, 150, 153, 178, 303, 304, 319
swords, 76, 257–58, 358
syllabaries, 217, 222, 226, 228–30, *229*, 232, 236, 260
syphilis, 199, 210, 212, 214, 217, 320, 357

Tahiti, unification of, 291
Tai-Kadai language group, 325, 328, 345, 351
Taiwan:
  Asian mainland connected with, *299*
  Austronesian expansion begun in, 339–40, 342, 343, 344
  languages of, *337, 339*, 342, 343–44
  Ta-p'en-k'eng culture on, 339–40
tamarind trees, 314
tannins, 128–29
Tanzania, languages of, 384
taro, *127*, 128, 148, 149, 186, 303, 304, 344, 388
Tasmania:
  cultural isolation of, 253, 256–57, 312, 313
  dogs adopted on, 164
  first human presence in, 300
  technological innovation abandoned in, 258, 312–13
taxation, 90, *269, 275*, 276, 279
technological advances, 239–64
  applications found after discoveries of, 242–43, 245
  autocatalytic tendencies of, 258–60
  commercial motivations for, 244–45
  cumulative development of, 245
  food production linked to, 261–62, 263, 311, 358–59, 364–65
  geographic/ecological factors and, 190, 256–58, 262, 263, 416
  heroic view of, 241, 244–45
  intercontinental differences in, 261–64, 358–59
  local invention vs. diffusion of, 254–55, 258–59, 364–65
  moderate political connectedness as optimal condition for, 416
  necessity as impetus for, 242–44
  population size and, 257, 261, 263, 313, 370, 407–8
  trial-and-error examples of, 246–47
technological advances, societal receptivity for, 154, 245–49
  diffusion conditions for, 255–58, 261, 413
  economic motives for, 247–48, 249–50, 260
  historical reversals in, 257–58, 311–13, 413, 416
  ideological atmosphere for, 250
  perceived advantage and, 249
  perceived need as motive for, 242–44
  prestige considerations in, 248
  in single societies or continents, 154, 251–54
  standard explanations for, 249–51
  vested interests in opposition to, 248–49
teff, *126*, 388
telegraph, 245

Tell Abu Hureyra, evidence of selection
     in plants gathered at, 144–45, 146
temples, 273, 274, 278, 280
teosinte, 137
territorial behavior, 174
Third Chimpanzee, The (Diamond), 40
tobacco, 188, 314
Tolstoy, Lev, 157, 175
Tonga, isolation of, 237
tools:
  bones used in, 39, 90
  for crop production, 88–89, 110–11,
     357
  metal, 361, 362–63, *362–63*
  natural resources for, 58, 64–65
  see also stone tools
Torres Strait, islands of, 298, 314–16
trade routes:
  diseases transmitted along, 205–6, 358
  of Indian Ocean, 392–93, 400
transistor technology, 248–49, 256, 417
trees:
  annual growth rings of, 96
  fruit, 119, 124–25, 156, 182
  oak, 115, 118, 128–29, 151–52
  sago palm, 147, 270, 305
tribal organization, *268, 269,* 270–73,
     277
tribute, *269,* 273, 274, 275, 276, 278,
     292
trichinosis, 198
tropical rain forests, latitude limitations
     for, 184
trypanosome diseases, 164, 186, 213,
     400
tsetse flies, 164, 186, 199, 400
tuber crops, *127,* 128, 132
tuberculosis, 196–97, 201, 202, 207,
     212, 214, 320, 357
turkeys, 142, 158, 188, 213
turnips, 125
Tutankhamen, 118
typewriter keyboards, letter sequence
     designed for, 248, 418
typhoid, 214, 320
typhus, 199, 209, 212, 320, 357

Ulfilas, 225
United States, ethnic diversity of, 322
upright posture, 36

vaccination, 200
Valverde, Vicente de, 71–72
Veddoid Negritos, 332–33

venereal diseases, 199
vicuña, 170
Vietnam, languages spoken in, 325, 336
village life, 35, *362–63*
violence, government curbs on, 277
volcanic islands, 58–59, 64–65

war:
  diseases transmitted by, 197
  horses used in, 75, 76–77, 91, 164,
     243, 358
  societal amalgamation fostered by,
     288–92
  technological advancement affected by,
     250–51, 255
Washington, George, 276
water buffalo, 159, *160,* 163, *167,* 330
watercraft:
  for Austronesian expansion, 339–42,
     351
  canoes, 258, 314, 341–42, 351
  cultural reversals of, 258
  earliest evidence of, 41–42, 44, 297
  Eurasian vs. Native American, 359
  for transatlantic crossing, 372, 373
watermelons, 118, 119 *127,* 182
water power, 358–59
Watt, James, 241, 244–45
wealth distribution:
  in chiefdoms, 274
  for elite vs. general population, 276–78
  in smaller social organizations, 272
weaponry:
  of Aboriginal Australians, 312, 316
  boomerang, 311–12
  bows and arrows, 258, 298, 312, 316,
     358
  cultural attitudes about, 257–58
  elite monopoly on, 277
  European advantage in, 358
  guns, 76, 241, 249, 255–58, 312, 343
  incendiary, 247
  multipiece construction for, 39
  muskets, 255
  of Native Americans, 74–75, 76
  of steel, 76, 358
  swords, 76, 257, 358
  technology diffusion of, 249, 255,
     257–58
weaving, 164, 253, 261
wheat:
  diffusion of, 330, 333
  domestication of, 97, 122, 120, 123–
     24, *126,* 133, 137, 145–46
  ease of germination of, 121

wheat (*continued*)
  einkorn, 133, 138, 141, 182
  emmer, 97, 138, 139, 141, 145–46
  nutritive value of, 125, 138, 142, 149, 151
  worldwide production of, 132, 148
Wheatstone, Charles, 245
wheels, 182, 190, 225, 248, 255, 262, 358, 359, 367, 369
Whitney, Eli, 242
whooping cough (pertussis), 199, 203, 207, 212
wild boar, 160
wild foods, decline in availability of, 110
Wills, William, 296, 321
wind power, 358–59
wolves, 158, 161, 166, 173
wool, 126, 159, 164, 170
Wright brothers, 241, 245
writing systems, 66, 215–38
  accounting records as stimulus for, 218, 228, 360
  alphabetic, 190, 217, 225–28, 230, 234, 235–36, 255, 259, 323, 333, 367, 400
  blueprint copying and modification of, 224, 225–28
  expressive limitations of, 233–36
  geographic and ecological barriers to spread of, 236–38, 400
  idea diffusion as source for development of, 224–25, 228–33
  independent invention of, 217–24, 219, 230, 236, 254–55
  language differences and, 216, 225, 226
  in Mesoamerica vs. Eurasia, 360
  as military advantage, 78–80, 215–16
  on Phaistos disk, 239–41, 240
  phonetic principle employed in, 220–22, 234, 417–18
  power of information transmittal through, 78–80, 215–16, 360
  printing technology and, 239–41, 259–60
  sites of origin of, 216, 236–37, 255, 362–63
  sociopolitical organization linked to early use of, 234–36
  spread of, 182, 190, 216–38, 352, 400
  state societies and, 280, 360
  three basic strategies used in, 216–17, 221
  in western Eurasia vs. China, 331
Wu Li, 232

Xhosa, 397

Yahi Indians, 374
yak, 159, 161, 161, 163, 167
Yali, 36, 38, 295, 405–8
yams, 127, 128, 148, 186, 303, 305, 310, 344, 388, 390, 391
yaws, 204
yellow fever, 204, 212, 214, 358
yucca, 125–26, 127
Yumbri, 352

Zaire, kleptocratic practices in, 276
zebras, 157, 163, 167, 171–72, 389, 398
Zhou Dynasty, 325, 331–32
Zohary, Daniel, 181, 181
zoos, breeding programs at, 168, 170
Zulu state, 290–91, 292